# Imperfect Justice

# Imperfect Justice

LOOTED ASSETS,

SLAVE LABOR,

AND THE

UNFINISHED

BUSINESS

OF

WORLD WAR II

## Stuart E. Eizenstat

FOREWORD BY ELIE WIESEL

PublicAffairs

NEW YORK

LIBRARY OF CONGRESS CATALOGING-IN-PUBLICATION DATA
Eizenstat, Stuart.
Imperfect justice : looted assets, slave labor, and the unfinished
business of World War II / Stuart Eizenstat ;
foreword by Elie Wiesel.
p. cm.
Includes bibliographical references and index.
ISBN 1-58648-110-X
1. Holocaust, Jewish (1939–1945)—Economic aspects. 2. Jewish
property—Europe. 3. World War, 1939–1945—Confiscations and
contributions—Europe. 4. World War, 1939–1945—Destruction
and pillage—Europe. 5. Forced labor—Germany—History—
20th century. 6. Gold—Europe—History—20th century. I. Title.
D804.7.E26 E59 2003
940.53'18144—dc21
2002036714

BOOK DESIGN BY JENNY DOSSIN.

FIRST EDITION

1 3 5 7 9 10 8 6 4 2

*To Fran, my loving partner in life,*
*whose support, encouragement,*
*and shared commitment to justice*
*for the surviving victims of World War II*
*made my efforts possible*

# CONTENTS

❧

# FOREWORD

୬

## BY ELIE WIESEL

THIS ABSORBING personal memoir by Stu Eizenstat deals with an aspect of the Holocaust with which I remain less familiar. But I have known the author for a quarter of a century. Our relationship goes back to the origins of the President's Commission on the Holocaust, culminating in the creation of the now world-renowned Holocaust Memorial Museum in Washington. His contribution to that project was of vital significance. Moreover, his relentless efforts to obtain compensation and restitution for Holocaust victims and for non-Jewish forced laborers, particularly from Eastern Europe, elicited admiration and gratitude. Making use of his experience in government service as well as his international legal expertise, he fought with skill, tenacity, and devotion for needy survivors, and prevailed.

At one point, in the late nineties, when the battle around the Swiss banks was raging in the international press, I was asked by the Swiss government to become president of its fund for Jewish Holocaust survivors. From various quarters, both in Israel and the United States, I was pressured to accept. Israel Singer and Elan Steinberg, of the World Jewish Congress, who together with their chairman, Edgar Bronfman, were among the first public figures to demand retribution and justice for Holocaust victims everywhere, presented convincing arguments. But I refused for two reasons: first, because I lacked even the minimum experience in matters of high finance and, second, because I felt reluctant to define the greatest tragedy in Jewish history in terms of money. I thought, how does one measure human suffering in terms of material reward? How much ought a government body have to pay a surviving mother for the murder of her child? To me, Auschwitz and Treblinka had to do with something other than financial evaluation. They had to do more with morality and even theology.

Is that why I chose not to do what Stu Eizenstat was doing? Those books I purchased with my pocket money in my childhood are lying in dust. Who can give them back to me? Who will give me back the *tephilin* of my father and grandfather?

I remember a little girl, a beautiful innocent little girl with golden hair and blue eyes, who had taken her most cherished possession with her, a beautiful scarf she had received as a Passover gift. Are there enough funds in the world to compensate her brother for that stolen scarf?

Eizenstat's approach was thankfully more realistic. After all, Hitler's Reich was not satisfied by murdering Jews; it also sought to enrich itself with their belongings. Due to his human qualities and professional skills, Eizenstat succeeded in persuading countless European institutions and authorities to imaginatively and ethically cope with their nations' past. Thus this book offers the reader an exciting story that has not been sufficiently known. But it also raises some questions: Why has this battle taken place generations after the event? Why this late concern for stolen money and wealth?

More than fifty years have elapsed since the Allied victory over Nazism and fascism uncovered the horrors of Birkenau, Majdanek, and Belzec. Innumerable testimonies have been published, witnesses interrogated, widely publicized trials held, criminals persecuted and, in some cases, punished.

Political scientists, psychologists, philosophers, essayists, psychiatrists, and historians have conducted invaluable research on what happened in those years of malediction and murder in the darkest of all places. Yet, somehow their simple economic dimension seems to have been utterly neglected.

Why?

Is it because many of us felt the remembrance of the Tragedy to be so sacred that we preferred not to mention its financial implications? Is it because the task of protecting the memory of the dead was conceived by us as so noble, so painful, and so compelling that we considered it undignified and unworthy to think of anything else, and surely not bank accounts? In truth, some of us feel reticent to talk about it even now.

Is it that intellectually and morally we could not accept the possibility that the Holocaust was, for the killers, only a combination of both perverse hate-filled idealism and convenient, cheap robbery?

There may have been other reasons as well. In the post-Holocaust years, survivors had more urgent problems to solve than demanding restitution or compensation. They had to adjust to freedom, society, and life, and their various challenges. Dwelling on the ruins of their lives in haunted invisible cemeteries, they needed to rebuild faith and hope. Those who aspired to go to Palestine found its gates locked by British soldiers; some went there illegally; others returned to their homes and were met by their neighbors' open hostility. In certain cities and villages, local inhabitants greeted former Jewish acquaintances with sneers: "What, you are not dead?" And sent them to DP camps in Germany. Or massacred them, as in Kielce.

When and how could traumatized survivors have found the means to organize immensely complex legal mechanisms, all necessary in obtaining documents and bank records? When, in the early fifties, Israel and Jewish organizations began meeting to discuss claims and reparations, not a single survivor was to be found in the American delegation.

Actually, the search for missing monies, apartments, and collections should have been undertaken long ago by the banks and governments themselves. The prophet's outcry to the king should have reverberated in their ears: "You have committed murder, now do you wish to become the victim's heir?" In Romania, Poland, Hungary, Lithuania, and elsewhere in the Communist empire, Jewish cultural and communal centers, synagogues, and libraries were confiscated, demolished, or transformed into storage rooms, stables, government shops, and offices; and nobody cared. People in influential circles chose to forget that the "Final Solution" targeted both communities and individuals, the living and the dead. For a long, very long, time all were forgotten.

Thanks to the Israel Singers, the Elan Steinbergs, and the Stu Eizenstats, a desire was felt to correct some of the injustices. I say "some" advisedly. The ultimate injustice, the one dealing with the extermination of 6 million men, women, and children for being Jewish, can never and never will be corrected. For them it is too late. As it is for some of their heirs.

Thus this book, filled with suspense and pathos, political intrigue and international diplomacy, is not really about money. In a deeper sense, it is about something infinitely more important and more meaningful; it is about the ethical value and weight of memory.

The duty to remember covers not only big accounts, huge palaces, and rare art collections but also less wealthy families, small merchants, cobblers, peddlers, school teachers, water carriers, beggars: the enemy deprived them of their pathetically poor possessions, such as a prayer book, a shirt, a comb, eyeglasses, toys.

In other words: the poor victims were robbed of their poverty.

What remains is their memory; it too silently permeates Eizenstat's story.

# Imperfect Justice

# A Fifty-Year Wait for Justice

T HAT THE life of Roman Kent, from Lodz, Poland, and mine, from Atlanta, Georgia, would intersect so intensely more than fifty years after the end of World War II is little short of astounding.

Roman was born in Lodz in 1929, one of four children whose life was brutally interrupted when the Germans occupied Poland in 1939. When he was ten years old, he and his family were forced into the Lodz ghetto. His memories of the ghetto were the constant fear of deportation and the methodical starvation of its inhabitants, even as the Nazis were "utilizing our diminished energies to produce goods for the German economy."

Roman was forced into slave labor, working in a factory without compensation to make uniforms and knapsacks for the German Army. He joined up to 10 million people throughout Europe, Jews and non-Jews alike, dragooned into coerced labor by the Nazis to keep their economy running while freeing up Germans for the war front. His father became one of 6 million Jews who would ultimately perish in the Holocaust when he died from malnutrition in the ghetto.

As a teenager Roman saw thousands become "walking skeletons in front of my eyes, just skin and bones. When going to sleep each night, many never woke up, while others simply died as they walked on the street." When this mode of murder was not fast enough for the Nazis, they liquidated the Lodz ghetto in 1944. Roman, his mother, and three siblings were shipped to Auschwitz, the notorious Nazi concentration camp in occupied Poland.

He told me he did not really know how long he spent there. "What I do know, however, is that one minute in Auschwitz was a day, one day was a year, and one month was an eternity. My response is, How many eternities can one have in one's lifetime? I do not know." To this day "the smell of burning flesh, the look of the tortured, the feeling of despair and helplessness, the agony, brutality, and bestiality, the shameful enjoyment on the faces of the German perpetrators" remain with him. His mother and one sister died in Auschwitz. He was sent to several other concentration camps, from Flossenburg, where he cut heavy stones for roads, to Sachsenhausen. The United States Third Army liberated Roman in 1945, as he and his brother were walking as prisoners to Dachau.

Here the coincidences in our lives began. Under a special American program for orphans of the war, he and his brother were settled with a family in Atlanta, Georgia, my hometown. Roman attended Grady High School, my high school a decade later, and studied at Atlanta's Emory University, as my sons Jay and Brian would do forty years later. Roman became a businessman in New York.

Like many survivors, he tried to put the Holocaust behind him, not to dwell on the horrific past but to marry, raise a family, and "make a living from ground zero." It took decades for him to be able to look back—in his words, to "distance myself from history." In 1980, with Benjamin Meed, a survivor of the Warsaw ghetto, he founded the American Gathering of Holocaust Survivors to develop the first list of American survivors and create a support network. A few years later, alarmed after learning from the *New York Times* Neediest Cases Fund list that many Holocaust survivors were destitute, Roman and Ben Meed joined the Conference on Jewish Material Claims Against Germany, the official organization charged with distributing German reparations payments to Jewish Holocaust survivors.

Roman and I first met in 1999, during the negotiations that I helped to organize to provide restitution to wartime slave laborers employed by German companies and the German government. Roman was vice president of the Claims Conference and an official member of the negotiating delegation; I was the undersecretary of state and special representative for the president and secretary of state on Holocaust issues. With his still heavily Polish-accented English, he joked that, as two southerners from Atlanta, we were the only ones who could really understand each other. As a result of my negotiations, in May 2002 Roman Kent received payment from the Germans for his slave labor almost sixty years earlier. But for him, much more meaningful was the apology on December 17, 1999, from German president Johannes Rau, begging forgiveness in the name of the German people. Roman received it standing next to me in Berlin, the former capital of the Third Reich.

The money represented for Roman a "token compensation so survivors know their suffering was acknowledged by the Germans." But the apology was more important, representing a "moral victory because," Roman said, "we can never equate morality and ethics in terms of dollars and cents."

Why did it take more than fifty years to provide imperfect justice to the civilian victims of Nazi barbarism, by which time most had died? The surprise is not that it took so long but that it happened at all.

Despite clear and repeated evidence that Jews, Slavs, Poles, Jehovah's Witnesses, Romanis (Gypsies), and political opponents were targeted by the Nazis, protection of their lives, let alone their assets, was a distant priority for the leaders of the wartime Grand Alliance. The most compelling testimony came from Jan Karski, the brave Polish diplomat who risked his life by twice going into the Warsaw ghetto to bear witness and who made his way to Washington to tell the story. He personally saw President Franklin D. Roosevelt, who ignored his accounts. When Karski met with FDR's confidant, Supreme Court Justice Felix Frankfurter, the great jurist said, "Sir, I am not saying you are lying, but I choose not to believe you."

The refugees were not much more of a priority after the war, when rebuilding a ravaged Europe and fighting the Cold War took precedence. The Cold War diverted Allied attention from the victims and threw up impenetrable barriers for those behind the Iron Curtain to trace their looted property. Like Roman Kent, the scattered survivors often tried to forget the painful past in order to build a better future. Tracking down assets a continent away, many of which had been nationalized by Communist governments, was at best intimidating and more often impossible.

It took a unique combination of events in the 1990s and a few enterprising people to raise world consciousness of those victims still alive and their need for justice.

Just as the Cold War pushed justice for victims off the world's agenda, the end of the Cold War redirected energies and opened archives. People behind the former Iron Curtain could finally travel and inquire freely. Jewish communities that survived the twin scourges of the twentieth century, Nazism and communism, wanted to reconnect to their religion and their obliterated institutions.

The coincidence of fiftieth anniversaries in 1994 and 1995 for D-Day, the Battle of the Bulge, and the end of the war in Europe led to retrospectives. Living in Europe during this time as the U.S. ambassador to the European Union, I was struck with how fresh were the wounds and grievances from World War II. Indeed, for my wife, Fran, and me the emotional highlight of our two and a half years abroad was the D-Day commemoration and the moving ceremony with President Clinton at the cemetery at Omaha Beach, with its seemingly endless rows of neat, sparkling white crosses and Jewish stars of those who made our freedom today possible. At the same time, Holocaust survivors reaching the end of their lives began to tell long-suppressed stories and now sought a measure of justice for what had been stripped from them.

People make history, and a few people provided the sparks that ignited the kindling of unsatisfied justice that was there after the end of the Cold War. Journalists like Peter Gumbel of the *Wall Street Journal* gave a human face to dormant Swiss bank accounts from the World War II era by highlighting the case of Greta Beer, who was blocked from even seeing records of the Swiss bank account her father had told her about on his deathbed. Edgar Bronfman, a wealthy and influential businessman, and Israel Singer, his close adviser, used the restitution issue to give new prominence to the World Jewish Congress, which they led. The United States was the only country that cared enough to take an interest at this late date and had the influence to make a difference.

The involvement of the United States government in the Swiss bank affair and all that followed was without precedent. With the Balkans in flames, the Middle East peace process and relations with Russia and China presenting daily challenges, the Republican-controlled Congress staging daily confrontations, and the White House in the midst of the Monica Lewinsky affair, why should the highest officials of the U.S. government, right up to the president, spend vast amounts of time intervening in class-action lawsuits involving purely private parties covering events that occurred over fifty years ago?

The question is easy to answer at one level. The Holocaust victims and others injured by the Nazis, many of whom were now U.S. citizens, were particularly deserving of some justice at the end of difficult lives. There were also traditional foreign policy concerns. Without American involvement, U.S. relations with friendly countries and close allies would be negatively affected by the lawsuits and the threats that surrounded them. The Swiss banks, and later the German, Austrian, and French companies who were sued, enlisted the help of their governments, which in turn wanted the U.S. government to find a solution in order to lift a cloud over their companies doing business in the United States. In Eastern European property restitution, my colleagues and I saw the advancement of property rights and respect for minorities as part and parcel of our efforts to transform these former Communist dictatorships into genuine democracies.

But there was another reason—domestic politics. Political and economic self-interest, realpolitik, is the primary force behind European foreign policy. Not so in the United States. Even the most sophisticated Europeans fail to appreciate that U.S. foreign policy is a unique and complicated mixture of morality and self-interest. Depending upon the president, the importance of realpolitik waxes and wanes in relation to moral issues like fostering democracy and human rights—waxing with a Nixon-Kissinger team, waning with a Woodrow Wilson or Jimmy Carter. The moral factor dominated in dealing with those victims whose rights were so devastatingly crushed in World War II.

But more than in any other industrial democracy, domestic politics always helps shape U.S. foreign policy, to the chagrin of Europeans and the American foreign policy establishment alike. Senator Alfonse D'Amato, the chief congressional antagonist of Bill and Hillary Clinton in the Whitewater investigation, brought his attack-dog tactics to the Swiss bank investigation. The administration believed it could not leave the field to him without risking a breach in U.S. relations with Switzerland, a major economic partner.

Were domestic Jewish political pressures also a major reason for sustained, high-level U.S. engagement in the Holocaust negotiations? Yes. Edgar Bronfman, the billionaire head of the World Jewish Congress, was politically well connected and a strong supporter of the president and first lady. He urged them, at a moment when the United States was the world's most powerful nation, to take a personal interest in providing belated justice to Holocaust survivors. And he spurred Senator D'Amato, facing a tough reelection campaign in a state with more Holocaust survivors than any other, to begin congressional hearings into the activities of Swiss banks during and after the war.

Yet there is nothing insidious about this. Jews are hardly the only group seeking to influence government officials. They are all part of a peculiarly American way of making foreign policy.

European parliamentary governments are largely immune from the political pressures of the well-organized groups that interact with the United States' more open, boisterous, contentious system with its independent congressional branch. Policy is made by the clash of interests. Organized labor and the big business community square off on everything from the minimum wage and health care to the benefits of free trade. U.S. steel companies seek protection from foreign competition, and agribusinesses higher price supports. Environmentalists pressure the U.S. government for environmentally friendly domestic laws and international treaties like the 1997 Kyoto Protocol on global warming.

Similarly, Greek Americans have long tilted U.S. foreign policy toward Greece and away from Turkey, a far larger and strategically more critical country. The U.S. policy of isolating Fidel Castro's Cuba is driven by the well-organized Cuban-American community in South Florida. African Americans helped change U.S. foreign policy to boycott South Africa, even during the conservative Reagan administration.

On a lighter note, Italian Americans insist on little, but make it a matter of pride to have one of their own named as U.S. ambassador to Italy. In the Clinton administration this led to the sudden reassignment to Italy of one of our most distinguished career ambassadors, Reginald Bartholomew, headed for a post in Israel, when his Italian ancestry was uncovered. In the George W. Bush administration, Rockwell Schnabel, already tapped for Italy and approved by its government, was precipitously moved to my former post, ambassador to the European Union, when the Italian-American community loudly objected that he was not one of them.

The Jewish community's influence on U.S. policy toward Israel has grown over the years. More recently the increasingly large Arab-American community is weighing in for a greater consideration of Palestinian interests.

Because Holocaust memory is one of the few uniting themes in American Jewish life, Bronfman's intervention with the president found an open door.

My own contribution was to bring a special level of commitment and perseverance. For me, this was not just another public policy challenge but a chance to help remove a cloud over the history of the United States, which had sacrificed so greatly to win the war but done so little to prevent civilian genocide and then help its survivors after the conflict. *Discipline* was my watchword. I pushed myself and my team unmercifully because we had a small window of opportunity and an administration willing to exploit a unique combination of historical developments. If we did not succeed now, when all the stars were aligned, there would be no more survivors left to help.

.     .     .

I GREW UP in modest circumstances in Atlanta, in a home in which Judaism was a pervasive influence but the Holocaust was never once discussed. Close friends of my father, Leo, called him by his Yiddish name, Leib. He was steeped in Jewish learning, which gave him great joy to maintain and pass on to me. Every Friday night, after my mother, Sylvia, had lit the Sabbath candles and prepared a traditional Sabbath dinner, he would take me on the couch in our den and review the week's reading from the Bible. Often he translated the difficult Hebrew writing of the great eleventh-century Torah commentator Rashi to explain its deeper meaning. At our synagogue in Atlanta, Ahavath Achim, which means "brotherly love," my father was known as the "pinch hitter." If the week's designated reader from the Haftorah (The Prophets) suddenly fell ill, the congregation could count on my father to chant with little advance notice.

All four of my grandparents were born in Eastern Europe, Russia on my father's side, Lithuania on my mother's. Yiddish was their native tongue, and they spoke English with a heavy accent. Yet the destruction of European Jewry during World War II was never a topic I heard them discuss, even though it had happened only a few years before my school days.

I was born in 1943, and growing up in the 1940s and 1950s, I cannot remember ever talking to a Holocaust survivor. I never studied these terrible events in elementary school, at Atlanta's Grady High School, or at the University of North Carolina at Chapel Hill. No college courses were offered on the subject, even if I had been interested. It was not until 1995, when, at Fran's suggestion, a researcher looked at the Lithuanian National Archives, that I discovered that three sisters of my maternal grandfather, Israel Medintz, perished in the Holocaust.

We often discussed the war itself. My father and his brother, Berry, both served stateside in the U.S. Army. My mother's brother, Coleman Medintz, was a brave Marine. His service was not in Europe but in the South Pacific, driving amphibious landing craft in the major invasions of islands, an experience far removed from the Holocaust.

My attachment to Atlanta and its institutions is deep and lifelong. Out of loyalty to Atlanta's premier product, Coca-Cola, we never had a Pepsi Cola in the house. Part of our family lore involves my grandfather Esar Eizenstat, a Russian immigrant, and Coca-Cola. Early in the century, he refused the entreaties of a salesman to buy shares of stock in Coke, telling my father, then a young boy, in his native Yiddish, *"Vayl keyner vet veln trinkn kolirteh vahse!"* (Because no one will want to drink colored water!). To this day my sons, Jay and Brian, lament the shortsightedness of their great grandfather in not buying even one share of Coke.

The memories of the 1913 lynching of Leo Frank, a Jewish leader falsely accused of murdering a young girl at an Atlanta pencil factory; signs at Mooney's Lake reading "No Jews allowed"; the Taylor brothers across the street beating me up as I returned from Hebrew school one day; Governor Ernest Vandiver's threat to close the public schools in 1959 in defiance of a federal desegregation order—these were the topics of our interest, not the Holocaust.

My earliest memory of confronting injustice had nothing to do with the Holocaust but with segregation. It is an early test that I failed. When returning from synagogue at the age of thirteen on a crowded, segregated Atlanta bus, I could not break with convention and permit an elderly black lady laden with shopping bags to sit in my seat in the whites-only section.

My experience in not confronting the Holocaust soon after the actual event was similar to that of most American Jews, indeed most Americans. The Holocaust scholar Michael Berenbaum has wisely observed a "paradox relating to the Holocaust: the more distant we are from the event the larger it looms." The growth of my own consciousness about the Holocaust roughly paralleled its increasing recognition by the general public. Without this heightened public sensibility my work on the restitution of Jewish assets would not have been possible, for the story would have had no context.

Immediately after the war, a shock ran through America and Western Europe with the full revelation of the Nazi death camps that had been liberated by the Allied forces closing in on Germany. So incomprehensible was the brutality that no less a figure than General Dwight D. Eisenhower, the supreme allied commander of the Western armies, publicly visited the camps so that he could personally testify to what had happened. The gaunt faces, the stick-thin bodies in their striped uniforms, the bulldozers piling heaps of the dead into trenches aroused a transitory horror when shown in newsreels across the United States.

The Nuremberg war crimes trials in 1945 detailed the master plan to destroy European Jewry. In prosecuting and convicting senior Nazi officials, the Allies established a new concept of crimes against humanity that would remain powerful five decades later. But in the late 1940s, attention waned as American policy shifted toward rebuilding war-torn Europe through the Marshall Plan and fighting the Cold War against the Soviet Union. The Allied program of punishing former Nazis and barring them from public office languished. It barely touched the vast number of German officials and private persons, including many important business and financial leaders, who supported Hitler's efforts and thereby directly or indirectly facilitated the Holocaust. Germany was to be rebuilt, its economy strengthened, and its crimes redeemed through membership in the North Atlantic Treaty Organization (NATO) and the European Coal and Steel Community, which later became the European Union, so that it could become a frontline ally in the defense against Soviet communism.

That efforts to help the 200,000 concentration camp survivors and those who survived the war in hiding were inadequate should come as no surprise. The fate of European Jewry had long been a secondary concern at best. Before the war's outbreak, the democratic nations sent Hitler a clear signal of their priorities by their reluctance to shelter Jews fleeing anti-Semitic laws in Germany and Austria. This was made manifest by their complete inaction at an international conference, held at the elegant French resort of Evian in July 1938, called to increase the intake of German refugees. In the United States, President Franklin D. Roosevelt resisted discussion of the plight of the Jews lest he lose domestic support for aiding Britain and, later, for the war effort itself, a crusade to protect democracy that he feared might be discredited as a "war for the Jews." Immigration quotas permitted only 155,000 European refugees to enter the United States from Hitler's rise to power in 1933 to America's entry in the war in December 1941. As the Nazi death machine accelerated its work, only about 20,000 Jews came to the United States from mid-1942 until the end of the war in Europe in May

1945—a much smaller proportion of the nation's population than even tiny, neutral Switzerland accepted in a more threatening environment. Britain permitted about 4,000 to go to Palestine. Canada took virtually none.

It can hardly be denied that the U.S. government knew what was happening. A book published in September 1943 by the World Jewish Congress titled *Hitler's Ten-Year War on the Jews* documented that 3,030,050 Jews had already been murdered and that property losses of European Jewry, excluding public communal property, were $6.317 billion.

Virtually the only senior official in the U.S. government who cared about the plight of European Jews was Secretary of the Treasury Henry Morgenthau, Jr., himself a Jew. He was so dismayed by the State Department's inaction that he commissioned his own report on U.S. policy toward European Jews. It was presented to him by junior members of his staff on January 13, 1944, and originally entitled *Report to the Secretary on the Acquiescence of This Government in the Murder of the Jews.* The report accused the State Department of actually hampering Jews' rescue, in particular through a policy, ordered by Assistant Secretary of State W. Breckenridge Long, of actively denying them entry visas.

Long was principally concerned that an influx of unsuitable foreigners would somehow pollute the racial stock of the United States, but for public consumption he usually relied on the argument, widely endorsed by government leaders, that wholesale admission of Jewish refugees would allow dangerous German agents to slip through. When Morgenthau presented his report to Roosevelt on January 16, it diplomatically carried a less inflammatory title, *Personal Report to the President.* Nevertheless, he dared not even leave a copy at the White House lest it leak out and damage Roosevelt politically in an election year.

Roosevelt, running for an unprecedented fourth term, finally recognized the political dangers of continued inaction—mainly a possible loss of Jewish support in key states—and followed Morgenthau's advice to create a War Refugee Board, belatedly leading to efforts to rescue refugees during the war's final months. Among other things, the board assisted Swedish diplomat Raoul Wallenberg in rescuing some of Hungary's Jews.

After the war the Jewish survivors were unwanted. Great Britain, exhausted, financially ruined, and desperate for access to Arab oil, blocked their efforts to emigrate to Palestine. The new Labour government of Clement Attlee rejected President Harry Truman's request to allow

100,000 refugees into Palestine as a humanitarian gesture, and from 1946 to 1949 Britain kept over 52,000 Holocaust survivors seeking entry to Palestine detained under guard for up to a year in squalid camps in Cyprus.

Those survivors who decided to return to their prewar countries and reclaim their homes and property faced a rude shock. In Poland and Lithuania, for example, the homes of deported Jews were occupied by people who had no intention of leaving. Polish and Lithuanian nationalists even murdered some of the Jews who returned. In the village of Eisiskes, near Vilnius in Lithuania, five of the few Jews who survived the Holocaust were murdered, with notes placed in some of their pockets: "This will be the fate of all surviving Jews." On April 21, 1946—Easter Sunday—five Jewish survivors of Auschwitz, Buchenwald, and Mauthausen were shot on the outskirts of Nowy Targ by members of the former underground forces of the Polish Home Army.

Unable to return home, hundreds of thousands of stateless refugees, drifting without hope and nowhere to go, found that the victorious Allied military forces were unprepared to deal with them. Twenty-two displaced person, or DP, camps were established in Italy, Austria, and Germany. Many refugees spent up to five years there. The largest concentration of DPs were located in the American Zone in southern Germany, occupied by the Third Army under General George S. Patton Jr. This famously daring armored-division commander, whose forces liberated concentration camps, ordered camp guards to monitor the refugees as if they were inmates in prison. Patton wrote in his diary on September 15, 1945, "Others believe that the Displaced Person is a human being, which he is not, and this applies particularly to the Jews who are lower than animals . . . a sub-human species without any of the cultural or social refinements of our time." On September 17, 1945, while he and Supreme Allied Commander Dwight D. Eisenhower were visiting a DP camp, Patton told Eisenhower, to the latter's dismay, that he anticipated converting a nearby German town "into a concentration camp for these goddamn Jews."

Although the overwhelming majority of U.S. military personnel treated the DPs with dignity, conditions in the DP camps were so deplorable that President Truman asked Earl G. Harrison, the U.S. representative to the Intergovernmental Committee on Refugees, to investigate. Harrison completed a scathing report, telling Truman, "As matters now stand, we appear to be treating the Jews as the Nazis treated them except we do not exterminate them. They are in concentration camps in large numbers under our military guard instead of SS troops. One is left to wonder whether the German people, seeing this, are not supposing that we are following or at least condoning Nazi policy."

As for property stolen, looted, or seized during the war by the Nazis, there was a burst of activity following the war and in the late 1940s to return it to the countries from which it was taken and then, if possible, to its owners. At the Potsdam Conference of July and August 1945, when the Allied leaders made their first postwar attempt to determine the fate of a defeated Germany, they directed the Allied Control Council to manage all foreign-owned German assets, many of which were in Switzerland. In November 1945 the Council formally confirmed its control of all external German assets in order to ensure they would not be claimed by the neutrals in payment of German war debts. The sole exception was gold, which the Allies recognized had been plundered by the Germans from conquered countries.

The largest trove of hidden Nazi gold was found during the closing days of the war at the Merkers Salt Mine, in the foothills of the Alps in the German state of Thuringia. Bedazzled American GIs found 3,682 bags and cartons of German currency, 80 bags of foreign currency, 8,307 gold bars, 55 boxes of gold bullion, 3,326 bags of gold coins, 63 bags of silver, 1 bag of platinum bars, 8 bags of gold rings, and 207 bags and containers of SS loot, everything from rings and bracelets to candelabras and gold fillings from teeth. The total value of the gold and currency was $520 million in wartime dollars. The mine also housed over four hundred tons of artwork and the records of the Reichsbank, the Third Reich's central bank. All of this loot came from the treasuries of the countries the Germans occupied or from individual Holocaust victims.

A gold pool, under the trusteeship of the United States, Britain, and France, was established at the Allied Reparations Conference in Paris late in 1945, with the looted gold stashed throughout Germany. In September 1946 the three allies established the Tripartite Gold Commission, with headquarters in Brussels. In a remarkable act of generosity by the countries that had borne the cost of defeating the Germans, the Allies placed 337 tons of looted Nazi gold in the pool for return to its owners.

The countries from whom the gold was taken got back about 65 percent of their looted gold from the Tripartite Gold Commission. The individual victims got none.

Allied negotiations with the wartime neutrals, especially Switzerland, to return gold looted by the Nazis and to liquidate German assets in their possession for the benefit of refugees were never given top priority, dragged on for years, and restored only a fraction of what was owed. Restitution programs to return looted property to the families from whom they were confiscated were woefully inadequate, as well, tailed off in Western Europe, and ended entirely when the Iron Curtain fell on Eastern Europe and all private property was nationalized by the Communist governments.

.　　.　　.

BY THE LATE 1940s, the attempted extermination of European Jewry had been buried in public consciousness or, as in the case in the 1950s of Anne Frank's *Diary of a Young Girl,* sanitized as a story of hope without moral outrage. Many authors had difficulties publishing their work on the Holocaust. Elie Wiesel was unknown, as readers turned away from the stark horror of this Auschwitz survivor's memoir and essays. Raul Hilberg, now one of the world's foremost Holocaust scholars, struggled for years to find a publisher for his monumental work of research, *The Destruction of the European Jews.* In 1962 Rabbi Irving "Yitz" Greenberg was denied permission to teach a course on the Holocaust even at Yeshiva University, so he had to call the course "Totalitarianism and Ideology in the 20th Century."

In Germany itself from 1945 to 1951, there was a deafening silence about the Holocaust. Israel's decision to start reparations negotiations with the Federal Republic of Germany in 1951 (the East German Communists abjured all responsibility) shattered the wall of silence between the two countries. For each government, this beginning represented a wrenching change.

Within Israel there were many who argued in favor of negotiating directly with West Germany. The Israeli economy was stretched to its limits, absorbing the flow of immigrants from Europe and from Arab states, developing a modern infrastructure, and strengthening its military capacity against surrounding Arab states that wanted Israel's destruction. Many Israelis also believed that Germany had a moral obligation, as first publicly defined in 1941 by Nahum Goldmann, head of the World Jewish Congress: "Who can doubt that we Jews have every right to international help for European Jewry after the war? If reparations are to be paid, we are the first who have a claim to them." At the same time, a large number of Israelis, particularly from the conservative Likud Party, found the idea of reparations distasteful.

With wartime wounds so fresh, Israel hoped to avoid direct negotiations with Germany. But when the Allies spurned Prime Minister David Ben-Gurion's request to negotiate on behalf of Israel, he moved ahead on his own. To avoid the appearance of direct talks, in October 1951 the Israeli government helped create the Conference on Jewish Material Claims Against Germany, known as the Claims Conference, with twenty-three Jewish organizations as members. Ferocious opposition arose, led by Menachem Begin, leader of the opposition Likud Party. Begin, who had fought the Nazis as a member of the Free Polish Army before coming to Israel and who lost many of his family in the death camps, angrily asked the Knesset, the Israeli legislature: "Who ever heard of some of the murdered going to the murderer for compensation?" Castigating Ben-Gurion as a "hooligan," Begin said, "Some things are dearer than life. Some things are worse than death." Violent protests erupted outside the Knesset. It was not until January 8, 1952, that the measure passed, 61–50.

Much like Ben-Gurion, West German chancellor Konrad Adenauer also had to strike a delicate balance among practical, political, and moral interests. Working independently of the government, Eric Luth and Rudolph Kustermeier founded a group called Peace with Israel in 1951 to press for reparations for Israel, after forty-seven countries announced they were ending their state of war with Germany without an official acceptance from the German government of responsibility for the Holocaust. Adenauer also knew that for Germany to return to the community of nations, it had to face its past. Restitution would be the price of acceptance. The U.S. high commissioner for Germany John J. McCloy, who as assistant secretary of war during World War II had rejected appeals to bomb the railroad tracks leading to Auschwitz, told the German people in 1949: "I assure you that while I shall do everything in my power to help you get a fresh start and win a dignified and responsible place in the family of nations, I shall not forget Dachau and Bergen-Belsen."

On September 27, 1951, Adenauer broke the official silence, proclaiming, "Unspeakable crimes have been committed in the name of the German people, calling for moral and material indemnity." From this grew the 1952 Luxembourg agreements between the Federal Republic of Germany on one hand and Israel and the Claims Conference on the other. Under these and later agreements that became known as the Federal Indemnification Laws, Germany has paid 100 billion deutsche marks—more than $60 billion—to 500,000 Holocaust survivors around the world. Germans believed these reparations should have closed the book on its responsibility for Hitler's Final Solution.

.    .    .

FOR MANY Americans and for me personally, the first major recognition of the Holocaust came in 1961, with Adolf Eichmann's dramatic arrest in Argentina and trial in Israel. He was the highest-ranking Nazi leader still known to be at large and was the official responsible for gathering masses of Jews and shipping them to the extermination camps. The televised image of an unrepentant Eichmann testifying impassively in his glass-enclosed, bullet-proof witness box was one of the first opportunities for ordinary Americans, and for me, to confront the Holocaust directly through the visage of one of its chief perpetrators.

The role of my own country was brought home to me while I was working in the 1968 presidential campaign of Hubert Humphrey and met a fellow campaign aide, Arthur Morse, whose groundbreaking book *While Six Million Died* had just been published. Arthur documented the shocking inaction of the Roosevelt administration in the face of clear evidence of the wartime slaughter of European Jews. His book and our conversations about it had a great personal impact on me. FDR had been so venerated in the Jewish community that there was a Yiddish joke that Jews believed in three worlds: "*die velt* [this world], *yenna velt* [the next world]—and Roosevelt!" To me, it was profoundly troubling that the president and his circle of White House advisers, several of whom were Jewish, knew about the murder of the Jews and did so little to stop it.

German-Jewish assets in the United States had been frozen in 1941 along with all other German property. Shortly after the war, the United States returned the property to the survivors or their heirs, but nothing was done about the assets of heirless Nazi victims, those who died without families. In 1954 Congress authorized up to $3 million in grants to Jewish charities, but it was not until 1963, almost twenty years after the war, that Congress, at President John F. Kennedy's direction, appropriated a smaller amount,

$500,000, to be given to the Jewish Restitution Successor Organization, responsible for heirless and unclaimed property.

During the 1970s and '80s there began an explosion of Holocaust-related books, not only from Hilberg, but Lucy Dawidowicz, Walter Laqueur, David Wyman, and others. Study of the Holocaust became part of such diverse disciplines as history, theology, philosophy, psychology, sociology, literature, film, and anthropology. In 1973 only two universities offered courses on the Holocaust; by the 1980s the number had exploded to 210. The Holocaust became a signature of evil incarnate, of humanity's basest instincts, of technology run amok. It raised questions about the nature of progress and civilization itself.

In 1974 Fran and I went on a weekend retreat at Camp Barney Medintz, named after my late uncle, sponsored by the Atlanta Jewish Federation. The guest scholar was Rabbi Yitz Greenberg, who had just returned from a year in Israel studying at Yad Vashem, Israel's memorial to and research center on Holocaust victims. We spent a dozen hours under his intensive tutelage, but I would never have imagined the ways I would put this knowledge to use when I went to work in the White House three years later as chief domestic policy adviser to my fellow Georgian, President Jimmy Carter.

Early in my tenure at the Carter White House, I learned firsthand how the Holocaust had become an intensely political issue. Without telling me, Mark Siegel, the White House liaison to the Jewish community and a deputy to President Carter's top political aide, Hamilton Jordan, asked a member of my staff, Ellen Goldstein, to find out which nations had built Holocaust memorials. This information was part of Siegel's background research in obtaining Senate ratification of the treaty against genocide. Ellen found that, apart from Israel, there were no such official memorials, and Siegel had an inspired idea: The U.S. government should take the lead in establishing a Holocaust memorial in Washington, D.C., to underscore the Carter administration's theme of putting human rights at the center of foreign policy. Siegel promptly sent a recommendation to Jordan, but nothing happened.

Months later, Ellen was reminded of her earlier research through a *New York Times* column by William Safire about a neo-Nazi march in Skokie, Illinois. Safire deplored the absence in America of "a vivid reminder of the horror of the final solution." She wrote me urging that Carter propose a Holocaust memorial. Aware that this might be taken as a public relations ploy to mollify American Jewish opinion (who were upset over a recent sale of military aircraft to Saudi Arabia), she suggested naming a committee of fifteen members to explore the idea and report to the president.

I was enthusiastic. American troops had helped liberate the concentration camps and had witnessed the aftermath of the Holocaust. And so it was only right that the United States should erect the first memorial outside Israel. In plain political terms, I also felt it would help the administration's frayed ties to the American Jewish community. On April 25, 1978, Robert Lipshutz, the president's counsel, and I sent President Carter a memorandum arguing for a memorial, citing his own human-rights initiatives, the increased interest in the Holocaust by Jews and non-Jews alike, and the age of the remaining survivors. A week later, Carter approved the recommendation.

I naively thought that this would be a simple and noncontroversial project. Instead, I learned a lesson that would stay with me for decades: Nothing about the Holocaust is free of controversy. It is politically radioactive. Everyone whom it has touched, directly or indirectly, holds strong and emotional opinions and seeks to claim it as theirs. Non-Jews, particularly Poles, Czechs, and Russians, demand similar attention for their grievous suffering during the war, often feeling that Jewish victims have received too much compensation at their expense.

Carter launched the project on May 1 at an elaborate ceremony on the South Lawn of the White House. Present were about a thousand rabbis from all over the country and Menachem Begin, who was now Israel's prime minister. I helped draft the president's speech, which referred to the impact of Morse's book. On that occasion, Carter gave Begin a 1944 photograph taken by a U.S. military plane of Auschwitz, with modern technology identifying the crematoria.

Carter had called me into the Oval Office to ask my recommendation for the chair of the presidential exploratory commission. Without hesitation I proposed Elie Wiesel. With Wiesel's support I secured the appointments of Rabbi Yitz Greenberg as director and the Holocaust scholar Michael Berenbaum as deputy director of the commission. That was the easy part. Two problems persisted for the better part of a year: first, who should serve on the commission and, second, how the Holocaust itself should be defined.

I explained to Weisel that we would need congressional legislation to establish a memorial, which would need broad public support and require non-Jews as well as Jews to be members of the presidential commission. He agreed, but successfully insisted that all appointees must have some connection to the Holocaust—either as survivors, families of victims, resistance fighters, or scholars. Overwhelmed by requests for appointments to the commission, we reluctantly decided to expand the membership and create a separate advisory council to handle the overflow. The commission thus had a mixed membership, including a number of prominent non-Jewish leaders. To deal with the overwhelming demands for membership by the Jewish community, the advisory committee was predominantly Jewish.

The same dispute broke out even more fiercely when, later in the year, the commission recommended creation of a U.S. Holocaust memorial museum to be headed by a council that would raise money and oversee construction of the museum and the collection and display of exhibits. We had to amend the original executive order creating the council to satisfy competing demands for Polish and Ukrainian Americans for representation. Carter instructed me to delete three proposed Jewish members and add three Americans of Eastern European background. As I struggled to find a politically acceptable balance, Wiesel became increasingly frustrated. We finally developed a diverse list of non-Jewish Americans including two African Americans, two members of Polish ancestry, and one each of Slovenian and Ukrainian backgrounds.

It was not only Eastern Europeans who wanted to be remembered as part of the Holocaust. Set Momjian, a leader of the Armenian community from the Philadelphia suburbs, was also named and brought his own agenda. He wanted to insure that any Holocaust memorial also recognize the death of an estimated 1 million Armenians under the Ottoman Turks during World War I. When the Turks learned of this, Turkey's ambassador to the United States, Sukru Elekdag, came to see me in my White House office. The ambassador's message was brutal. If the Armenian massacres were included in the museum, Turkey, which had protected its Jewish community for five centuries, could no longer be responsible for its safety. He warned of negative effects on Turkey's relations with the United States and on Israel's relations with Turkey—the first Muslim country to have full diplomatic relations with the Jewish state. The dispute between the Turks and the Armenians would bedevil the museum for years.

Most discouraging was the fierce and fundamental dispute over the very definition of the Holocaust itself. Was it indeed, as Wiesel and I believed, a distinctively Jewish event? Wiesel put it to me eloquently: "Not all victims were Jews, but all Jews were victims." Aloysius Mazewski of the Polish American Congress did not see it that way. He told Rabbi Greenberg that the 3 million Polish victims of World War II shared the Holocaust with the 6 million Jewish victims. For over a year this debate raged. At the first Days of Remembrance service in the Capitol Rotunda on April 24, 1979, President Carter referred to "11 million innocent victims exterminated—6 million of them Jews," upsetting the Jewish survivor community and Wiesel in particular, who saw it as diluting the distinctive Jewish nature of the Holocaust. His presidential commission in September recommended another definition, stressing the extermination of 6 million Jews as a central act of the Third Reich. Michael Berenbaum wanted a more universal definition, similar to one I had recommended to the president, the one incorporated into the president's executive order creating the U.S. Holocaust Memorial Council: "six million Jews and five million other peoples." When Wiesel came up with another suggested definition, President Carter scribbled an exasperated note to me: "Stu—use the same exact definition as was used in EO 12169; delay announcement if you wish or we simply delay any names." Tensions ran so high that the administration canceled the second Days of Remembrance service, in 1980. Wiesel wrote me an angry letter accusing the White House of "deplorable manipulations" and of emphasizing "politics, not loyalty to the dead."

In the end, a more inclusive council and Holocaust definition, still recognizing the particular Jewish dimension, gave the museum the broad support and moral force that have made it an unqualified success.

The struggle over the museum was not my only White House encounter with the lessons of the Holocaust. In 1979 the shah of Iran, a close ally of the United States, was forced by a revolution to flee his country. A sizable Jewish community, which had lived peacefully in Iran for 2,000 years, feared for their lives as a radical regime of Islamic fundamentalists gained control. Tens of thousands of Iranian Jews fled. Desperate to find a way into the United States, they besieged the U.S. consulates in Rome, Vienna, and elsewhere in Europe. The consular officers rejected them and told them to return to Iran. They were not eligible for employment, visas, student visas, or even visitors' visas, nor could they be considered political refugees, because the administration did not want to antagonize the new revolutionary regime in its formative stages.

I was determined not to repeat the mistakes of my predecessors in the Roosevelt administration, who could have saved hundreds of thousands of Jews and other refugees but did not. After extensive consultations within the administration and with groups outside government, I developed a solution. On November 26, 1979, Carter signed Executive Order 12172, granting visitors' visas to the Iranian Jews that would expire only when the status quo was returned to Iran—that is, when the shah was restored to the throne. Some 50,000 Iranian Jews entered the United States as a result, spared from the Khomeni regime, and others already in the United States before the revolution were spared from being expelled and having to return to Iran. Almost all are now American citizens.

By the time I returned to government service in 1993 as the U.S. ambassador to the European Union, Holocaust remembrance was in full swing. The American Gathering of Holocaust Survivors, formed by Roman Kent and Ben Meed, had held its first major conference in Washington, D.C., in April 1983, bringing together 20,000 Holocaust survivors, many of whom located members of their families they had not known to have survived. The gathering was addressed by the president of the United States, Ronald Reagan.

Steven Spielberg's cinematic masterpiece *Schindler's List* was dramatizing to the world in 1993 the enormity of the Holocaust. The tragedy was the subject of many other films (including Claude Lanzmann's landmark 1985 film, *Shoah*), novels, memoirs, and historical studies, as well as an accepted field of academic inquiry. And in September 1993, I had a quiet sense of pride as I saw President Clinton preside over the formal opening of the U.S. Holocaust Memorial Museum.

All of this coincided with my own personal experiences. Virtually every Jewish friend Fran and I made in Brussels and Antwerp during my diplomatic posting in Belgium was a survivor of the Holocaust; most of those our age had been hidden as children during the war. In all my first fifty years in America, I had never had such personal encounters, but they were daily fare for Jews in Europe. Even more gripping were our visits to the ancestral villages of my two grandfathers—to the killing field outside Ukmerge, Lithuania, where three of Israel Medintz's sisters were likely shot by the Nazis; and to Zagalie, Belarus, where the oldest man in town vividly described the roundup and slaughter of the Jews of the shtetl, which Esar Eizenstat fortunately left for America at the beginning of the twentieth century.

Fran and I once accompanied a delegation of Belgian officials and Jewish community leaders in a government-provided airplane to visit Auschwitz-Birkenau. We were led around by Henri Kichka, a Belgian survivor who had donned his inmate's cap. We entered the chilling gate with its false inscription, *"Arbeit macht frei"* (Work brings freedom). He showed us the barracks in which he had been housed, the remains of the crematoria, the tiny museum with the remnants of shoes, human hair, and personal effects. He described the brutal conditions of his daily effort to survive death all around him, the almost intolerable conditions, including the morning lineup outside the barracks, wearing the thinnest of clothing in weather as bone chilling as the day we were there. Fran said out loud that she felt guilty wearing her fur coat.

I would soon receive a call from Washington that would start me on an odyssey into the epicenter of a belated effort to do justice to Holocaust survivors and others brutalized by the Nazi regime. By then, both the world's consciousness and my own had been heightened about the Holocaust. Without my experiences and the world's knowledge having come together in my middle years, the work on which I would soon embark would have been impossible.

# CHAPTER ONE

# Through the Valley
# of the Dry Bones

O
N A TYPICALLY dreary, wet winter day in Brussels in January 1995, I was working in my office at the United States Mission to the European Union. Carolyn Keene, my longtime assistant, told me that Richard Holbrooke, assistant secretary of state for European affairs, was on the line. Dick and I had been friends and colleagues for almost twenty years. I had brought him to Atlanta in 1976 as a foreign policy adviser to Jimmy Carter's presidential campaign, for which I was the chief policy adviser. After Carter's victory, I helped Dick become the youngest assistant secretary of state in modern history. I respected his boundless energy, creativity, and dedication to public service. And I recognized his ambition for higher office.

This call would change my life. It would also help propel onto the world's agenda many shameful events that had long been buried in memory, often deliberately, and that only now were coming to light. Dick asked if I would undertake a special "limited mission" that he assured me would take only a few months. He offered me the position, in addition to my regular duties in Brussels, of the State Department's special envoy to encourage the return of property confiscated from religious communities by the Nazis and then nationalized by Eastern European Communist governments. I would concentrate primarily on the Jewish communities facing the greatest barriers.

Holbrooke explained that this would help the spiritual rebirth of religion and religious institutions suppressed by Communism. But property restitution was to be part of a broader U.S. policy to encourage the rule of law, respect for property rights, tolerance toward minorities, and the creation of nonpolitical administrative and judicial processes in the former

Communist countries. It was an essential part of what we called "civil society," without which the transition to viable democracy is not possible.

That I was in Brussels at all was a quirk of fate. I had worked for Bill Clinton's election in 1992, but having been President Carter's chief domestic policy adviser in the last Democratic administration, twelve years before, was actually a disadvantage in getting a post in the new administration. Bill Clinton resented Jimmy Carter, believing Carter's decision to place Cuban prisoners from the Mariel boat lift in Fort Smith, Arkansas, contributed to Clinton's defeat in the 1980 Arkansas gubernatorial election. Nor did he want his administration to look like Carter redux, given Carter's crushing defeat by Ronald Reagan. An offer in May 1993 by President Clinton's chief of staff, Thomas F. "Mack" McLarty, to be his deputy evaporated. After telling me the president needed my experience in the White House, McLarty withdrew the offer, and it was given to one of Vice President Gore's top aides, someone who had never served in the executive branch. So I was off to splendid exile in Brussels. Being sent to Europe was a way of keeping Carter people as far away as possible. It would take me several years of hard work to convince the Clinton insiders of my complete loyalty to Bill Clinton.

There was a special twist to Holbrooke's call. The previous spring, I had expected to be promoted to Holbrooke's position. He had hosted a dinner for Fran and me at his residence in Bonn, where he was serving as U.S. ambassador to Germany. Dick took pride in showing us the small framed picture of his grandfather, a German Jew, in full World War I military regalia, steel-pointed helmet and all, prominently displayed on an end table in his living room. He wanted his German guests to know that his grandfather had fought for the Kaiser—and by extension, to recognize the contributions that Jews had made to their country before, as he privately put it, "they killed them all" in the Holocaust.

As always, Dick was one step ahead of the news. He startled me by saying the post of assistant secretary of state for European affairs would soon fall vacant and that I would be asked by his other guest of the evening, Undersecretary of State Peter Tarnoff, to return to Washington and take the job. Sure enough, Peter pulled me off in a corner after dinner and made the offer. I told him I was flattered and would call him after discussing it with Fran, since we were enjoying our time abroad.

My senior staff in Brussels unanimously urged me to accept this broader platform to influence policy. When I finally decided to take the job a few weeks later, Tarnoff was suddenly hesitant. I later learned from Secretary of State Warren Christopher that I would not get the job after all—but that Holbrooke would. Christopher, clearly uncomfortable, told me that because of the rising troubles in the Balkans, Dick's negotiating experience made him the better choice. Dick had worked for me in the 1976 Carter campaign, but now I would be reporting to him. Had I gotten the job in Washington, I would never have had the opportunity to deal with the unrequited injustices of World War II, and Holbrooke might not have had the opportunity to negotiate the Dayton Accords ending the war in Bosnia. Sometimes things have a way of working out unexpectedly.

When Holbrooke called with his offer to be special envoy for property restitution in January 1995, I again did not immediately accept. It would divert attention from my full-time job in Brussels, where I dealt with a range of interesting issues between the two halves of the Western world. A mission to Eastern Europe, cut off from its Western neighbors for half a century, was unlikely to produce any tangible short-term results, and I would find myself caught between the governments of the new democracies and the Jewish communities that felt mistreated by them. What's more, the American ambassadors in the capitals of Eastern Europe would regard me as an intruder on their turf pursuing an unpopular issue.

I called one of those ambassadors, Alfred Moses, an old friend from the Carter White House who now held the post in Romania. He gave me the same warnings and added: "Why you? Because you are Jewish? You will be shot at from every direction." But in the end, with Fran's support and encouragement, I put aside such warnings and told Holbrooke I would take the job. There were too many deep emotions and my own sense of Holocaust history tugged too much at my conscience to refuse.

Holbrooke's call did not arise from a sudden brainstorm. He was under political pressure from Edgar Bronfman, a friend of President Clinton's and the president of the World Jewish Congress; Israel Singer, its flamboyant, creative general secretary; and Elan Steinberg, a gifted publicist and the head of the congress's North American division, who were already deeply involved in encouraging property restitution in Eastern Europe. All three were leaders of the World Jewish Restitution Organization (WJRO); Bronfman was also its president. Singer, joined by Steinberg and Maram Stern, the World Jewish Congress' European director, had met with Holbrooke to seek the administration's support in restoring confiscated Jewish property. Holbrooke, whose highly developed political antenna could not let him forget Bronfman's close relationship with President Clinton, agreed and asked who should lead the government's effort. Stern, based in Brussels, had already briefed me on the problem. Without advising me in advance, he told Holbrooke I was the right person.

This is a perfect example of a nongovernmental organization pushing its cause at the right time and using the levers of power to influence government policy. The leaders of the WJRO knew that they needed the U.S. government's help to accomplish anything in the former Communist lands. An umbrella body representing ten Jewish organizations, the WJRO was established in 1992 by the World Jewish Congress and the Israeli government to represent the interests of world Jewry in regaining Jewish property after the fall of Communism. On September 10, 1995, less than two months before his assassination at a peace rally in Tel Aviv, Israeli prime minister Yitzhak Rabin wrote Bronfman a letter endorsing the WJRO's quest and reaffirming that the WJRO represented the interests of the Israeli government and the Jewish people. In 1992 Bronfman had supported Rabin over Shimon Peres for leadership of the Labor Party. Rabin's letter was a political reward. But more important, it removed a headache for the Israeli government, which would otherwise be thrown into conflict with the new governments of the former Communist nations they wished to court for broader political support on other political and economic issues. Just as the Israeli government had created the Claims Conference to negotiate with the Germans in the 1950s, so here they created a nongovernmental body for property restitution to keep a difficult problem at arm's length.

Bronfman was armed not only with the exclusive mantle from the Israeli prime minister but also the endorsement of the president of the United States. On September 8, several months after I had begun my work as special envoy, President Clinton sent Bronfman a letter reaffirming my role as the administration's point man and specifically supporting the work of the WJRO. The president noted that "progress will be neither easy nor simple," and that Jewish property "seized during more than 50 years of war, occupation, and dictatorship is a complex and emotional subject." This double-barreled clout gave Bronfman the prominence that would make him an indispensable force in my property restitution efforts and in my subsequent negotiations with the Swiss, Germans, Austrians, and French.

My mission in Eastern Europe did not capture the attention of senior officials in Washington, and it was rarely even a talking point for President Clinton with any senior Eastern European leader. My office in Brussels was thousands of miles away from the seat of power in Washington. I also had to obtain support from U.S. ambassadors who had many other issues on their agendas, and this one never stood at the top. It was often only my visits that spurred them to act and follow up, which—to their credit—most eventually did with enthusiasm. I was largely on my own, slogging it out country by country, property by property. There were no external pressures from lawsuits or from the U.S. Congress, even though I wrote regular reports to congressional leaders on my visits, pointing out progress and difficulties. Aside from a 1995 European Parliament resolution generally encouraging property restitution, we received no support from the European Union, which could have used the leverage of its own admission process to encourage prospective member states in the former Communist world to adopt modern property laws and to return property confiscated during the Nazi and Communist eras.

Even more difficult to accept was the Israeli government's reluctance to use its political capital with the governments of Eastern Europe to help the reawakened Jewish communities. Despite several direct appeals to prime ministers Benjamin Netanyahu and Ehud Barak, in which I told them that Israel should be embarrassed by its disengagement, little was done for the cause of Eastern European property restitution. Israeli diplomats in Eastern European countries were unhelpful because they felt that anything that might assist the Jewish community to strengthen its roots in Europe would impede immigration to Israel and because they believed they had more pressing issues to pursue. It was ironic that the government that purports to represent the interests of world Jewry would have left the field to the U.S. government.

.    .    .

IN FACT, in ways neither Holbrooke nor I nor anyone else could have imagined at the time, his "limited mission" would lead me down a far different, unforeseen path, one that would wind for six more years and end with a final financial accounting for the crimes of World War II. Ahead lay tortuous, tumultuous, tension-filled negotiations involving a Shakespearean cast of colorful characters: with Switzerland over dormant bank accounts of Holocaust victims; with Germany and Austria over slave and forced laborers—Jews and non-Jews alike—and looted personal property; and with France over the financial legacy of its dark Vichy past.

Yet this first step was essential, though it lacked the dramatic fireworks of what was to come. It laid the groundwork for what would follow, creating the precedent of the United States government, at the zenith of its power in the world, intervening in a World War II issue involving what normally would be a quintessential internal matter, the disposition of property.

My work on the property restitution issue introduced me to realities for which I was unprepared. I came face-to-face with the Holocaust survivor community of Eastern Europe, which had lived through both the Nazi massacre and the Communist repression that followed. I coined a term to describe them—"double victims." I saw in their faces the brutality of our time, but I also recognized an indomitable spirit in the new young leadership that arose after the fall of the Berlin Wall. No longer were these victims anonymous people. Their quest to rebuild their religious community, together with similar efforts by their Catholic, Orthodox, and Protestant counterparts, steeled my determination and provided a sense of urgency to complete the job before it was too late for the wartime survivors.

I also became a witness to the rebirth of the decimated Jewish communities of Eastern Europe, once the flower of Jewry's religious, cultural, and artistic traditions. I saw new Jewish museums sprout up, daily synagogue services resume, Jewish newspapers flourish, kosher restaurants open, community centers bustle with activity, Jewish day schools filled to capacity from Budapest to Vilnius, from Kiev to Tallinn. A particularly moving experience occurred on a rainy night in Vilnius, Lithuania, a great center of Jewish culture that had been eradicated by the Nazis and then buried by the Communists. The experience exemplified for me the effort to reconnect to the traditions of the past. I visited a small class learning Hebrew in the basement of a dilapidated building and came across an elderly woman struggling with this alien language. "Why are you trying to learn Hebrew now?" I asked. She replied, "I just wanted to hear the language of my ancestors before I died."

I also learned a great deal about the challenges of life in post-Communist Eastern Europe that would lead me in my later negotiations to insist that their governments have a seat at the bargaining table. I saw the harshness of life as they tried to create capitalist economies. I found a seething bitterness that their citizens, also Hitler's victims, had never received compensation from the Germans comparable to the billions paid to Jewish Holocaust victims. And I learned how difficult it was for these former Communist countries to cast off their authoritarian yoke. Democracy is more than free elections. It is a set of institutions, a way of thinking, a respect for minority and property rights foreign to many of the countries with whom I dealt. There was a clear correlation between their progress in democratization and their willingness to return religious property still in their hands from Communist days.

My restitution work in Eastern Europe had one last, more personal impact, which carried over into my later enterprise. It ended the comforting feeling I had had from childhood that, as devastating as the Holocaust had been for the Jewish people, my family had been left untouched.

In a diplomatic visit in 1995 to Lithuania, the ancestral home of my mother's family, I discovered a stark and shocking reality. An 1895 census in the Lithuanian State Archives showed the location of the house of my maternal great grandparents, Orel and Simcha Medintz, in the village of Vilkomir, now Ukmerge. Their eight children, including my grandfather, then thirteen, were also listed. But only my grandfather and five of his siblings would emigrate to Chicago. What about the other two sisters, Rasha and Gena-Sora, then five years old and ten months old, about whom I had never heard?

With my prodding, elderly relatives in Chicago recalled hearing that the two sisters had made their way as far as Cuba when the storm clouds of war grew in the late 1930s, only to be turned back. In a later trip to Lithuania in 1998, I visited Ukmerge's old Jewish quarter, by which time the archivists had mined another family gem, a 1932 marriage certificate of yet another sister of my grandfather, Sonia, not born at the time of the 1893 census. An old survivor, Hirshas Pekelis, who accompanied me on the trip to Ukmerge, startled me by exclaiming that he had been an apprentice to one of the witnesses cited in the marriage certificate.

All three sisters and their families were almost certainly killed in the 1941 murder of the town's Jews in the nearby Pivonijos forest. With a steady rain falling, my guide, Regina Kopelvich, scooped up some of the wet soil in an envelope from that killing field and handed it to me, with tears streaming down her face. From that day forward, the crimes of World War II were no longer to me merely a historical event.

.    .    .

IN VISITS OVER the next several years to twelve Eastern European countries, I faced five basic barriers: competing wartime claims; government complicity in appropriating valuables; the absence of the rule of law, with the lack of efficient and transparent judicial and administrative systems; many governments' refusal to return secular communal property, such as schools and community centers, though agreeing to return religious properties, like churches and synagogues; and most disturbing, rivalries between local Jewish communities and the WJRO, based in New York and Jerusalem, over who were the rightful owners of the communal property I hoped to have returned.

These problems were by no means limited to the Jewish communities. For example, the sizable prewar landholdings of the Catholic Church in Czechoslovakia were confiscated by the Communist government, and the governments of the two successor countries, the Czech Republic and Slovakia, have shown great reluctance to restore them. None of the religious communities in Ukraine is satisfied with the slow pace of restitution of their properties. But in general the Jewish communities had the greatest problem because of lingering anti-Semitism in segments of the Eastern European public. Suffusing all of these problems was resentment that properties would be wrested away from their current owners and occupants.

My experience with the Czech Republic underscored the first of the barriers I faced, the complexities of competing claims lingering five decades after the war. I had been introduced a decade earlier to the Jewish treasures in Prague by Marc Talisman, a man of enormous talent and energy. As an aide to U.S. Representative Charles Vanik, author of the law restricting trade with Communist countries like Czechoslovakia, he had spent more than ten years negotiating with the Czechoslovakian Communist government to have on temporary exhibit in the United States what became known as the "Precious Legacy." This was a collection of the best Jewish religious artifacts stolen by the Nazis from Bohemia and Moravia, regions within Czechoslovakia, and stored for eventual use in Hitler's imagined "Museum to a Dead Race." By the time I made my first visit to Prague, in 1995, property restitution to Jewish and other religious groups had made a fitful start. In 1990 a law granted the Catholic Church, other Christian denominations, and the Jewish community the return of their religious communal properties. But one order of nuns was mistakenly given convents that did not belong to it, and the entire restitution process was stopped dead in its tracks in 1992.

The drive to reinvigorate the return of Jewish communal property was led by Tomas Kraus, the dynamic young executive director of the Federation of Jewish Communities who exemplified the new generation of Jewish leaders in Eastern Europe, dedicated to reviving their dormant and decimated communities after the Cold War. We first met to discuss the problems facing his community and other religious groups in the Swan restaurant in Prague, in the building once owned by the father of Madeleine Albright, then the U.S. ambassador to the United Nations.

Kraus took me on a tour of Prague's old Jewish quarter, which filled me with a deeply spiritual, almost mystical feeling. Six synagogues are clustered closely together around a cemetery and museum. Together they portray the long history of Czech Jews. The oldest grave in the cemetery of Avigodor Karo dates back to 1389. Because Jews historically could not bury their dead outside the old ghetto, eleven generations are layered, one on top of the other, creating a mélange of gravestones in bizarre patterns. The oldest house of prayer is the Altnueschul, literally the "Old-New" synagogue. The "new" one was built around 1270 on the foundation of one even older. Its small sanctuary has high vaulted ceilings with Gothic windows thirty feet high, the only source of light aside from candles, which create an eerie glow. Here I prayed.

But it was the Pinkas Synagogue that fused in my mind the Nazi and Communist periods in Eastern Europe as nothing else. Between 1954 and 1959 the Jews of Prague began a unique project to honor their Holocaust dead. Painstakingly they painted on the walls of the Pinkas Synagogue the names of each of the nearly 78,000 victims from the Czech lands of Bohemia and Moravia. When the brief flowering of expression known as the Prague Spring was crushed by Russian tanks in 1968, a party-line Communist, Gustav Husak, was installed in power, and he cracked down on intellectuals, dissenters, and reformers. Several of the leading Communist reformers of the Prague Spring movement were Jewish, so his purge had ferocious consequences for the Jewish community.

The Husak government saw the Pinkas Synagogue as a hotbed of Zionist propaganda, especially in the aftermath of Israel's decisive victory in the 1967 Six-Day War, which had prompted the Communist governments to break diplomatic relations with Israel. The government ordered Pinkas closed, ostensibly to control humidity from the ritual mikvah bath that was supposedly threatening the walls. Husak's regime used this as an excuse to close the synagogue for over twenty years and to paint over the names of the Holocaust victims so lovingly inscribed on the walls.

When the tiny Jewish community of 10,000 emerged with the fall of Communism in 1989, it regained control of the synagogue. One of the first acts to reassert its identity was to spend three years, from 1992 to 1995, painting back the names and adding a display of children's drawings from the Terezin concentration camp. This was more than a symbol of the past. It demonstrated the spirit of the remnants of the huge prewar European Jewish population in the Czech Republic and throughout Eastern Europe to stay and rebuild their shattered communities.

Kraus had joined with the Civic Democratic Alliance, one of the major post-Communist political parties, to draft legislation returning religious property in government hands. His position and the Alliance's was that there were over two hundred Jewish communal properties stolen by the Nazis and nationalized by the Communists and the state should not keep them.

But Prime Minister Vaclav Klaus, of the conservative Civic Democratic Party, refused to support the measure, and the bill failed, on the argument that much of the property was in the hands of municipalities, which could not be ordered by the national government to return it. These properties under municipal control, like schools and community centers, had been converted into revenue-earning facilities for the cities and towns, and they did not want to dispose of them. The properties held by the national state, such as synagogues and cemeteries, required substantial maintenance and repair, which the Czech Jewish community could not afford.

On September 8, 1995, I met with Klaus to urge him to support full property restitution to all religious communities, Jewish and non-Jewish. Klaus, then fifty-three, was a brilliant economist who saw himself as the architect of a new capitalist Czech economy. He was tough, stern, and self-confident to the point of arrogance. One does not have a conversation with Vaclav Klaus but receives a tutorial from him. In Brussels they joked that Klaus thought the European Union should join the Czech Republic, rather than the other way around. Unyielding, he told me he had already issued a decree returning fifty Jewish communal properties held by the central government, but the rest were held either by local communities or had already been converted to private ownership. This free-market advocate then said bluntly, "I will do nothing that slows down the process of privatization." I questioned whether property confiscated from the Jewish community should be sold outright to private owners. I urged him to consider alternatives that would avoid interfering with privatization but would provide some benefit to the prior owners.

But Klaus was frank enough to tell me that he had a more fundamental concern. "Mr. Ambassador, if large amounts of Jewish property are returned I will have problems with the Sudeten Germans." These were the ethnic Germans who had provided the pretext for Hitler to annex the country in 1938 and who were accordingly expelled without mercy by the Czechs, with Allied acquiescence, after the Russians liberated the country in 1945. I told the prime minister I saw no parallel between the Jewish and Sudeten German claims; the former were for communal property of the victims of Nazism, the latter for private property of Nazi supporters. He brushed aside this crucial distinction, and I left the meeting feeling that he would not budge.

On the same visit, I also met with President Vaclav Havel, then fifty-nine, who had become the conscience of not only the new democratic Czech Republic but all of post–Cold War Eastern Europe. Havel and Klaus were bitter political enemies. No two people could have been more different or had more divergent views of the direction the Czech Republic should take in the post–Cold War world. Havel, a gifted playwright, was the champion of human rights who led the Czechoslovakian intellectual opposition against Communism during the Prague Spring. After the brief opening was crushed by Soviet tanks in 1968, Havel was targeted by the hardline-Communist Czech government, and his works were banned. He became a key figure in the Velvet Revolution of 1989, uniting opposition groups in his democratic forum, and that year became the first non-Communist president of Czechoslovakia.

During the same time, Klaus labored in obscurity under the Communists as an employee of the central bank, quietly studying the works of the Western economists in the bank's library. Klaus was lean, taut, tightly controlled. Havel was broad-chested with thick hair, a flowing moustache, and large features. He exuded an enormous personal warmth and empathy.

But their differences went far beyond appearance and personality. Klaus's center-right coalition was driven by his determination to quickly privatize the old Communist order, to follow strict market principles. He was suspicious of European integration. Havel, by contrast, wanted to maintain a more humane social structure in the process of developing a free market system and saw his country's future integrated into the European Union.

Klaus had little sympathy for the reemerging Jewish communities and saw property restitution to all religious communities as a nuisance, an impediment to his free market goals. Havel's sincerity about bringing justice to the surviving Jewish community showed me instantly that he was an ally in the restitution battle. He had worked closely with many Jewish intellectuals and supporters of democracy in his Charter 77 underground opposition movement from the late 1970s until the fall of Communism. I appealed to Havel to make public statements in order to put his immense prestige behind broad property restitution. He promised to do so, and shortly after I left Prague, he began speaking out frequently, much to the consternation of Klaus, his political rival.

Even though the return of the fifty properties promised by Klaus did not proceed easily, the community did regain its great historic synagogues, communal buildings, schools, and cemeteries. One of the most important was the State Museum of Prague, containing the Precious Legacy that Talisman had labored so hard to expose to the world.

In 2000 Klaus's decree was formally enacted into law by a Social Democratic government under Prime Minister Milos Zeman and broadened by the Czech Parliament, returning communal property still in state hands and offering compensation for privatized property. A new foundation was created by the government and the Jewish community, funded by three hundred million crowns ($7 million) from the Czech government. Part of the money will help the Jewish community restore the cemeteries and synagogues that are returned to them, part will be used for education, day care centers, and benefits for Holocaust survivors, and the last third will be given to orphans born of Czech parents who died in the Holocaust.

Even the Sudeten German claims were quietly dispatched with political goodwill and the mediation of Rabbi Andrew Baker of the American Jewish Committee. After Gerhard Schröder of Germany's Social Democratic Party won the chancellorship in the 1998 election, the German government withdrew its support for the claims of the displaced Sudeten Germans, many of them nationalists who had long supported the Christian Democratic Party of Helmut Kohl. This policy turnabout—by a German chancellor whose father had been killed fighting as a soldier in Eastern Europe—helped not only German-Czech relations but Jewish restitution as well by removing the political concern from years earlier that Klaus had expressed to me.

Although problems remain, the Czech Republic is a success story. The government has come a long way in its attitude toward property restitution, and the small Jewish community of 10,000 is stable and vibrant.

Slovakia, the Czech Republic's neighbor, illustrates the second of the problems I faced: government complicity in the robbery of valuables from the Jewish community.

Fero Alexander, the young, handsome head of the Central Union of Jewish Religious Communities in Slovakia, which represents no more than 1,500 people, came to my Brussels office in 1995 for help in what I called the "Strange Case of Slovak Gold." Alexander gave me a brief history. There have been two independent Slovak republics, one born of evil intent by the Nazis in 1939 and the other the product of a peaceful separation from Czechoslovakia in 1993. Czechoslovakia was first carved out of the Austro-Hungarian Empire after World War I, then carved up again by Hitler two decades later. Suddenly over 90,000 Jews in Slovakia found themselves in a virulently anti-Semitic state. Next to Germany, wartime Slovakia had some of Europe's toughest anti-Jewish laws. It even agreed to pay five hundred reichsmarks to Germany for each Jew the Germans took off its hands for "resettlement and requalification," the only country in Europe that paid Germany for the deportation of its own citizens.

But where did the Slovaks get the money? From the Jews themselves, of course. They confiscated the assets of Slovakia's Jews, who thus effectively paid their assassins for their own murders. Between March and October 1942, 57,600 Slovak Jews were deported; only 282 survived. The Slovak government in turn paid Germany 200 million Slovak crowns, then worth about 18 million reichsmarks.

When I returned Alexander's visit to Brussels with one to Bratislava, the Slovak capital, in September 1995, I was told that approximately $3.5 million worth of Slovak Jewish gold confiscated during World War II was in the vaults of the Czech Republic's central bank. I was shown an unofficial document with the precise dates of and people involved in the transfers of this gold. The current head of the Czech Central Bank was in no hurry to relinquish the official document, to say nothing of the gold.

Slovak Jews had deposited their gold, rings, wristwatches, and other personal items for safekeeping in the Slovak central bank as the clouds of war descended upon them. After the Jews were deported, the fascist government wanted to sell the gold in Switzerland. A courageous man, Imrich

Karbas, the wartime head of the bank, refused to allow the sale, insisting that the gold was not the property of the state but had been deposited by Slovak citizens for safekeeping. On his orders the twenty-seven boxes of valuables were transferred from Bratislava to the small town of Kremnica. First the Germans and later the Russians inquired about the boxes. They were informed the boxes contained old bank records and never bothered to look inside.

After the war, the gold objects were returned to the Bratislava branch of the state bank of the reunited Communist Czechoslovakia and then, in 1953, to the bank's headquarters in Prague. The documents show 149 kilograms of gold was smelted into bars. The watches were used for official gifts. Fero Alexander's research had uncovered detailed records of 60,000 deposited items, of which only about 4,000 had been returned after the war. The rest belonged to those who were killed or, as Alexander recounted to me, to people like his mother, who was so anxious to put her shattering wartime experiences behind her that she threw away the receipt for her personal effects.

Resolving this situation would take the cooperation of both governments and the nations' Jewish communities. I raised the matter in both capitals and with senior officials of the central bank of the Czech Republic in Prague, where the gold was supposedly housed. An investigation was promised by all the parties. Buoyed by my visit and the documents they found, the Slovak Jews wrote the Czech central bank requesting their gold. Jan Vit, the vice governor of the bank, met them in Prague. His first words were "Gentlemen, we have nothing." All he had was one piece of paper indicating the gold had been moved in 1953 from Bratislava to Prague.

Alexander jumped at this news. That document, he cried, was the "missing piece of the puzzle." It fit with the accounts discovered in the archives in Bratislava. In response to Alexander's assembled records and my intervention, the Czech government in the summer of 1997 returned the gold, though without interest, valued at 32 million Czech crowns, or just under $1 million. Two-thirds went to the Jewish community of the Czech Republic, and one-third to the Slovak Republic's Jewish community. The Slovak portion has been deposited in a new foundation to support a home for the aged and a day care center for the young.

A third overriding barrier I found throughout much of Eastern Europe not only created a challenge for me in restituting communal property but more generally retarded democratic and economic development throughout the former Communist region. That was the absence of the rule of law. New administrative and court systems, formerly political arms of their Communist regimes, have been slow to develop norms of transparency and independence.

Generally, this became more of a problem the farther east I traveled, where ancient Russian autocracy and Soviet-style Communism cast a deeper shadow and Western values were more distant. In Belarus, President Aleksandr Lukashenko controls the country with an iron fist, muzzles the press, and in 1998 even locked out the American and other Western ambassadors from their diplomatic residences. Property restitution cannot proceed in such an environment.

Disregard for the rule of law also bedevils the large (400,000 strong) Jewish community of Ukraine, with five hundred organizations led by the dynamic, entrepreneurial, American-born Orthodox rabbi Yaacov Dov Bleich and Joseph Zissels, chair of the secular Association of Jewish Organizations and Communities of the Ukraine. Despite having lavished hundreds of millions of U.S. dollars on Ukraine, no one in Washington was willing to press its president, Leonid Kuchma, to follow through with his 1992 order to local governments to restore Jewish and Christian properties. The Catholic, Orthodox, Muslim, and Jewish communities have formed a joint council, and the heads of eighteen ethnic communities have pressed the government on this issue, but to no avail.

But nowhere is the problem more obvious than in Bulgaria, where the government to this day has refused to follow a decision of its own Supreme Court to return a valuable piece of property to the Jewish community.

This is particularly sad, given the exemplary history of the government and the Bulgarian Orthodox Synod in protecting the country's Jewish community from the Nazis, even when the government was formally allied with Germany during the war. Long a homeland for a heterogeneous population of twenty-seven ethnic groups, Bulgaria inherited the Ottoman Empire's tolerance for diversity after gaining its independence in 1878. At the start of World War II there were 50,000 Bulgarian Jews, none in any ghetto. After the Nazis began mass deportations from neighboring Macedonia and Thrace, in northern Greece, Bulgarian citizens petitioned the king to stop his cooperation. Twelve bishops of the Orthodox Church signed a declaration against further deportations, and a large demonstration was organized in Sofia by the unions and the Communist Party. Then the pro-fascist majority in Parliament, led by Deputy Speaker Dimiter Peshev, petitioned against the persecution and deportation of Jews. Although Jews were required to wear yellow Stars of David and some were put into forced labor camps, no more Jews were deported from Bulgaria for the rest of the war.

Bulgaria was also the only Communist country that permitted unrestricted Jewish emigration to Israel after the war. Bulgaria's frustrating conduct after the Cold War despite such a notable past demonstrates that the difficulty of restoring property taken during the war is partly a function of developing efficient and transparent administrative and judicial systems respected by the government and by the public.

True to its traditions, post-Communist Bulgaria got off to a good start on restoring communal property with a decree from Prime Minister Philip Dmetrov. More than ninety different buildings, cemeteries, apartments, and synagogues were returned. Yet the most vexing problem was the Rila Hotel and the building at no. 9 Suborna Street behind it, both of which had belonged to the Jewish community before the war. The hotel is profitable, especially because it now houses a gambling casino. In 1992 the Supreme Court of Bulgaria ruled that the Jewish community owned substantial interests in both properties, with the city of Sofia owning the balance. But the central government repeatedly ignored the decision of its own highest court to undo the Communist nationalization. Ownership in the name of the Ministry of Trade and Tourism continued through the post-Communist years.

During my first visit to Bulgaria in 1996, I met with Stephan Sofianski, the handsome young, newly elected mayor of Sofia. He was a natural ally because the court's decision recognized the municipality's majority interest in the hotel. But the central government was as unresponsive to him as to me and to the capable U.S. ambassador, Avis Bohlen.

Nothing had changed when I returned three years later, in February 1999. The minister of trade and tourism, Valentin Vasilev, told me the Rila hotel "presented a complicated legal situation," which he had referred to his lawyers—this some seven years after the Supreme Court decision. He conceded that the Jewish community had owned the hotel before the war but argued that Shalom, the chief Bulgarian Jewish organization, had not proven its "heritage rights" to represent the Jewish community. "The question is, who is the real successor to Jewish ownership rights?" he asserted.

Shalom had presented documents to the court and to him, but Vasilev refused to accept them.

The rental income from its share of the hotel would go a long way to supporting the Bulgarian Jewish community and ensuring its future. The only possibility of breaking the deadlock lies in the election of Simeon Saxe-Coburg-Gotha (the son of the wartime king) as prime minister, along with gaining the hitherto unexpressed interest of the U.S. government. Simeon spent his early adult life as a businessman in Spain and brought with him to Bulgaria an entourage of Western-trained financial experts—and, one would hope, a greater respect for the rule of law.

Few governments have made a greater about-face from their World War II and Communist past than Lithuania. Yet Lithuania points up the fourth barrier I faced: the refusal to include valuable secular communal properties like sports clubs, community centers, theaters, and schools in the package of religious properties being returned.

As in so many Eastern European countries, so in Lithuania there was a dynamic leader of the Jewish community pressing the case for property restitution: Emanualis Zingeris was a member of the Lithuanian Parliament and of the Council of Europe.

On my first visit, in October 1995, I saw Lithuania through Zingeris's eyes. Before the war its capital, Vilna, now Vilnius, was known as the "Jerusalem of the North," boasting 150 operating synagogues, several famous yeshivas, and seven theater groups. It was Lithuania's Oxford and Cambridge combined. During the war, Lithuanian nationalists served as willing Nazi executioners. Of Lithuania's Jewish community of 250,000, some 220,000 were murdered, leaving a population today of only 4,000, mostly Russian Jews.

I met Lithuanian president Valdas Adamkus in his presidential palace. He is an impressive figure, with a broad face, a shock of graying hair, a twinkle in his eye, the ease of a natural politician. He is dedicated to facing Lithuania's past and creating a new, democratic future. He was born in Lithuania but left for the United States before the war, was raised in Chicago, and worked for the U.S. Environmental Protection Agency. Remarkably, he returned after the end of the Cold War and successfully ran for president. I urged him to encourage broad property restitution and to consider creating a commission to examine the role of Lithuanians in World War II, both as victims and perpetrators of war crimes.

To my surprise, he agreed. But he made clear that it would be politically essential for the commission to examine not only the Nazi occupation but the Soviet period as well. "After all, we suffered twice in this century," he observed. "We cannot examine one without the other." And so the commission was established in 1998 with two committees, one to examine the German occupation and the other to study the Russian. Emanuel Zingeris heads the investigation of World War II.

The Lithuanian president was less flexible on the return of secular communal property. Although I stressed the importance of liberally interpreting the term "religious property" in their restitution law, Adamkus would promise only to review the problem. In Lithuania, as elsewhere in Eastern Europe, this artificial distinction between "secular" communal properties (schools, social and sports clubs, community centers) and "religious" properties (synagogues, churches, cemeteries) continues to impede restitution. Properties that the Jewish communities would readily use or sell remain in government hands, whereas religious properties in poor condition are returned. The issue was sensitive, because the broader the interpretation of "religious property," the more Lithuanians would have to be ejected from former Jewish or Christian community property. The most I was able to do in 1995 was help convince the Lithuanian government to return hundreds of Torah scrolls in the basement of the Lithuanian State Museum to the Lithuanian Jewish community. With the tiny community's agreement, the government in early 2002 began to redistribute the scrolls to synagogues around the world.

The last and most tragic problem I encountered was the struggle between the World Jewish Restitution Organization and the local Jewish communities of Eastern Europe. It is one thing to do battle with recalcitrant governments. It is another to watch bickering within the Jewish community impede progress. From Lithuania to Slovakia to Ukraine the complaints are the same. As one Slovakian leader put it, "We can't leave it to the WJRO, who treats us like retarded children."

The problem is most pronounced in Poland, where the existence of a huge physical Jewish heritage with a minuscule community to use and care for it presented a unique dilemma. Here, more than anywhere else in Eastern Europe, an unseemly power struggle between the WJRO and the tiny Jewish community of some 5,000 Poles, many recent emigrants from the former Soviet Union, stymied progress on communal property restitution with a receptive Polish government. The feud turned on several questions: Which group is the legitimate heir to the decimated Jewish communities—only the tiny band of survivors and the new young leadership or the WJRO, representing the interests of Polish survivors the world over? Can the local community manage the properties when they are returned? There is enough blame to go around for the impasse that developed. The Polish government refused to negotiate with the WJRO, preferring to deal with the small, weak Polish Jewish community. The local Jewish community overstated its capacity to manage thousands of properties.

But a principal responsibility lies with the WJRO. Almost all the Polish Jews who survived the Holocaust live either in the United States or Israel. Many share a loathing for Poland, a distrust of its government, and a suspicion, often disdain, for its small Jewish community. None harbors these passions more strongly, it seems, than Ambassador Naftalie Lavie of the WJRO in Jerusalem, a brave Holocaust survivor from Poland who saved his younger brother, Israel Meir Lau, now the Ashkenazi chief rabbi of Israel, by literally carrying him over vast stretches of Europe. Ambassador Lavie told me repeatedly that the small Jewish community cannot be the legitimate heir to the huge amount of property owned by the large prewar Jewish community and has neither the resources nor ability to manage it.

Poland was the heart of prewar European Jewry. The importance of Poland's 3.5 million Jews to Jewish culture, history, and religion cannot be exaggerated, and numbers alone cannot measure their importance. Poland was the site of some of the most important yeshivas in the world and had the largest and most creative Yiddish theater and cinema. When the Communists ran the country and Jews numbered at most several thousand, the government considered Jewish communal property abandoned and confiscated it.

Centuries of anti-Semitism, often inspired by the influential Polish Catholic Church, should have created solidarity among Jews about Poland. Yet divisions between the small Jewish community and the WJRO brought to a complete standstill my efforts to achieve the restitution of as many as 5,000 properties that could reinvigorate Jewish life, because there was no consensus on who should control them.

Since the fall of Communism, there has been a new, positive attitude in the top levels of the Polish government toward healing the bitter Polish-Jewish rifts of the past. President Aleksander Kwasniewski—short, stocky, with a direct manner—defused a number of politically sensitive issues, like taking down the crosses erected by local Catholic priests outside the Auschwitz-Birkenau camp, and opposing commercial development nearby. In July 2001 he issued a moving apology for Polish citizens' participation in the 1941 murder of 1,600 Jews in the village of Jedwabne.

My first visit to Poland, on May 9, 1995, was considered so sensitive that the Polish government insisted that it receive no publicity. The prime minister declined to meet with me and sent a more junior representative instead. But when the government recognized that I was on a mission not to castigate them but rather to cooperate with them in facilitating property restitution, their attitude changed.

After several trips, which included meetings with President Kwasniewski and other leading officials, the government submitted to Parliament a proposed "law on the relationship between the state and the Jewish religious communities." It was passed and became effective on May 11, 1997. Jewish communities were granted a legal status similar to eleven other recognized religions, including the Catholic Church, that the government had recognized soon after the end of the Cold War. The new law was imperfect but reasonable and fair. It gave the Union of Jewish Religious Communities in Poland (JRCP) five years to locate and claim their religious properties; other religious communities got only three because they and their records had not been subject to such destruction.

But squabbling between the JRCP and the WJRO prevented timely research on property claims. An April 1998 understanding between JRCP head Jerzy Kichler and the WJRO collapsed when the two sides could not agree on membership of a foundation to manage the properties and on who should control the properties. The fundamental conflict persisted between the needs of the local community and the demands of the former Polish Jews overseas. What should have been a partnership developed into deep enmity. Andrzej Zozula, the JRCP's executive director, told me the WJRO questioned the "legitimacy of our existence" and wanted to drain off the proceeds of the restored property for programs in Israel and around the world.

I encouraged both sides to compromise. On July 13, 1998, I brought both sides together for dinner at a kosher restaurant in Warsaw, a meeting led by Ambassador Lavie from Israel and the JRCP's Jerzy Kichler. I warned the local community that they needed the financial, technical, and managerial assistance of the WJRO to deal with the properties that would be returned. I lectured the WJRO that its officers needed to respect the local community, which was trying to rebuild Jewish life in Poland. I suggested a compromise: Wherever the local community had sufficient numbers, a "critical mass" I called it, in a particular area to manage the restored properties, it should do so. Where there was no surviving community, restored property should be controlled by the Foundation for the Preservation of Jewish Heritage in Poland with joint WJRO-JRCP membership. Both sides indicated a willingness to work within my proposal.

I offered the mediating services of a member of my staff, Ambassador Henry Clarke, a career diplomat with great experience in Eastern Europe. After a year's arduous effort, he obtained an agreement in November 1999 on a division of the property between the local communities and the foundation, with the sweetener of an offer by the WJRO to help fund the process of researching claims. But the good feeling engendered by the compromise did not last long. The WJRO's financing never materialized. There were disputes and vitriolic exchanges over the foundation's composition and governance. Both sides operated as if time could be suspended, even though every day brought closer the end of the five-year period to file claims under Poland's law.

On June 14, 2000, Clarke's wise mediation finally bore fruit. An agreement was reached in which nine local communities would control their own restored property and property in other regions would be controlled by our proposed foundation. Five members each would come from the WJRO and the JRCP, with Ronald Lauder, the former U.S. ambassador to Austria, serving as a neutral chair with the power to break tie votes. Lauder's family foundation had generously funded schools, camps, and other Jewish activities throughout Central and Eastern Europe.

At last everything seemed set. On January 22, 2001, both sides signed an agreement to register the foundation and to have Henry Clarke serve as its CEO, after his retirement from the State Department. But continued infighting over the powers to be given the CEO caused him to resign in frustration. Lauder decided to take matters into his own hands. In March he created a separate foundation to be partners with the JRCP and offered his own funding to start the laborious research necessary to support claims. But following a stormy WJRO meeting in New York, Lauder backed off as the WJRO feared an end-run was being made around it. He told Kichler he could not go forward without the WJRO as a partner. Everything went back to square one, where it had been two and a half years earlier, when I first brought the parties together in Warsaw.

It was not until the early months of 2002, after several more rounds of mediation, now including the American Joint Distribution Committee, that the foundation finally became operational. The new board of the Foundation for the Preservation of Jewish Heritage in Poland met for the first time on February 5, 2002, in Warsaw. The JRCP's Kichler and Kalman Sultanik, president of the Federation of Polish Jews in the United States, were made cochairs. The foundation has submitted 3,500 claims in twenty-seven of the forty-nine Polish voivodships, or regions, where it will own and manage the properties. Local communities have submitted 1,700 claims for the other twenty-two voivodships in which they will control the properties. All the debilitating squabbling exhausted the filing deadline of May 11, 2002, under the 1997 Polish law I had encouraged. But again showing its goodwill, the Polish government led by Prime Minister Leszek Miller has agreed to extend the time period for the Jewish, Catholic, and other religious communities to perfect their claims.

Yet with all of the difficulties surrounding property restitution in Eastern Europe, substantial progress has been made, and hundreds of properties are being returned. We had successes in unlikely places. The main synagogue in Kiev, Ukraine, stolen by the Nazis and converted by the Communists into a popular puppet theater, was returned to the Jewish community. The tiny Estonian Jewish community got a piece of property adjoining its day school to permit its expansion. With the enthusiastic help of U.S. ambassador to Hungary Donald Blinken, we brokered an agreement with the WJRO and the local community that led to the Hungarian government creating the Jewish Heritage Foundation and endowing it with 4 billion forints ($15 million). The Hungarian government also returned a number of properties and restored the magnificent Dohany Street synagogue in Budapest. To settle outstanding property claims, the Hungarian government in 1998 gave the Hungarian Jewish community an annuity that will distribute about 700 million forints ($2.7 million) annually.

The future of the Jewish communities of Eastern Europe hangs in the balance. They have bravely rebounded from Nazi genocide and Communist suppression. The battle for their lost property has made significant progress but still faces substantial barriers. That fight must continue if these communities are to lay the basis for a future Jewish existence. To those who wonder why mere property should loom large, the reply is that every great religion has always been anchored by its monuments—the temples of the Nile, the Parthenon, the awesome mosques of the Middle East and Central Asia, the great medieval cathedrals of Europe, and the Western Wall of the great temple of Jerusalem, destroyed almost 2,000 years ago.

The communities of Eastern Europe will never again dominate the Jewish cultural and religious world as they did before World War II. Most are stabilized at small numbers, and many are continuing to lose population to the United States or Israel. Still, a new generation of young leaders is fiercely determined to preserve their heritage. Young people who never knew they were of Jewish heritage during the Communist era have discovered they have a Jewish parent or grandparent. Jewish children saved from the Holocaust by being hidden with non-Jewish families are only now learning of their heritage in their twilight years and are telling their own children. The Jews of Eastern Europe are living, functioning communities, not museum pieces, and they deserve respect and support. Their spirit and optimism is exemplified by Yevgeny Ziskind, who shared with me his Ukrainian humor: "When the last Jews leave Ukraine, there will be 10,000 Jews waving them goodbye."

The role of the U.S. government continues to be crucial for more than the spiritual rebirth of a tiny community or the survival of other religious groups. To the degree that property restitution becomes a regular process and is broadened in countries like Poland to cover private as well as communal property, it will help the countries of Eastern Europe to become healthier democracies.

In my work with the reemerging Jewish communities of Eastern Europe, I was reminded of the Biblical prophet Ezekiel, who was carried into exile in Babylonia and inspired his own and scores of later generations with the prophecy that their shattered lives would be made whole again, that despair would give way to rebirth. In Ezekial's vision of the Valley of Dry Bones, God instructs him to "prophesy over these . . . dry bones. Behold I will cause breath to enter into you and you shall live. . . . Behold, I will open your graves, and cause you to come up out of your graves, O my people."

With these efforts continuing in Eastern Europe, I was about to begin work in Central and Western Europe that would put the redress of unsatisfied grievances from World War II back on the world's agenda.

# CHAPTER TWO

# Greta Beer and the Swiss Bank Affair

G RETA BEER is a striking, elegant woman with graying hair cropped short, fine features, and a regal bearing, with only a slight stoop betraying her seventy-plus years. Her story of the rude treatment she received from Swiss bank executives in trying to locate her late father's World War II–era bank account made her the symbol for victims in the Swiss bank affair. Her life became a metaphor for all those Jews whose families had trusted their secretive bankers in Zurich and Geneva and were betrayed by them.

Greta was born in Cznerowitz, then a center of Jewish commerce and culture in northern Romania, and educated in Swiss boarding schools, where she became fluent in five languages. Her father, Siegfried Deligdisch, was a wealthy textile manufacturer and retailer between the wars whose suppliers ranged from Egypt to Germany. He drove only American Nash automobiles. His bankers were the Swiss, keepers of the most stable continental currency of the day.

As the Nazis rose to power, Siegfried repeatedly reassured his wife, Rachelle, and their children, Greta and Otto, that if anything happened to him, the family's safety net was a *chifre*—literally, "a number"—his secret account in a Swiss bank. Ironically, the Nazis never got Siegfried, who was relatively well protected as a wealthy citizen of Romania, a fascist country that was allied with the Nazis. Instead, Siegfried succumbed to disease. In 1940 he contracted a kidney infection. He went to Budapest for treatment, but his health grew progressively worse. While he was on his deathbed, Greta implored her father to tell her which bank held his account, but by then he was too ill to communicate. He lapsed into a coma and died in September 1940.

Greta's family fled to Brasov, in the Carpathian Mountains, living in an apartment owned by a Romanian officer friend. Otto was conscripted for forced labor, but the family survived the war. When Greta returned to Bucharest, Soviet troops were in control, and the borders were closed. But she also met her future husband, a physician, Dr. Simon Beer. Separately they made their way to Vienna. Greta had to jump off a train and was smuggled through Hungary in a truck loaded with contraband cigarettes. Simon and Greta married, and in 1951, after spending three years in Italy, they emigrated to the United States as stateless refugees. She brought her mother and brother over several months later.

Adapting to life in their new country was enough of a challenge without returning to Europe to track down a lost Swiss bank account. But when Greta's mother decided to return to Europe and settled in Switzerland, the two women decided to begin the search. They went from bank to bank in Zurich, trying to match the *chifre* for Siegfried Deligdisch's account. Every possible roadblock was erected. At one bank they told Greta it was unlikely her father would have placed his money in a Zurich bank because, they dissembled, Zurich was only a village at the time of the war. Another bank seemed interested only in the details of her father's death, whether by violence or natural causes, even asking if he died with a gun to his head. In vain, Greta and her mother examined records at the federal justice ministry.

Greta Beer was not alone. The stonewalling she and her mother received was part of a concerted plan by the Swiss banks that affected thousands of others. The banks knew full well they held accounts that Jews had opened under duress to keep their assets out of Hitler's clutches. Yet they held onto these accounts as if they themselves owned them, putting every possible roadblock in the survivors' way.

An official Swiss commission report released in March 2002 found that the banks time and again "would bring bank secrecy into play in order to legitimize their reluctance to provide information while at the same time charging high search fees for conducting investigations." These fees could cost as much as 750 Swiss francs, or $450. In addition, the banks charged administrative costs to the dormant Holocaust accounts, often running the accounts down to zero. "Due to the deduction of such fees, unclaimed accounts, deposits, and safe-deposit boxes could also disappear in the space of a few decades," the report concluded. It is ironic that bank secrecy laws were invoked against the families seeking their accounts, since these strict laws had been passed in 1934 to provide a safe haven from the Nazis by using agents, false names, or secret numbers like the one Greta Beer's father had given her. Now the laws were being turned on their head and used to prevent owners from recovering their funds.

Greta and others like her did eventually receive some support for their cause. Under pressure from Switzerland's small Jewish community and the American and British governments, the Swiss Parliament passed a law in 1962 ordering the nation's banks to review their old dormant accounts and to return the money to the owners or their heirs. They had ten years to do so, except for those owners declared ineligible because they lived under Communist rule—their private accounts would most likely have been expropriated by their governments if returned.

From 1964 to 1973 the banks announced the location of more than 10 million Swiss francs, or about $6.25 million, in 1,000 dormant accounts. About 7,000 claims were filed, but the great majority were denied, like Greta Beer's. Of the 10 million Swiss francs, 1.4 million went to surviving owners or their heirs, another 2.4 million to Jewish charities for cases where there were no survivors, and more than 5 million were swallowed by the Swiss banks themselves.

The banks considered the whole issue behind them by the mid-1970s. Nevertheless, the bank matter was kept alive in books published in French and German. Early in the 1980s, a German documentary series on looted Nazi gold that had passed through Swiss banks ran on the major Swiss television channels. A landmark book by the Swiss historian Jacques Picard, *Switzerland and the Jews, 1931–1945,* was published in 1997 and took a particularly harsh view of wartime Switzerland. Older generations found his criticism unfair.

But consciousness had been raised to the point that in 1995 President Kasper Villeger first publicly acknowledged and apologized for the closing of Switzerland's borders to fleeing Jewish refugees after 1939 and for the infamous "J" stamp that had been introduced in September 1938 on German passports at the request of the Swiss themselves to make it easier to identify unwelcome Jewish refugees. Villeger spoke out at Switzerland's fiftieth anniversary commemoration of the end of the war in Europe, and he did so without external pressure.

With the demise of Communism following the fall of the Berlin Wall in

1989, people who had been trapped behind the Iron Curtain were free to travel to the West and try to track down Swiss bank accounts their relatives may have opened before Hitler's forces could confiscate them. At the same time, Swiss banks, the backbone of the Swiss economy, decided it was time to go global and become major players in the world economy. For banks, that meant New York City, the hub of the international financial system, where the Swiss banks needed a major presence in order to be world-wide players. Suddenly, they were expected to live up to international standards of disclosure. Swiss and Israeli newspapers began raising embarrassing questions about Swiss bank behavior during and after the war, leading the Swiss Federal Banking Commission to ask their banks to reexamine their World War II–era accounts. The crowning blow occurred with a front-page story by Peter Gumbel in the June 21, 1995, issue of the *Wall Street Journal*. Gumbel had been doing a series of reports about the fiftieth anniversary of the end of war in Europe. Here he focused on Greta Beer's travails. His portrait of Greta gave a human face to the victims of the Swiss banks' deceitful conduct.

I read the article at my desk in the U.S. Mission to the European Union in Brussels and immediately saw the connection to the property restitution work I was doing in Eastern Europe. I called Dick Holbrooke in Washington, for authorization to extend my field of activity to include restitution of Holocaust-related bank accounts in Switzerland. Holbrooke granted my request without hesitation. No one in Washington held any meetings or weighed the pluses and minuses of my entry into what would roil Swiss-U.S. relations as no other incident in our 140-year-long diplomatic relationship. I just plunged in, initially with no goal other than to find out the facts about the numerous dormant bank accounts in Swiss hands for over five decades. There were no grand plans or strategies; these came later. As Sergeant Friday used to say on the old TV program *Dragnet*, "I want the facts, ma'am, just the facts."

The facts got uglier and uglier. What began as a simple investigation into dormant bank accounts turned into a diplomatic debacle, forcing Switzerland to reexamine its role as a neutral nation.

During World War II Switzerland followed its official neutrality dating back to the 1815 Congress of Vienna, doing business with the Allies and with Nazi Germany. The Swiss National Bank, Switzerland's central bank, became the principal money changer for the Third Reich. The bank converted what it knew as early as the autumn of 1940 to be looted gold bullion from the countries overrun by the Wehrmacht into hard currency that Berlin used to pay other neutral countries for the raw materials that fed the German war effort. The Germans needed a way to pay for these, and they found it in Switzerland.

The Germans did not stop at looting gold from the central banks of the nations they occupied. They also stole gold from individual Jews. They extracted gold from Holocaust victims' teeth and confiscated watches, wedding bands, and other jewelry. The Prussian Mint and the Degussa Company, based in Frankfurt, smelted this loot into gold bars and embossed them with the Reichsbank's stamp to make it appear as if they had come from its coffers. These were sent to the Swiss National Bank.

In 1943 and again in 1944, the Allies issued declarations warning the neutrals, principally Switzerland, Portugal, Spain, Sweden, and Turkey, that all of their transfers of property from German-occupied territories were invalid. This was meant to stop them from accepting what were in essence stolen goods. The various Allied warnings and demands, powerfully reinforced by Allied success in battle, gradually persuaded most of the neutrals to curtail or even stop trading with Germany. But not the Swiss. They traded in gold right down to the closing weeks of the war. Switzerland was also the biggest recipient of looted art, fencing the majority of the Nazis' vast plunder of paintings.

After the war, when there was no German threat, the Swiss resisted Allied demands to disgorge the looted gold they had acquired and to liquidate German assets in their country, such as businesses and real estate. They dragged out negotiations until an agreement was finally reached in 1952, more than seven years after the war's end, which obligated them to pay only a small fraction of what they possessed.

Many Swiss citizens were unaware of the contemptible behavior of their country's bankers and politicians, but not all. The sharpest internal criticism of Switzerland's bankers naturally came from the left. A satirical ditty published in 1946 in the Basel Communist newspaper *Vorwärts* laid bare the facts:

How the bars are stacked up high
Really pure and heavy gold.
No one asked where they came from or why,
Even glad for robber's gold.

All a-sudden now, poor Swiss,
They make you shell out a bit;
But you take it quite amiss—
Fight like bell-hops for a tip.

Terrible to yield at last!
How they've persecuted you!
Neutrality holiness is past
And is now of darker hue!

Did they talk that way before
'Mid the blood and bullets hiss?
No, they then just prayed for more:
"Give the gold to us Swiss."

The story of the Swiss reparations process is not a story of easy successes or idyllic justice. The Swiss banks were at best insensitive and at worst antagonistic to the Greta Beers of the world. The Swiss government was not cooperative. Only through the diplomatic efforts of the U.S. government, threats of sanctions and boycotts by lawyers and Jewish organizations, class-action lawsuits, and heated negotiations did my colleagues and I help produce results far beyond anyone's expectations. In the process we also exposed unhealed wartime wounds.

I could never have conceived that our investigation into Swiss bank behavior would have such ugly consequences; that the historically amicable U.S.-Swiss postwar relations would fall apart; that anti-Semitism would revive in Switzerland; that the far-right populist Christoph Blocher would use the dispute to significantly strengthen his party; that the Swiss would be forced to face a more complicated wartime history than they had taught themselves to believe; that poor Greta Beer would never locate her father's account; and that I would be mediating massive class-action lawsuits against Swiss banks demanding they pay the price for their misconduct fifty years before. Most unexpected, the Swiss affair would galvanize the world's attention on Holocaust assets and set in motion across Europe a process that became the final accounting of World War II.

I was about to enter a drama far more complicated than anyone in the Clinton administration had bargained for.

# CHAPTER THREE

# Enter the Players

W HAT BEGAN for me as an interest, spurred by an article in the *Wall Street Journal*, in obtaining information on World War II–era bank accounts, exploded into a full-fledged investigation into the behavior of the Swiss banks during and after World War II. Almost immediately, interested parties sprang out of the woodwork. And they all had different motivations. At the simplest level, the victims' representatives wanted to exact the maximum price from the banks for their misdeeds in mishandling wartime bank accounts, whereas the banks wanted to pay the least to end their problem. But the reality was far more complex.

The Swiss bank affair brought together a rich, varied, combustible mixture of players, which made my job particularly difficult. The first and most important of the players was Edgar Bronfman and his top aide, Israel Singer. I was first brought into their orbit on September 13, 1995, when I hosted a dinner at my official residence in Brussels for them and other top officials of the World Jewish Restitution Organization (WJRO) from Eastern Europe and Israel. I had arranged this dinner in order to discuss the state of property restitution efforts in Eastern Europe.

Bronfman and Singer were the dominant figures that evening, as they would remain for the next three years during the Swiss bank affair. They are the proverbial odd couple. Although they were separated by only thirteen years, Bronfman was more like a father than an elder brother to Singer. Bronfman was a billionaire. In his midsixties, he cut a dashing figure—tall, handsome, and debonair, standing ramrod straight in his perfectly tailored suit. A business leader who owned a 39 percent interest in Seagrams, the worldwide distillery, he was self-assured, blunt, and at times provocative. He was used to getting his way.

Bronfman was born in Canada in 1929 into a secular Jewish home, with few religious attachments. Beyond a bar mitzvah, Judaism was not a significant part of his life. His immigrant father, Sam, whom he idolized, sent him to an Anglo-Protestant prep school and then to Williams College. Sam had started a small liquor distillery in Canada, which acquired the Seagram brand in 1928. The Seagram family at the time owned race horses and a distillery. Edgar still laughs at the Seagram family's fateful decision to keep the horses and sell the distillery to Sam Bronfman.

Edgar Bronfman moved to New York City in 1955 and became an American citizen and a registered Republican of the liberal Rockefeller-Javits variety. After Sam's death in 1971, Edgar became CEO of Seagrams and his brother Charles, who stayed in Montreal, became executive vice president and cochairman. They made two brilliant business decisions. In 1974 the brothers sold Seagrams's holdings in Texas Pacific Oil and Gas for $2.3 billion at a huge profit, thanks to skyrocketing oil prices. They also sold 25 percent of Dupont for $7 billion at another large gain.

While Bronfman was prospering in the rarified atmosphere of corporate boardrooms, Israel Singer was teaching political science at Bar-Ilan University in Israel and at the City University of New York and protesting on the streets of New York, long hair and all, against the Vietnam War and in favor of civil rights—unusual in itself for an Orthodox rabbi.

Singer's middle-class background was starkly different from Bronfman's. His parents fled Austria soon after the Anschluss in 1938, were expelled after seeking refuge in Switzerland, and made their way to France, where they were arrested and put in a camp as enemy aliens. They escaped and made their way to the United States. Israel was born in Brooklyn in 1942, was given a religious education, and graduated in 1964 from Yeshiva Torah voDaath in Brooklyn as an ordained rabbi. He later got a joint law and international relations degree at New York University and the City University of New York.

Whereas Bronfman was polished and suave, Singer was flamboyant and mercurial. Singer wore a black knit yarmulke at an angle, and at times an old-fashioned, Italian-made fedora, which gave him a charming yet roguish quality. Singer joked that you could judge his mood by the color hat he wore. He was brilliant, fast-talking, a gifted speaker, magnetic. He could be witty and charming one moment and truculent the next, his engaging smile turning to a scowl. He was an extraordinary negotiator, tough in pursuing his goals, yet possessing a sixth sense for when it was time to cut a deal.

Singer and I were not strangers to each other. We had met twice during my time as President Jimmy Carter's chief domestic adviser in the 1970s, when Singer was a young representative of the World Jewish Congress. But our paths first intersected ten years earlier. When I was working on President Lyndon B. Johnson's White House staff in the late 1960s, Singer was among a group of antiwar professors LBJ called in to convince them of the rightness of his cause. He gave a piece of advice the young radical never forgot: "Gentlemen, you can do one of three things. You can come inside my tent and piss out; you can be outside the tent and piss in; but what you cannot do is come inside the tent and piss on me." His eyes twinkling, Singer says the trick in Jewish communal life is to be in the tent pissing on the governmental decision makers with support from the crowd outside.

Despite their differences in age and temperament, Bronfman and Singer were both products of post–World War II Jewish politics. As the dimensions of the Holocaust and the general passivity of the Jewish community in confronting President Franklin Roosevelt during the war gradually seeped into American Jewish consciousness, the phrase "Never again" became the motto. The goal was not just to avoid another Holocaust but never to remain quiet when Jewish security was involved, whether in Israel, the Soviet Union, or anywhere around the globe. In 1956, as anti-Semitism in the United States drastically declined after the war and Jews came out of the closet politically, the American Israel Public Affairs Committee was founded to lobby Congress and presidents on behalf of Israel. It has long been one of the most effective lobbying organizations in Washington. The Conference of Presidents of Major Jewish Organizations, chartered in 1959 and catalyzed by the 1967 Six-Day War, has come into its own as a uniting force for over fifty Jewish organizations today.

Bronfman and Singer came from the same school of thought and shared a highly developed American Jewish consciousness. They saw the Holocaust as a product of historic Jewish weakness in Europe and a lack of effective political influence in the United States. They brought a confrontational approach to problems, even if it came at the cost of an anti-Jewish backlash. That drive would be at the heart of the Swiss bank affair.

This unlikely pair was thrust together by the World Jewish Congress, which was founded by Jewish leaders in Palestine in 1936 to combat the rise of Hitler's anti-Semitism and had grown into a powerful umbrella group for eighty-two organized Jewish communities around the world. It was the famed Nahum Goldmann, president of the WJC from 1949 to 1977, who put the WJC on the world map and brought Bronfman and Singer together. Goldmann spoke out vigorously in favor of German reparations to Holocaust survivors and was the seminal figure in the creation of the Conference on Jewish Material Claims Against Germany (the Claims Conference) to negotiate and distribute reparations.

Goldmann handed the reins of the WJC to Edgar Bronfman in 1982. Bronfman was at a point in his life when he could have retired with his wife to his luxurious home in Sun Valley, Idaho. Instead he plunged into the thorny world of Jewish politics, spending thirty to forty hours a week overseeing the WJC. For this man who seemingly had everything such work was particularly sweet. Bronfman's beloved father, Sam, had never risen above vice president of the WJC. The presidency was one thing he could accomplish his father had not.

Singer caught Nahum Goldmann's eye for a different reason. When Goldmann was harshly criticized in 1969 for meeting with Anwar Sadat of Egypt, Singer—then on the faculty of the Orthodox Bar-Ilan University and, like Goldmann and Bronfman, left of center on Middle East peace issues—defended Goldmann before the faculty and student body. Goldmann never forgot the support. In 1971 and again in 1975 he invited Singer to attend conferences in Brussels focusing on the plight of Soviet Jews, and in 1975 he helped secure Singer's election to the WJC's executive committee. Singer had been moving restlessly from teaching to serving in New York City mayor John Lindsay's office. The WJC gave him a chance to direct his social activism to the Jewish world writ large.

It was at a WJC conference in 1975 that Bronfman and Singer met for the first time. Israeli prime minister Yitzhak Rabin addressed the group in Hebrew. Singer translated for Bronfman, who was impressed by Singer's knowledge and embarrassed by his own lack of Jewish education. When he became president of the WJC, he asked Singer to become the top staff man, secretary general.

Each learned from the other. Singer learned from Bronfman how to run large organizations, delegate details, and mix with captains of industry and leaders of government in the United States and abroad. Bronfman learned the meaning of Judaism from Singer. He was taught to see things, as Singer put it, with a Jewish *optik*, a view of the world based on the concept of *tikkun olam*, literally "repairing or healing the world." In 1979, when they were traveling together in Bronfman's private jet to an event for Jewish students at Harvard Business School, Bronfman saw Singer reading the Talmud and asked what it was. Singer explained that it was a practical interpretation of Jewish law dating back more than a thousand years. For the next six years Bronfman studied Judaism. Singer arranged for daily lessons in the Bible and Prophets, and as Singer put it, "Bronfman really worked at it."

They complemented each other, as well. Singer helped offset Bronfman's short attention span, his refusal to suffer fools gladly, his tendency to get hot under the collar quickly. Bronfman helped ground Singer in the practical steps needed to run a worldwide organization. Not everyone admired the pair. In Israel, because of their dovish views, they were unpopular with Likud prime ministers Menachem Begin and Yitzhak Shamir, who blamed Singer for moving Bronfman in what they considered the wrong direction. Shamir called Singer "Rasputin" and Begin declared him a modern-day Cardinal Richelieu.

The organization Bronfman and Singer took over was moribund. It was tens of millions of dollars in debt and lacked a clear mission. Bronfman helped stem the tide of red ink, partly out of his own ample pockets and partly by establishing a strong fund-raising base. Singer supplied the ideas and direction. The WJC needed a niche to make itself distinctive among the pantheon of Jewish organizations, and Singer helped find it.

First, Bronfman and Singer made the cause of freeing Soviet Jewry their top priority. Because of the strange reverence for successful businessmen in the Soviet Communist state, Bronfman had direct access to Soviet presidents. He also helped win over skeptical Soviet Jews who thought he was simply a rich man with little interest in their plight. On crutches after a skiing accident in 1985, he climbed up five flights of stairs and stood for over an hour to meet with Soviet dissident Yuli Edelstein and a group of Soviet Jewish refuseniks.

In 1986 Bronfman and Singer found another issue: Kurt Waldheim. During a 1986 world assembly meeting of the WJC in Jerusalem, a leader of the Austrian Jewish community handed Singer an embarrassing picture of Waldheim, twice secretary general of the United Nations and now a candidate for the presidency of Austria. It showed Waldheim in a Nazi uniform.

When Bronfman wrote Waldheim for an explanation, the Austrian denied his Nazi past, saying he had served only briefly in the Wehrmacht and then had been a student for the balance of the war. The WJC's research showed this to be a blatant lie. The solid research and confrontational tactics that the WJC employed against Waldheim gave the organization worldwide exposure and laid the groundwork for what I would see deployed against the Swiss, Germans, and Austrians years later during my negotiations.

It was Bronfman's and Singer's third issue that brought us together—their determination to see the return of property in Eastern Europe owned by the Jewish community before World War II, confiscated by the Germans, and nationalized by the Communists. In 1987 they convinced East German Communist president Erich Honecker to pledge for the first time to compensate Holocaust victims. But property restitution became a major issue with the fall of the Berlin Wall and the transformation of Eastern Europe from Communist to democratic governments. Jews in Hungary and Poland and throughout the former East bloc—the "double victims" of Nazism and Communism—urged Bronfman and Singer to help return the properties necessary to rebuild their shattered religious communities.

By the time the Swiss bank affair began to gain prominence, Bronfman had become a globe-trotter and the face of the international Jewish community to foreign governments. Using his business skills, he controlled an interlocking set of institutions, extending his influence. He was not only president of the WJC but also president of the WJRO and chair of the finance committee of the Claims Conference. Singer served in top positions in all these organizations, as well.

Bronfman had also become politically powerful in the United States. Feeling increasingly comfortable in the Democratic Party, he was one of the largest donors to Bill Clinton's presidential campaign, and neither the president nor the first lady ever forgot his generosity. President Clinton attended Bronfman's sixty-fifth birthday party at the Waldorf-Astoria in 1994, along with a thousand of Edgar's other friends.

It was at the height of Bronfman's political power and worldwide influence and of Singer's creativity that our interests crossed at my 1995 dinner party in Brussels. The discussion turned that evening from Eastern European property restitution to dormant World War II–era Swiss bank accounts, which Bronfman and Singer saw as a new issue to maintain the WJC's visibility and obtain justice for claimants.

Immediately after our dinner in Brussels, Bronfman and Singer went to Bern to meet with the Swiss Bankers Association about the dormant bank accounts of Holocaust victims. The SBA decided to deal directly with Bronfman and the WJC because of Bronfman's political preeminence. Other Jewish organizations might have been less confrontational in their approach to the Swiss, but they also lacked the clout needed to get an audience.

The Swiss visit had a special meaning for Singer. Not only had his father and mother been refused refuge after fleeing from Austria, but his wife, Evelyne, had deep Swiss roots. Her mother was a third-generation Swiss Jew, with family ties going back to 1852. Her father, Julius Kuhl, had come to Switzerland in 1924 from Poland, and after Hitler's invasion in 1939 he was appointed consul to the Free Polish Government in Bern. His attempt to get Polish Jewish refugees into Switzerland was rebuffed by the Swiss minister of interior and police, and after the war the Swiss refused to let Kuhl stay in the country, declaring him a stateless person of Polish origin.

The Bronfman party first paid a courtesy call on President Kasper Villeger to thank him for his recent apology for Switzerland's restrictive wartime refugee policy. Bronfman personally praised Villeger for his courage. This was to be one of the few positive meetings between Swiss and Jewish officials for the next several years. The very next meeting started a downward cycle that seemed irreversible.

Bronfman's party walked the few blocks from the president's office to the Grande Société in Bern, a private dining room in one of the city's most impressive historic buildings, to meet with SBA officials. Bronfman remembers being shown into a wood-paneled waiting room with no chairs and left with his entourage to stand for some ten minutes. By the time the delegation of Swiss bankers arrived, Bronfman, who has a low boiling point, had become impatient and annoyed.

After very brief pleasantries, Bronfman recalls that a lectern was plunked down in the waiting room. The SBA's president, Dr. George F. Krayer, stood behind it and read a prepared speech. He announced that the bankers' ombudsman had thoroughly reviewed the dormant accounts of the Swiss banks and had found that only 774 dormant accounts from World War II had any possible Holocaust relationship, worth a mere 38 million Swiss francs ($32 million). By this time Bronfman was fuming. He later told me: "They thought we were a bunch of *schnorrers* [a Yiddish word for someone who begs or solicits money]. They just wanted to get rid of us."

Krayer asked what Bronfman thought about the discoveries of the dormant bank accounts. Bronfman answered that he was not interested in a lump-sum settlement but in establishing a reliable process for finding out what was actually in the accounts and paying them to their rightful owners. Over lunch in the adjoining dining room, the situation turned from bad to worse as the Swiss bankers cast scorn on the notion that Jews still had large amounts in old, dormant bank accounts; most had been paid after the war, they insisted. They kept asking Bronfman how much money he wanted to settle the matter, which he and Singer felt was humiliating. Bronfman demanded that international auditors review the accounts of the Swiss banks. The Swiss agreed to the idea but not on how to accomplish it.

The Swiss may not have been aware how deeply they had offended Bronfman with what he called their "atrocious manners." "If they had behaved properly at the first meeting, it would have cost them less in auditors and lawyers," Bronfman later said. But the uncooperative and imperious posture they took eventually "destroyed their reputation," in his view.

The Swiss sharply contradict this account. Krayer wrote Bronfman on March 13, 1997, a year and a half later, recalling that the cocktails and meeting started late because of Bronfman's unplanned visit to President Villeger and that everyone at the Grande Société—the Swiss and Americans—had remained standing. He denied that the SBA's press release amounted to a diktat and apologized "for not having invited you to be seated on one of the many chairs in the Salon Rouge." The Swiss insist that they treated Bronfman and his party with courtesy and dignity and would have been foolish to do otherwise. These utterly divergent accounts of the same meeting were to typify the way the American and Swiss sides continually misunderstood each other, a level of misunderstanding that soon ripened into deep distrust.

This was not just a clash of egos. The misunderstanding at the meeting demonstrated that the Swiss banks—perhaps because of a long insularity they were just beginning to shed, perhaps because they carried with them the banks' deeply ingrained antipathy toward Jewish account holders seeking their assets—were always behind the curve. This would be evident in event after event. If, at the initial meeting with Bronfman and Singer, the banks had been forthcoming about opening their old account records to an independent audit, the whole affair might have ended right there.

More broadly, the banks' conduct pointed up that if ever a country was unprepared for the harsh spotlight of international scrutiny, it was Switzerland. No democratic country's style of government more sharply contrasted with the United States' boisterous democracy. Switzerland is an insulated, carefully balanced multicultural state divided into four linguistic regions. The federation created in 1848 was consciously modeled after the U.S. federal system and was originally composed of twenty-two cantons that still have substantial local power. It has a deliberately weak executive branch, a seven-person Federal Council whose presidency rotates annually and makes decisions by consensus. Traditionally neutral to a fault, the Swiss refused for decades in popular referendums to join either the United Nations or the European Union. Only in 2002 did the electorate narrowly approve UN membership.

Having stood aside from international institutions and their tough debates, the Swiss in the late 1990s did not possess a robust sense of the give-and-take of politics that is normal in the United States and elsewhere. Their political insularity was further aggravated by Switzerland's unique form of democracy, which complicates the country's ability to make prompt decisions. The nation is the closest to a direct democracy of any national government in the developed world today. Its referendum process, which can be initiated by a minimum of 50,000 signatures, is similar to the state of California's, but the issues can be far more personal; citizens in some cantons even vote to grant citizenship to individual applicants and, in one notorious case, refused to naturalize a handful of settled refugee families from the former Yugoslavia. This legislation-by-referendum was a factor in our negotiations over the missing bank accounts. The Swiss negotiators knew that the conservative People's Party, led by billionaire populist Christoph Blocher, could easily obtain the signatures necessary to put any settlement with the foreign Holocaust claimants to a popular vote that might overturn it. This sword of Damocles kept the Swiss government at a safe distance from the negotiations and put the banks in the front lines to defend themselves.

As if politics was not complicated enough, the Swiss and American legal systems are drastically different. Swiss lawsuits are usually decided in a discreet trial, and out-of-court settlements are rare, especially large ones. The concept of a vast American-style class-action lawsuit representing tens of thousands of people who may have no knowledge of a case being brought on their behalf is foreign to the Swiss. They are also unaccustomed to settling cases by deals between the parties and especially to the kind of rough justice based on moral claims that may flout ironclad legal precedent.

In the three months following their meeting with the SBA in Bern, Bronfman and Singer did not receive another proposal from the Swiss. During this time I was racing around Eastern Europe working on property restitution while keeping a distant eye on the Swiss banks, preparing for my own visit to Switzerland. But the action was shifting from Bern and Brussels, where I was still based, to Washington.

Bronfman and Singer realized it would take external pressure to convince the bankers of the seriousness of the WJC's concern. So they played the political card for the first time, going not to me or to President Clinton initially, but to one of Clinton's archenemies, New York senator Alfonse D'Amato, the powerful chair of the Senate Banking Committee, which has jurisdiction over all banking and financial issues and institutions.

On December 7, 1995, Bronfman and Singer met the senator in his Washington office. Bronfman expressed his intense grievance at having been, at least to his mind, cold-shouldered by the imperious Swiss bankers and presented with what he considered a derisory offer. If he could not on his own persuade the Swiss banks to cooperate, then he would pull his political levers to do so. He told D'Amato that, although he still hoped to quietly resolve his differences with the Swiss, he wanted to be able to call on the senator's help if necessary. Bronfman was not seeking massive payments from the Swiss banks at this stage. He simply wanted the banks to match up dormant accounts with their owners and to give the WJC control over heirless accounts for the benefit of all Holocaust survivors.

D'Amato smelled blood. He saw what Bronfman described to him in terms of political bargaining. That Bronfman had increasingly liberal leanings and was a strong supporter of the Clintons, and that D'Amato was an equally passionate conservative Republican, was irrelevant. They needed each other, Bronfman to pressure the Swiss, D'Amato to find a winning issue for his 1998 reelection campaign. Always a serious champion of his New York constituents' interests—D'Amato was called "Senator Pothole" by the New York press for his legendary attentiveness to local problems usually considered beneath the dignity of a senator—he also represented the state with the largest population of Holocaust survivors. The Swiss bank affair was a godsend, a chance, as he later told me, to combine good works and good politics—the magic combination every politician tries to find, from president and senator to county commissioner and dogcatcher.

And for D'Amato this magical mix came at a particularly opportune time. D'Amato was leading the charge in the Senate's investigation of "Whitewater," President Clinton and Hillary Clinton's business dealings with a failed savings and loan. D'Amato's investigation was going nowhere and had hurt his standing among New Yorkers, who were generally fond of the Clintons. The Swiss issue gave him the opportunity to change focus from a political loser to a political winner, or so he hoped.

In a sea of blandness on Capitol Hill, Al D'Amato was the genuine article. He wore his emotions on his sleeve. The fifty-nine-year-old slight, balding grandson of Italians who came to America in the great wave of immigration around the turn of the last century, he epitomized his fore-bears' preeminent value of family and community loyalty. The senator's father, Armand D'Amato, was born in New Jersey and trained to be a teacher, but his Italian name made it hard for him to find a job. Al's mother made it clear that she would "change husbands if you change your name." Her ethnic pride engraved a moral lesson on the future United States sen-ator: ability, not ethnicity or skin color, must be the basis for advancement.

Legally blind until corrective eye surgery at the age of ten, Al D'Amato blossomed after the family moved to the Long Island suburbs. He also entered the world of politics at an early age. His father was close friends with Joseph Carlino, the Speaker of the New York State Assembly, who helped young D'Amato climb the greasy pole of politics through the county attorney's and the U.S. attorney's offices, then to win election as Nassau County's top tax collector and town supervisor in Hempstead, Long Island.

But his biggest break in politics came in 1979, with the prosecution of Joseph Margiotta, the most powerful Republican politician on Long Island, for accepting kickbacks from insurance companies. Margiotta's conviction opened the way for D'Amato to take over the powerful local Republican machine and position himself for higher office. In 1980 he ran for the Senate, and with the liberal vote split between two opponents, Rep-resentative Elizabeth Holtzman and Senator Jacob Javits, he made it to Washington.

I liked Al D'Amato. I had worked closely with him for years on many foreign-policy issues, including the law he sponsored to impose sanctions on Iran and Libya for abetting terrorism. We developed a mutual respect, and I admired his remarkable energy, gusto, and political instincts that come straight from the gut. A ferocious champion of his constituents' inter-ests—including middle-class and Orthodox Jews who have increasingly deserted New York's classic New Deal liberalism in favor of Republican candidates—he was both warm and wily, unpolished, quick thinking, often distracted by doing three things at once.

But before Bronfman unleashed D'Amato, there was still the very real opportunity to avoid a major public contretemps. The WJRO and the Swiss Bankers Association even reached the bare-bones outline of a deal five days after Bronfman's initial meeting with D'Amato: The banks would open their files for a review of the dormant accounts, and the Jewish side would inspect them in confidence. But then on February 7, 1996, the Swiss bankers made a fateful decision by declaring in a news conference that they had found even fewer dormant accounts than they thought. This unilateral public declaration was the work of Heinrich Schneider, whose inept handling of this and other matters would cost him his job as deputy chief of the SBA within eighteen months. Bronfman felt he had been tricked. It seemed like a repeat of their disastrous September lunch in Bern, with the Swiss trying to buy them off. The WJC concluded that the only way to deal with the Swiss banks was through a public campaign similar to the one they had mounted a decade before against Waldheim in Austria.

Shortly after the disastrous Swiss news conference, Bronfman and Singer called D'Amato to formally ask for Senate Banking Committee hearings. Now D'Amato had his chance, delivered to him on a silver platter by Bronfman and by the fumbling tactics of the Swiss bankers. He pivoted: out went Whitewater, in came the Swiss. He intended to make the most of this high-profile project. For the next two and a half years he milked the Swiss controversy for everything it was worth. His first step was to announce a hearing in the Senate Banking Committee for April 23, 1996.

Both D'Amato and the WJC wanted the hearings to be as sensational and provocative as possible. They needed facts to back up their rhetoric. In March, a month before the D'Amato hearings, the WJC hired Miriam Kleiman, a young, bright, and determined researcher, to comb the National Archives for embarrassing information about Swiss conduct during the war in general and about the Swiss banks in particular. D'Amato was not far behind. He asked Gregg Rickman, a talented member of his staff, to work on the Swiss project. Rickman, who by coincidence had just returned from a visit to the concentration camp in which his father-in-law had been incarcerated, leapt at the chance. Soon Miriam and Gregg were working hand-in-glove to find sensational materials. I tried to help by encouraging the declassification of documents. Greg Bradsher, a senior official at the National Archives facility in suburban Washington, helped Kleiman and Rickman locate the materials they needed by unlocking the mysteries of World War II documents gathering dust in the bowels of the archives.

On her second day at work, Kleiman located a U.S. government Safe-haven report from July 1945, which described the program the Allies established during the war to track looted assets going out of Germany. The report noted that one bank alone, the Société Général de Surveillance, listed the names of dormant account holders, with accounts worth $20 million. (This figure should be compared to the Swiss banks' offer to settle with Bronfman for a little over $30 million for all their banks.)

By the summer of 1996 over a dozen young interns were working with Kleiman and Rickman. They uncovered a treasure trove of materials that the WJC and D'Amato used over the next several years to pique press interest and keep the Swiss on the defensive—from a September 1944 OSS report on the extensive receipt of looted Nazi gold by Swiss banks to graphic photographs of American troops uncovering tons of looted gold and fabulous works of art hidden in the Merkers Salt Mine in Germany.

The research at the National Archives had a frenetic, Marx Brothers quality. The little-known archives facility in College Park, Maryland, was suddenly besieged by researchers from all the parties. Soon there was a battle not only in the halls of Congress and in the courts but among researchers. Greg Bradsher told me that he often felt like a referee between competing researchers, each hoarding boxes of important documents and spying over one another's shoulders. The Swiss researchers called Rickman "devil boy." At the battle's height in 1997, there were almost fifty researchers working for the Swiss Bankers Association, for lawyers representing the Swiss and the Holocaust victims, and for the State Department, all trying to elbow their way into a small area to examine documents.

With the D'Amato hearing looming, the Swiss bankers realized that they needed to deal with the budding controversy. Rainer Gut, the chairman of Credit Suisse/First Boston, understood more than any other Swiss banker the potential damage that the spiraling controversy could cause to his bank's American business, which measured in the hundreds of millions of dollars. He left the majesty of playing golf at the fabled Augusta National course to deal with the emerging crisis, meeting in Washington with Swiss ambassador Carlo Jagmetti and the lawyers for the Swiss banks, Marc

Cohen and Lloyd Cutler. Gregg Rickman, of D'Amato's staff, had fore-warned the lawyers that "D'Amato will do a scorched-earth hearing; it will be cut and burn." Gut told Jagmetti that the Swiss government needed to become directly involved as soon as possible, and Jagmetti agreed that the impending Senate hearings were not simply a private matter for the banks.

Pressure was now building inexorably. Sensational findings were period-ically released from the National Archives, some accurate and some not. For example, the WJC asserted that Hitler's publisher, Max Amman, had an account at the Bern branch of the Union Bank of Switzerland to deposit the royalties from *Mein Kampf,* which were Hitler's principal private source of income. When this disclosure was reviewed by Cutler's investigators, it turned out that Amman did have an account, but there was no documented proof it contained *Mein Kampf* royalties or that Hitler received income from the account, although both were plausible.

But the damage was already done. Time and again, the facts never caught up with inferences and rumors, because the Swiss banks never developed an effective public strategy, partly out of fear they would be hit even harder if they fought back too aggressively. Media attention soared. And still the Swiss banks refused to open their secret wartime accounts to an independ-ent audit. The Swiss banks had a tin ear for the realities of American poli-tics. Their natural pension for secrecy was their enemy. They knew that an independent audit had real risks for them in light of their postwar stonewalling tactics and their treatment of dormant accounts. But on any balance of risks they would have been far better off to take their medicine, since an audit would have taken years and would have removed them from the spotlight. But they failed to react quickly enough and paid a stiff price as the allegations broadened.

At one point, Curtis Hoxter—a German-born émigré from the Third Reich and now a well-connected international business consultant based in New York with a diverse clientele in Switzerland, Germany, and Austria— tried to bring the Swiss and Israel Singer together. The Swiss would later jokingly refer to Hoxter as a "double agent," but in reality he was Singer's man, a shadowy but effective figure who mysteriously turned up at key moments. When the Swiss controversy first burst into the open, Hoxter had gotten Singer and Hans Bär, one of his clients, together at the Berkshire Hotel to try to quietly find a solution. Bär was the head of Bank Julius Bär, a 110-year-old Jewish-owned Swiss institution, and had spent the war years as a teenager in the United States; the Swiss saw him as their own Jewish banker. Initially Singer's proposal fell on deaf ears. But as the D'Amato hearings loomed even closer, Marc Cohen faxed Singer a proposal for an independent audit of the Swiss banks, hoping to avert the D'Amato hearing. Singer, visiting his mother in Florida, insisted he never received the fax. More likely, he simply did not want to step on D'Amato's headlines or Bronfman's. Things had gone too far to cut them off now.

Bronfman and Singer were now smelling blood, too. Their researchers were finding plenty of embarrassing evidence of Swiss misbehavior during the war, and the two were now determined to broaden the attack beyond dormant accounts in private Swiss banks to the role of the Swiss National Bank, Switzerland's central bank, in handling looted Nazi gold, and to a general inquiry into Jewish wealth that had been looted, laundered with Swiss banks, and never returned.

Realizing the depth of the allegations and getting no response from Singer, the Swiss Bankers Association, in a state of panic, quickly wrote D'Amato offering an independent audit. Their letter arrived just hours before the hearing. Meanwhile, they deployed Bär to persuade Bronfman to temper his testimony. By coincidence, Bronfman was hosting a fundraising event for the Democratic Party that evening at his home in Manhattan, with First Lady Hillary Clinton as the guest of honor. When Singer told Bär that Bronfman could not meet him because of a meeting with Mrs. Clinton at his apartment, Bronfman's stature increased exponentially in the eyes of the Swiss. They also realized they were in big trouble. Bronfman had political clout they could never match. Bronfman used the occasion itself to good purpose, presenting a *New York Magazine* article about Greta Beer to the first lady. After he asked her to tell the president of his personal involvement, she wondered if "we could get the Swiss banks" to meet their obligations. Bronfman replied pointedly, "Yes, with your husband's help." Mrs. Clinton called later with the news that she had arranged for Bronfman to see President Clinton after his Senate testimony.

It was now my turn to deal with D'Amato. Three weeks earlier, on April 2, I had left my position in Brussels to serve Secretary of Commerce Ron Brown as his undersecretary for international trade. I had lunch with Ron in Paris the weekend before Fran and I left, hosted by U.S. ambassador Pamela Harriman at an elegant luncheon club near the U.S. Embassy. It was the last time I saw him alive. The day after I landed in the United States, we went to my mother's house in Atlanta for the Passover holidays. My son Brian called and told me to turn on CNN. Ron's plane had crashed in Croatia. I was devastated. Three days later, on April 5, I arrived at the huge Commerce building in Washington, where with Fran by my side, I was sworn into office before a stunned crowd of senior Commerce Department officials. The department was like a giant morgue. A dozen senior people from Commerce had been killed in the crash of Ron's plane, including my dear friend Assistant Secretary Charles Meissner. Soon after, I took up my duties at the department. Brown's successor, Mickey Kantor, honored Ron's promise that I could bring along my property restitution and Swiss bank portfolios to the position at Commerce and would testify for the government before D'Amato. This was my issue and no one else in the government wanted to touch it.

The day before the D'Amato hearing, Bronfman, Singer, and Elan Steinberg, the head of the WJC's North American division and a tough, confrontational press spokesperson, came to see me. They were no longer willing to quietly resolve their disagreement with the banks. They demanded a full examination of all wartime Swiss accounts and insisted that the Swiss government impose a settlement on the banks. I agreed to support their efforts to broaden the investigation. Lawyers for the Swiss banks also met with me before the hearing and assured me that the Swiss had searched the dormant accounts thoroughly and that every effort would be made to find the heirs.

The next day, as the government's witness, I testified first. The thrust of my testimony was to promise to put the full weight of the U.S. government behind the search for the truth about the dormant accounts and to assure the return of all assets to the families entitled to them. My testimony was not the stuff of headlines. The limelight belonged to D'Amato, who was chairing the hearing.

He made good on his promise—or threat—to focus on Swiss collaboration with the Nazis in moving gold from the conquered countries of Europe. He theatrically waved the documents Rickman and Kleiman had found, making it appear he had just gotten them declassified. (In fact the documents had been open to the public but ignored since the 1970s.) D'Amato's star witness was Greta Beer. The World Jewish Congress had sponsored Greta's trip to Washington and put her up at the stylish Madison Hotel. Rickman interviewed her the day before her hearings and put her on the phone with D'Amato, who at that moment was visiting his mother in New York. Informed by Rickman that Greta spoke Italian, the senator opened the telephone conversation with a warm and ebullient *"Buongiorno,* Greta." When she responded in her fluent Italian—far beyond his—D'Amato quickly put his mother on the line so the two elderly women could chat. On the stand the next day, Greta Beer delivered her sensational story as promised.

Poor Hans Bär did his best to indicate that the Swiss banks would try to search for more dormant accounts and announced the banks' willingness to accept an independent audit. But his testimony was seen simply as a reflection of the banks' party line. Bronfman dropped the biggest bombshell of the hearings by producing documents from the National Archives indicating that most of the Nazis' stolen gold had been converted into negotiable Swiss francs by the Swiss National Bank. The gold had not only been taken from conquered central banks but been melted down from Jews' stolen jewelry and even their gold teeth. Now it was not just a matter of private bankers cheating the heirs of the Jews. Swiss officials were being accused of willingly serving as Hitler's bankers—and his ghouls.

From Capitol Hill, Bronfman proceeded to the White House to talk with President Clinton and his chief of staff, Leon Panetta, in the historic basement Map Room where Franklin Roosevelt planned the military moves of World War II. Briefing the president on the Swiss role in the war and its aftermath, Bronfman sought his support. Clasping the top of a high-backed chair as he stood near a giant globe, the president pledged to help and told Panetta to inform federal agencies to cooperate. Then he asked a political question prompted by D'Amato's Whitewater probe: Was it really necessary for Bronfman to work with D'Amato? Bronfman reminded the president that D'Amato had jurisdiction as chair of the Senate Banking Committee and that any legislation would have to go through him. The president paused and then said, "Edgar, this is so important, I'll even work with D'Amato." The president's support for Bronfman was formalized in a letter of May 2, 1996, viewing the return of Jewish assets as "a moral issue and a question of justice" and expressing the president's continuing support for "the return of Jewish assets in Swiss banks."

It is difficult to exaggerate the impact the D'Amato hearings had in Switzerland. Although D'Amato was derided as a venal politician merely chasing the Jewish vote, his hearings were viewed with utmost seriousness. They were carried live on Swiss television and summarized under front-page headlines. The Swiss hardly noticed that no American television program carried the news and the U.S. newspaper reports ran on inside pages; they thought Americans were discussing the disclosures from morning to night in the same way the Swiss were.

Propelled by the dramatic D'Amato hearings, the idea of having the wartime accounts audited by a joint committee of the Swiss and the WJC gained strength. After several days of intense bargaining between Singer and Hans Bär, the Swiss bankers assembled at Bronfman's headquarters at the landmark Seagram Building on Park Avenue for the final stormy negotiations. At one point, Avraham Burg, head of the Jewish Agency in Israel, questioned how the Jewish side could trust the Swiss bankers to implement the agreement. Josef Ackerman, the powerful chairman of Credit Suisse/First Boston, became furious that his word was being challenged. The key issue was the scope of the audit. At the last minute, Singer added "looted assets" to the agreement, broadening the scope of the audit beyond individual dormant accounts of Holocaust victims to accounts opened by Nazis to deposit Jewish looted assets. The Memorandum of Understanding was signed on May 2, 1996, by three parties: Bronfman and Singer on behalf of the WJRO, Avraham Burg and Zvi Barak of Israel's Jewish Agency, and Hans Bär, George Krayer, and Josef Ackerman for the Swiss bankers.

The memorandum called for an independent audit to be conducted by professionals under the guidance of an Independent Committee of Eminent Persons consisting of six people, three appointed by the WJRO and three by the Swiss banks. A seventh member, serving as chair, would be chosen by both parties and would have the decisive vote in case of a tie. For the Swiss banks, with their historic penchant for secrecy, this was a major leap into the unknown.

After going through a variety of people to chair the commission, from former Canadian prime minister Brian Mulroney to Jimmy Carter, Henry Kissinger, and Elie Wiesel, the Swiss and WJRO finally agreed on Paul Volcker. Why Volcker? Although the Swiss would have preferred one of their own citizens, they knew the WJRO would never accept anyone from Switzerland. If they had to accept an American, Volcker had a number of advantages. As the former chairman of the U.S. Federal Reserve Board of Governors under presidents Carter and Reagan, he had earned a reputation for strict integrity that would give any audits conducted under his auspices instant credibility. He was also a board member of the Swiss corporate giant Nestlé. For the WJRO, Volcker was attractive because he was based in New York City and had spent most of his career there. The organization also believed his unassailable record of public service in the United States would insulate him from Swiss pressures. Now the WJRO just had to convince him that he was their man.

Hoxter was again the go-between, the first to approach Volcker. Then Bronfman sounded him out, telling him the committee needed someone of his stature to head it. Volcker, who stands six feet, seven inches tall, joked with his wry wit, "I'm tall, if that's what you mean!" Bronfman said, "No, we need someone of unimpeachable honesty." Volcker asked for time to think the offer over. Singer asked me to persuade him to take the position. I called and told him the Clinton administration would give him our full support.

I knew Volcker from the Carter administration. In 1979, with inflation raging and the president's popularity plunging, Carter asked his full Cabinet to submit letters of resignation and accepted several, including that of the secretary of the treasury, Michael Blumenthal. Blumenthal's replacement was G. William Miller, then chair of the Federal Reserve Board, leaving an opening for this key position at a crucial time in the administration's history. After several people turned down the job, we turned to Paul Volcker, then president of the Federal Reserve Bank of New York. Volcker made it plain to the key economic advisers in the Carter administration and to the president himself that, if selected, he would be completely independent of any political pressures and would consider drastic monetary measures to bring inflation under control. This made many of us nervous, but President Carter believed the economic situation was dire, and he wanted someone who would apply tough medicine, regardless of the political consequences.

Within months, I learned firsthand that Volcker's intimidating physical size and equally large intellect were combined with a single-minded determination and independence. Volcker figuratively and literally looks down on the rest of us mortals. Within weeks of taking the job, Volcker applied a new, more forceful monetary policy that over time broke the back of inflation but also broke the political back of the Carter administration, leading to double-digit interest rates that were an unbearable burden for the president. It was Ronald Reagan and the nation that eventually benefited.

It took four weeks for Volcker to decide to take the job as chair of the

Independent Committee of Eminent Persons (ICEP). His Jewish friends urged him against it, arguing that it was a lose-lose position between fiercely contending forces. He asked Michael Bradfield, who had been his general counsel at the Federal Reserve, to scout for him in Switzerland. Bradfield met with a former member of the Swiss Federal Banking Commission, who warned that the banks would not be able to find any more dormant accounts than they had already discovered, that records did not exist, and that the banks were simply engaged in a public relations exercise. Bradfield's advice to Volcker when he returned was, "Don't do it. You will not be able to accomplish a lot, and both the Jews and the Swiss will be mad at you." Volcker ignored the advice and took the plunge. He believed that a thorough accounting of dormant accounts was important to Switzerland and to the integrity of the international financial system to which he had devoted his life. And on a personal level he could not turn down the entreaties of his good friend and fellow Nestlé board member Fritz Leutweiler, who had headed the Swiss National Bank during Volcker's tenure at the Fed.

The first meeting of the ICEP was held on August 14, 1996, at Volcker's Manhattan office. He was immediately selected as chair, and the committee quickly became known as the Volcker Committee. Bronfman attended the initial meeting. But both Volcker and Bronfman, once among the most powerful leaders in the world, were used to being in control. Bradfield, Volcker's counsel for the committee, recalled that the meeting was "not big enough for both of them." There was a clash of two titanic egos. At one difficult moment when Volcker was trying to get agreement on the scope of the audit, Bronfman barked, "Who made you God? You're not chairman of the Fed now!" Bronfman wisely never attended another meeting.

A fierce fight immediately broke out at the meeting over the scope of the audit. The Jewish side insisted it cover not only dormant individual accounts but also those opened by Germans with looted Jewish assets. The Swiss vehemently asserted this was beyond the scope of their agreement. Volcker wanted an audit from top to bottom. The Jewish side suggested a compromise: To the extent the auditors found looted assets during their review of dormant accounts, they would report them. The Swiss refused. The meeting quickly became acrimonious. The Jewish side rose and threatened to walk out. Volcker persuaded them to stay by saying he would consider their request. Shortly after the meeting, and over the strenuous objection of the WJC representatives, Volcker ruled that the audit would cover only accounts of Holocaust victims or their heirs. Volcker reasoned that, after half a century, it would be impossible to prove that funds in bank accounts had been looted.

The initial meeting almost ended over the selection and payment of the independent auditors. Bronfman said to George Krayer, "You pay." Krayer joked, "You think I'll pay for my clients to find out what bastards their grandfathers were?" But the Swiss agreed to pay the full expenses of the outside audit. It would cost over $200 million for the three principal Swiss banks to foot the bill for the international accounting firms Arthur Andersen, Coopers & Lybrand, Deloitte & Touche, KPMG, and Price Waterhouse.

This bombastic meeting was a precursor of the committee's future internal dynamic. Bär became the leader of the Swiss side. On the Jewish side, the two Israelis, Zvi Barak and Avraham Burg, were the most belligerent toward the Swiss. Singer often played a mediating role within his group, which constantly made bitter accusations against the Swiss and frequently threatened to walk out. Thankfully, Volcker was there to calm the competing parties. He brought the same fierce focus to this job that he did to reigning in inflation in the Carter years. He had one and only one goal: a thorough, complete, searching audit of Swiss bank accounts to determine how many were Holocaust related. Ironically, the very qualities that unquestionably made him the right person for the job—probity, integrity, taking no grief from anyone trying to distract him from his mission—became a mixed blessing. His rigid focus on his mission would cause major complications for me later.

Despite Volcker's coolheadedness, there was a great deal of dissension, particularly among the Israelis, who, according to Bradfield, were in constant commotion, conducting discussions among themselves in Hebrew and allowing their cell phones to interrupt business. In a June meeting in Jerusalem, the Israelis attacked the Swiss bankers and Volcker personally. People interrupted and shouted at each other. Volcker, who had always prided himself on running important meetings with dispatch, became so disgusted that he threatened to resign. He joked to me later that he would not like to make his living negotiating with Israelis. But his sense of duty kept him going.

The most contested issue became what Volcker called the "but for" accounts—those accounts that would still have been in existence but for the fact they had been closed by the banks. The balances had often been eaten up with service charges and fees or, after lying dormant for years, been closed or suspended and transferred to the banks' bottom-line profit. The Swiss were shocked that Volcker's auditors planned to examine these accounts, yet they accepted it with remarkably little opposition. It was on these vanished accounts that the Volcker auditors would spend the bulk of their time and from which they mined their most successful discoveries. Initially, Volcker and Bradfield, old hands at standard banking practices, found it hard to believe that reputable Swiss banks could have engaged in such conduct. Yet the ICEP found 983 accounts closed and transferred to bank profits, 1,322 closed because they had been consumed by fees, and 417 accounts paid to Nazis at the request of the Reichsbank.

Volcker took another significant step. At the suggestion of the WJC, he retained Helen Junz to study prewar Jewish wealth in Europe. An economist and former colleague from the U.S. Treasury, Junz had grown up in Holland and had been hidden from the Nazis as a child. Volcker wanted to know how much money might have been transferred to countries like Switzerland. Junz based her estimates on the prewar populations of various Jewish communities and the estimated incomes of the occupations Eastern European Jews typically entered. Her final estimate of Jewish prewar wealth in six countries was $12.9 billion.

Meanwhile, counsel Michael Bradfield adopted his own unique method: He matched the names of Holocaust victims listed at the Yad Vashem Holocaust center in Jerusalem against the names of the dormant accounts. He was amazed at how many accounts he matched—and the Swiss had not—but also saddened at how many would never be identified; perhaps up to two-thirds remain unclaimed.

Another perplexing difficulty was estimating a current value for old accounts. Volcker retained the noted Wall Street economist Henry Kaufman, a refugee from Nazi Germany as a child. Stock prices in managed accounts had increased by seventy-five times since the end of World War II, and the Jewish representatives pushed for this huge multiple. But Kaufman reckoned that only a select number of the Holocaust accounts had been personally managed accounts; the overwhelming majority were deposit accounts sent to Switzerland for safety, not for investment in growth stocks, which was rare in those days for any except the richest investors. The

Volcker Committee settled on Kaufman's recommendation of a multiple of ten—what investors would have earned if they had invested in long-term Swiss bonds and been able to keep pace with half a century of increases in the cost of living.

.    .    .

THE D'AMATO hearings not only catalyzed the agreement for the Volcker Committee but led as well to my own trip to Switzerland in May. In a meeting with Chairman George Krayer and other leaders of the Swiss Bankers Association, I applauded their progress, urged that they account for all assets, and expressed the hope that unclaimed assets would be used to help the Holocaust survivors I had seen on my many visits to Eastern Europe. But it was clear there were still things left unsettled, such as the final disposal of the unclaimed money, the level of proof of ownership required to reopen a dormant account, and the burden of paying for a search for a missing account. The Swiss bankers told me that an ombudsman would help claimants find accounts and would insist on a lower standard of proof than in past decades. Search fees would be waived in needy cases.

By the end of the summer of 1996, the Swiss banking controversy was contained. The Volcker Committee was off and running, and an international audit of Swiss bank accounts would soon begin—the goal of the WJC and of the U.S. government. I had put the prestige of the U.S. president behind a thorough audit. The Swiss Federal Banking Commission promptly decided to waive bank secrecy so the new committee could "have full and unfettered access to all relevant files in the banks" to determine "whether there are any dormant accounts and other assets and financial instruments that were deposited before, during, and immediately after the Second Word War in banks located in Switzerland." Things seemed to be progressing.

But in America's litigious society, it was too much to hope that all of the publicity would not catch the attention of lawyers looking for a suit against the vulnerable Swiss banks. The lions were on the prowl.

# CHAPTER FOUR

# Enter the Lawyers

THERE ARE MORE lawyers in the city of Washington, D.C., than in the whole of Japan and about the same number as in all of Great Britain. In Europe, lawsuits are handled without publicity and resolved by judges in trials or quiet settlements. In the United States, trials are often public events, splashed across newspaper headlines without regard to their possible influence on juries. In the case of the Swiss bank affair, lawsuits raised the stakes by changing the nature of the debate from negotiation to the adversarial electricity of Anglo-Saxon law.

Any hope of containing the controversy by quiet diplomacy and the Volcker audits ended when a group of class-action lawyers got wind of the D'Amato hearings. The lawyers hijacked the Swiss bank dispute. They and their cases, more than the Volcker Committee or Bronfman, would now be in the driver's seat. Such is the power of lawyers and lawsuits in the United States today.

The class-action lawyers who entered the scene were a witches' brew of egos and mutual jealousies, greatly complicating my responsibility to keep the Swiss affair from careening out of diplomatic control and, once the suits were filed, impeding my ability to develop a coherent bargaining unit with which the Swiss could deal. Despite their different personalities, strategies, and goals, all the lawyers employed that uniquely American phenomenon, the class-action lawsuit.

Class-action suits are specifically recognized in the Federal Rules of Civil Procedure and by most states of the Union. These suits permit a few individuals to bring a case on behalf of hundreds, thousands, or even millions of others who have supposedly suffered similar injuries and who can recover if the suit is successful, even though they may know nothing about the case or even about the potential injury. Class actions are often legal platforms to raise politically sensitive issues. The principal attraction of the system is that large numbers of people may have legitimate claims—often small ones individually—and could never gain redress any other way. The suits are an increasingly effective way to hold companies publicly accountable for mass injuries. For example, class actions have held pharmaceutical companies accountable for defective drugs, tobacco companies for addictive cigarettes, and oil companies for environmental damage from spills. They are also used in cases arising from civil rights discrimination and other broad social concerns.

Class-action lawsuits are despised by most U.S. companies and feared by foreign corporations doing business in the United States. The Swiss government and Swiss banks, like other foreigners, did not understand the breadth of issues that class actions could raise. In a class-action suit, a marginal or even concocted wrong, like an unexpected drop in the price of a stock, can be elevated to a multimillion-dollar damage claim if enough people are involved.

It takes the special personality of a high-stakes gambler to make a living as a class-action lawyer. These attorneys' pay is contingent on a victory; hence they earn only what are called contingency fees. Major cases, such as the one against Exxon in the huge oil spill from the tanker Exxon *Valdez* off the pristine coast of Alaska, can drag on for years—more than a dozen, as of this writing—without a penny paid of the $5 billion awarded by the jury. Because corporations have such deep pockets to pay for appeals, lawyers may walk away empty-handed after years of research and argument. The stakes are enormous, emotions run high, and the infighting among class-action lawyers can be ferocious.

Had the class-action lawyers who emerged with the Swiss banking affair merely raised the issue of individual dormant accounts—the basis of the Volcker audit—their lawsuits might have been easily managed. But instead the lawyers contended that the private Swiss banks had accepted deposits not only from Hitler's victims but also from Germans depositing assets looted from victims and even from German companies depositing profits derived from their use of slave laborers. Further, they wanted to review Swiss conduct during World War II, not just by the few Swiss banks sued in the United States but also by the Swiss government in barring refugees.

I immediately recognized these allegations as new challenges, with arguments that might have little legal merit but were politically charged. The lawyers were not in it to find the historical truth. Most were in it for the money.

The class-action lawyers fell into two broad groups. The race to the courthouse was improbably won by Edward Fagan, who organized the first group. Charming, intelligent, and friendly, with curly hair and an air of innocence, at age forty-six Fagan had no class-action experience and was a neophyte to big-time litigation. Yet he was the first to file what became scores of Holocaust-related lawsuits over the next several years against Swiss, German, Austrian, and French companies. He had a dual personality: The picture of politeness and innocence inside the negotiating room, outside he was attracted to the press and the public limelight like a hummingbird to nectar. His tactics were maddening, upsetting, and disruptive. He constantly held press conferences, shamelessly using elderly Holocaust survivors as props. He was the attorney most disliked by his own colleagues and one of the most constant sources of annoyance to the Swiss and to me. Fagan nevertheless raised the visibility of the cases and did the legwork to sign up more plaintiffs than any of the other lawyers.

Fagan was born in the small town of Harlingen, Texas, to a Jewish family that later moved to San Antonio. As a young man, he became progressively more Orthodox, spending 1971 to 1974 at the Itry Yeshiva in Israel. During the 1973 Yom Kippur War, he was the banjo player for a group that entertained Israeli soldiers with American pop songs. A year later he helped rehabilitate the survivors of a terrorist massacre of Israeli high school students and later worked for an Orthodox youth group. He returned to the United States and attended Cardozo Law School at Yeshiva University, learning tort law firsthand by defending big companies in asbestos and tobacco suits for three years. Then he ran his own law firm in New York City, but he joked to me that he was not an ambulance chaser. "I had the ambulance come to me, usually. I had a lot of friends who were doctors." Then he made a more aggressive move: He placed a Yellow Pages ad for his law firm opposite the page giving the details of how to dial 911 for emergencies. "It was a hell of a gamble. It cost a lot of money. But it brought in good cases," he told me. Soon Fagan was managing sixteen other lawyers in an office on lower Broadway. It happened to be John D. Rockefeller's old executive suite and was adorned with Tiffany chandeliers and bronze doorknobs.

Fagan's life changed on a late September Sunday in 1996 with a phone call from his mother-in-law, who directed him to a *New York Times* article about the wartime conduct of Swiss banks. Fagan immediately envisioned a courtroom full of defendants, but there was one problem: no plaintiffs. He clipped the article, figuring that one day an aggrieved Holocaust survivor would walk into his office and ask him to file a complaint. He did not have long to wait.

Gizella Weisshaus had been the executrix of a relative's estate, which included a house purchased with German reparations. The state of New York seized the property for estate taxes. As Weisshaus's lawyer, Fagan lobbied to regain the property on the ground that it represented tax-exempt reparations. Weisshaus paid Fagan with Friday-afternoon gifts of sponge cake and kugel. On one visit he showed her the article, and she poured out a torrent of information. Her father had gathered up deposits from members of his community in Sighet, Romania, and, along with his own money, deposited them in Swiss banks. As the war crowded in on him in 1944, her father assured her that he had money for the family in Swiss banks. He was killed by the Nazis. After the war, she hired lawyers to find the money, but to no avail. Fagan had found his first plaintiff.

Fagan finalized a bare-bones complaint on his laptop computer while attending a playoff game at Yankee Stadium and filed it the next day, on October 3, 1996, in the U.S. District Court for the Eastern District of New York in Brooklyn, against the Union Bank of Switzerland (UBS) and Swiss Bank Corporation (SBC). It alleged that UBS and SBC, as well as scores of other Swiss banks, held dormant accounts from Holocaust victims from which they had unjustly profited for half a century. Establishing the pattern he would follow, Fagan produced Ms. Weisshaus at a news conference covered by a number of reporters.

A tort lawyer's instinct told Fagan that he needed an even more sympathetic victim. He found that person in Estelle Sapir. A frail and elderly but feisty woman who weighed no more than ninety pounds, she had a dramatic story that made her, in D'Amato's own words, a "poster child" for the cause. Estelle Sapir was born in 1925 in Warsaw to a wealthy investment banker, Joseph Sapir. Their apartment in Warsaw was filled with fine furnishings, silver, and art and staffed by live-in servants. When the Germans invaded Poland, her parents were traveling in Paris, and they got Estelle out of Warsaw. The Sapirs fled to the south of France, ruled by the vassal Vichy regime but temporarily free of Nazi troops. The French began their roundups in 1942 at Nazi insistence, starting with foreign refugees. The entire Sapir family was arrested. Estelle's father and brother were sent to a concentration camp in Rivesaltes in southern France, her mother to work in a hospital attached to the camp. Estelle, then seventeen, went first to a prison in Perpignan but later was transferred to the same hospital at Rivesaltes, first as a patient, then as a laborer.

Once during her imprisonment, she saw her father on the other side of the barbed wire. He could only put one finger through the wire to touch her. He implored Estelle to have courage to survive even if he did not. He then told her, "Don't worry for money. You have plenty of money in Switzerland." He named the different cities in which he had placed money in Swiss banks and made her repeat them to ensure she would remember. What she most remembered was Credit Suisse, but she also recalled other banks in Zurich, Basel, Geneva, and Lausanne. Moreover, all this was written down in the notebooks her father had left hidden in the family's Paris apartment. The next day he was sent to the Majdanek concentration camp outside Lublin, Poland, and was never heard from again.

Estelle and her brother and mother escaped from Rivesaltes and were taken in by French partisans. Estelle worked with them until the liberation in 1944, made her way back to the apartment, and retrieved the notebooks. One had the name of Credit Suisse in Geneva, and in 1946 she went to the teller's window there. The teller asked her to write her father's name and address on a slip of paper. He returned with a manila folder on which Estelle could see the name "J. Sapir." The teller told Estelle that she would need to talk with the manager, a tall man with beautiful gray hair and a demeanor so cold that it reminded her of the Gestapo. At his request, she produced an identity card showing she was the daughter of Joseph Sapir. He asked for her father's death certificate. When she said she did not have one, he told her to return to Paris, fetch the certificate, and bring it to the bank. He refused her request to see her father's folder. "This belongs to us; this is not your business," the bank manager said.

When she returned to Paris, she went to the French ministry handling deportees but could find no death certificate. She returned to Credit Suisse and saw the same manager, who still insisted on a death certificate. "There is no such thing, and you know it," she shouted. "Do I have to bring my father back to life?" Again the bank manager refused to permit her to see her father's folder. She returned again in 1957 but came away empty-handed.

Only in 1978, after she had moved to the United States, did she receive some written confirmation of her father's death with the publication in France of a registry of Jewish residents who had been deported. Joseph Sapir was listed as having been sent to Majdanek, the only official notation in Estelle's possession to mark her father's death. "I cherish this. This is all I have. I don't have a grave," she explained.

In 1996 she heard on French radio that the Swiss were going to unblock Jewish accounts. Later she learned about the D'Amato hearings. After Fagan's lawsuit was filed, she finally got a call from Credit Suisse informing her that, after reviewing her father's files, they did not know what had happened to the money in the account. She went back to Switzerland but, lacking a proper visa, was detained by the Swiss police at the Zurich airport. After paying seventy-five francs, she was released and made her way to Credit Suisse. Again she was told she needed a death certificate. Estelle became hysterical and ran out of the bank screaming and crying.

Estelle tracked down her father's accounts in French and English banks but never in Switzerland. She lived on his money, on reparations from the German government, and on U.S. Social Security. Before she died in April 1999, at the age of seventy-three, she explained that she was pursuing her father's funds in accordance with his plea to her never to forget. She said, "I can die tomorrow or an hour from now. I want when I go back upstairs to heaven, when I meet my father, to tell him, 'I done this for you. I went. I done. I found.'"

In September 1998, when Fagan took Estelle and several other survivor clients to the remains of the Majdanek concentration camp, they found an open pit of ashes had been preserved as a monument. The wind whipped ash in their faces. Fagan heard Estelle say, "Oh, God!" and asked if she had dust in her eyes. She shook her head, saying, "These are people." Then tiny Estelle climbed down into the pit to scoop out ashes so she could bury what was left of her father.

Meanwhile Fagan gathered his team. By December 1996 it included Burt Neuborne, an experienced civil liberties lawyer and professor at New York University Law School; Professor Richard Weisberg of Cardozo Law School; seasoned trial lawyers Bob Lieff and Irwin Levin; Michael Witti, a German lawyer; and a prize catch, Robert Swift of Philadelphia. Swift had brought a class-action against Philippine dictator Ferdinand Marcos and his family on behalf of Philippine citizens, alleging that Ferdinand and his wife, Imelda, had robbed the country and tortured and executed thousands of political opponents. Swift had based his case on one of the oldest laws on the books, the Alien Tort Claims Act of 1789, passed by the first Congress, which permitted aliens to bring suit in U.S. courts for "a tort only, committed in violaton of the law of nations or a treaty of the United States." Swift won an uncontested judgment for $150 million which was upheld on appeal. After years of further legal effort, he obtained a court order freezing Marcos's assets, much of which were in Swiss banks.

Swift, fifty-two, was an atypical class-action lawyer: the consummate gentleman, understated, calm, reserved, and flexible, with none of Fagan's flamboyance. He was a Vietnam veteran who had learned to handle class actions for a leading antitrust attorney, but his passion was the new field of human rights law. He wanted to convert the concept of criminal responsibility from the Nuremberg trials into civil liability in favor of human rights victims, still a novel theory of law.

When Swift was approached by Fagan to use the Alien Torts Act against the Swiss banks, he was skeptical. What torts, or wrongs, could be alleged against the Swiss banks? Simply having provided financial assistance to the Nazi violators of human rights would not be enough. But as Swift reviewed Fagan's complaint, he could see the nub of a case against the banks for aiding and abetting the Nazis' torts by knowingly accepting their loot and for failing to return the money of Holocaust victims.

For Fagan the suits were the opportunity to earn one of his first big paydays and achieve the celebrity status he craved. Like Fagan, Swift believed in getting paid for his work, even if it was representing Holocaust victims. Their team wanted attorneys' fees and the quickest settlement possible, even if it meant settling for less than they might get later at the trial.

·     ·     ·

A SECOND group of lawyers was organized by Michael Hausfeld, an experienced Washington-based class-action attorney, and another well-known Washington lawyer, Martin Mendelsohn, who had created the special Nazi-hunting unit at the Justice Department under President Carter in 1977. On October 21, three weeks after Fagan's suit, the rival Hausfeld group filed a broader and more thoroughly researched class-action suit in the same

Brooklyn federal court, adding Credit Suisse to the two banks Fagan sued. In addition to the dormant-account charges in Fagan's complaint, Hausfeld alleged that the Swiss banks knowingly accepted assets looted by the Germans, as well as profits from German businesses employing slave laborers. Fagan soon amended his complaint, adding Credit Suisse and including Hausfeld's additional charges.

Michael Hausfeld was nothing like Ed Fagan. Short, chunky, and intense, with a cherubic face, Hausfeld could be sweetness and light at one moment and anger and darkness the next. He was unpredictable and at times unreasonable in his demands, but he was central to any successful negotiation because he had a keen sense of where the bottom line was beyond which he could not push. At fifty-two, he had successfully handled high-visibility class-action cases, including a major employment discrimination suit against Texaco.

This fight was also a personal one for Hausfeld. His father escaped from the village of Tulste, Poland, in 1940, but most of the family was killed by the Nazis. Hausfeld grew up in a Jewish area of Brooklyn, where his family belonged to an Orthodox synagogue, and his father organized and led the Tulste Society of Survivors. To the extent the survivors discussed their memories at all, they mourned their loss. Their lives were swathed in guilt for having survived while others perished. At Kol Nidre, the solemn evening service that commences Yom Kippur, the Day of Atonement, Hausfeld remembers survivors shaking with emotion and sobbing uncontrollably.

As early as 1981 Hausfeld and Martin Mendelsohn brought an unsuccessful suit against the former Croatian minister of interior Andrija Artukovich, who ran slave labor camps during the war. The case was dismissed because of the lapse of time and the court's belief that it presented political, not legal, questions. When Bronfman and D'Amato brought the complaints against the Swiss banks to light more than a decade later, Hausfeld was ready. Several victims contacted him, along with the American Jewish Congress and the Simon Wiesenthal Center, with whom he and Mendelsohn had a long-standing relationship. The Center helped supply him with victims willing to sue. Before filing his suit, Hausfeld hired Miriam Kleiman, the same archivist and historian who had helped prepare the D'Amato hearings for the World Jewish Congress. She spent six months researching the conduct of Switzerland's banks during and after the war. Hausfeld then pored over her results for another two months to weave a tapestry of financial offenses by the banks. But Hausfeld felt he needed added legal horsepower and turned to Mel Weiss of New York City, arguably the dean of American class-action lawyers.

The gruff and brilliant Weiss had a history of making sophisticated and successful complaints against a wide range of corporate financial practices, becoming the bane of existence for large multinational corporations. Perpetually scowling, he combined a razor sharp legal mind with a natural negotiator's temperament for the endgame. Weiss was the wealthy head of a firm of 170 lawyers—plus forensic experts, economists, and scientists. He often flew to our negotiations aboard his private plane. When Hausfeld proposed donating the firm's services, Weiss immediately agreed. Neither wanted the many impoverished survivors to have what might be their meager portions diluted even further by the legal fees that traditionally eat up one-third of a class-action settlement. Instead, Hausfeld, Mendelsohn, and Weiss were willing to work pro bono, free of charge. For them, the Holocaust was a driving force motivating them to compel the Swiss to come to terms with their history. Because they had less riding on the outcome from a personal and financial standpoint—they were already successful, established lawyers—they were the most uncompromising, the most belligerent toward the Swiss, and toward me.

Fagan's tactic was to try to embarrass the Swiss and to get publicity for himself by press appearances with his Holocaust survivor clients. The Hausfeld-Weiss team's strategy was entirely different. They abhorred Fagan's histrionics. But they recognized the shaky legal basis of their cases, so they determined to bring political pressure on the Swiss. For them the class actions were a vehicle to make their case to the court of public opinion as well as the court of law.

That Edward Korman would be the judge handling the explosive Swiss bank cases was a fluke, or perhaps a stroke of destiny. Through the normal rotation system known as "the wheel," lawsuits in the Brooklyn federal court were arbitrarily assigned by the court clerk among various judges. The Fagan and Hausfeld groups had brought the cases in Brooklyn because a large Holocaust survivor population resided there and the lawyers hoped the judges, as a result, would be more open-minded to the novel legal arguments they were making. In short, they were "forum shopping," a time-honored tradition in big cases. The clerk gave the Swiss bank cases to Judge John Bartels, who was in his nineties and in poor health. Judge Bartels asked Judge Korman to take the cases from him, but Korman declined, knowing how contentious they would be. So the Swiss bank cases went back to the wheel. Korman's name came up anyway.

Judge Korman's life had intersected in a strange way with both mine and with Senator Al D'Amato's. Korman and I crossed paths as young lawyers, when he was an associate at the distinguished New York law firm Paul, Weiss, Rifkind, Wharton & Garrison helping to try a case in Atlanta before the federal judge for whom I was then serving as a law clerk. And in an ironic way, Korman had helped to advance Al D'Amato's political career. Korman had been the federal prosecutor of Long Island political boss Joseph Margiotta, whose conviction cleared the way for D'Amato to take his place. D'Amato later joked to Korman that "you did me a *mitzvah*"—Hebrew for good deed—by prosecuting Margiotta, even though D'Amato had not supported the case against his fellow Republican.

Korman's career, in turn, owed quite a lot to his relationship with Al D'Amato. Korman had been appointed to his judgeship under a unique arrangement between D'Amato and his Democratic Senate colleague, Daniel Patrick Moynihan, giving both political parties a voice in nominating Federal judges to ensure a quality Federal bench in New York. Korman, though not a Republican, was grateful to D'Amato for the appointment and made it his business to drop by the senator's office when he was in Washington. He was well acquainted with D'Amato's endearing habit of sitting down with visitors while continuing to run his office like a circus ringmaster, taking phone calls, shouting requests at his staff, and making asides to whomever happened to come into the room. Korman was always careful not to share his thoughts on the Swiss Bank case with D'Amato; he could never know in which ring of the circus his ideas might suddenly appear. Still, Al D'Amato would never have been permitted the role he would later play in Judge Korman's chambers but for their unusually close relationship.

Korman faced two competing sets of class-action lawyers—Fagan-Swift and Hausfeld-Weiss—with similar cases in his Brooklyn courtroom, each with sharply different goals and strategies, each fighting to become the lead counsel and dominate the executive committee of plaintiffs' lawyers that normally manages the litigation, negotiations, and relations with the judge in complicated class-action cases like these. The already poisonous atmosphere between the two groups was hardly improved by the fact that Hausfeld had left the Washington office of Swift's Philadelphia law firm after an acrimonious split. The lawyers themselves failed to agree on who could best represent the full class of clients, and so they came before Judge Korman on March 6, 1997, to have him impose a compromise. Accusations were traded furiously over which team had more clients and more experience. Judge Korman had to gavel down shouting attorneys in what he later described to me as an unseemly fight, considering the tragic genesis of the cases.

Fortunately for everyone's sanity, the glue that held the two fractious groups tenuously together was Burt Neuborne, a quiet, studious, fifty-seven-year-old professor of law at New York University (NYU) Law School. Time and again during the next several years, he brought calm and rationality to an emotional, often irrational process.

At this hearing Neuborne was sitting quietly in the courtroom as Swift and Weiss went literally chest to chest. Neuborne had worked for twenty years as a lawyer for the American Civil Liberties Union and had argued cases against Korman when the future judge was a senior government lawyer. The judge quieted the other lawyers and asked Neuborne how committed he was to Fagan's team. Neuborne replied that Fagan's people had sought him out but that, unlike them, he sought no fees, and in any case he had offered to serve "as a library" for all the plaintiffs' attorneys, paid or unpaid.

"Good, you'll be the swing vote," ruled the judge, taking him off Fagan's legal team and appointing him an independent member and chief organizer of the lawyers' Executive Committee. Neuborne's role was to develop a coordinated position from the fractious crowd and be the liaison to Judge Korman. Through tortuous negotiations that only a lawyer could relish, Neuborne rejected an even split of five members from each team lest too much of the legal tactics pivot on his tie-breaking vote. He gave Hausfeld's team five members because of its superior resources, Fagan's team four, and himself veto power by being able to deadlock negotiations among the lawyers with his single vote, an outcome no one relished.

Neuborne turned out to be the indispensable person not only in the Swiss bank cases but also in the German slave labor cases that followed. Analytic, reflective, and level-headed, Neuborne rose above the warring factions among the class-action lawyers. To me he was their intellectual force and ballast. But there was a sadness to his demeanor, a pall over his face, and for good reason. Although Neuborne described himself as a "relentlessly secular Jew," his daughter Lauren, who had suffered from a weak heart since childhood, had been drawn toward religion while young and was a rabbinical student at Hebrew Union College. A few months before the cases came before the judge, she suddenly died of a heart attack. Her father saw his work as a living memorial to his lost daughter.

The Executive Committee was an uneasy coalition of egos. Life among the lawyers was not exactly smooth after Neuborne took over, especially with Fagan, who had little experience in sophisticated litigation. He rarely attended the committee meetings and, when he did, constantly jumped up to talk on his cellular phone, prompting Neuborne to joke, "Someone must have put Ritalin in his coffee." Fagan continued searching as far afield as Israel for more plaintiffs. When he found them, he seemed to spend more energy putting them on the courthouse steps for the television cameras than preparing the cases for the court.

The Executive Committee held its first meeting late in February 1997 at NYU Law School. Fees were the first item on the agenda. Hausfeld and Weiss persisted in their agreement to waive their fees. Fagan, Swift, and their team said they could not afford to work without pay. Neuborne argued that, though Weiss and Hausfeld were wealthy enough to waive their fees, they could not require everyone else to do so. He proposed a fee structure established in civil rights statutes: legal charges for hours actually spent to advance the cases, with a small bonus for exceptional contributions, to be determined by the judge. Neuborne believed that Fagan and his team agreed to this arrangement at the NYU meeting, but Swift later denied it. Attorneys' fees would remain an unresolved issue for years after the Swiss banks settled.

On the Swiss side, the lawyers were more in synch. Every major bank retains a Washington law firm to deal with Congress and the numerous government agencies that regulate the U.S. banking industry. The Swiss Bankers Association was no exception. They retained the prestigious firm of Wilmer, Cutler, & Pickering, whose senior partner was Lloyd Cutler, the Swiss banks' éminence grise within the Washington legal establishment. He and I had worked together in the Carter White House on a daily basis when he served as counsel to the president. Lloyd has a remarkable legal mind and wise political judgment, which I saw him use to great effect in helping resolve the Iran hostage crisis in the last months of the Carter administration. Suave and articulate, he was sent from central casting for the part of the quintessential Washington lawyer. Only white hair and a slight stoop revealed his eighty years.

When the class-action suits were filed by the two warring camps of lawyers, Cutler and one of his young partners, Marc Cohen, sent their Swiss clients a memorandum setting forth a three-part strategy.

First, they would try to have the suits dismissed on traditional legal grounds. They would argue that the demands for the Holocaust accounts were a political issue to be debated by governments, not fought in courts of law. They would also contend that the dispute was more appropriately covered by Swiss, not U.S., law. They decided not to base their arguments on the passage of time lest that produce a political backlash. They recognized that in the public's mind, almost any serious case involving the Holocaust could no more be subject to a statute of limitations than a murder case.

Second, the Swiss should settle the cases. Winning in court might save money for the banks in the short term but would be counted as a huge loss in the court of public opinion. A legal battle would tarnish their reputations as responsible fiduciaries especially on Wall Street, at a time when they sought a larger presence in global financial markets.

Third, they could use the Volcker audit to argue against any discovery of bank documents by the class-action lawyers, on the ground that it would impede the Volcker Committee's work.

Although both the Swiss banks and their government hoped to dispose of the whole dispute as quickly, painlessly, and cheaply as possible, they held profoundly different agendas. Whereas the Swiss banks wanted to salvage their plummeting reputations, the Swiss government simply wanted to push the whole crisis away from itself and onto the shoulders of the three private banks. The government refused to take any part in the class-action negotiations or to pay any amounts, thus dodging the threat of a public referendum it feared it would lose and avoiding a confrontation with the raw political feelings the controversy was engendering in the Swiss public. The government did take small steps to calm the controversy along the way, but essentially it continued to insist the problem was only for the banks sued in court, failing to appreciate that the entire country's reputation was at stake.

The first small step the Swiss government took after the filing of the class-action suits in Brooklyn was a decision by Foreign Minister Flavio Cotti to appoint a young diplomat, Thomas Borer, to head a special task force to coordinate the government's response to the growing crisis. Borer, who had spent three years in the Swiss Embassy in Washington and understood the United States and its complex politics, was given the rank of ambassador at large. He spoke perfect English with only the barest hint of an accent. For the next three years, Borer briefed Cotti almost every morning at 6:30 A.M.

Borer was a most unusual diplomat, particularly for a reserved country like Switzerland. His finely chiseled, handsome features, blond crew cut, and bold, direct manner became the public face of Switzerland in the United States as he flew over—frequently with his wife, a former Texas beauty queen—to testify before Congress, to hold press briefings, and to meet with me and my colleagues in the U.S. government.

But for all his charm, Borer was in a particularly difficult spot. He was given no authority to negotiate solutions but only a mandate to contain the political fallout. He confided to me later that he was as unprepared as his country for the crisis it faced and that, if the private banks had had a consistent strategy of openness and transparency, "they could have settled more cheaply early." As he struggled with his difficult job, he became a polarizing figure in the United States. Weiss found him "despicable," and Bronfman was even less charitable, telling me later that it was odd for the Swiss to have appointed "someone who looked like an SS captain."

Although I had my differences with Borer, particularly as the endgame approached, I recognized he was caught between growing public resentment at home and the need to show an accommodating Swiss face in the United States. He often got a bad rap. After Borer visited the Holocaust Museum for two hours—and, as he told me, was deeply moved—some newspapers wrongly reported that he had dropped by the museum only briefly as a public relations stunt. My first exposure to Borer came during his visit to my office on December 6, 1996. I was instantly attracted by his directness. He assured me the Swiss government was willing to shed "full light" on its activities during and after World War II through the creation by the Swiss Parliament of the "Independent Commission of Experts Switzerland—Second World War: Switzerland, National Socialism, and the Second World War," to be led by Professor Jean-François Bergier. Interim reports would be issued regularly until the final report was ready. The commission's mandate was to examine as completely and exhaustively as possible Switzerland's political, economic, and financial links with the Axis powers, the Allies, and the other neutral countries.

I was encouraged by this additional proactive step, and after meeting with Professor Bergier in Washington and Switzerland, I never doubted the sincerity or probity with which he would undertake his work. His later reports on the extent of looted-gold transactions with Nazi Germany and the failings of Swiss refugee policy were written without equivocation. But as a professor of medieval history, he worked on an academic timetable more suited to the Middle Ages. His final report was scheduled for completion in 2002.

That did not help my cause. Borer insisted that, beyond distributing any dormant accounts found by Volcker, the Swiss government would take no further action until Bergier's final report was completed. This was a complete misreading of the angry American mood and the political pressures already coming to a boil. Borer knew it, but he had to follow his instructions from Bern. Back in their capital, the Swiss were naive and misguided in believing that everyone would stand still while a commission of professional historians, however objective, went about their careful research and deliberations. The world would not wait six years.

And the class-action lawyers would not wait six seconds. They were already jockeying for position. To me, their cases seemed distant, a matter between private parties that should not occupy the time of the United States government. And while I realized the cases would be a bone in the craw of the Swiss, I saw no way of removing it for them. To me, the Volcker Committee's audits, buttressed with a long-term study of Swiss wartime conduct by the Bergier Commission, were the best ways to achieve justice for victims with the least damage to the United States' bilateral relationship with Switzerland. This naive hope would soon be overtaken by events.

CHAPTER FIVE

᛭

# All That Glitters

EVERAL EVENTS coincided within a few months that polluted the atmosphere between Switzerland and the United States and set back my efforts to bring some order out of the growing chaos.

On September 26, 1996, Edgar Bronfman wrote to his friend President Clinton, indicating that the World Jewish Congress's research in the American wartime intelligence documents confirmed that Nazi Germany sent $500 million worth of gold in 1945 dollars to Switzerland, whereas the Allies recovered only $60 million in gold from the Swiss after the war. Bronfman also informed the president that of the 337 metric tons in looted Nazi gold, worth $4.18 billion, the Allied soldiers found after the war 6 tons remained under the jurisdiction of the Tripartite Gold Commission (TGC) and had never been distributed. Two of that 6 tons were in the Federal Reserve Bank of New York, and the rest in the Bank of England. The great bulk, about 330 metric tons of gold, had been given over the past fifty years to the central banks of the ten European countries from whom it was stolen, "but not one ounce has gone to Holocaust survivors or victims of Nazi persecution." Bronfman concluded that the World Jewish Restitution Organization should be given the remaining 6 tons for the benefit of Holocaust survivors.

A month later, on October 25, Bronfman got more specific. Together with Lord Greville Janner, a member of the British Parliament and chair of the Holocaust Education Trust, affiliated with the WJC, Bronfman wrote to Secretary of State Warren Christopher. He sought Christopher's assurance that the residue of 6 tons in the gold pool "will not under any circumstances be distributed before all the options have been fully investigated by your Government and the other two TGC authorities [Britain and France]."

Bronfman and Janner asserted clearly for the first time that they believed some of the residue of the 6 tons still in the gold pool had been taken from Holocaust victims and melted down into disguised gold bars. In view of the doubtful source of the entire gold pool—some monetary gold from central banks of the countries occupied by the Germans and some from victims—they argued that the remaining gold, worth $88 million at the 1996 price, should not be distributed until "its origins are investigated."

Both letters clearly indicated the Clinton administration was entering an entirely different phase with the Swiss, one separate from the lawsuits that were just being filed and from Volcker's audits of dormant accounts in private Swiss banks. The scope of the inquiry was about to be broadened to the role of the Swiss National Bank in receiving looted Nazi gold and of the Allies themselves, the United States included, in handling—or mishandling—it after the war. Perhaps the three victors—France, Britain, and the United States (the Soviet Union did not participate)—had, unwittingly, given the countries from whose treasuries the Nazis plundered not only their gold but that of the victims, disguised as gold bullion from central banks!

After reviewing the first of the two letters, Sandy Berger, President Clinton's national security adviser, called and asked me to stop the distribution of the last 6 tons of gold pending a determination of its origin. He also asked me to undertake an interagency study into the origins of the gold in the TGC gold pool.

The president replied to Bronfman on October 30. He noted that several weeks earlier the State Department had announced a new study undertaken with the U.S. Holocaust Memorial Museum. He told Bronfman that he was broadening that research project and that he had asked me, as an extension of my role as special envoy for property restitution in Central and Eastern Europe, to coordinate the project, which was "already underway." President Clinton noted that "the subject of allied and neutral nations' actions during and after the war to handle Nazi assets and dormant accounts is both important and complex" and that "I have asked Ambassador Eizenstat to look into the matter thoroughly and consider your views."

The Bronfman letters and Clinton's reply added a sense of urgency and focus to what I had already commenced. My office was being bombarded by requests for documents and appearances at hearings before the Senate and House Banking Committees. The WJC and the class-action lawyers were selectively leaking historical tidbits from the National Archives with disturbing regularity. Moreover, we had permitted Senator D'Amato and the WJC to define the issue their way, without access to all the facts. Now we felt it necessary to provide a detailed and coherent historical picture. The politically astute U.S. ambassador to Switzerland, Madeleine Kunin, believed we needed to avoid letting D'Amato get the headlines and shape the story. More than any of us, she recognized the sensitivities on both sides of the Atlantic. Born to a Swiss Jewish family, she emigrated to the United States at the age of ten and later became governor of Vermont. As critical as she was of D'Amato, she also thought that the Swiss themselves believed that the whole affair would vanish if "only D'Amato and the Jews go away." That was not the case. The world, including the Swiss, had to understand that the U.S. government took the matter of Holocaust assets very seriously.

While the administration's historical research was quietly proceeding, and just when it seemed that the Swiss had taken sufficient action to calm the controversy by agreeing to the Volcker audits and by appointing the Bergier historical commission, three political avalanches occurred. They landed within days of each other, sweeping away Swiss complacency but replacing it with a defensive sense of persecution and righteous indignation. First, the Swiss president revealed himself as at best insensitive and inflexible. Second, the Swiss ambassador to the United States was sabotaged by the leak of an undiplomatic cable. Last and most notorious, one of the Swiss banks was discovered destroying its own apparently incriminating records.

The first avalanche occurred in the traditional year-end press conference for Swiss reporters by the person who holds the rotating presidency of Switzerland's federal council—in this case, Jean-Pascal Delamaruz. Delamaruz charged that Jewish organizations were trying to "blackmail" Switzerland into paying them large sums of money to destabilize Switzerland and destroy its banking industry. The basis for this statement was Thomas Borer's confidential cable sent two weeks before, reporting that Singer and Bronfman had warned that if Switzerland did not create a large humanitarian fund, Jewish organizations would take action against the Swiss. Without Borer's knowledge, the head of the Swiss Foreign Ministry circulated his cable to all members of the Federal Council, including Delamaruz. The outgoing president put the worst possible interpretation on Singer's and Bronfman's warning, and his inflammatory language caused an uproar.

Borer read the interview on a skiing vacation and immediately recognized it as a disaster. He later told me it showed his president's insensitivity to American Jews "fighting for truth and justice" on behalf of those who had been killed. In response to Delamaruz's remarks, Singer came out swinging. He threatened a boycott—a term he had not used before—of Swiss banks and companies unless Delamaruz's comments were "rejected by Switzerland and its bankers clearly and decisively."

The Swiss cabinet moved quickly to control the damage. On January 7, 1997, it offered to create a compensation fund from the $32 million already found in dormant accounts by the ombudsman for the Swiss banks. The WJC rejected this as inadequate and hit back again. They released a 1946 memorandum found in the National Archives in which the Office of Strategic Services (OSS), predecessor to the CIA, gave details of "how the Swiss National Bank sent truckloads of gold looted by the Nazis to Spain and Portugal in vehicles bearing the Swiss emblem."

Paul Volcker called me to report that Delamaruz's remarks were affecting his committee's work; the Jewish members were refusing to attend meetings until the Swiss apologized. This took ten days because Delamaruz's letter of apology had to be approved by the Swiss Federal Council. Borer called me to concede that Delamaruz's words had "destroyed a lot of good will."

Just as the furor was subsiding, a mid-December cable from Ambassador Carlo Jagmetti to his superiors in Bern was leaked on January 25 to the Swiss paper *Sonntags Zeitung*. Analyzing the pressures on Switzerland, Jagmetti recommended that the government adopt a more aggressive strategy and "wage war" against its opponents. For a diplomat with thirty-five years of experience, this was an injudicious thing to put in writing. Jagmetti was in his last few months of a distinguished career, but this put an ignominious end to it. He looked for support from the Swiss Federal Council and was met by silence.

One of the most uncomfortable meetings I have ever had was with Jagmetti on January 27, hours after he was forced to resign. Still flabbergasted—his own word—he told me he had been trying for a year to awaken his government to the increasingly aggressive American attitude toward Switzerland. He admitted that his cable contained strong words but insisted "not one word" reflected any anti-Semitism on his part. He explained that he did not mean Switzerland had to win a war against the Jews but wanted to "save the integrity of Switzerland and to save relations with the United States." The war, he told me, was against adversaries like Senator D'Amato and the press, and the Swiss strategy must be to "win the war against ourselves not the Jews." Those who had leaked his confidential memo in Bern were "really criminals," he angrily confided.

No one ever discovered which of Jagmetti's enemies leaked the cable that forced him out. Some believed, without proof, that it was the work of Borer, seeking the prized Washington diplomatic post. While I had little sympathy for Jagmetti's inflammatory language, it was impossible not to feel sorry for him as a person and as a diplomat trying to do his job. Fortunately for Switzerland and for the United States, he was succeeded by Alfred Defago, Swiss consul general in New York. Defago was the first of his government's representatives to fully appreciate both the raw feelings in his country and the emotional resonance of the Holocaust in the United States.

The third and final blow was the Meili affair. This did more than anything to turn the Swiss banks into international pariahs by linking their dubious behavior during and after the war to the discovery of a seemingly unapologetic attempt to cover it up now by destroying documents. The incident also occurred in January 1997, only three weeks after the Swiss banks' American lawyers had signed an agreement that their clients would not destroy any potential evidence in the class-action suits.

Christoph Meili was a full-time security guard at the Zurich headquarters of the Union Bank of Switzerland. His job was to check windows and doors at 45 Bahnhofstrasse, watch the distribution of money from UBS to smaller banks, and pay particular attention to construction sites at the bank.

On the fateful day of Wednesday, January 8, 1997, he was working the afternoon shift, making his five o'clock rounds and turning off the lights. As he entered the bank's shredding room, a number of unusual things caught his eye. Two metal bins were overflowing with ledgers dating back to 1864. One ledger involved records from 1864 to 1970 for UBS, the Swiss National Bank, and the Eidgenossische Bank, taken over by UBS after its bankruptcy in 1945. Meili's suspicions were particularly aroused by finding records of the country's central bank in the UBS shredding room. With the bank's employees gone home for the evening, he had time for an inspection.

Meili quickly noticed two big black books from Germany's Reichsbank listing stocks and real estate held during World War II. They held entries for a number of German chemical companies, such as Bayrische Sodawerke (now BASF); DeGussa, the German company that smelted much of the looted Nazi gold into ingots with markings disguising their source; and Degesch, which made the Zyklon B chemical used to kill inmates in Nazi concentration camps. Some of the transactions dated from the final months of World War II, in 1945. On some of the pages next to the names of German companies were large numbers, like 10,000 or 20,000 reichsmarks, with notations recalculating the stock values. The last pages of the books contained entries from 1933 to 1945 regarding real estate transactions in Berlin. Attached were typed white papers noting that they were forced sales and giving the prices in reichsmarks. Here, Meili realized, were obviously records of real estate confiscated by the Nazis and placed in secret Reichsbank accounts in Switzerland. That real estate now belonged to UBS. After the Berlin Wall fell, the bank had laid claim to properties that had been nationalized by the Communist East German government.

Meili had read about the D'Amato hearings, and he also knew that in 1996 the Swiss government had issued an edict forbidding the banks from destroying any documents covering their activities from 1933 to 1945, Germany's Nazi era. He immediately ripped out about sixty pages relating to real estate and took these pages and three other ledgers home with him. He discussed his discovery with his wife, Giussepina, who shared his view that something seemed wrong, that somehow the documents "belonged to the Jewish people." Meili had recently seen the movie *Schindler's List* and felt he shared certain characteristics with Schindler, a Nazi businessman who protected his Jewish forced laborers. Meili also belonged to a socially oriented Protestant denomination, the City Mission Church, which emphasized feeding the poor and helping the homeless and elderly. He later told me that he saw it as his duty as a Christian to help Jews.

But what to do now with this explosive information about the very company where he worked? After pondering for another day, he called the Zurich newspaper *Tagesanzeiger;* they were uninterested. Then he called the Israeli Embassy and was told simply to send in the documents. Meili called the Israeli Cultural Center in Zurich, went there by car, and left the documents with two security guards. The Israeli officials, fearing a trap by some unfriendly Swiss persons to enmesh the Israeli government in the Swiss bank controversy, told him to hire a lawyer and finally put him in touch with Gisella Blau, a journalist for the Jewish press in Zurich. He called Blau on Sunday and gave her some of the documents.

What followed demonstrated the Swiss banks' consistent inability to develop a strategy for damage control. As soon as Borer heard of Meili's dis-covery at UBS, he talked with Mathis Cabiallavetta, the bank's president, and urged him to take the matter seriously and to congratulate Meili for preventing the destruction of documents. Instead, the chairman of the bank, Robert Studer, angrily attacked Meili on Swiss television, suggesting that the discovery was a setup to frame the banks. Borer urged Studer either to produce proof that Meili had acted improperly or to apologize to him. The chairman did neither.

Meanwhile the Swiss police investigated Meili for taking the ledgers and UBS for planning to destroy them in violation of a recent government decree preventing destruction of materials that might be useful in examin-ing the dormant bank accounts.

Just as Meili acted innocently, indeed courageously, the bank may have been acting innocently, if naively. Its archivist was cleaning out old records mainly from well before World War II, including the nineteenth-century financing of Switzerland's famous railway tunnels. These could have no bearing on Nazi loot. But the discovery brought to life what until now had to some seemed yet another morally ambiguous wartime incident, this one involving old bank accounts best left dead and buried. It demonstrated a consistency over time in Swiss thoughts and deeds, from the wartime acceptance of looted assets, to the postwar stonewalling of legitimate account holders, right up to today's seeming cover-up. And finally, it led D'Amato's congressional colleagues to see his investigation in a new light, as much more than just an election stunt.

World attention focused on the unsophisticated, young Meili, who quickly became a pariah in his own country. The Swiss Jewish community wanted him kept under lock and key, because it feared anti-Semitic reper-cussions. The security firm that employed Meili suspended him with pay. Meanwhile the various American groups—the class-action lawyers, Jewish groups, and Senator D'Amato—all tried to exploit Meili's courage to advance their own causes, some to his benefit, some not. Most tried to bot-tle up his testimony for their exclusive use. Ed Fagan showed up in Switzer-land and persuaded Meili to give a two-hour deposition so he could prepare a lawsuit. The Anti-Defamation League (ADL) contributed generously to Meili's legal defense fund. Abe Foxman, head of the ADL, held a news con-ference with Meili and ran advertisements around the world soliciting more money for the fund. This created a backlash against Meili in Switzerland

and, by Foxman's own admission, made the Swiss Jewish community "ballistic," worried that the growing controversy, fed by U.S.-based Jewish groups, would stir up latent anti-Semitism against them.

Meili accepted D'Amato's invitation to testify before the Senate Banking Committee, even though the ADL had warned him that doing so might sever his ties to Switzerland. On February 25 he arrived with his wife and two children at Kennedy Airport in New York en route to Washington. Sheltered in a VIP lounge, he took an urgent transatlantic conference call from Werner Rom of the Israeli Cultural Center in Zurich and his own Swiss lawyer, Marcel Bossonnet. Rom warned Meili that the Swiss banks' newly professed interest in creating a Holocaust victims fund might vanish if he testified. Bossonnet warned his client that he would no longer represent him unless he returned home. Frightened, Meili and his family fled to Fagan's house in New Jersey without their luggage, which had been checked through to Washington. Fagan's wife, Elizabeth, threw them out of the house lest D'Amato retaliate against the Fagans for persuading Meili to snub his Senate hearing. Arguing that "D'Amato just wants to use you" and perhaps fearing the worldwide publicity might attract competing lawyers to represent him, Fagan persuaded Meili to take a late-night flight back home. Rom met him at the Zurich airport with flowers.

These were the only flowers the unfortunate young international whistle blower ever got. Meili was fired from his security job. He received bomb threats and hate mail alleging that the ADL support proved that the Jews had paid him to steal bank documents. He had to change his telephone number. The Swiss press, influenced by the banks, printed false stories about his past. He could not find a job. By the end of April Meili had had enough. He left Switzerland, formally retained Fagan, and agreed to testify before D'Amato's Senate Banking Committee.

D'Amato saw the hearing in apocalyptic terms. He told me that, in contrast to their pristine Heidi image, the Swiss now seemed "part of a sinister conspiracy aimed at destroying people" who had tried to prevent the shredding of documents. On May 6, Meili told his compelling story to Congress and asked for help to remain in the United States. D'Amato, vindicated before Senate colleagues who had felt he was just pandering to the Jewish vote, pushed a special bill through Congress giving Meili U.S. citizenship because of the death threats in Switzerland. Meili and his family settled in Orange County, California, where he later enrolled at Chapman University.

Ultimately the Swiss police investigations against Meili and UBS were dropped without charges. Following the Meili affair, the Volcker Committee found that in 1998 there had been three other incidents in which UBS documents disappeared in error, one of which the bank said involved the cleaning people simply taking the wrong box. UBS was not the only bank to attract suspicion. There were also a series of mysterious fires at the American warehouses of Credit Suisse that destroyed bank records.

Though they claimed they were free of guilt in the Meili affair, the Swiss banks astutely realized the need for immediate damage control. At the suggestion of Rainer Gut, chairman of Credit Suisse, the SBA announced the formation of a "Humanitarian Fund for the Victims of the Holocaust," chaired by Dr. Rolf Bloch, head of the Swiss Jewish community, to which the three major Swiss private banks in the class-action lawsuits would contribute a total of 100 million Swiss francs ($70 million).

Gut emanated authority. An imposing, elegant man, he was the clear leader of the Swiss bankers. I agreed to meet him on Sunday, April 6, and praised him for initiating the Humanitarian Fund, even under such pressure. It took a great deal of courage, as gauged by the reaction of the Swiss themselves. "I am appalled," Gut told me, "at the 'fan mail' I have received since I suggested the fund. I didn't believe there was still this much anti-Semitism." He also gave me early warning that any government reparations would be approved only after a referendum and its success was highly uncertain. Gut explained that the Swiss middle class opposed the whole reparations process, that anti-American sentiment was growing in Switzerland, and that the Swiss resented the scrutiny of their wartime behavior. Why were they, a neutral country, being attacked? But Gut felt otherwise. "We would be guilty if we didn't clean things up," he said. Gut and SBC chairman Marcel Ospel urged me to make a positive public statement about the fund, which I did.

On March 6, 1997, the Swiss National Bank offered to contribute more money to the fund, the first and only such offer. Even right-wing leader Christoph Blocher approved, as long as the gesture was not perceived as an expression of guilt. But the Swiss government contributed no taxpayers' money to the Humanitarian Fund—or to anything else. The money came from the country's central bank, which had been the main vehicle used by the Nazis to convert their looted gold into hard currency. The bank now offered 70 million Swiss francs (about $50 million) to the fund. A group of

Swiss companies also pledged 46 million Swiss francs (about $30 million) as a humanitarian gesture.

This was the high-water mark of the Swiss government's response. The new Swiss president, Arnold Koller, made a special address to the Swiss Parliament on March 5, 1997, proposing an additional "Foundation for Solidarity," with capital of 7 billion Swiss francs ($4.7 billion), to be created by revaluing the Swiss National Bank's gold at its fair market value. From this fund, the government would donate up to 300 million Swiss francs ($210 million) annually to various humanitarian causes—"victims of poverty and catastrophes, of genocide, and other severe breaches of human rights such as, of course, victims of the Holocaust."

But Christoph Blocher could not stomach this latest generosity. He accused the banks of admitting guilt when "Switzerland had no reason to apologize for doing business with Nazi Germany in order to survive as a neutral country." Blocher threatened to force a referendum on the Solidarity Fund and suggested using the revalued gold to increase Swiss old-age pensions. That brought the Solidarity Fund to an immediate halt. To this day, it has not been set up by the Swiss government.

Meanwhile I was busy assembling the report President Clinton had ordered me to undertake in October 1996. My goal was an objective examination of the conduct of Switzerland and the other neutral and non-belligerent nations (Spain, Portugal, Sweden, Turkey, and Argentina) throughout World War II. All told, eleven federal agencies, from the intelligence agencies, the FBI, and the Defense Department to the State, Treasury, and Justice Departments and the National Archives, helped compile records and gather information. It is rare for such a massive study to be undertaken and still rarer to see the degree of cooperation and dedication its participants displayed. The project demonstrated the awesome resources the U.S. executive branch can muster when it receives presidential backing. I was amazed at the powerful story that was emerging by drawing from the data banks of these different federal agencies.

The report owed much of its eventual success to the direction of a remarkably wise, able, and fiercely honest man, William Slany, the historian of the State Department. It was Slany who laid out a work plan: investigate what the Swiss had done to facilitate the exchange of looted gold; examine the postwar negotiations with the Swiss and other neutrals; review the wartime Safehaven project to identify Nazi assets; determine what had been done with Nazi gold and German assets in Switzerland and other neutral countries to help refugees.

One of our early decisions was to declassify all of the documents we unearthed and to make more accessible those documents already declassified under a 1995 executive order from President Clinton. In the end we made public close to 1 million documents, the largest single declassification in U.S. history. And with the sterling help of Greg Bradsher, director of the Holocaust-Era Records Project; Michael Kurtz, assistant archivist; and their colleagues at the National Archives, a master index was prepared for more than 15 million pages of records for use by scholars, journalists, and the general public. One of my jobs was to help Slany free up documents from recalcitrant agencies.

When Slany was stymied by lack of access to OSS documents, I persuaded John Deutch, director of the CIA, and then his successor, George Tenet, to cooperate. In fact the CIA's active and unusual cooperation made a crucial contribution to our report. The most sensitive intelligence documents were intercepts from the supersecret National Security Agency of Swiss cables between 1946 and 1950, which indicated the Swiss negotiating positions in the Allies' difficult postwar talks with them. We declassified them, despite our concern that it would only feed Switzerland's growing paranoia. The Defense Department also created a special unit in the Department of the Army to comb U.S. Army records for information on the looted gold found by our soldiers in the war's closing weeks.

Several principal themes began to emerge from the wealth of documents. The Germans had used vast amounts of looted gold, worth as much as $580 million then (some $5 billion in 1997), to finance their war effort. Between $398 million and $414 million of gold—almost $300 million of it looted—was sold by Germany to the Swiss National Bank and to private Swiss banks. We determined that the Swiss National Bank knew they were dealing in looted gold, both because the sums they were receiving from the Nazis vastly exceeded the known gold reserves in the Reichsbank and because they received specific Allied warnings as early as 1943. The gold was converted by the Swiss into hard currency, which the Germans used to purchase critical war materials from the neutrals—for example, ball bearings from the Swedes. The Swiss were not only Nazi Germany's bankers but also facilitators for other countries that would not trade directly with Germany. So Portugal sold its critical tungsten ore to Germany through the Swiss. In short, the Swiss repeatedly violated their own professed neutrality.

As these facts became clear, the WJRO pressed me to push the Swiss to pay out more funds. At the same time, I came under pressure from the State Department not to do so. Dick Holbrooke, by then the United Nations ambassador, the person who had been my partner from the outset on property restitution, called me on March 12 to warn that the Swiss felt threatened, and bluntly said, "Don't hurt the bilateral relationship."

As our self-imposed end-of-March deadline approached for publication of the report, I was shaken by two events. The first was an anguished telephone call to my home at 11:00 P.M. on February 6 from one of the interagency team working on our report, Eli Rosenbaum, the head of the Justice Department's Office of Special Investigations, assigned to tracking down Nazi fugitives. Rosenbaum, who had been the lead lawyer for Bronfman's World Jewish Congress investigation into the Waldheim affair in Austria during the mid-1980s, told me he felt we had not sufficiently investigated the Nazi gold transferred to Switzerland, and thus whether the Tripartite Gold Commission created by the allies after the war had mistakenly transferred some victim gold to the countries seeking the return of their central bank gold. This was the very heart of what Bronfman had requested from the president months before.

Rosenbaum followed up his call with a startling letter to William Slany, the chief historian for our report, on March 17, only days before our publication date, making clear he would not sign off on our report unless we "dealt candidly with certain questionable aspects of postwar conduct by U.S. officials," in particular why the Truman administration accepted an inadequate postwar gold settlement with the Swiss and suggested to the U.S. Congress that the Swiss had purchased less Nazi gold than the government knew it had. There was deep concern that this letter would leak and undermine our whole report. I was furious. Rosenbaum had been involved in all our deliberations and could have expressed his concern to me privately, as he had done the month before in his late-night phone call. I faced a dilemma. We had announced a March 27 publication date, and a delay would give rise to rumors and further angst in Switzerland. But not delaying would mean we would not have the unanimity from all eleven agencies required to make it clear the entire U.S. government stood behind our findings. I concluded on the spot that it was better to be criticized for an embarrassing delay than to have sniping at the report after its publication. In the end, however questionable his tactics, Rosenbaum did us a great favor. The report was strengthened substantially by our additional work.

With the postponement, we got our second wind. Barrie White, Rosenbaum's historian at the Justice Department, did a great detective job of using Nuremberg trial documents from the Prussian Mint to identify specific gold bars that had been smelted down from victims' personal gold. Her research showed that after smelting the gold, the SS transferred it to the Reichsbank and deposited it in a special "Melmer" account, named for the SS officer who handled the transfers. The bars were given disguised markings to make it appear as if they had come from the Reichsbank's own inventory. After the war, the U.S. Army found Reichsbank gold that could be traced to the Melmer account stockpiled in places like the Merkers Salt Mine. But the Army had made no serious attempt to segregate monetary gold stolen from the central banks of the countries the Germans occupied from the nonmonetary, or victim, gold. White used 1946 Army records to trace by serial numbers a Prussian Mint operation in which looted Dutch guilders had been smelted into disguised gold bars and mixed with 37 kilograms of victim gold from the Melmer account. More than three-fourths of these bars were traded to the Swiss National Bank.

Slany, Stan Turetsky of the U.S. Holocaust Memorial Museum, and others on our team agreed that White had established that the Allied gold pool after the war did include victim gold, raising unanswerable questions about how much of the Tripartite Gold Commission gold pool transferred to the ten countries had actually been victim gold. With this consensus and a more thorough description of the reasons behind the United States' postwar reluctance to press the Swiss for a better settlement, Rosenbaum was satisfied.

In light of the difficult facts we were uncovering, I thought the report needed an executive summary for easier reading and a foreword to put our findings into a broader context and to confront serious questions about the nature of Swiss neutrality. Two underlying issues, both of which were explosive, had jumped out at us over the months of our investigation. One involved the nature of neutrality in the context of a world war against a regime that was evil incarnate. The other involved the cumulative impact the neutrals had on prolonging the war and costing hundreds of thousands of lives. Had the Swiss been willing accomplices of Nazi Germany out of greed? Or were they forced to do business with the Nazis in order to survive the war as an independent democratic state? Had their actions, together with those of other neutrals, prolonged the war?

We chose Bennett Freeman, a gifted writer with a touch of flamboyance and a keen intellect who had worked for Secretary of State Warren Christopher, to write the executive summary and to do a first draft of my interpretative foreword, which I then completed.

We strove to make the report objective, balanced, and not entirely accusatory. I insisted that since we were holding a harsh light on other countries, we bend over backward to ensure that we emphasized the United States' shortcomings, as well. For example, despite the admitted inadequacy of Swiss refugee policy, we pointed out that on a per-capita basis, the Swiss took in far more refugees under more difficult circumstances than did the United States. We also specifically recognized that neutrality was firmly rooted in Swiss history and ingrained in the country's social fabric, having been officially recognized by the family of nations as far back as the 1815 Congress of Vienna, and was not a reaction to Nazi Germany. We indicated that Switzerland felt threatened by the German Army, particularly in the early years of the war. We also reported that Swiss neutrality had advantages to the Allies as well as to Hitler's Germany. In December 1944 Secretary of State Edward Stettinius, Jr., declared Swiss neutrality beneficial since Switzerland was a listening post for the OSS and had accepted American prisoners of war who had escaped from the Germans.

This clash between neutrality and morality was hardly limited to Switzerland. Turkey, anxious to preserve its neutrality, set adrift the ship *Struma* in February 1942, carrying 801 Jewish refugees, which had sought safety in Istanbul's harbor. It was torpedoed and sunk the next day. The United States, during its neutral period, turned the ship *St. Louis* back to Europe in June 1939 carrying 900 Jewish refugees, most of whom were later killed in the Holocaust—a point we noted in the report.

But under Bill Slany's skillful guidance, the more information we stitched together into a coherent tapestry of wartime action by the neutrals—in particular the Swiss—the more our collective blood pressure rose. This clearly colored the foreword I wrote.

The neutral nations repeatedly violated their neutrality on behalf of the Nazis. Sweden protected German shipping and allowed German troops to cross its borders. But it was Switzerland that was central to the economic dimension of Nazi Germany's aggression. The Swiss government allowed German trains to cross Switzerland regularly to supply fascist Italian and German troops. Swiss arms and munitions were shipped to Germany. German businesses were cloaked by the Swiss to prevent their detection by the Allies. Each of the neutrals supplied critical war materials without which the Germans could not have prosecuted the war: ball bearings and iron ore from Sweden, chrome ore from Turkey, wolfram (tungsten ore) from Portugal and Spain. And to pay for all of these the Germans sold gold to Switzerland, which its central bank took in full awareness that it had been looted, and received hard currency in return.

We found that Switzerland was so important to the Nazi war machine that in 1943 Karl Clodius, the Third Reich's minister of economics, remarked that it could "not continue even for two months without carrying out foreign exchange transactions in Switzerland." Nothing in Swiss law or its political neutrality obliged the Swiss National Bank to accept looted gold. It was a choice. And they made it.

As early as January 1943, the Allies issued a formal declaration warning the neutral nations that all of their transfers of property from German occupied territories were invalid. But the Allied appeals to Switzerland to stop or at least limit their help to Nazi Germany were ignored. In February 1944 the Allies issued another declaration, specifying that they would not recognize the wartime transfer of gold from Nazi Germany. The most unequivocal warning against trading with Nazi Germany was issued in April 1944 by U.S. Secretary of State Cordell Hull, who declared: "The Allies could no longer acquiesce in these nations drawing upon the resources of the Allied world when at the same time they contribute to the death of troops. We ask them only, but with insistence, to cease aiding the enemy."

In February 1945, when the German war machine was all but destroyed, Lauchlin Currie of the U.S. Treasury reached an agreement with Walter Stucki, former Swiss ambassador to Vichy, whereby the Swiss government would block all German assets, take a census of German assets in Switzerland, purchase no more gold, and stop the transfer of looted assets. The agreement did not last. One week later, Emil Puhl, the Reichsbank's deputy head, arrived in Switzerland and persuaded the Swiss to accept more gold.

Why did the Swiss accept Nazi gold in the first place? They always maintained that their actions during the war were motivated by a fear of German attack. But in fact there was a chasm between the Swiss people and their business and government leaders. The Swiss citizenry was vigorously anti-Nazi, determined to maintain its independence and its democracy. The Swiss citizen army manned the tunnels and passages in the Alps to block any possible German advance. Although the Swiss may not have appreciated the fact, Hitler had no need to invade Switzerland. Rather, he relied on Switzerland as a business partner, and its elites gave him all he wanted. Major Swiss companies used some 11,000 forced laborers in their plants in Germany and permitted German companies to operate under cloak of Swiss charters.

With Slany's help, I concluded that during the early stages of war, Switzerland could make a strong case that it felt genuinely threatened. But with German defeats on the eastern and western fronts in 1943 and 1944, from Stalingrad to Normandy, and the Allied advance to Switzerland's borders by September 1944, the end of the war—and eventual German defeat—loomed. As the tide of war turned sharply against Germany, with each month the element of greed grew larger and fear grew smaller among the Swiss elite, until sheer greed trumped legitimate fear. Switzerland alone among the neutrals continued its trade with the Germans almost to the bitter end.

But what troubled our research team even more was Swiss conduct after the war. As the neutral nation that had profited the most from commerce with the Nazis, Switzerland paid the Allies the least as a proportion of its profits and took longer to do it than any of the other neutrals. After the war, the Allies wanted the Swiss to give up all the looted gold they had acquired and to liquidate German assets in their country, such as businesses and real estate. The Swiss negotiators, Walter Stucki and Alfred Hirs, a member of the central bank's governing board, at first denied all knowledge of looted gold, then claimed that Switzerland had come by all German gold legally, citing Emil Puhl as their authority. Only when confronted with Puhl's own testimony to Allied interrogators that he had told the Swiss the gold had been looted were they forced to recant their story. But they still insisted they owed the Allies nothing and that international law gave the Allies no right to recover German assets in their country.

The Swiss had profited immensely from their role as Hitler's foreign exchange dealers and fought with great determination to hold onto their financial gains, which helped provide the foundation for Switzerland's great postwar prosperity. The Swiss refused to return any looted gold or other German assets until the Truman administration agreed to unblock $1.5 billion in Swiss assets held in the United States, frozen by the United States during the war, along with the assets of other neutral countries, out of fear they could be diverted into German hands. The negotiations dragged on for months. Finally, the Allied-Swiss Accord, signed in Washington, D.C., on May 25, 1946, and known as the Washington Accord, struck a compromise. The Swiss agreed to return the paltry sum of $58 million in looted gold, regained their assets frozen in the United States, won the right to keep half of the liquidated German assets, and promised to contribute 50 million Swiss francs—about half the total fund—to a reparations fund created by the Allies for the relief and resettlement of refugees.

But even with this victory in their hands, the Swiss continued dragging out repayment of the German assets as long as possible, haggling over such matters as the exchange rate of gold. In 1948 they paid only 20 million of the 50 million Swiss francs pledged for refugee relief. No final agreement with the Allies was reached until August 1952, as the Swiss refused to implement the 1946 Washington Accord until they settled their claims against Germany and other countries for losses of Swiss assets and because of disagreement over currency exchange rates. Thus the Swiss avoided the full impact of the Potsdam Agreement and the decisions of the Paris Reparations Conference, by which the Allies had laid formal claim to the stolen German gold and other German assets from the neutrals. Much of the Swiss share of the looted gold ended up in the vaults of the Swiss National Bank, and a major share of German assets also remained in Switzerland.

Although supposedly searching diligently for the bank accounts of heirless Nazi victims, the Swiss government concluded secret agreements with the Communist governments of Poland in 1949 and Hungary in 1950 to dispose of some of those very same accounts. In exchange for settling the claims of Swiss companies and individuals whose property had been nationalized by the two Communist governments, the agreements permitted money from the accounts of mostly Jewish citizens killed in the Holocaust to be identified, despite vaunted Swiss bank-secrecy laws, and handed over to the two Communist governments. Swiss industrialists received compensation from that same pool of unclaimed Polish and Hungarian Holocaust money for their nationalized businesses. Holocaust victims and their families lost twice. But the Swiss were no more cooperative in paying the Communist states of Eastern Europe than in returning looted Nazi money to the West. They did not finally settle with Poland and Hungary until 1973, paying them only about $200,000 each.

The Swiss got away with all of this because of the Cold War. Reparations had become secondary to the need to rebuild Europe and especially Germany as frontline states in the war against Stalin's aggressive Communist empire in Eastern Europe. In the new struggle, Washington was in no mood to antagonize its friends. When I asked Seymour Rubin, one of the chief U.S. negotiators in the late 1940s, why the United States accepted such a small fraction from Switzerland of what it legitimately owed, Rubin said simply, the Swiss "wore us down."

It was against this background of discovery that my foreword was drafted. At our last meeting on May 1 before the report was sent to the CIA printer to ensure security, Ruth van Heuven, the State Department's office director for German, Austrian, and Swiss affairs, warned vehemently that anything that seemed to attack Swiss neutrality would cause grave problems in Switzerland. But Bill Slany felt the report was the uncomfortable truth.

The conclusions in my foreword, penned by Bennett Freeman and accepted by me, were clearly directed not solely at Switzerland but at all the neutrals we investigated. "In the unique circumstances of World War II," it stated, "neutrality collided with morality; too often being neutral provided a pretext for avoiding moral considerations." All of the neutrals were "slow to recognize and acknowledge that this was not just another war. Most never did. Nazi Germany was a mortal threat to Western civilization itself."

Another especially explosive issue involved the cumulative impact of the neutrals' actions on Germany's capacity to wage war, an issue I took on myself, again making clear that we were pointing a finger not at Switzerland alone but at all the neutrals. Slany was convinced that, if the neutrals' imports had been cut off as late as the end of 1944, when Germany presented little threat to these countries, perhaps a million civilians and tens of thousands of Allied soldiers could have been saved from death. White of the Justice Department also agreed. My foreword therefore concluded: "The neutrals continued to profit from their trading links with Germany and thus contributed to prolonging one of the bloodiest conflicts in history."

I was torn about the conclusions in the foreword. I spent hours agonizing over them with Freeman, Slany, and van Heuven. I knew I was taking the position of a moralist and historian rather than a diplomat. But I found it difficult to ignore the implications of what we were uncovering or to obfuscate judgments. Had this not happened all too often during the war?

I felt my presidential mandate was to set forth the facts and the conclusions, however harsh, in order to force all of the neutrals and the rest of the world to confront the complexities of dealing with an evil regime under the pressures of war. My dilemma mirrored the dual role I was playing. I was responding both to the domestic political demands of the White House to try to help the victims and, at the same time, to the pressures within the State Department to keep the Swiss relationship on an even keel. These conflicting pressures would remain and even intensify throughout the Swiss affair and, indeed, throughout all my Holocaust-related negotiations.

There were consequences of moving into moral and subjective judgments. I was an American diplomat trying to salvage a relationship with a valued U.S. friend. For all its contributions to the historical record, our report would roil the bilateral relationship I had struggled so hard to maintain against pressures from D'Amato, the WJRO, and the plaintiffs' attorneys. Although I was not yet involved in trying to settle the class actions, my foreword would harden Swiss public opinion and complicate the ability of the banks to settle their suits without looking as if they had sold out their country's honor.

A few ill-chosen words in my foreword would set off the final avalanche with Switzerland. In retrospect, the same points could have been made less provocatively. But I believe even more strongly now that the report's conclusions and my own personal observations in the foreword are accurate and will withstand historical scrutiny. The Swiss myth about their conduct during the war that they had sold to themselves and the world—the brave neutral bastion, the haven and rescuer for refugees with the St. Bernard dogs—was only partly true. But accuracy and sound judgment, reality and public perception, are two different things. I led with my diplomatic chin, succeeding at one task—presenting the unadorned historical facts—but failing at the other. Without greatly compromising the truth, for example, I could have reached the same hard conclusions but stated them more diplomatically—for example, saying that the neutrals helped "sustain" the German war effort rather than "prolonging" it. I was also applying to the conduct of the 1940s the sterner morality of the 1990s, which contained the threads of postwar human rights that had been the centerpiece of President Carter's foreign policy during my time in the White House two decades earlier. By choosing the more daring course, I made a judgment that would have more long-term historical value to the Swiss and to others by clarifying the historical record and dispelling the Swiss myth. But that came at the expense of poisoning U.S. relations with Switzerland, coming on top of the Delamaruz, Jagmetti, and Meili incidents. The Swiss considered my foreword diplomatic piling on. In this they were right.

No other neutral nation highlighted in the report or my foreword complained. But it hit the Swiss hard. Formally given the bureaucratic title *U.S. and Allied Efforts to Recover and Restore Gold and Other Assets Stolen or Hidden by Germany During World War II—Preliminary Study*, it was immediately dubbed the "Eizenstat Report" by the Swiss.

Initially, the Swiss reaction was tepid. On the day of the report's publication, May 7, 1997, Foreign Minister Cotti, on behalf of the Federal Council, released a mild statement welcoming the study as an important contribution to knowledge of gold transactions but asking for understanding of "the extremely difficult situation in which our country found itself." The *New York Times* reported on May 9 that the Swiss viewed our report "with a yawn." For a brief moment we thought we had been able to do the impossible. Unfortunately, that yawn soon turned into a yell of outrage.

The Swiss press made it appear that the report's condemnation was aimed only at Switzerland. Public opinion turned quickly as the Swiss increasingly felt victimized. They were outraged by America's attack on their neutrality and by the incorrect assessment that they themselves were being held responsible for causing untold civilian and military deaths. What had been viewed up to this point by many Swiss as an attack by American class-action lawyers and Jewish groups against private Swiss banks turned suddenly into the United States attacking Switzerland's whole sense of itself.

As Ambassador Borer would later tell me, my report turned public opinion. "Until early 1997 most Swiss were sympathetic to Jewish requests; they do not like Swiss banks," he said. But the sentences "taken out of context by CNN and Fox News hurt the Second World War generation in Switzerland." Before, the accusations had been "an issue with the banks," but now the "man in the street was accused," he said. The Swiss felt the U.S. government had attacked them for having, as one attorney for the Swiss put it, "blood on their hands for U.S. soldiers and Holocaust victims." The Swiss government, rather than confronting the essential facts in the report, succumbed to popular outrage. The Federal Council went into a defensive crouch. Things got so nasty that seventy members of Parliament recommended a boycott of U.S. goods.

The Swiss government's increasing bitterness was reflected in two formal comments, first by the Federal Council and then by Foreign Minister Cotti. On May 22 the council issued a declaration attacking my foreword, which "contains political and moral values which go beyond the historic report." The government defended its postwar negotiations, and Swiss wartime profits, and asserted that the council "regards the representation of Switzerland as the banker of the Nazis as a one-sided package judgment." They argued that Swiss neutrality had not only protected their own citizens but permitted Switzerland to act as a haven for "tens of thousands of refugees and as an oasis of democracy and freedom in a totalitarian Europe," a point we had carefully made in our report. On only one point would the Swiss yield: that their fainthearted refugee policy concerning Jews was inexcusable.

On June 20, Cotti addressed a seminar for Swiss parliamentarians with even stronger invective. He reckoned that Switzerland's share of the German war effort came to "just 0.5 percent" and rejected the charge that Switzerland's conduct prolonged the war. For his own domestic political audience, Cotti was clearly ignoring that we had held responsible all the neutrals and not just Switzerland. He asserted that the United States did "not understand what 'neutrality' means." He pointed to the 22 million Swiss francs donated to postwar relief by the Swiss people between 1944 and 1948 and said, "This is not mentioned anywhere in the Eizenstat Report."

My foreword, however unfairly or selectively used by the Swiss press, had worsened an already difficult situation and triggered a diplomatic crisis with Switzerland—not just between private Swiss banks and class-action lawyers, the World Jewish Congress, or Senator D'Amato but between the governments of Switzerland and the United States. There was a special irony to this. I am an innate conciliator. Confrontation is not in my nature. I had been serving as the voice of moderation, a vigorous opponent of sanctions that were being threatened against Swiss businesses and banks, an outspoken supporter of the recent efforts Switzerland was making to face its past through the Volcker audits and the Bergier historical commission. Now the tables had turned. Suddenly I was cast as the villain responsible for the "Eizenstat Report." I had moved in Swiss eyes from peacemaker to pariah, creating a serious and lasting breach in U.S.-Swiss relations. For me, this was a personal low point.

I received some solace from positive American press reports, and from President Clinton, who told Edgar Bronfman that "the Eizenstat Report was a landmark on morality." But former Congressman Robin Beard, just back from Switzerland, informed me that I had the dubious distinction of replacing Al D'Amato as the focal point of Swiss anger. I attempted to limit the damage by giving Swiss television an interview in late August, which was well received. In part to try to mollify the Swiss, we launched a second, year-long investigation, whose report was published in June 1998, which focused more clearly on the conduct of the other neutrals. But nothing helped.

At least the international reaction to our report stood in stark contrast to that of the Swiss. The report spurred an international collaborative effort to complete the unfinished business of World War II. In response to Bronfman's request, the United States had already blocked the last disbursement of looted gold pending my review. Now, armed with the finding that some portion of the gold pool had come from victims and led by Randolph Bell, a dedicated member of my team from the State Department, we decided to convince the ten countries with claims on the last six metric tons of gold still in the postwar gold pool to release it for the benefit of victims. But to get to first base with this idea, we first had to persuade the United States' cotrustees in the Tripartite Gold Commission, France and Britain, and then the ten claimant countries to forgo their legal claim to the balance of the gold.

The British reacted quickly, thanks in large part to the efforts of Lord Greville Janner. Lord Janner had served with the British Occupation Forces in Germany after the war in their War Crimes Investigation Unit near the Bergen-Belsen concentration camp and had worked for twenty years as a member of Parliament to pass a law permitting the prosecution of war criminals in Britain. He was one of the early discoverers of the connection between Nazi gold and Switzerland, having obtained U.S. archival material from the WJC in the fall of 1996 indicating that British Intelligence knew about the use of looted Nazi gold transferred to Switzerland to pay for critical raw materials.

We also opened a contact with Claude Martin, a senior official in the French Foreign Ministry, who also was receptive. With the French and British, we agreed on separate but coordinated démarches to the ten countries, noting the findings in the 1997 U.S. government report and raising the possibility of distributing the remaining treasure, with the countries' consent, to Holocaust victims. Along with Bill McDonough, president of the Federal Reserve Bank of New York, where some of the gold bars were located, Alan Greenspan, chairman of the Federal Reserve Board, applied his great prestige by seeking maximum information from the central banks of the other gold pool members about the identity of the gold they accepted during the war. Deputy Treasury Secretary Lawrence Summers wrote his counterparts abroad seeking support in declassifying records.

At the same time, with pressure from Lord Janner and with my office's full support, British foreign secretary Robin Cook invited more than forty countries, including the ten gold pool countries, to a December conference in London. This was Janner's idea, but one that meshed completely with the interests of the U.S. government's and the WJC. It was important for the meeting to be convened by a government other than the United States, so it would not appear that the entire restitution effort was simply an American idea driven by the American Jewish community.

As a prelude to the London Conference on Nazi Gold, I called a meeting in September at the TGC's drab offices in the British Embassy in Brussels, only a few blocks from my former offices at the U.S. Mission to the European Union. The purpose was to prod each country to donate its pro-rata share of the remaining six tons of gold.

The meeting itself exceeded my fondest hopes. I was able to announce a major $25 million U.S. contribution. This contribution would serve as a moral gesture for the pittance of $500,000 the U.S. government had paid to Holocaust victims from German assets frozen in the United States, and then not until almost twenty years after the war. The French, normally prickly about their sovereignty, agreed that aid should be multilateral and announced their own contribution. Then Ambassador Hans Winkler of Austria, whom I knew to be committed to rectifying his country's many wrongs during World War II, pledged all of Austria's remaining share and declared: "We all have a moral obligation to the survivors of the Holocaust, and to make their remaining days better." Winkler also led support for our team's concept of the hybrid charitable structure that was eventually adopted: an international fund composed of national accounts from which money would be disbursed by each nation according to agreed-on general guidelines.

One country after another made its own moving act of sacrifice. The Belgians, whose gold reserves vanished during the war while stored at the Bank of France but were repaid anyway, announced they would consider contributing as a moral gesture. The Czechs, who had just established a national fund for their own Holocaust survivors, nevertheless announced their support for this multilateral fund. The Greeks spoke of "a positive step not only to show human kindness but to help turn the page of a disturbing chapter of history." The Dutch and Polish supported the fund, as well. The Italians alone demanded that the gold commission remain open—to collect more gold from the recalcitrant wartime neutrals. Only Slovakia expressed undiminished and unrequited pain. Supporting the fund, the Slovaks nevertheless launched a passionate attack on Germany for refusing not only to compensate 13,000 non-Jewish victims of the Nazis but even to discuss the request—and this from the country that sold its Jews to the Reich!

Armed with this support, our U.S. team then turned toward the London conference. Forty-one governments met in London on December 2–4, 1997, for the first international conference since the Paris peace talks of 1946, to focus on the unfinished business of World War II. Indeed, it was the first conference ever in which the Allied victors, the Axis vanquished, the neutrals, and the countries occupied by the Germans had joined in one place to review their wartime roles. It gave international visibility to Nazi gold, which in turn put pressure on the Swiss. Our principal goal, beyond committing the last of the gold pool to charitable purposes, was to have each country open its wartime archives—including those of the Reichsbank, the former Soviet Union, and the Vatican.

I had a feeling of exhilaration when the conference opened. Not only governments but six organizations representing the survivors and the institutions that actually handled Nazi gold gathered to review the process through which the Nazis looted gold and the ways in which their own actions and inaction had made the tragedy possible. This represented the first collective acceptance by the world community of the need to rectify the effects of the Holocaust, and a very belated counterpoint to the Evian Conference in 1938, when the world turned its back on victims.

Robin Cook opened the conference with a statement of firm commitment: "We are here to clarify one of the darkest episodes in human history. We are here to look for compensation for a suffering that can never be expiated. We are here to ensure we do not forget the most awful memory known to man." He then announced the formal creation of the Nazi Persecutee Relief Fund, which I had negotiated in Brussels. Nine of the ten claimant countries—Austria, Belgium, the Czech Republic, Greece, Italy, Luxembourg, the Netherlands, Poland, and Slovakia, excluding only Albania—had donated all or a substantial portion of their share of the remaining gold. Spain, Argentina, France, and Britain announced contributions as well, along with ours.

I told the conference: "We are taking an important step toward completing a significant portion of the unfinished business of the Second World War. We are doing so in a way which extends both a moral gesture and a material contribution to justice, however little and late, for Holocaust survivors." I have rarely been more proud of my country than when I formally announced our contribution of $25 million over three years, approved without dissent by Republicans and Democrats in Congress, with the special leadership of Senator D'Amato and Representative James Leach, chair of the House Banking Committee. The American money was to pay for food and social programs for elderly Holocaust survivors in Eastern Europe.

Then the national participants recounted confiscation of their wealth by the Nazis. The German delegation confirmed the looted gold flows to Switzerland and estimated that $14.5 million in gold was taken from concentration camp victims.

For the first time the Swiss had to defend their wartime conduct before an international audience. They admitted that as early as 1941 the Swiss National Bank was aware it was taking looted gold, but insisted that the action was justified because they were encircled by the Nazis and that their conduct was morally correct.

I had an immense sense of satisfaction. The London conference was a rare moment of real success. The forty-plus countries united around a common goal—to get the long suppressed facts of the looting of assets in World War II out in the open. As countries recounted for the first time their role in handling Nazi-looted assets and what happened to their Jewish citizens, it helped further marginalize revisionist historians who were denying the Holocaust had taken place. The London conference prompted nations to open their archives and establish historical commissions—now twenty-eight in all. It formalized the new international Persecutee Relief Fund for survivors, helping people before it was too late. And it also served one other broad purpose: It reinstated on the international agenda the issue of justice for Holocaust survivors and other Nazi victims, who had been virtually ignored by diplomacy for half a century.

# CHAPTER SIX

# Kabuki Dance

HE GLOW FROM the success of the December 1997 London conference may have taken some of the sting out of my Nazi gold
report and pushed the Meili affair and the Delamaruz and Jagmetti
tempests off center stage, but the class-action lawsuits now took the spotlight and never relinquished it. They undercut the Volcker audit and gradually drew me into their powerful vortex—an unprecedented involvement
by a senior government official in purely private lawsuits.

After they filed their suits in the fall of 1996, the lawyers from both sides
engaged in a long mating process, trying to decide whether to submit their
dispute to mediation and, if so, whether I would be an attractive mediator.
I had just moved from the Commerce Department to the State Department to become undersecretary of state for economic, business, and agricultural affairs, working for my longtime friend Secretary of State
Madeleine Albright. This new position gave me direct access to the diplomatic lines of power in the State Department and greater contact with the
White House. I took the Holocaust portfolio with me. Having since then
been preoccupied with my duties at State and with producing the Nazi gold
report, I had not focused on the details of the lawsuits. I had hoped the Volcker audits of dormant bank accounts would deal with the main issues covered by the lawsuits. And Bronfman and the World Jewish Congress were
not parties and did not press President Clinton to get me involved in the
suits, as they had in other aspects of the Swiss bank affair. Neither Secretary Albright nor the White House had any interest in the suits at this
stage. The Swiss government was not being sued and sat on the sidelines,

eager to improve its tarnished reputation but also fearful of a nationalist backlash if it yielded to foreign pressure.

My first direct exposure to the lawsuits came during a visit on December 2, 1996, by Michael Hausfeld and Marty Mendelsohn, two leaders of the Hausfeld-Weiss group of lawyers. When they explained their case to me, it was immediately apparent that it went well beyond the Volcker audits. Volcker was exploring actual bank accounts and trying to match victims, whether living or dead, to the accounts. The lawsuits went into areas Volcker had refused to go: allegations that Nazi officials had deposited looted Jewish assets in Swiss banks and that German companies employing slave laborers had deposited some of their profits in the same banks. These additional allegations seemed to me a legal stretch. I did not see how it would be possible for the lawyers to link individual plaintiffs with looted assets and slave labor profits. I did not express my doubts about their cases, but listened. The two did not ask for my direct involvement, but they were clearly testing the waters.

Hausfeld and Mendelsohn initially had modest goals. They told me they had indicated to Ambassador Borer that they would drop their suits if the banks' books were opened to them, an offer that was refused. They then asked for complete authority to review Volcker's audits and for a seat on the Bergier Commission reviewing Switzerland's wartime history. In return they promised not to seek crushing punitive damages. Bergier refused the proposal, telling me it was impossible to have nonhistorians, particularly lawyers suing Swiss companies, on his historical commission.

On the same day I met with Hausfeld and Mendelsohn, I had my first of what would be numerous meetings and conversations with Paul Volcker. This was my first significant contact with him since our mutual public service in the Carter administration.

It was immediately evident, and became clearer over the ensuing months, that Volcker despised the class-action lawyers, seeing them as greedy egomaniacs more interested in burnishing their shingles than serving their long-suffering clients. He considered the lawsuits frivolous and inflammatory in attempting to reach beyond actual dormant accounts to looting and slave labor profits. And he told me the suits were not necessary to locate dormant accounts; that was the purpose of his audit. He had staked his worldwide reputation for probity and competence on getting to the bottom of the mystery of the missing Holocaust accounts, and nothing was going to stand in his way, certainly not these class-action lawyers. He had no intention of involving them in his audit and giving them free discovery for their lawsuits, even though I tried for months to find an acceptable formula.

The opinions each side had for the other were mutually poisonous. Volcker's suspicions of the lawyers' motives were matched by their belief that his objectivity was compromised because he was on the board of directors of Nestlé, the huge Swiss multinational. I thought the lawyers' concerns were absurd, given Volcker's absolute rectitude and imperviousness to pressure or influence. But at bottom the lawyers' real fear was that Volcker's audit was a device established by the Swiss banks to bury their lawsuits. This ignored the fact that the audits had been forced upon the banks by Bronfman and Singer. Still, it remained their unshakable conviction.

On December 5, only three days after my meetings with the class-action lawyers and Volcker, I met for the first time with the Swiss banks' American lawyers, Roger Witten and Marc Cohen, partners in the firm of my former White House colleague Lloyd Cutler. Cohen and Witten attacked the lawsuits as lacking any legal merit, arguing that Volcker's audit was justice enough. Witten, a superb trial lawyer, added in a moment of candor that the "Swiss have awakened after a long and not too glorious sleep and decided to resolve the dormant accounts in a fair and speedy manner. They are headed in the right direction—to relieve themselves of the assets of Holocaust victims."

But for the first time, Witten suggested the U.S. government might use its influence to involve the WJC in the settlement, as well as the class-action lawyers. His worst fear was to settle with the lawyers, only to have the settlement attacked by Singer as inadequate. At this stage I was purely in a listening mode, acting as a sounding board, passing along ideas presented to me from one side to the other.

Before directly involving me, the plaintiffs' attorneys had to satisfy themselves that they could not settle the case without outside help. Mel Weiss, the most celebrated of the class-action lawyers and one of those who had agreed to serve without a fee, told a caucus of the plaintiffs' lawyers that he had reason to believe from Swiss newspaper accounts—which were incorrect, as it turned out—that the banks would be willing to settle for $5 billion. But Weiss reckoned this meant the bidding on the plaintiffs' side had to start at $9 billion and work down. Mel Urbach, who left Fagan's team to represent the World Council of Orthodox Jewish Communities, raised the ante to an opening bid of $10 billion. Robert Swift, one of the most experienced and legally inventive of the lawyers, regarded Urbach with scorn: "You have never tried a case in your life or even taken a deposition. How can you demand such a figure?" Perhaps it was precisely because this corporate lawyer had so little courtroom experience that Urbach wanted to outbid the others, to show his toughness. Swift and Fagan wanted much lower numbers.

The executive committee, which Judge Korman had cobbled together under Neuborne's chairmanship to present a united front among the warring lawyers and to encourage a settlement, met in December 1996 in the conference room of Cutler's Washington, D.C., office for their first discussion about how much money the Swiss banks might pay to settle. The class-action lawyers had been unable to agree in advance on a common position, partly because they had no documentary evidence to support any figure. In front of the bank lawyers, Swift implied he could accept a settlement in the hundreds of millions (in a letter to Witten, without Weiss's knowledge, he later suggested a $500 million settlement). Weiss shot back in his typically gruff manner: "This case will never be settled unless the amount starts with a *B*." He suggested $9 billion. Witten, a tough, often irritating, but effective negotiator, essentially stopped the meeting by declaring, "Forget about it." Among the lawyers this became known as the $9 billion meeting. There would be no other negotiations until I was brought in.

My first contact with Mel Weiss came on June 9, 1997. He was up-front with his strategy, without nuances. He wanted to exert external political and economic pressure in the form of threatened sanctions against the Swiss banks, and he wanted a united bargaining group with the WJC. That was the trouble. He believed the Swiss were co-opting Singer and Bronfman through the Volcker process, on which the WJC was working with the Swiss bankers. Weiss alone among the lawyers understood the need for the WJC's cooperation.

What Weiss did not understand was a fundamental fact: Singer and Elan Steinberg harbored a suspicion of the lawyers bordering on outright antagonism. They believed that litigation would be lengthy and uncertain and that, although the Hausfeld-Weiss group was working pro bono, other lawyers would insist upon a substantial contingency fee straight out of the pockets of Holocaust survivors. But there was another factor: The WJC saw the lawyers as stealing what had been their show. And so Singer and Steinberg rejected Weiss's initial entreaties with disdain.

Throughout the Swiss negotiations, the WJC's priority was control of the "heirless" assets, the unclaimed bank accounts that neither the lawsuits nor the Volcker inquiry would be likely to pry loose from the Swiss banks. Singer and Steinberg had recognized from the start that only a small number of families would be able to identify bank accounts dating back half a century. Most of the money in Swiss banks would never be matched with living claimants, since so many of the depositors and their entire families had been consumed in Hitler's ovens. They wanted to ensure that these heirless assets would be taken from the banks, bypass the lawyers, and go to the WJC to help aging Holocaust survivors, most of whom had no connection whatever to the Swiss banks. So the WJC operated like a third party, refusing to cooperate with the class-action lawyers despite their shared interests.

The mating process of getting me directly involved in the lawsuits proceeded like a Japanese Kabuki dance. Neither the class-action lawyers nor the Swiss bank lawyers wanted to definitively ask me to mediate without being certain the other side would agree. I was not volunteering for the thankless task, certainly not without the consent of both sides. My involvement would not be a personal one; it would be on behalf of the United States. The government had to be extremely careful to involve itself only in private lawsuits that affect a clear U.S. interest. That interest in these cases was beginning to form in my mind: both helping U.S. citizens recover their lost assets and resolving lawsuits that threatened to further roil already troubled waters between the United States and Switzerland, two traditional friends. With Weiss's threats of sanctions ringing in my ears, my involvement seemed all the more necessary.

On June 25 Cutler's legal team gathered at my State Department office to set possible terms for my involvement. They informed me of the imminent release of the first list of dormant accounts, dating so far only to the latter days of World War II, to be followed by the establishment of a new claims process under the Volcker Committee. But for the first time, they said the Swiss wanted to negotiate a "global solution" to the cases and were willing to pay another $25 million to $100 million to settle the suits, in addition to what the Volcker Committee would determine they owed for dormant accounts. I believe they had gotten wind of the tough tactics Weiss and the WJC were proposing to employ and were looking for a quick way out of the suits. They wanted the U.S. government to engage in a "major push for settlement," as Witten put it, so the Swiss banks could put the matter behind them once and for all. They said the banks and the Swiss government were ready to accept me as a mediator to settle this out of court.

I later learned that the lawyers for the Swiss had been trying for months to persuade their clients and the Swiss government to appoint me. But the Swiss needed some distance from my Nazi gold report before they could accept me as a neutral party. As Marc Cohen confided to me, "After the Eizenstat Report, it took a lot of capital to convince the Swiss you were the best person to serve as mediator."

A delegation of the class-action lawyers came to see me shortly afterward. Once again, they argued vigorously that Volcker's examination would be insufficient to expose all the Swiss' ill-gotten gains. They also urged the U.S. government to develop a policy that could resolve the cases. Like the Swiss, the class-action lawyers were willing to consider a global settlement, but as Weiss said, "We're talking about billions and they are talking about millions."

I held interagency meetings in late June and early July, which included the White House National Security Council staff, to decide if the U.S. government should become actively involved in trying to settle the cases. We examined every option, including doing what the Swiss government was doing—sitting on our hands and doing nothing. The Justice Department, the agency charged with representing the United States in court, was reluctant for me to get the U.S. government involved in private litigation. They urged me to wait for Judge Korman to rule on the Swiss motions to dismiss the cases. But I feared we could not wait that long. Ultimately we came to the conclusion that there was too much riding on the lawsuits—justice for thousands of U.S. citizens and the United States' relations with Switzerland. Moreover, both sides were now actively seeking our intervention. Swift had long urged the plaintiffs' executive committee to bring in an outsider to stimulate negotiations. As Fagan recalled, "You were the natural person; everyone liked you in those days."

But both the Clinton administration and the class-action lawyers struggled with the role I should play. Should I be simply a convener or an active mediator? Most of our government team thought I should moderate, not mediate. I decided, however, that I could not simply convene meetings. I needed to be actively involved in shaping an agreement. If the matter was important enough to merit my involvement, I could not do it halfway. But it was a tricky decision. After all, we were groping for a model to fit a situation without precedent in American legal or diplomatic history—intervention by a senior U.S. official to help settle lawsuits between private parties.

As my State Department team moved inexorably toward getting involved, two events occurred to shape the nature of my engagement. One was a dispute between Volcker and Israel Singer over the class-action suits. Volcker sought his committee's support for a letter he wanted to send Judge Korman complaining that the lawsuits were "impairing our work, potentially to the point of ineffectiveness" by antagonizing the Swiss and hinting he might resign if the judge allowed the cases to proceed. Singer was against sending the letter. He feared it would add the committee's prestige to the Swiss banks' motions to dismiss the suits. Volcker sent the letter anyway, angering Singer.

The second event was the hearing before Judge Korman on July 31, 1997, on the Swiss banks' motions to dismiss. Burt Neuborne ruefully joked that the motions and the accompanying documents, designed to undercut the plaintiffs' allegations, filled so many boxes that they would kill him if they fell on him. At the close of the hearing, Korman forced each side to consider an out-of-court settlement. He indicated that he had grave doubts about the class-action lawyers' allegations on looted assets and slave labor profits. But he also told the Swiss bank attorneys that he was unlikely to dismiss the entire case, particularly the issue of identifiable dormant deposits. He lectured the Swiss that they were constructive trustees for those accounts and bore a high degree of responsibility to reach out to their depositors in distress. He made it clear to the Swiss that at least this part of the case might eventually go to trial.

Neither side had it good. The plaintiffs' lawyers realized that large parts of their case were at risk. The judge made it clear how difficult it would be for them to prove that the banks accepted funds knowing they had been looted or were the profits of forced labor. Meanwhile, the Swiss had to worry that the trial might move forward. That could be disastrous. Disclosures about their past conduct, including shocking stories by sympathetic Holocaust survivors describing their difficulties in regaining their families' money, could harm the banks' reputation in the United States. They worried about their status on Wall Street and about the possibility of sanctions by local political leaders and questions from the New York State regulators who oversee foreign banks.

For over a year Korman refused to rule one way or the other on the Swiss motion to dismiss the cases, leaving both parties in a state of suspended animation. When the lawyers realized what the judge was doing to them by essentially freezing their cases in place, they wryly described it as "Kormanizing." Judge Korman later explained the reasoning behind his deliberate inaction. He wanted to give Volcker time to finish his audit. He also had his eye on the settlement negotiations that were just getting started under my auspices, about which he read in the *New York Times* and the Jewish press, and he wanted to let my efforts ripen.

By cannily keeping both sides in suspense, Korman showed wisdom and sophistication. In this way he maintained leverage over a dispute that could easily have spun out of control. "He played it beautifully," Burt Neuborne confided to me after it was over.

After the Korman hearing, Volcker called and accused me of strengthening the plaintiffs' hand by not taking a position against them on behalf of the U.S. government. I explained to Volcker that I had a different position from his. Both sides were considering me as a catalyst for settlement, and I could not afford to antagonize either side. Volcker also warned that Singer was losing control to the lawyers and wanted the class actions to stop. In fact, Singer's position was more equivocal; he also distrusted the lawyers but favored anything that would get more money out of the Swiss banks.

But Volcker also suggested a compromise that later helped me develop the framework for a settlement. His committee would maintain control over the individual dormant accounts of Holocaust victims, while the lawyers could negotiate for the more uncertain sums constituting their allegations of looted assets and profits of companies employing slave labor. These two categories would later become the heart of our negotiations.

Following Judge Korman's hearing, the class-action lawyers knew their legal cases were hanging by a thread that the judge could cut at any moment by issuing a ruling. So they introduced a new and sinister element that would occupy a great deal of my time and pit me directly against them and the WJC: sanctions against the Swiss banks.

One of the first lessons I learned at Harvard Law School was from Professor Milton Katz. He joked that, when the facts in a case are against you, argue the law; when the law is against you, argue the facts; when both are against you, bang on the table and yell like hell! That is what Mel Weiss now decided to do. To bolster the quicksand on which the bulk of his legal allegations rested, he began organizing outside pressure against the Swiss through sanctions against their banks. His choice for chief enforcer was Alan Hevesi, the comptroller, or chief financial officer, of New York City, who controlled billions of dollars of pension fund investments and business deals with the city and who had visions of being mayor one day.

These types of tactics are all too familiar in class-action cases. Lawyers for plaintiffs in major personal injury cases in states like Mississippi often work black churches in the area from which the jury pool will be chosen. Lawyers for defendants hire public relations firms to put the best spin on their position for the media. Still, the type of direct pressure Weiss envisioned was a step beyond the normal. We now had a genuine three-ring circus—or for the Swiss a three-front battle: the Volcker audits, the lawsuits, and the threat of state and local sanctions.

Hevesi was an obscure politician who wielded an enormous amount of power. The grandson of the chief rabbi of Budapest, and the nephew of a refugee who survived the Holocaust by hiding in the sewers of that city, his family was close to Raoul Wallenberg, the savior of tens of thousands of Hungarian Jews. Hevesi thus had an emotional attachment, as well as a political interest, in helping Holocaust victims.

Hevesi aggressively managed New York City's mammoth pension funds in ways he boasted gave him "leverage." But even before Hevesi became comptroller, the New York City pension system had been wielded as a political tool. It was used to discourage publicly held American companies from following apartheid laws in South Africa and from discriminating against Catholics in Northern Ireland. It was employed to pressure Exxon to clean up the *Valdez* oil spill in Alaska and Texaco to curb racial discrimination. The threat to divest the funds of a company's stock had always been implicit. The Swiss banks were the first to receive direct threats.

Hevesi had been enlisted early on and in person by Weiss, himself a leading figure in New York Democratic politics, as well as by the WJC's Singer and Steinberg. Edgar Bronfman insisted to me that it was "never a question of a boycott, but just not doing business with the Swiss," an unclear distinction that was cold comfort to the Swiss banks. Because of Hevesi's family background, political constituency, and political ambitions, he readily agreed. The city pension system owned 360,000 shares in the three major Swiss banks—Union Bank of Switzerland (UBS), Credit Suisse, and Swiss Bank Corporation (SBC).

More important, the three banks did business with the city, and Hevesi wrote their chairmen on May 6, 1996, pointedly reminding each of them that, for example, Credit Suisse dealt profitably in the city's bonds and New York's Bureau of Asset Management conducted short-term trades with the bank's American subsidiaries. He noted increasing evidence that Swiss banks held millions in unclaimed assets of Holocaust victims and "have been less than forthcoming in returning these monies to the survivors and rightful heirs." He asked the chairmen to take specific steps in collaboration with the Jewish community to return the money. In a later letter, Hevesi noted tellingly that, as long-term investors, the city's pension funds had found that "a company's public image is one of its most valuable assets. Similarly, we have found that contingent liabilities—such as potential boycotts or even the expense of lobbying against such boycotts—are often undervalued. As investors in many Swiss companies, we do not want to see their values diminished." This was hardly a subtle message.

In May 1997 Hevesi went to Switzerland for meetings with senior government officials and bankers. Afterward he held a press briefing, proposing that American pension fund managers work together to ensure that Switzerland returned Nazi loot to Holocaust survivors. In July he invited nine hundred public finance officers across the United States—state and local treasurers, comptrollers, and public pension fund managers—to join him in monitoring Swiss efforts to return unclaimed assets. Hevesi was beginning to capture the attention of the Swiss. He continued to apply the pressure, urging Swiss companies whose shares were held by the New York City pension funds to contribute to the Swiss Humanitarian Fund for the Victims of the Holocaust, established following the Meili affair. His office began publishing a regular newsletter on the rapid advance of events.

I held my first formal meeting with Hevesi on September 4 and expressed my concern that threats of financial retribution would only inflame already overheated passions. Hevesi was not to be put off. He invited public finance officials from around the country to a December 8 conference on looted and stolen assets. It would become a watershed event, meticulously planned, right down to the kosher lunch at the Plaza Hotel for the more than one hundred officials who accepted his invitation. Edgar Bronfman flew in from his Sun Valley skiing vacation especially for the meeting.

An Executive Monitoring Committee was created, headed by Hevesi and consisting of senior financial officials from California, Maine, Pennsylvania, and New York State. At my urging, to give our negotiations a chance to succeed, they agreed not to act until March 31, 1998, in effect giving the Swiss a ninety-day moratorium on sanctions.

The Jewish organizations were by no means united on the threat of sanctions. They were opposed by Abe Foxman, himself a hidden child in Poland during the war and the longtime, widely admired head of the Anti-Defamation League, and by Rabbi Morris Sherer, the esteemed leader of the Orthodox Agudath Israel and no neophyte to New York or international politics. Rabbi Sherer told me sanctions would be counterproductive and urged me to put "Edgar [Bronfman] on a steady keel, or he will play rough." American politicians, he added, "want to play political games and cater to Jews."

The banks themselves had given Hevesi, the WJC, and the class-action lawyers a potential hostage of their own. UBS and SBC, two of the three banks sued in the class actions, had announced plans in December 1997 to merge to form Europe's largest bank. This presented their attackers with a fat and irresistible target and a powerful lever, because the New York State banking authorities as well as the Federal Reserve Board in Washington had to approve the merger of their U.S. operations.

At Senator D'Amato's request, Elizabeth McCaul, the acting superintendent of the New York State Banking Commission, had already begun investigating the wartime accounts of the New York City branches of SBC, UBS, and Credit Suisse. SBC had shown such a shocking lack of cooperation—"boxes of documents kept disappearing," she told me—that she backed up her demand with a court order obtaining the bank's cooperation. This investigation cost the banks tens of millions of dollars. In a formal request, D'Amato also urged Federal Reserve chairman Alan Greenspan to oppose the merger until the banks came clean about the dormant Holocaust accounts and "their record of collaboration with the Nazis during World War II." The banks' most important business strategy now depended on settlement with the Holocaust survivors. They had little choice but to negotiate, and soon.

Negotiations were risky for everyone. For the U.S. government it meant sailing into uncharted waters as a mediator with conflicting objectives—helping Holocaust victims and soothing U.S.-Swiss relations. For the class-action lawyers it meant accepting less than their most grandiose hopes for a big victory in court. But for the three Swiss banks, the stakes were even higher. They opened themselves up to fierce criticism at home by negotiating with what the Swiss public saw as greedy lawyers, under my auspices as the author of a report critical of their wartime and postwar conduct.

But the alternatives to negotiation were even worse for everyone. Prolongation of the litigation held risks for both parties because of the uncertainty of Judge Korman's ruling on the motions to dismiss. The banks also worried that a cloud of sanctions would follow them, impeding their access to the U.S. market and approval of the UBS-SBC merger. And I believed that the longer it took to resolve the cases, the greater the threat to U.S. relations with the Swiss, and the more Holocaust victims or their heirs would die without any justice from the Swiss banks that had dealt so cavalierly with them. Negotiations seemed the safer choice. Everyone was ready to jump off a cliff together, without knowing whether we were heading for a soft or a hard landing.

To start to bring order out of the chaos, I set several goals. I needed to unite the victims' side by bringing Singer and Bronfman into an alliance with the fractious class-action lawyers in order to give the Swiss one cohesive group with which to strike a deal. I also wanted to get the Swiss government engaged in the negotiations in order to collect money from them for the settlement pot I would need to create and to assure that they would not undercut any deal we reached with the banks. And I wanted to try to integrate the Volcker audit process into our negotiations.

The least productive effort was trying to get the Swiss government off the sidelines and into our negotiations. I fielded one of our heaviest guns: I persuaded Madeleine Albright to become the first U.S. secretary of state to visit Switzerland since 1961. She and I went to Bern on November 15. Her message was conciliatory, expressing appreciation for Switzerland's reexamination of its past. At a private meeting with her Swiss counterpart, Flavio Cotti, she declared her opposition to state and municipal sanctions. I then reiterated her message in public. She informed Cotti that I would lead a U.S. team to help resolve the class-action lawsuits. Although the cases had been brought against private banks, I told the Swiss officials that the suits directly affected the reputation of their country as a whole. But the Swiss politicians were simply unwilling to risk their political capital on the most challenging issue to face the country since World War II. Although the Swiss government was delighted to have the U.S. government involved, it refused to serve as a negotiating partner.

I had no more success in persuading Volcker to accept some kind of observer status on his committee for the plaintiffs' lawyers, even though the Swiss banks, the class-action lawyers, and I were all of one voice in recommending it. The most he would do was provide periodic reports on the progress of the audits to the attorneys. Paul Volcker is the kind of person you only push so far.

Jealous of Singer's direct pipeline to the Swiss bank CEOs, the class-action lawyers insisted as a condition of commencing formal negotiations under my direction that I produce the CEOs for a meeting with them. This was no small order. Normally, CEOs will not meet with lawyers suing their companies; they leave that to their corporate general counsels. I told the class-action lawyers that I would try, but I laid down one cardinal rule: no discussion of dollars for settlement. This meeting was to be solely an initial introduction to each other and a preliminary sharing of perspectives—not a formal negotiation. To put money first would put the cart before the horse and prevent any eventual agreement. Everyone agreed.

To my pleasant surprise, the Swiss CEOs readily consented to meet with the class-action lawyers, on a Sunday no less, which was the only day I could fit into my demanding travel schedule as undersecretary of state. I arranged for a half-day stopover in Zurich, landing early on the tranquil morning of December 14, 1997, with a light snow on the ground accentuating the city's beauty. I went straight to the Savoy Hotel for breakfast with Paul Volcker, who was there for a meeting of his audit committee. Although Volcker would not be a part of our talks, they could succeed only with his blessing, because the results of his committee's work would have to be part of any final settlement. Conscious of his deep suspicion of the class-action lawyers, I wanted to assure him that no settlement would compromise the integrity of his audits. Volcker told me he supported our efforts so long as they did not supplant his own.

I then went to the opening of the talks in a conference room in the same hotel. By agreement of all parties the meeting was supposed to be secret, and no one in the press was even to be told of its existence, let alone its time and location. But Ed Fagan, who was not a participant, had come to Zurich and was scooping up publicity by holding press briefings; he almost certainly was the source of a leak to Saturday's *Neue Zürcher Zeitung*, which announced the meeting in advance. When I emerged from Volcker's breakfast into the lobby of the Savoy, I was besieged by cameras and reporters shouting questions. The Swiss delegation received similar treatment. None of us said anything, but we were all steaming mad that our meeting was now public news.

The Swiss all wore suits and ties, dress-down weekends not yet having reached the Zurich banking establishment. The three CEOs, Mathis Cabiallavetta of UBS, Marcel Ospel of SBC, and Lukas Mühlemann of Credit Suisse, were an imposing group. Bennett Freeman, who had become my senior adviser, a free spirit and a daring dresser, joked to Cabiallavetta that he liked his tie, which had dinosaurs on it. The Swiss were not amused.

Cabiallavetta had taken the helm at UBS only on March 1 and had cautiously welcomed the proposal for a Humanitarian Fund by Rainer Gut of Credit Suisse. Only a month before this meeting, he had also issued an apology expressing his full support for "the efforts to bring this emotionally delicate chapter of history to a fitting conclusion." This represented a refreshing change of the guard. After all, UBS was the bank where Christoph Meili had worked, and Cabiallavetta's immediate predecessor, Robert Studer, saw the Holocaust accounts as a minor affair and had suggested that Meili had ulterior motives for blowing the whistle on UBS.

Marcel Ospel, who would be number 2 to Cabiallavetta when the two banks merged, was widely viewed as a straight talker and was the principal force behind the merger. He was almost a chain-smoker, leaving some of the American participants gasping for fresh air. (The no-smoking rules now common in the United States did not apply in Switzerland.) Lukas Mühlemann, of Credit Suisse, had attended Harvard Business School, worked for IBM, and been a senior director of the management consulting firm McKinsey & Company. He was thoroughly familiar with the United States and its business methods.

The plaintiffs' attorneys were represented by Mel Weiss, Michael Hausfeld, and Robert Swift. Everyone was "excited about the meeting," as Swift put it, because it was seen as the first breakthrough. Even Weiss, the crusty and experienced litigator, found the scene "remarkable." Three of Switzerland's most important bankers were sitting across from them, listening to the lawyers' account of what had happened decades ago as the result of a discredited philosophy of the Swiss government and banks. For making this face-to-face meeting possible, Weiss and his colleagues credited the U.S. government.

It was obvious that the CEOs did not relish this meeting. It was the only time they were to be in the same room with the lawyers, and there was an air of tension and distrust. I sat at the head of a long conference table with the U.S. team from the State and Justice Departments on the right, the Swiss CEOs and their team on the left, and the plaintiffs' attorneys ranged between us around the far end of the table. Next to me was the U.S. ambassador to Switzerland, Madeleine Kunin, who had been amazed only a few months before to find her mother's name on the first list of dormant accounts published by the banks. I welcomed everyone and expressed my appreciation for the bankers' attendance and their banks' recent cooperation. I explained that we felt a special urgency to do justice for elderly Holocaust survivors, many of them Americans wronged by private interests during the war, "before it was too late." Likewise I stressed that we sought to restore good relations with Switzerland, now impaired by lawsuits and threats of sanctions. Pointedly noting Singer's absence, I emphasized that he and his colleagues eventually would have to be included to conclude a durable deal.

Mühlemann thanked me for convening the meeting but said he was overwhelmed by publicity, which made it difficult "to do more than listen." Still he was open to future talks. He made it clear the three banks could speak only for themselves, not for all Swiss banks, not for the Swiss National Bank, and not for the Swiss government. Ospel and Cabiallavetta sat impassively.

Roger Witten praised his Swiss bank clients for supporting the Volcker audit, the Humanitarian Fund, the proposed Solidarity Fund, and the Bergier historical commission. He said the banks would not tolerate sanctions and "must be free from all supposed pressure." As this distinguished Washington lawyer completed his statement, Weiss passed a note to Hausfeld: "This guy is a schmuck." They never deviated from that attitude toward Witten.

I then presented the outline of the settlement, which was based in part on a discussion paper Witten had presented to me weeks before: The banks would accept the assessment of claims, interest, and fees from Volcker's audit and would pay living claimants or their heirs through an arbitration panel an amount ten times that remaining in each bank account—a multiple already agreed to by the Volcker Committee. For those accounts that no one was alive to claim, the balances would be paid to the Humanitarian Fund, with its mixed Swiss-WJRO membership. This would provide the bridge for which I was searching, from the lawyers and banks in the lawsuits to Singer and the WJRO. Finally, since the Volcker audits would not cover looted assets or slave labor profits deposited in Swiss banks, Witten suggested the banks would be willing to pay an additional amount, to be allocated by Judge Korman, to a victims fund for "rough justice"—a term I adopted in these and later negotiations for legally uncertain but morally compelling claims.

The class-action lawyers were not entirely comfortable with my framework. Swift worried about singling out one group, the WJRO, to distribute funds. Weiss warned that failure to settle the suits would have a severe effect on the banks' reputations and their ability to do business in the United States. He did not spare the rhetoric, warning the Swiss that there was a "serious cancer growing within your country" and that the class-action suits "can be like an excessive dose of radiation which will produce real side effects." Unresolved, the litigation would eat away at the Swiss banks for years. Then he warned that the plaintiffs' lawyers "will do what we need to do to get justice," and in the most dramatic part of the meeting, he characteristically began to define justice in figures.

Weiss told the bankers that the amount in the Humanitarian Fund, now approaching $200 million, was "not meaningful" when compared with the magnitude of claims for looted assets and forced-labor profits. Hausfeld concurred with Weiss and then declared that the damage caused by the Swiss during and after the war amounted to $10 billion. The Swiss CEOs were so angry they threatened to walk out. They stayed only when I urged them to listen to the lawyers, even if they chose not to respond. Then I admonished the lawyers not to talk about money until we had agreed on a structure for distributing it.

At 1:00 P.M., over two hours after we started, I felt we had gone as far as we could in an opening session, and I was relieved that we had avoided a blowup. As the meeting broke up, Mühlemann said to Hausfeld, "This is not going to be easy." That was an understatement. To feed the frenzied press and avoid conflicting statements, everyone agreed I should make brief remarks. In my statement I stressed that this was only an initial discussion, not a negotiation, that no specific figures were mentioned, and I reiterated that the U.S. government was involved both because we valued our relationship with Switzerland and wanted justice for Holocaust survivors. The next day the *Neue Zürcher Zeitung* commented that the fact I was involved was "a positive development for Switzerland," but it bemoaned the lack of any Swiss government participation, noting that Foreign Minister Cotti saw this only as "the banks' business," which cut the banks adrift even though they had operated in wartime with the express direction of the Swiss government.

As soon as I returned to Washington, I focused on bringing Singer and Bronfman into the negotiations as part of a united team with the class-action lawyers. But trying to corral Singer and Bronfman was like taming bucking broncos. They preferred to freelance, traveling frequently to Switzerland to deal directly with the CEOs of the three banks. The degree to which Singer and Bronfman insisted on working on their own, behind the backs of the class-action lawyers and me, had been vividly demonstrated by their decision at the end of August 1997 to ask Mort Zuckerman, the real estate magnate and media mogul, to cut a deal with the Swiss to settle the lawsuits. Singer and Bronfman believed that Zuckerman's business credentials would carry weight with the Swiss bankers. This was a stunningly brazen act. They had no involvement in the lawsuits, knew of the efforts to engage me in the process, and yet acted without consulting or even warning me. The lawyers were seething, and I was not far behind.

Zuckerman, it turned out, was like a comet. He lit up the sky for a brief moment and then disappeared, as I made progress in roping Singer into our talks.

I met Bronfman, Singer, and Zuckerman in Bronfman's hotel suite in London on December 1, 1997, the day before the start of the London conference, which we were all attending. Singer belittled the lawsuits and said the Swiss would "only respond to pressure." He demanded that the Swiss government apologize for their conduct. Bronfman suggested a settlement of the suits, to which the WJRO was not even a party, of $300 million for each of ten years, or $3 billion. When Mathis Cabiallavetta, president of UBS, heard this huge figure he told Zuckerman, "What do I tell my mother about paying such money to settle these suits?"

Singer disavowed Bronfman's $3 billion settlement figure and foresaw the need for a settlement of $1 billion to dispose of the lawsuits. He told me he wanted to conclude the dispute in an honorable way, but the "bankers shouldn't get the feeling that it is easy; they should not feel comfortable." He recommended that I get everyone in one room—the Swiss bankers, the WJC, the class-action lawyers—and forge a settlement before Judge Korman ruled on the motions to dismiss. This was just what I wanted to hear. But converting that talk into reality was still months off.

Singer played his cards brilliantly, though for me it was like trying to capture lightning in a bottle. By maintaining his own private channels with the top leadership of the Swiss banks, by convincing them that no deal they might reach with the class-action lawyers alone was worth the paper it was written on, he made himself indispensable. He was also driving Weiss and the other class-action lawyers to distraction. As Weiss told me, he found Singer utterly exasperating and "as bad as anyone I've ever dealt with." This was not simply a clash of egos. It involved the fundamental issue of who at the end of the day would control the bulk of any money the Swiss would pay—the World Jewish Congress, through their control of the WJRO, or the lawyers.

Meanwhile whatever goodwill I had managed to build at the Zurich meeting in mid-December was soon erased. I had called on all the parties for a time-out on provocative statements, but my admonition had fallen on deaf ears almost from the start. Just two weeks after the Zurich meetings, Flavio Cotti, the Swiss foreign minister, made a remarkable New Year's statement as he was about to begin his year as president, containing shades of Jean-Pascal Delamaruz's statement a year before. Attacks on Switzerland, he said, "come from limited geographic areas, for example, the East Coast of the United States, and in particular from New York." It did not take imagination to read this to mean the Swiss bank affair was only a Jewish concern. Thomas Borer worked furiously to try to explain away this obvious interpretation, rejecting any allegation of anti-Semitism. Enough backing and filling was done to permit a trip to Switzerland by First Lady Hillary Clinton to proceed as planned, including a meeting with Cotti.

Then, on January 13, 1998, the Wiesenthal Center of Los Angeles published a report by an American historian, Alan M. Schom, contending that 70 percent of the Jewish refugees admitted into Switzerland were required to perform work in Swiss labor camps that he compared to Nazi death camps. The director of the Wiesenthal Center, Rabbi Marvin Heir, called for a Swiss apology. State Department historian William Slany and Ambassador Kunin in Bern confirmed the existence of the camps but said the account of conditions there was significantly exaggerated. I publicly denounced the report, as did the Swiss government and even the Swiss Jewish community, but this offered more grist for the political mill in Switzerland that the country was being unfairly attacked.

Not to be outdone, in early March Bronfman gave an interview to the

*Jewish Bulletin* of Northern California calling for "total war" against Switzerland and publicly demanding $3 billion to settle all claims. This was utterly out of bounds. When I called to chastise Bronfman, he retreated into the classic excuse that his remarks had been taken out of context. I asked him to keep his thoughts to himself in the future so we could reach a settlement. I then called Elon Steinberg, Bronfman's public relations chief, and asked him to try to clean up the mess. He promised to tell the press that Bronfman had been misquoted and that the WJC and its chair wanted no war with the Swiss but "total peace." The next day Bronfman gave a conciliatory speech to the Commonwealth Club of California commending the banks for cooperating and "reaching out the hand of friendship to them." But the damage was done. Witten told me the Swiss bank CEOs felt that Bronfman's remarks had "put us back to zero." "You know what happened to the last person who said 'total war,'" Witten said. "It was Hermann Göring." Wearily I reminded both sides that I had called a time-out on recriminating statements. It was like talking to toddlers.

Finally, in back-to-back meetings in mid-March, I brought Singer together with the Swiss bank attorneys and then with the class-action lawyers. I had no time to lose. With the moratorium on New York City comptroller Hevesi's sanctions about to expire at the end of March, Hevesi's Executive Monitoring Committee had set a hearing for March 26 to determine if there had been any progress in our negotiations.

I needed breathing space from Hevesi, but to get it I needed to show him that we had gotten Singer into the talks as part of a united bargaining team with the lawyers. When I brought all the parties together, Roger Witten warned that the Swiss would not negotiate under a threat of sanctions. Weiss snarled, "The only way to get the banks to move is to hold them to a sword. I hope it's a very sharp one and it is right up to their throat." Trying to be the peacemaker, I assured them if the talks failed I would not blame either side. Witten, ever looking for an advantage, looked at me and said, "Speaking of offense, I'm sitting next to the guy who said Switzerland prolonged the war." I had to bite my tongue hard to restrain myself.

All finally agreed to have one united bargaining team to address the Swiss. But with Singer nothing was ever easy. Just when I felt I had everything nailed down, it all slipped through my hands. Singer suddenly insisted that before the WJC would join the talks, he had to receive a personal, written invitation from the three Swiss bank CEOs themselves, welcoming him to help negotiate what he called a "global agreement." He also refused to forswear Hevesi's sanctions, as the Swiss banks' attorneys had demanded, telling me that "every time we blink they see it as a sign of weakness."

The day of Hevesi's sanctions hearing had arrived. After much delay, the CEOs agreed to the language of a letter to Singer, welcoming "the direct involvement of the WJC" in the negotiations under my aegis. Their worst fears were quickly realized as Singer trumpeted this as a global agreement, one covering all Swiss sins, leaving them to shoulder the burden for the entire country's conduct during the war. With the CEOs' letter in hand, I testified, with a sigh of relief, that we were making progress and that Singer would be joining the talks. I again urged a moratorium on all sanctions and released a joint statement with the Swiss government opposing sanctions. It was the closest the Swiss government ever came to involving itself in the entire process. Hevesi announced he would postpone sanctions until the end of June, the new deadline sought by Weiss.

I phoned the top officials of the Swiss banks. Mühlemann of Credit Suisse thanked me and said that Hevesi's postponement made the banks more willing to cooperate. Cabiallavetta of UBS called to thank me for treating them with "class" but complained about Singer: "The way he talks to us is unbelievable, his tone and his manner." SBC chairman Marcel Ospel said he was impressed with my work in helping to delay sanctions and bring Singer into the talks. But he was blunt and pained because the Swiss public "accuse us of betraying Swiss interests and giving in to blackmail."

There was a brief period of optimism. Marc Cohen, one of the banks' lawyers, and Ambassador Borer were exultant at the ninety-day postponement of sanctions, celebrating in the SwissAir lounge at Kennedy Airport. But by the time they landed back in Switzerland, things had gone into reverse. Singer announced a breakthrough far beyond the intent of the CEO letter. He incorrectly contended that the Swiss banks had committed to an "all Switzerland" settlement to include not only the banks but industry, the insurance companies, and the Swiss National Bank. The Swiss press lacerated the banks for capitulating and presuming to negotiate for the entire country.

Nevertheless, Singer was now on board, there was a temporary truce between the Hausfeld-Weiss and Fagan-Swift groups, and I could now focus on a structure for our negotiations. After weeks of intense negotiation, we agreed on April 6, 1998, to the "Structure for Settlement of Swiss Bank Class Actions and Related Issues," with which all sides were comfortable, including Paul Volcker. It was similar to what I had proposed at the December meeting with the CEOs in Zurich. There would be two separate but integrated parts. The first involved actual bank accounts found by the Volcker audits. The Swiss banks obligated themselves to pay on those that "belong to or could possibly belong to a Holocaust victim" and to provide "additional interest and refund of fees." These included accounts that were still open but dormant since May 9, 1945, and those that were closed but would have been open and dormant "but for" improper action by the Swiss banks in closing them. For accounts that the Volcker Committee matched against living claimants, payment would be made immediately. For accounts for which there were no living heirs, the banks would pay the assets into a Class Action Victims' Distribution Fund to be overseen by Judge Korman.

The second process would be a negotiated lump sum for a "rough justice account" to settle the class-action lawyers' claims for looted assets and slave labor profits and any other claims against Swiss banks arising out of World War II.

What remained to be done made everything else seem like a tea party: money. As Weiss barked, "If you gave $10 billion to the Humanitarian Fund you set up for Singer and $9 billion for us, I don't care what structure we use!"

# CHAPTER SEVEN

~

# Scorpions in a Bottle

I F MONEY TALKS, the Swiss heard it first. Without informing me, Singer, or even their fellow class-action lawyers, the Fagan-Swift team cut a deal with the Swiss for one of their most sympathetic class-action plaintiffs, Estelle Sapir. Ed Fagan, Robert Swift, and Senator D'Amato immediately recognized the positive impact of a settlement. For Fagan and Swift this would mean quick money to a needy victim and a precedent for the Swiss paying a claim, at least under compelling circumstances. For D'Amato, helping to broker a settlement would thrust him again into the political limelight for a worthy cause, near the time of his 1998 reelection campaign.

At D'Amato's urging, Credit Suisse agreed to a meeting. Late in the winter of 1997–98, Sapir and Fagan went to Credit Suisse's New York offices and demanded $5 million. The Swiss team, clearly aghast, left the meeting without comment. D'Amato was shocked by the lawyers' audacity, exploding, "Are you crazy?" He said the Swiss were more likely to settle for one-tenth of her demand. That was the figure—$500,000—agreed to on March 4, 1998, over Estelle's reluctance to break with the class members and accept so little.

On the Swiss side, it was both unusual and risky for a defendant in a class-action to concede a settlement to the lead plaintiff. But Estelle's story of repeatedly being denied access to her murdered father's bank account because of the absence of a death certificate from his concentration camp showed such callousness that it reinforced the repellent image of the Swiss treatment of Holocaust depositors. The banks were better off getting this tiny ball of energy and indignation out of the picture. Estelle made them look bad. They needed to show they could do the right thing when the evidence warranted. And finally, there was the human element. As Roger Witten put it, even the Swiss lawyers liked her and believed her story. Moreover, he observed, "She was sick, and we didn't want her to die; it would be a disaster if she died and we hadn't settled."

Nevertheless, the other class-action lawyers were distressed by the loss of this perfect plaintiff. Although they dared not object, this unilateral settlement exacerbated already serious tensions among them.

Now we were ready to start talking about money for all the claimants. On one hand, the Swiss bankers, who had made great profits from tainted transactions with the Nazis, tried to create the impression that money was secondary to maintaining their national honor and restoring the credibility of their vaunted banks. The class-action lawyers and the WJRO, on the other hand, liked to talk about justice to Holocaust victims. But ultimately both sides had to express themselves in terms of dollar amounts. Reaching agreement on how much was necessary for each to accomplish its goals took tough negotiations, employing unusual tactics, in the context of external pressures I found difficult to control.

My dilemma was that I had no Swiss government counterpart. I effectively had to be a mediator, but I was hardly neutral in the strictest sense. Indeed, I was torn between conflicting missions—to help U.S. citizens and other Holocaust survivors achieve justice and, at the same time, to beat back any efforts, including sanctions—even though these might force the banks to settle—that might further strain already tense U.S.-Swiss relations.

Since we had agreed in our April 6 "Structure" that the banks would pay whatever the Volcker Committee determined they owed on actual bank accounts, our negotiations would focus, so we all thought, only on the "rough justice amount." This would cover all of the looted assets, slave labor profits, and other claims made against the Swiss banks arising from the war and would be controlled by Judge Korman.

Given the absence of evidence, the rough justice figure would have to be determined by hard bargaining and not objective calculations. The whole concept of rough justice was itself a novelty, a new theory to accommodate what amounted to a political negotiation, not a legal principle. In any traditional lawsuit, the injured parties must establish a clear nexus, a direct relationship, to the party from whom they seek to recover. This could be done with the bank accounts Volcker was auditing. It could not be done with looted assets and slave labor profits, which had been at the expense of people who, if they or their heirs were even alive, could not tie their losses to the three Swiss banks sued in the class actions.

Both sides had an incentive to keep the banks' liability for actual bank accounts separate from the rough justice negotiations. For the Swiss banks, now that they were paying the enormous audit fees for several international accounting firms, it was critical to their international reputations to have the stamp of approval from Paul Volcker that they had cooperated and divulged all that their predecessors had hidden. For the class-action lawyers, they had given up having any control over Volcker's audits and wanted to focus their attention on the rough justice negotiations, which they would manage through Judge Korman. Singer, as usual, had his foot in both camps, working with the Volcker Committee and as part of the victims' "united" bargaining team with the class-action lawyers, though with them unity was a scarce commodity.

In nine negotiating rounds between April 27 and June 26, I found the only way to bridge the huge divide between the parties' expectations was to combine an estimated amount for the Volcker audits and the rough justice amount. I knew that it would be difficult for three private banks to meet the high expectations of the class-action lawyers, particularly the Hausfeld-Weiss group. So I decided to make a last-ditch effort to persuade the Swiss government and the Swiss National Bank to share the financial load.

I got nowhere with a personal appeal to President Cotti or with the Swiss National Bank, which remained steadfast in its refusal to contribute. The central bank's president, Hans Meyer, a tall, balding man, stern and tight-lipped, with no patience for small talk, listened impassively at a breakfast meeting at the Swiss ambassador's Washington residence on April 17, when I declared it was "unfair to the big three commercial banks to carry the entire burden." He pointed out that his central bank had already made a contribution to the Humanitarian Fund and that legislation was being prepared that would permit the central bank to revalue its gold holdings and contribute to a new Solidarity Fund for victims of disasters, including Holocaust survivors. The bank's archives were now open, and although he was not defending their wartime actions, he could do no more. The commercial banks could settle accounts however they wanted, Meyer said, but "the Swiss National Bank is not a party to the problem." It made no difference whatsoever to him that my Nazi gold report and an interim Bergier report documented the Swiss National Bank's profitable role in laundering stolen gold for the Nazis. In fact, the central bank had been a worse actor than the private banks, which handled little looted gold. Meyer shrugged that off: "[We] can't turn the clock back, and have to live with history."

With the Swiss government and its central bank firmly rooted on the sidelines, I turned my attention to negotiating a final settlement that the three private Swiss banks would have to fully shoulder.

There was so much animosity between the class-action lawyers and the Swiss bank lawyers that I decided not to put them in one room together with me but to organize what in diplomatic parlance are called proximity talks. This now-standard diplomatic procedure was first used to great effect by Ralph Bunche of the United Nations in negotiating a truce to the 1948 war between Israel and the Arabs. Since the Arabs refused to recognize the existence of the new Jewish state, Bunche put the parties in separate rooms and shuttled between them to narrow their differences, for which he won the Nobel Peace Prize.

I was no Ralph Bunche, and this was not a shooting war. But I believed the two groups of lawyers would be better off separated because of their intense mutual antagonism. To avoid inflaming passions, their opening bids would be made to me, not to each other. Over the course of the negotiations, I would shuttle from room to room, passing along the other side's views, trying to find areas of compromise.

Although I took care to reflect the arguments made by each side to the other, I would convey initial offers of settlement amounts only if one was within range of the other. I would need to decide what, if any, credits the banks should deduct from any settlement—for example, for money paid into the Humanitarian Fund; to require each side to justify its numbers; and to explain one side's justifications to the other side as if each were arguing in court.

To establish this procedure I brought all the parties around my conference table in the State Department on April 27, 1998. For the first time everyone was in one room: Singer and Gideon Taylor, legal counsel for the WJRO; the class-action lawyers; the Swiss bank representatives; and our U.S. government team. I laid it on the line: no more public relations stunts. The negotiations over money must remain extremely confidential since, I said, "leaks will fry the process as well as the negotiations."

But I knew more rhetorical admonitions would be useless with this crowd. So I produced a stipulation and order that I asked everyone to sign and that was filed with Judge Korman and signed by him the next day. This Confidentiality Order required all the parties to hold in strict confidence the economic positions each side would be taking, bound them to make no comment on the substance or conduct of the negotiations to anyone outside their own team, and forced them to promise that, if the talks fell through, the positions taken would not be used in any way in the pending litigation. A breach of the order would bring potential sanctions by Judge Korman. Everyone signed, including Singer and even me and the members of my governmental team.

The negotiations over money that followed were like a boxing match, with many rounds but few rules, certainly not those of the Marquis of Queensberry. There were rabbit punches, low blows, and verbal insults on all sides. It took us months to move from the opening round to the final round about money, and each negotiating session featured the pounding of heavyweight prizefighters.

My problems in reaching an agreement were aggravated by the serious internal disputes among the victims' lawyers and between them and Singer. Just as frustrating, the WJRO was rent with division between Singer and Avraham Burg, the fiery head of Israel's Jewish Agency, who saw the talks as a way of advancing his goal to be the next prime minister in a Labor Party government. (He is now Speaker of the Knesset.) Burg was itching for a fight to show the Israeli public how tough he could be toward the Swiss. He had already made a public broadside against the negotiations themselves.

I had my own confrontation with Burg, warning him that his public attacks on the negotiations were harming the interests of the survivors. I faced him squarely and said, "If these talks break down over internal bickering, and this leads to years of fruitless litigation while victims die every day, it will be a heavy burden of history on your shoulders. You need to decide if you need headlines or results."

Burg retorted angrily: "As long as the Swiss play an outside and inside game, I will too. Have I come all this way to be rebuked? This is none of your business as the U.S. government, it is only the business of the Swiss government." He suggested rotating negotiations in Israel, the United States, and Switzerland. "I won't behave differently than the Swiss," said Burg. "If we squeeze enough, they will settle." He concluded by promising to give negotiations a try, "but I hope they don't work."

To find ways to bridge the gulf between the two sides, I solicited ideas for conducting the negotiations from experts in mediation, like Ken Feinberg (who in 2001 would be named the arbitrator of the September 11 claims fund created by Congress). I finally landed on what seemed a clever approach, suggested by Mel Weiss, one that he had seen used in resolving financial disputes. Each side privately presents the mediator with four numbers: an estimate of what it believes will be the opposing side's opening offer and of what it will ultimately pay, along with its own opening and final demand. The mediator shares the figures with neither side but uses them to reckon each side's range and then to narrow the gap between them.

The opening round of the proximity talks on April 27 immediately demonstrated that the parties were miles apart. I began with the class-action lawyers and the WJRO, who presented a $5 billion opening demand, with Mel Weiss taking the lead. They estimated the banks' opening offer at $800 million to $900 million and believed the banks would ultimately be willing to settle at $3.5 billion. These numbers were simply not in the banks' universe. The lawyers refused to credit what the banks had recently put into the Humanitarian Fund, the huge fees they were paying to the auditors Volcker retained, nor even the small amounts the banks had paid in dormant accounts between 1962 and 1974.

Then I went down the hall to meet with the Swiss side. Their opening offer was $300 million over three years for their rough justice account, offset by the $70 million they had paid into the Humanitarian Fund, or $230 million in new money, plus whatever they would be judged to owe in the Volcker process. They guessed the victims' side would open with a $3 billion rough justice demand but that the class-action lawyers and Singer would ultimately settle at $500 million.

I returned to the class-action lawyers and told them they would have to justify their $5 billion demand to me. I warned them that they needed not just present a litany of Swiss misdeeds, as they had just done, but to link their demands with facts connected clearly to the banks. In fact, they had no evidence upon which to base their demands. They made a feeble effort to cite my own 1997 Nazi gold report and some documents from the U.S. National Archives, but these hardly justified their figures. They were unresponsive when I asked them to assess the relative strength of their various allegations: "They're all equal," Hausfeld pronounced.

Not that the Swiss figures were more soundly based. Their predictions were based on various numbers dangled by the other side over the past several months—Bronfman's public demand of $3 billion, Singer's discussions with the bank CEOs indicating his willingness to take $1 billion or even less, and an early signal from Fagan and Swift in the $500 million range. Roger Witten injected a political element: Swiss public opinion could tolerate only a settlement based upon facts and not on "extortionate" demands. The Swiss saw themselves as "under attack" and felt "no one should leave the field."

When I asked the Swiss to defend their numbers, they launched a detailed attack on the class-action cases, attempting to minimize the banks' profits on gold, silver, platinum, stocks, and looted art to a mere $4 million. They dismissed the slave labor claims as "worth zero" in court. As for looted assets, the World Jewish Congress's own report had shown that only $20 million in Reichsbank gold had gone to private banks before 1942, when the Swiss government decreed that all gold must go through the central bank. Nevertheless, the Big Three private banks were willing to pay several hundred million dollars to end the threats of litigation and sanctions. They said that amount would be payment for the "inconsiderate treatment" that heirs had received after the war in vainly searching for their family bank accounts. But Witten insisted that "wealthy Jewish families sent their money to the U.S., Argentina, and the UK" rather than Switzerland. I found this an astonishing statement but considered it purely a negotiating point and saw little to be gained from arguing with Witten when the Volcker audit would present the full picture.

At 6:00 P.M. I returned to the plaintiffs' lawyers to give them a sanitized briefing of the banks' arguments. The only numbers I mentioned were the banks' prediction of the plaintiffs' demand and the basis for their guess. Hausfeld said that his team could not "microevaluate" evidence, because the banks had refused to open their books. Singer launched into a tirade, detailing the banks' wartime improprieties: $20 million in Nazi gold had made its way to private banks in Switzerland, including dental fillings yanked from victims' mouths; the Antwerp diamond exchange was closed by the Nazis and the industry moved to Zurich, where Credit Suisse played a major role; Swiss dealers fenced their looted art with the help of the banks; and Credit Suisse had helped the Swiss Bally company acquire shoe companies that had been seized from Jewish owners and "Aryanized." It was clear that Singer had done his homework, but less clear how these incidents justified any particular figure the banks should pay.

The conclusion of the meeting was most disturbing. Weiss suddenly set an ultimatum: "Unless we resolve the negotiations by the end of June, the process has to end." I felt this was ridiculous and unfair and said so. This was the first day of real negotiations over money and already Weiss was setting an arbitrary sixty-day deadline. But my objections did no good. At a later round of negotiations on May 20, Singer stuck to the same June 30 deadline. There was nothing random about the date. This was the end of the moratorium Hevesi had given on the imposition of sanctions.

Over the three rounds we conducted in May, there were high and low points as I tried to convince the two sides to think outside the box. At the May 11 session there was a brief note of levity when Weiss asked Witten to sign a greeting card. "What card?" Witten asked. Weiss produced a card addressed to Judge Korman which said, "Thinking of you." Witten signed and everyone laughed.

There were other light moments. At the opening of the May 20 round I was pleased to introduce Bobby Brown, the official representative of Israeli prime minister Benjamin Netanyahu, who, unlike Burg, was fully supporting our negotiations.

Weiss, not knowing Brown, asked, "What position do you play?"—knowing that the New York Yankees had a third baseman in the 1950s named Bobby Brown.

Brown got the reference immediately and extended the joke: "Third base, but if you were under thirty-five, you'd say I was Whitney Houston's husband!"

Hausfeld conceded, "There is a resemblance," as everyone laughed with the short, stocky, jovial Israeli.

But these few moments of laughter were like slivers of sunshine on a stormy day. In general, the mood was tense and divisive. Weiss was angry that Borer was urging the small Swiss Jewish community to press the lawyers for a quick settlement. Worse, we did not seem to be getting anywhere. I continued to pound the plaintiffs' attorneys for some solid evidence to support their rough justice demands. Hausfeld admitted he could not supply a connection that would stand up in court. If I needed any reminder that we were in a political, not a legal, negotiation, Weiss tartly supplied it: "Look, the question is going to be how hard we squeeze their balls or how hard they squeeze ours!" Here he believed he had the whip hand because of the looming threat of sanctions.

But this was not enough for me. I warned the plaintiffs that the banks would need some rational basis for settlement, one they could sell to a skeptical Swiss public. Even if they could not establish a sufficient relationship between the damages the plaintiffs sought and the actions of the three banks to hold up under the strict rules of evidence in a U.S. court, there had to be some plausible linkage to justify the banks' large payments; they could not simply be seen to bend to pressure. Hausfeld ruefully joked that there was a difference between "rational" and "rationale." He could either present a number and build a rationale for it or develop a rationale and allow them to build a number around it. Either way it could not withstand strict legal scrutiny.

At our May 20 session, Hausfeld produced a twenty-one-page letter signed by himself, Weiss, Swift, and Singer. At one level it was an impressive compilation of Swiss bank misdeeds, demonstrating the deep involvement of the three major Swiss banks "in every form of financial transaction with Hitler's Germany," as the letter noted. But it was not an accounting of the precise amount by which the banks profited through their misconduct. I recognized again that the class-action lawyers and Singer would never be able to quantify the losses for which they were demanding reparations, and this realization drove home yet again the unique, political dimension to our negotiations. This simply confirmed what Hausfeld argued before: If both sides could agree upon a number, we could find a rationale to support it.

But the atmosphere for reaching an accommodation was becoming increasingly charged. The Swiss were upset by a bill passed by the New Jersey State Assembly that would have forced the state's pension funds to divest themselves of all their stocks in Swiss companies. This was the first legislative body to pass a sanctions bill. A Credit Suisse spokesman responded that it "undermined the ongoing discussions between the Swiss banks and Jewish organizations" that I was mediating. I agreed. I had written New Jersey officials a few days before that "sanctions will only slow down the ongoing process to settle these problems."

But far more serious was the threat to block the UBS-SBC merger, which was critical to the banks' expansion in U.S. and world capital markets. The pending bank merger had cast a shadow of uncertainty from the time I entered the fray. But now a June 4 deadline for New York State banking authorities to rule on the merger intersected directly with my own negotiations. Roger Witten warned me bluntly that "my clients will walk away from the negotiating process if the merger is not okayed. They are losing money and are obsessed with it and willing to sacrifice."

As was so often the case, Singer became the indispensable person. Witten demanded that Singer go on record, at the very least, as not opposing the merger. When I called Elizabeth McCaul, the acting New York bank superintendent, she sought the same assurance, fearing that, without Singer's tacit blessing, she would anger the person who had recently appointed her, New York governor George Pataki, a champion for Holocaust victims, as well as New York's Jewish voters. Senator D'Amato had already written to her and to Federal Reserve Board chairman Alan Greenspan, urging that the merger be blocked because of UBS's and SBC's actions during and after the war.

It was not my role to tell McCaul how to rule on the merger. But I did tell her to make her decision on the merits, not the politics of the matter. She told me frankly that she was under tremendous pressure from the WJC and was "really getting beaten up." Since the Federal Reserve Board also had to approve the merger, I called Alan Greenspan with a similar message. But I was pushing on an open door. Greenspan, not subject to the kind of political pressures being applied to McCaul, readily assured me that D'Amato's letter would have no impact on him. He would insist that the Fed make a strictly legal decision based on the merits.

Senior officials of the U.S. government frequently advise developing nations to adopt transparent, nonpolitical regulatory processes like those in place in the United States. And so it drove me to distraction that the class-action lawyers and the WJC were trying to pollute our own regulatory system, however sympathetic the cause. I enlisted William McDonough, president of the Federal Reserve Bank of New York, to warn McCaul of the dangers to New York's reputation as a financial center if regulatory matters became hostage to politics. But my insistence on not politicizing the merger only seemed to make matters worse.

When I convened the lawyers in my conference room for our next round of talks on May 26, Witten insisted that Singer demonstrate that he did not oppose the bank merger. He accused Singer and the WJC of trying to stall the approval. Weiss immediately cut him off: "Why should Singer be forced to write a letter?" In a Talmudic response worthy of his rabbinical degree, Singer said, "Until I write a letter opposing the merger, I'm not opposed." This stopped discussion of the issue.

It had become clear to me, from the first two rounds in May, that we did not have the luxury of leisurely negotiations and we were not going to get anywhere unless I came up with a number for our May 26 session. In the preceding days, my team and I had met to decide how to bridge the gap between the parties and how to allow each side to declare victory. We came to two main conclusions. First, I decided on some creative accounting to try to satisfy both sides. In order to build up the total to help the victims' side while actually lightening the Swiss's burden, we should spread the payments over seven years. By doing so, the nominal dollars would seem large but their present value would be considerably less because of what economists call the time value of money. One dollar today is worth less if paid over several years, due to future inflation and forgone interest. Second and more radical and risky, we should estimate up front Volcker's eventual audit figures for actual bank accounts and combine them with whatever number we negotiated for "rough justice." This could add several hundred million dollars to the settlement. But it also meant departing from the watertight separation between the Volcker process and our negotiations in the April framework agreement. How else could I square opening offers that were so far apart?

From my first involvement with the negotiations, I instinctively felt that there was a deal to be had at around $1 billion, that the class-action lawyers would be satisfied with nothing unless it had a *B* in front of it, as Weiss had said months before. And I believed, in part from some back-door intelligence from Curtis Hoxter, the international business consultant who continued to serve as a go-between for the Swiss and Singer, that the Swiss would ultimately settle for something just under $1 billion.

I had no better legal basis for my number than the two sides had for theirs. I needed to choose an initial number high enough to keep the class-action lawyers from walking out but not so high as to push the Swiss off. My team and I had to come up with a figure that was considerably less than the class-action lawyers' initial demand of $5 billion, yet well above the opening offer of $230 million by the Swiss.

Rather than provide one number, we decided I should provide a range to each side in their separate conference rooms, in the hope of pulling both parties inside my sphere. I chose a payment range of $1.25 billion to $1.8 billion to be spread over seven years, combining Volcker and rough justice amounts. Thus, for the low-end, $1.25 billion figure, if we assumed the Volcker payments would total $500 million, the nominal rough justice amount would be $750 million. But with a seven-year payout, the real present value—the actual burden on the banks—would be only $474 million.

My proposal landed with a thud. The Swiss were flabbergasted by my negotiating range. Witten told me his side had all taken bets on what I would propose, but no one bet this high. "This is a very challenging offer; we felt your offer would be lower," he said.

I immediately went down the hall and presented my range to the class-action lawyers. I told them the banks were shocked at the size of my proposal. They asked to caucus and within an hour accepted the upper end of my range, $1.8 billion, but to be paid over three years rather than seven. This, of course, drove up the present value and the burden on the banks. Weiss insisted that "you were lower than our walk-away number" and said it "took a lot for us to come into your range." Impulsively, he demanded a forty-eight-hour turnaround for the banks to accept their counteroffer. I told him this was not bargaining in good faith. The banks needed time to digest the numbers.

I believed Weiss was posturing. Even though the payout period was shorter, the fact that the class-action lawyers and Singer so quickly lowered their demand from $5 billion to the top of my range gave me qualms. Had I pitched the settlement range too high? I regretted that I had not had a lower bottom range and realized the seven-year payout was simply an artifice to lower the real cost to the banks, a gimmick that meant an unrealistically long wait for elderly survivors.

Clearly, the Swiss thought the same. About an hour later Witten called me from his office to say that the range I had proposed was questionable if it "was so high the plaintiffs could accept it in one hour." He calculated that all of the Volcker accounts would still total only about $200 million even when adjusted for the passage of time—and my proposals more than doubled this figure.

I repeated that I needed a number within my range to take back to the class-action lawyers. The Swiss said there would be no new offer without approval of the UBS-SBC merger. I became so furious at their single-minded focus on the merger, on which I was already working so hard, that I slammed down the receiver on Witten and Cohen, only to call back in twenty minutes and apologize once I had calmed down.

Over the next few days the merger issue, to my great dismay, hijacked my negotiations. Witten assured me that if New York State approved the merger, the Swiss would "more than double" their offer of $230 million in rough justice money. As Marc Cohen put it, "This is what will be on the table if the merger is approved. There will be nothing if it is not." But they refused to permit me to transmit their higher offer to the victims' side before June 4, the deadline for New York State to decide on the merger. It was painfully clear to me that the talks would fail if the UBS-SBC merger was denied. Witten said bluntly that the class-action lawyers did "not have much leverage in the lawsuits even with a Jewish judge" but they did with sanctions, like holding the merger hostage.

SBC chairman Marcel Ospel called to say the threat to block the merger was "the straw breaking the camel's back" and that "we will not accept a settlement that is the product of extortionate threats." He emphasized that it was critical that New York State and the Federal Reserve approve the merger, and if it was approved, he promised, "We will not lowball a counteroffer."

By not allowing me to give the class-action lawyers a number, the Swiss banks were hamstringing me. All I could tell Weiss, Hausfeld, Swift, and Singer on May 29 was that I had received a "constructive counterproposal" with a significant increase but that I could not share the number with them because the banks did not want to be seen as trying to buy approval of the merger with their new offer.

It was at this point that I unwittingly sowed the seeds of distrust, particularly with Hausfeld and Weiss. I told them that all I could say was that the banks' proposal would bring them close to the bottom of my range and I did not believe it would be their last offer. I based my assumption on Singer's insistence that the Volcker audits would produce between $600 million and $750 million, to which I added at least $460 million in the rough justice funds—double the banks' previous $230 million offer—that Witten had promised if the merger was approved. Hausfeld and Weiss later accused me of conning them into dropping their objection to the merger on the understanding the banks were within my range. But I was careful about what I conveyed. I believe now as then that Hausfeld and Weiss were wrong. But I understood their possible confusion, given the divergent assumptions about what Volcker would find.

Although they welcomed the promise of a higher offer, Hausfeld and Weiss were concerned that it would be withdrawn once the merger was approved. They asked me to guarantee the new offer would stay on the table. Although I told them I would not do this, I double-checked with Witten and was reassured that the improved offer would not be pulled if the merger was approved.

With all eyes on the June 4 merger decision, I called for a June 5 meeting in New York City to receive the new offer from the banks if the merger was approved. I was in a tricky spot, underscored by Hausfeld's warning that my opposition to sanctions and efforts to avoid blocking the merger showed "a balance toward Switzerland." If the banks felt my range was too high, "we felt you were too low," Hausfeld said. He demanded $1.8 billion, "no terms, no concessions, no offsets."

On June 3, I received an aggravating phone call from Lloyd Cutler and Roger Witten. Suddenly, they were not so sure they would have the authority to more than double their previous offer. Because of the time difference with Europe, they would not be able to contact the three banks' CEOs to get firm authority until Friday, June 5, at 8:30 A.M. New York time—just when our negotiations were set to commence. This would cut the matter too close for comfort. I felt with a growing sense of doom that they were now backing off their promised increase. If they did and the merger was approved, I would be blamed for having lost the plaintiffs' biggest bargaining chip.

On June 4 Elizabeth McCaul announced that she was approving the merger, saying that her decision was influenced by the fact that UBS and SBC had finally agreed to permit New York bank inspectors to review records of the banks' activities in the United States during the war, including records that could have belonged to Holocaust victims. "We now have trust in the bank management; we didn't have that before," she intoned.

When I congratulated McCaul, she told me, "I have put my personal reputation at stake." I assured her that she had enhanced her reputation, at least with me.

I had breakfast in Manhattan with Paul Volcker early the next morning to see if he could give me any help. He told me that well over half of the dormant deposits his auditors were finding would be unmatched—no living heirs—and most of these were probably Holocaust accounts on which the banks would eventually have to make good under the 1996 Memorandum of Understanding. But again, he disappointed me with his unwillingness to project even an estimate of what he would find. I bit my tongue, but I was privately agitated. Given Volcker's unwillingness, or inability, to estimate a range for his audits and given the opposition of both sides to combining his numbers with the rough justice figure, I realized I had no choice but to focus solely on the rough justice amount.

The first unmistakable sign that the negotiations were in serious trouble appeared in no less public a place than a headline story by David Sanger in the *New York Times* on the morning of June 5. A leak. What little hair I had left stood on end. I cannot ever remember being more angry. The article laid out in detail the state of our negotiations but with incorrect numbers, stating the Swiss banks had offered a settlement of more than $1 billion. Someone had flagrantly violated the confidentiality agreement filed with Judge Korman. I was certain that Singer was the source, since he was not a party to the suits and may not have been subject to the court's discipline through its contempt provisions. When I met with the two sides that morning at the Four Seasons Hotel in midtown Manhattan, I asked Singer, Steinberg, and Gideon Taylor to leave the room where everyone had assembled.

I asked whether both sides wanted to exclude the WJRO representatives from the talks and seek a contempt citation from Judge Korman. They wanted to do neither. Weiss snapped, "I didn't know that Sanger of the *Times* signed the confidentiality order." I was not amused. Weiss blamed the banks for putting themselves in this position because they wanted to include Singer in the hope that he would agree to a lower number than the lawyers. Then I met separately with Singer and his two colleagues and accused Singer of the leak. He angrily denied responsibility but agreed to a total freeze on all contacts with the press for ten days. A few years later Fagan confessed to me that he had been the source of the leak, and apologized.

When we broke into separate groups, the Swiss gave me their new, post-merger rough justice offer. It was $450 million, roughly double their previous offer of $230 million. In addition, they would still pay whatever Volcker discovered in dormant accounts. I also suggested negotiating an estimate for the "but for," or closed, accounts and adding it to the rough justice figure. The banks would have to pay the auditors millions of dollars to verify these "but for" accounts; surely it would be better to pay the money to victims rather than accountants.

As soon as I dangled these numbers before the victims' lawyers, I knew I was in trouble. I had hoped the sweetened Swiss offer would help settle things, but Weiss immediately said, "We feel betrayed. This is not even at your negotiating floor."

Although as the mediator I could not say so to the lawyers, I was also disappointed. Still, I pushed them to consider the latest Swiss proposal—$450 million in rough justice money, plus $70 million already paid to the Humanitarian Fund and as much as another $600 million (if Singer's guess was correct) to make good on the Volcker accounts. "I've worked hard to get the banks here; give them a chance," I pleaded.

Hausfeld countered, "If I were impatient, we'd have left this process weeks ago. We expected a number on May 26; we expected a number on June 5." With growing animation, he accused the banks of dragging their feet until the merger was approved—and now, "we're finally where we were six months ago. This is not a game! No one is blaming you, but the banks have to understand the process has to yield a result."

Things were beginning to fall apart. We were entering the familiar period in negotiations when each side tries to shift blame for a failure to the other. Weiss and Hausfeld declared that the negotiations were effectively over and wanted to walk out. Swift disagreed. He suggested giving the banks a range and letting them walk out if they could not accept it.

I told the Swiss we were on the verge of a breakdown. They had been in touch by telephone with the banks' CEOs in Zurich. First Lloyd Cutler and then Roger Witten dangled figures slightly higher than they had already discussed. Cutler, the senior statesman, said, if they knew this was the "endgame," they could go to $600 million plus a $200 million guarantee for the Volcker audit. Witten went further and suggested $750 million for rough justice if this would settle the matter, plus a guaranteed amount for my idea of the "but for," closed accounts. Although they did not have final authority from the banks, they promised to push for it.

It was now 1:00 P.M. I returned to the victims' side and gave them the new, higher rough justice range of $450 million to $750 million, and Cutler's and Witten's promise to recommend it vigorously. The lawyers sounded interested and asked if some of the money could be paid immediately. When I went back to the Swiss side, they told me they could no longer reach their clients in Zurich because of the time difference, which seemed dubious. But Witten repeated he would "vigorously recommend" a range of $450 million to $750 million over three years, with the first payment immediately, plus a range of another $50 million to $150 million for Volcker's "but for" accounts (believing they would save this much in additional audit fees). In addition they restated that they would pay for anything more for which Volcker found them responsible in actual bank accounts.

I felt I really had something. Perhaps we had reached the precipice at which really tough negotiations can only be resolved. We were nearing the magic figure of $1 billion.

For the rest of the day, I shuttled back and forth discussing details. "This has been a very constructive day, surprisingly so," said Cutler. Swift, speaking for the plaintiffs' lawyers, likewise admitted, "This was a productive and constructive day; we'll stay with the process." Far from collapsing, the talks had a new lease on life, combining, as I had proposed on May 26, the rough justice account with an assumed amount for the Volcker audits. I was beginning to smell success for a historic negotiation, and I felt a great sense of relief. Hausfeld even told me he believed the "handwriting is on the wall," because Swift, Fagan, and Singer all wanted to settle.

But the deal that seemed so tantalizingly close began to unravel. Once more the Swiss banks shot themselves in the foot, this time declaring that the deal breaker was the "but for" accounts. The banks had learned that a negotiated agreement would save only $30 million in audit fees, not the $50 million to $150 million that Witten had suggested. The same day that I received the bad news from the Swiss, Weiss and Hausfeld told me they were going to bring a lawsuit against the Swiss National Bank to pressure it into contributing to the settlement. I urged them not to do so. I told them of my many unsuccessful attempts to persuade Hans Meyer, the bank's chairman, to contribute. I explained that the suit would provide no leverage because as a government institution the Swiss National Bank was immune from being sued in U.S. courts. Moreover, I implored them to focus on our negotiations, where we were making real progress. Another suit would be at best a distraction and at worst could derail the talks. But they went ahead anyway.

The next day, June 9, Ospel of SBC and Mühlemann of Credit Suisse flew to Washington to give me an equally negative message. Perfunctorily thanking me for my efforts on the UBS-SBC merger, Ospel said, "We will only pay what the claims are worth based upon facts." He reviewed the figures and then cut to the political fundamentals: The banks were under pressure from their stockholders and from Swiss public opinion, and the best they could deliver was a rough justice number of $450 million. I pressed them to come within my range and warned them this was their last chance to avoid a confrontation with Hevesi, the lawyers, and the WJRO. They said they would go back to their boards and ask for additional flexibility to go to $520 million. But even that was far below the $750 million for which their own lawyers had promised to fight. The higher figure, which would be above 1 billion Swiss francs, was "not explicable" to the Swiss public, let alone the banks' boards and stockholders, who, they said, did not take seriously the claims of looted-asset and slave-labor accounts in their bank.

I ended the meeting by saying that, unless I had a new number soon from the banks, "I am done. There is nothing more I can do."

For the next few days calls ricocheted between Washington and New York with threats of sanctions, old proposals in new guises, and mutual insults: Singer against the class-action lawyers, Hausfeld against his colleagues, everyone on the victims' side against the Swiss. I felt like the manager of an insane asylum; if the inmates had not actually taken it over, they certainly had been let out of their rooms.

When the Swiss presented their new proposal to me on Thursday, June 11, I called the class-action lawyers and told them the banks had added another $110 million, for a total of $560 million in fresh money, thus coming within the rough justice range of $450 million to $750 million but nowhere near the top. I was bitterly disappointed. The fact was that, with the UBS-SBC merger approved, the Swiss CEOs simply rejected the advice of their American legal team, believing the pressure was off. It was yet another miscalculation for which they would pay dearly.

Singer and the lawyers rejected the banks' proposal but asked to negotiate a number now for the banks' future obligations on Volcker's audit findings of dormant accounts and combine it with the sum for rough justice. Thus they had come full circle, back to my original idea to negotiate one sum combining Volcker and a rough justice number. Alas, this was still anathema to the banks and to Volcker as well. The banks still had a mortal fear that they would be accused of having aborted Volcker's efforts to investigate all the Holocaust-era accounts. Volcker resented the encroachment on his work. As his counsel, Michael Bradfield, put it, "What's the need of doing the audit?" Peter Widmer, the Swiss lawyer for the banks, told me that completing the Volcker audit was crucial to "restoring our honor and the confidence in the banks by disproving the allegations against them."

Weiss tried a direct contact with Thomas Borer in a breakfast meeting in New York on June 15, along with Phil Baum of the American Jewish Congress. But the meeting went badly, with Borer saying, "The Swiss can be very stubborn. If this negotiation fails there will be a major trade war by the Swiss with Israel and the U.S."—as if the United States would be the loser by being shut out of Swiss ski resorts.

Then a remarkable thing happened, even by the standards of this negotiation. On June 19 the Swiss banks peremptorily released to the Swiss press a last rough justice offer of $600 million, plus whatever they would eventually owe under the Volcker audit. Not only did it breach the Confidentiality Order, but I regarded it as an act of personal betrayal. Whatever leaks had occurred on the victims' side, this brazen act of publicly announcing a final offer in the midst of a negotiation represented a new low. I called my longtime friend Lloyd Cutler to complain that the banks had gone public when the negotiations still had some life. He replied defensively that "it was not our idea" but offered to "reconstruct $1 billion by creative means."

In a final effort to break the impasse, I called a meeting at the State Department on Tuesday, June 23, with the key plaintiffs' attorneys and the Swiss lawyers in separate rooms. I knew this was my last shot. Hevesi's sanctions and Weiss's self-imposed June 30 deadline were only a week away. I could see that Weiss and Hausfeld were seething with rage. In my exclusive meeting with the class-action lawyers and Singer I began by venting my own anger at the Swiss, hoping to defuse theirs. I called the Swiss press statement a "slap in the face" to the U.S. government. Singer railed against their "unilateral offer in the newspaper; they threw money on the table and said take it or leave it," just as they had done with him and Bronfman two years earlier in their first meeting in Bern. Then I reviewed the several stages we had gone through to arrive at this last effort, from my combined Volcker–rough justice range of $1.25 billion to $1.8 billion over seven years, to a separate rough justice range of $450 million to $750 million over three years when both parties rejected a unified package.

At this climactic meeting I now repackaged my compromise idea. To enhance the deal's image in the eyes of each side's constituency, I proposed a unified settlement of $1.05 billion over three years, combining rough justice and Volcker. Given the three-year payout period, the Swiss could claim this as less than a $1 billion settlement in present-value terms. I told the plaintiffs' lawyers that my new proposal would provide "real and tangible justice for your clients" and was my best offer to achieve "as much justice as can be obtained from these three banks." I also reviewed the hurdles they would face in court. I wanted a yes or no answer by Wednesday night.

Weiss replied with a tirade. He said that if I relayed my latest package to the banks, it would undermine his side's ability to resolve the matter. The banks, he said bitterly, had already stalled with "sham negotiations" to buy time for their merger to be approved. They had misled everyone into believing they would negotiate in my range, he said, and "they screwed us. We could have delayed the merger beyond June 30." Singer was so angry he threatened to throw a monkey wrench into the Volcker audits.

I immediately called Volcker for one last effort to give me an estimate, but he said, "I am very frustrated that I can't tell you more." So was I. Weiss made their final demand: $1.5 billion over three years in equal payments, $750 million for the rough justice account and $750 million for claimants to the Volcker accounts. They would drop all their suits including against the Swiss National Bank.

I went down the hall to present the Swiss side with their $1.5 billion combined Volcker–rough justice package. I pledged for the first time that I would agree not to reopen the 1946 Washington Accord on gold and German assets in Switzerland and would seek no more money from the Swiss government. They asked for time to digest the offer, especially what Witten called my "new and valuable" concession on the Accord, which would help Swiss industry. That, in turn, would make it easier for the banks to pass the hat to other Swiss companies to help make up the sum, since a potential threat would be removed from the whole country.

Then the Swiss suddenly shifted gears. Witten upped their offer for rough justice to $650 million and offered to consider a guaranteed floor under the money for the Volcker accounts. This was movement in the direction of the unified Volcker–rough justice package I had been pushing. I relayed the offer to the plaintiffs' attorneys. They wanted the certainty of a lump sum and did not want to wait for Volcker to conclude his audit.

By this time the plaintiffs' lawyers themselves were split; Weiss and Hausfeld thought they would have greater leverage by turning up the heat with Hevesi's sanctions, as his moratorium expired June 30. They judged that sanctions would force the Swiss to settle for more than they would get through my negotiations. But Swift thought this course of action was a greater risk than settling, since it might further stiffen Swiss resolve. Singer confided that "everyone is in a terrible mood." He said, "We do not have a $1 billion figure from them, only from you." He feared sanctions would create a bad environment, but that was where they were heading. The plaintiffs were starting to bank on sanctions.

From the Swiss I got only suspicion. Ambassador Alfred Defago accused me of extortion in my offer not to reopen the 1946 agreement and said he doubted the Swiss Federal Council would think much of it. When I again appealed to the Swiss National Bank and the Swiss government, they flat-out refused to contribute any money to the settlement. Ambassador Defago said that the "bashing of Switzerland" had taken its toll. Still, I pulled out all the stops. At my request, Bill McDonough of the New York Fed asked Hans Meyer of the Swiss National Bank for help in filling the gap but reported back that, regardless of the consequences, Meyer was inflexible and "planning to tough it out." I called President Cotti directly, reaching him in his dentist's office. In a courteous but labored voice, he declined. My call must have been more painful than the dentist's work.

I was not surprised when, at the last round of negotiations on June 26, the Swiss lawyers stepped away from my "jumbo proposal" combining a rough justice fund with Volcker. The three banks had already determined they would get little from others if they "passed the hat." Witten said about his Swiss clients, "They can't get to $1 billion, and whether they are as short-sighted as their predecessors, that's where they're at." To add insult to injury, Hausfeld and Weiss boycotted the meeting (along with Singer) and then sent a blistering letter on June 29 accusing me of trying to "exploit perceived differences" among plaintiffs' counsel by meeting only with Swift. Weiss wrote that it was one thing for the Swiss banks "to try to divide out inter-ests," but "it is a disgrace for you to do so." My last-minute phone call to the Jewish groups and lawyers in New York to ask that they consider the last Swiss offer was angrily rejected. When I appealed to Singer to show flexi-bility, he told me that if he did so, Weiss would accuse him of selling out.

At this point, I was completely deflated. I had lived with the Swiss bat-tles since 1995 and had been directly engaged in the negotiations for six solid months. The two sides simply could not take the last step necessary for set-tlement. The banks refused to give me a combined Volcker–rough justice offer at or near $1 billion, and the class-action lawyers, particularly Hausfeld and Weiss, were holding out for $1.5 billion.

I was now in a damage control mode. The guillotine of Hevesi's sanc-tions was hovering over our negotiations, putting me on a collision course with Hevesi and with Weiss and Singer, who were prodding him on.

I knew the power of sanctions. Throughout much of the Clinton admin-istration, I called myself the administration's "sanctionsmeister," the point man on dealing with a range of sanction initiatives from the U.S. Congress and from states and localities. I had negotiated with the European Union to avoid U.S. sanctions against European companies investing in Cuba and Iran under the Helms-Burton Act and the Iran-Libya Sanctions Act. I had persuaded the Clinton administration to ask the U.S. Supreme Court to strike down a Massachusetts law that sanctioned companies doing business with Burma (the Court so held). The Swiss sanctions threat was simply another irritant in a long line I was handling. In all of these I had to balance domestic and international interests.

I told Hevesi from the start that his proposed sanctions interfered with the conduct of our foreign policy and with our trade with Switzerland. He replied, "I am not making foreign policy, but I am deciding who to do business with." And yet, with all the effort I had put into forestalling Hevesi's sanctions, I was hardly oblivious to the hard fact that they had gotten the attention of the Swiss banks in ways I alone could not. This never led me to pull my punches with Hevesi or, earlier, with Elizabeth McCaul on the UBS-SBC merger, but it was a reality.

Part of the reason we had reached this sanctions crisis was that for all their emphasis on secrecy, the Swiss banks could not keep our negotiations secret and had undercut any shred of trust by publicly announcing their $600 million rough justice offer. It not only torpedoed my negotiations; it made Hevesi feel personally betrayed. He believed the Swiss had agreed during one of his hearings to negotiate a global settlement; they had even drunk champagne in his office to seal their commitment. Hevesi later recounted to me the way events looked to him: "The Swiss go home. They get a terrible reaction when the press reports the right-wing reaction. There had been some pretty ugly anti-Semitic responses all along, ugly cartoons and comments and so on. And the Swiss government announced the following Tuesday they would not be party to any such deal. There is no deal. They reneged. And the banks too—the banks were pulled out."

The intensity of everyone's emotional engagement was not lost on the more sophisticated officials of the Swiss banks, particularly those based in New York. Robert C. O'Brien, managing director in New York of the Swiss subsidiary Credit Suisse/First Boston, is an Irish American who grew up in the ethnic neighborhoods of lower Manhattan. His father fought the Germans during World War II. O'Brien understood the passions engendered by the Holocaust far better than the remote Swiss bankers. He had testified before the New York City Council on sanctions it was considering, and debated on television against Abraham Foxman of the Anti-Defamation League, as well as Hevesi. On one late-night debate, Hevesi told him, "Boy, am I glad I have my side of the issue and not yours!"

Some of O'Brien's Jewish friends stopped speaking to him. He recalled a breakfast with one of them: "All of a sudden this guy breaks out in tears and he says, 'You don't know, I had twenty-seven relatives die in the Holocaust, and you can't understand that.'" O'Brien tried to explain the Swiss bank position, and his friend exploded again: "You cannot know, you cannot understand." From this O'Brien wisely learned the lesson that "logic was not going to work in dealing with this issue. It was just too emotionally charged. What can be more profound than the events of the Holocaust, and what can have a more profound impact on somebody's soul and emotion?"

O'Brien is buoyant, tough, and combative in the New York manner. He had stood up to unions trying to stop his bank from financing anti-union companies and to pressure groups who wanted the bank to stop lending in countries with undesirable regimes. But with Holocaust controversies he had "never seen anything of this order or magnitude." When he heard Estelle Sapir tell her story, it brought tears to his eyes. But with thirty-two years of banking experience, he realized he might have done the same as the Swiss: "If I was sitting in a branch over at the Chase Manhattan Bank, and somebody walked in and said, 'My grandfather had an account at this branch and I'd like to get the money,' I'd ask the same questions." Yet O'Brien knew that in the special circumstances of the postwar environment, the Swiss bank bureaucrat who demanded Estelle's father's death certificate was simply "following the letter of the law without fully understanding and appreciating the emotion of the individual herself."

Such was the state of affairs when we assembled on July 1 for Hevesi's Executive Monitoring Committee of state and local public finance officials to consider sanctions. Before the hearing, Weiss, Singer, and Hausfeld met with O'Brien and his colleague Joe McLaughlin in Hevesi's office. Hevesi tested the waters at a level just under $1 billion. Singer was tempted to go along. But again, Weiss prevailed and said no to anything under $1 billion. Weiss had judged that sanctions would force the Swiss to settle for more than they would get through my negotiations.

As O'Brien was waiting to testify before the committee in the dusty old conference room in New York's Municipal Building, he spotted a Bible on the bookshelf over his shoulder. He reached back, pulled it onto the table, and trying to break the tension, joked to Roger Witten, "Well, let's see what the Lord will give to direct us." Opening the book at random, he blindly placed a finger on a verse. O'Brien opened his eyes and read from II Chronicles 34:16–17: "All that was committed to thy servants, they are doing. And they have emptied out the money that was found in the House of Jehovah and have delivered it into the hand of the overseers, and into the hand of the workmen." O'Brien, smiling, said to Witten that it "was just incredible that we could have this thing there." Just then Israel Singer walked into the room. O'Brien said, "Israel, you wouldn't believe what I found in the Bible there." Singer joked, "Leave the Bible to me. I'm the rabbi." O'Brien later framed the passage and displayed it in his office.

When his time came to testify, O'Brien had a good story to tell, but not to this audience. Forceful and direct, he pointed out all the ways this generation of Swiss bankers had faced up to the actions of their wartime predecessors, including engaging in the current settlement discussions under my direction. Next he explained that their $600 million settlement offer had not been well understood by reporters, because they failed to stress the additional several hundred million dollars that the banks would pay on dormant accounts uncovered by Volcker. Then he pleaded that the sins of the Swiss National Bank should not be visited upon the private banks, since the central bank had conducted most of the wartime trade in Nazi gold. Imposing sanctions on private banks for what the Swiss central bank had done, he argued, was "about as rational as imposing sanctions on Citibank because gold stored in the vaults of the New York Federal Reserve Bank could have been resmelted from gold the Nazis took from concentration camp victims."

But O'Brien's harshest and most passionate words were directed against sanctions. "As righteous as the cause is, it does not justify squeezing us to pay for the acts of others. We are entitled to fairness, too. The crass exercise of economic leverage over us because we do business here, as a means of pressuring others, would not be a sound exercise of your governmental powers. On the contrary, they are unjust." Indeed, he added, sanctions would impede negotiations and "make the political climate in Switzerland completely hostile to any resolution."

In my testimony, delivered by speakerphone from Washington, I also spoke out against the sanctions, insisting that they were contrary to the foreign policy interests of the United States. I also declared publicly that my negotiating role had ended for now, though I would reenter if the parties wished.

O'Brien's arguments and mine fell on deaf ears. The Executive Monitoring Committee had already decided that the sanctions were the only way to force the banks to settle for more, and I knew what was coming. To the credit of Hevesi and his committee, they decided to employ both an iron fist and a velvet glove. They decided sanctions would not go into effect until September 1, thus publicly encouraging resumption of negotiations and prudently allowing a cooling-off period for the expected negative Swiss reaction.

But what kind of sanctions might work? Interviewed after the hearing by a *New York Times* reporter, Mel Weiss dramatically took off his gold Swiss watch and suggested that like-minded people send in their Swiss watches so the gold could be melted down and given to the victims—and meanwhile not buy a new watch from Switzerland.

On a more practical level, Hevesi and Carl McCall, the New York State comptroller, held a press conference the next day that went beyond generalized threats. They announced that, if sanctions were imposed in September, they would keep short-term government deposits out of Swiss banks, prevent Swiss banks and investment firms from selling city and state bonds and notes, and disallow Swiss banks from providing letters of credit on New York City debt. If the impasse continued, an escalating set of even tougher measures would be phased in, eventually covering all Swiss companies, not just the banks. Singer quipped, "If you can't make it in New York, you can't make it anywhere."

Financial officers in Vermont, Rhode Island, and Kentucky were already considering sanctions, and the Executive Monitoring Committee wrote to all eight hundred state and local finance officials suggesting they follow the initial sanction steps by September 1. Not to be outdone, Matt Fong of California, with his eye on a race for governor, announced that California (which had some $3 billion invested in Swiss enterprises) would immediately stop investing in the U.S. subsidiaries of Swiss banks and signing contracts with them.

I persuaded Secretary of State Albright's chief spokesperson, Jamie Rubin, to condemn the sanctions as "unjustified, unwarranted, and counterproductive," preventing the country from speaking with one voice in foreign policy and calling into question the openness of American financial markets. But I privately believed that the Swiss banks, by their unilateral public offer, had undercut the ability of the U.S. government to prevent state and local sanctions.

Rubin's admonition was given short shrift, and the sanctions movement escalated. On July 3 Barbara Hafer, a member of the Executive Monitoring

Committee and the treasurer of Pennsylvania, announced that her state would begin phasing in its own sanctions. The Chicago City Council considered an ordinance limiting its dealings with Swiss banks. Governor Christie Whitman of New Jersey ordered her state not to increase investments in Swiss financial institutions until the dispute was resolved. The New Jersey legislature gave renewed attention to its bill requiring the state to divest its $66 million worth of UBS stock. Bill Nelson, the insurance commissioner of Florida, said he was considering breaking contacts with Swiss insurance companies. Carl McCall and Sheldon Silver, the Speaker of the New York State Assembly, stood dramatically on the steps of New York City Hall threatening legislation against democratic Switzerland that would be as draconian as the commercial and financial sanctions against South Africa in the era of apartheid.

In full anticipation of what was to come, Swiss bank stocks declined, producing a swift and predictably sharp political reaction. The Swiss Federal Council declared that the sanctions were "counterproductive, unjustified and illegal" and "constitute a danger to the good bilateral relations between Switzerland and the United States." The president of the Swatch watch company demanded a Swiss boycott of U.S. goods if the U.S. imposed sanctions on Swiss banks. The Swiss banks said they would file lawsuits to block the sanctions. O'Brien and UBS's Richard Capone threatened to sue Hevesi and warned that he could cost 12,000 jobs in the banks' New York subsidiaries.

Criticized by a *New York Times* editorial on July 12 calling the sanctions "misconceived," Hevesi replied in a letter to the editor the next day: "We are preparing to bring sanctions because the diplomatic solution advocated by *The New York Times* has failed after nearly two years."

By mid-July, the class-action lawyers were deeply split. The Hausfeld-Weiss group wanted to keep up the sanctions pressure. The Fagan-Swift group could see their case and their attorneys' fees flying out the window. Dramatically, Swift and Fagan broke publicly from their hard-line colleagues. On July 15 they called a press conference and announced they would be "flexible" if the Swiss increased their offer.

Within hours of the press conference, the banks announced that they were ready to resume negotiations. Hans Bär, the head of his Jewish family's bank in Switzerland, called Curtis Hoxter to say it was time to cut a deal. At the same time, Credit Suisse had come under a new kind of pressure. Not only was it secretly in merger talks with J. P. Morgan—which refused to agree to any deal until the suits were settled—but its American subsidiary, Credit Suisse/First Boston, was the object of a whispering campaign among its Wall Street competitors for its Swiss parent's involvement in the suit.

Weiss was livid about the Fagan-Swift press conference. He viewed their departure from the $1.5 billion figure as nothing short of treason. He sent all of his colleagues a memorandum warning them that he was appealing to Judge Korman to remove Swift from the lawyers' Executive Committee. The committee convened amidst a level of rancor that was high even by its exacting standards. Weiss bellowed accusations of treachery at Swift and Fagan. Hausfeld showed his disdain by sitting in the corner of the room facing the wall. Bemused, Swift listened and stated an obvious point: Someone had to get negotiations going again.

Swift and Fagan urged the lawyers to bring me back into the negotiations. But Weiss and Hausfeld refused, believing I had sold them out by convincing them to lift their hold on the UBS-SBC merger, by opposing Hevesi's sanctions, by discouraging their suit against the Swiss National Bank, and by counseling further compromise. I immediately persuaded the White House to issue a press statement calling for the parties to get back together, believing this would have more weight than one issued from the State Department.

For my part, I kept my promise to both sides not to cast blame on either if the talks reached an impasse. But that did not prevent me from having my own deep disappointment, for myself and my team, who had put in hundreds of hours of time. We had brought the parties to within a few hundred million dollars. A settlement was within reach at $1 billion.

I was also bitter at both sides for taking up enormous amounts of senior U.S. government officials' time. It was now clear that Weiss and Hausfeld all along had used me to get the most out of the Swiss but in the end had relied upon Hevesi's heavy club of sanctions to get still more, at a heavy cost to U.S. relations with Switzerland. I was angry at Weiss's and Hausfeld's intransigence in sticking to their $1.5 billion demand and for refusing to permit me to rejoin the talks. I took this as a personal insult and, worse, an insult to their own government, which had worked so hard to achieve a fair settlement.

I was equally annoyed at the banks for not going to $750 million, the top of the rough justice range their American lawyers promised; for not agreeing to combine a negotiated sum for the Volcker audits with a rough justice sum that would have capped their liability; and for breaching our confidentiality agreement by going public with their last offer. They were oblivious to the political fallout from their unilateral announcement and failure to settle.

But my greatest wrath was privately reserved for the Swiss government and the Swiss National Bank. In any international negotiation it is always important to take into account the political constraints of the other government. I certainly knew how difficult the right-wing political leader Christoph Blocher had made the controversy, from which he derived great political profit. But at no point did the Swiss Federal Council try to lead public opinion or to take on Blocher and try to isolate him.

The studied passivity of the Swiss Federal Council fell far short of what any diplomatic negotiator should expect in modern governance. Swiss politicians and officialdom continued to treat the entire controversy as if it were purely a private bank matter, even though the commercial interests and the international image of their country were at stake. The full cost would fall on the banks, though the reputation of the country itself was at risk. The Swiss National Bank had been the real culprit in World War II, and now the private banks were paying for its sins.

The Swiss government was perfectly willing for the U.S. government to bloody itself in trying to settle the cases, to resist sanctions, and to publicly praise the Swiss for their many positive gestures once the crisis began. But the Swiss withheld even the most modest diplomatic and political help. They wanted to restore the bilateral relationship that existed before but at no cost to themselves. Roger Witten himself shared his frustration, telling me that the Swiss government was "hopeless" and that the banks had asked it in vain to help close the gap.

Rather than lick our collective wounds, I made one last stab at Hans Meyer of the Swiss National Bank. When he repeated his refusal to consider paying anything until the Bergier Commission issued its final report in 2002, I told him bluntly that the commission's already published interim report had everything he needed to know about the central bank's misconduct during World War II. He replied stubbornly, "We will not change our opinion; there is no way we will change our approach."

I met on July 21 with Edward Brunner, a former Swiss ambassador to the United States, who represented the Swiss business federation. He indicated that Swiss businesses wanted to help with a settlement since the Swiss government is "afraid of using taxpayers' money." But Swiss industry was also divided, and Brunner's offer came to naught.

I felt it was important to make clear that the negotiating process had broken down, in order to put maximum pressure on both sides to resume. On July 22 I told D'Amato's Senate Banking Committee in a hearing that "I consider my role in this phase of the matter closed." I knew this would strengthen Hevesi's hand in applying sanctions, and sure enough, Hevesi wrote to President Clinton the following week, arguing that my settlement talks would not have stalled "had the Swiss government been at the table or had at least indirectly supported and participated in these talks." Conceding that sanctions were extreme measures, he told the president he had no choice given the "absolute refusal of the Swiss government to meet any moral obligations, even after the devastating findings of Switzerland's own Bergier Commission." He asked President Clinton to encourage President Cotti of Switzerland "to come to the negotiating table and make rightful restitution to innocent victims of one of the greatest horrors the world has ever seen."

The financial gap between the parties was small by the time I concluded my negotiations, but the psychological and emotional divide was enormous. The two sides were like scorpions in a bottle. I had negotiated many complicated agreements with foreign governments during the Clinton administration, but I could not reach an agreement with the unreasonable and irrational private interests here. It was a crushing personal defeat and an embarrassment for the U.S. government. Passions were so high that only a new outside force could bring the parties back to rationality. Roger Witten made a revealing remark: Perhaps, he said, Judge Korman—an independent federal judge—could push the parties to take the last step by imposing a figure, to "inflict pain on both sides to settle. Both sides will suffer, and maybe this is needed to bring things to resolution. The judge needs to get some glass broken."

# CHAPTER EIGHT

# The Settlement

J UDGE EDWARD KORMAN played the Swiss bank cases like Jascha Heifetz played the violin. For over a year, he cleverly sat on the Swiss motions to dismiss the cases, both to allow the Volcker audit to be completed and to give my negotiations a chance to succeed. He put the fear of the Lord in both teams of lawyers, giving each reason to question the strength of its case. To the class-action lawyers, he indicated that much of their case rested on thin ice. To the banks, he indicated that at least on the issue of dormant accounts he would allow the case to go to a jury.

Now he could wait no longer. He had to act. The Volcker audit was nowhere near being finished. My negotiations had imploded but had put the parties within shouting distance of each other. He had to take my baton and carry it over the finish line.

He had several advantages. The Hevesi committee's new deadline had real teeth in it. Bob O'Brien of Credit Suisse/First Boston made clear to me that Hevesi's threatened September 1 sanctions meant "time was running out" and that, although the banks would have preferred to let Volcker complete his orderly audit process, "September 1 was coming down the pike." The bottom line for corporations the world over is their own bottom line, their financial accountability to their shareholders. Defending themselves in the U.S. market they needed so badly simply became too high a cost for the Swiss banks to pay, however strongly Swiss public opinion might oppose a settlement and however unhelpful their own government in Bern might be.

But Judge Korman brought another indefinable asset besides his sagacity—the respect of the independent judiciary. It would be easier for the

Swiss to accept a negotiated figure from an American judge than from an American government official like me.

The banks had come to another conclusion that would greatly help the judge. After rejecting for months my recommendation to build up their offer by combining our negotiated "rough justice" figure with an assumed number for the Volcker audits, they now did an about-face. For one thing, they saw no other way to bridge the gap with the class-action lawyers and Singer. For another, their balance of risks had begun to shift. Initially they had seen the Volcker process as shielding them from criticism, but now Volcker was finding far more dormant accounts than they had imagined. Better to negotiate a cap to their Volcker liability before his final report, when the WJRO representatives could press for expensive conclusions. Finally, a quick settlement might short-circuit Volcker's review, save additional auditing costs, and give them legal protection against future suits.

Lastly, Hausfeld and Weiss might have stiffed me but not a sitting federal judge before whose court they would have other cases in the future. I was reminded of the statement by Judge Newell Edenfield, the federal judge in Atlanta for whom I served as a law clerk after working on the White House staff of President Johnson. He said, "Hell, Stu, I have more power than the president of the United States you worked for. As a district court judge, I can enjoin the president from doing anything I damn well want!" The United States invests a great deal of authority and confidence in its judges. Judge Korman justified that trust.

Burt Neuborne got things moving by taking matters into his own hands. The scholarly and judicious NYU law professor had served in the thankless job as Judge Korman's appointed chair of the lawyers' Executive Committee, riding herd on the committee's pride of unruly lions. Now he could see the settlement he wanted slipping away—the settlement he saw as a memorial to his late daughter. He sent an e-mail message to Korman urging him to intervene. Neuborne thought he had simultaneously informed the Swiss by copying the message to their lead lawyer, Roger Witten. But he hit the wrong computer key and realized the error only the next day, when Witten learned of the message and exploded that he had never seen Neuborne's e-mail.

Nevertheless the message had the effect Neuborne desired. The judge decided to intervene.

Judge Korman called the parties into his chambers at 3:30 P.M. on July 27,

1998, for what turned into a five-hour meeting. His office on the fourth floor of the federal courthouse in Brooklyn has an old government-issue desk and conference table, with papers and books scattered all around. But its dreariness is compensated for by a lovely view of the Manhattan Bridge and the Empire State Building. Korman told both sides he knew only what he had read in the papers about my negotiations. He asked them to lay out their opposing positions.

The plaintiffs went first. Weiss summarized the negotiations and what he called the banks' "take it or leave it" offer. But so many numbers had flown around in the last days of my negotiations, the parties could not even agree on where the negotiations had left off. Weiss repeated the plaintiffs' demand for an all-inclusive $1.5 billion settlement package.

The judge dismissed this as "a public relations figure" and told Weiss and his colleagues that, given their clients' ages, they would be better off if they were awarded two-thirds now of what they might win in a trial several years later. He warned that he would not allow discovery of Swiss bank records, would not rule on the motions to dismiss the suits, and would do nothing to jeopardize Volcker's audits. Weiss and Hausfeld attacked the Volcker process, leading the judge to ask, "Why would Israel Singer sit on Volcker's board if he was a liar?"

Then it was the Swiss lawyers' turn. Witten gave Judge Korman the banks' justification for their offer of $600 million plus Volcker's findings. "What if the banks pay $600 million now and negotiate an additional amount later?" asked the judge, looking toward the time that Volcker would be able to determine what the banks would have to pay on their dormant accounts.

Witten replied that it offered no advantage to the banks to settle piece-meal instead of wiping the slate clean. He argued that the claims for looted assets and slave labor profits banked in Switzerland were worth far less than the $600 million the banks were offering, which meant that their figure included plenty to pay "for outrage."

Maintaining the pressure, Judge Korman called the plaintiffs' lawyers into his chambers again on July 30. He asked them to justify their demand for $1.5 billion. Hausfeld came armed with a notebook four inches thick containing research drawn from Helen Junz's studies of prewar Jewish wealth in Europe. But in the confines of the judge's chambers, where the rules of evidence dominate any discussion, Junz's imposing study could not be the basis of a credible legal argument. Judge Korman reminded the lawyers that it was unlikely a particular victim would ever be linked to any Swiss account holding looted assets or profits from German industry. That was an unmistakable signal to the lawyers not to push their demands to unreasonable heights.

The judge told them they needed a "rational way" to push the Swiss closer to their $1.5 billion. Why not present Junz's research to the Swiss side, the judge suggested. Hausfeld replied it would be a waste of time unless they could make their presentation without interruption and cross-examination. Hausfeld knew the weakness of his legal argument and did not want to expose himself to Swiss inquiries. The judge listened, absorbed, but did not tip his hand. He asked whether the lawyers would permit him to speak to me; Hausfeld and Weiss refused. Korman was hamstrung because the Code of Conduct for U. S. judges precluded him from contacting non-parties unless all the parties agreed. Nevertheless it was obvious that he was quietly picking up the threads of my process. Judge Korman declared that the gap between the two sides "was not unbridgeable," and the lawyers agreed to try to close it in negotiations lasting four to six weeks.

Then the judge met with the Swiss lawyers. They too repeated their demands, presented a full history of the banks' efforts to deal with dormant accounts, and showed the judge the same charts of wartime money flows they had presented to me months earlier in order to deflate their opponents' claims. The judge politely expressed his appreciation and asked if they would hear Hausfeld's presentation. At first Witten scoffed at the idea, but he finally agreed.

What happened next demonstrated that carefully researched argument weighed far less than straightforward, tug-of-war bargaining. To Korman's surprise, the Swiss lawyers asked him to recommend a number to settle the lawsuits. Korman protested that he knew little of the case because I had done all of the work to date. He said he could only act like King Solomon cutting the baby in half and that would mean a settlement just a bit higher than $1 billion. The only other alternative was worse: flipping a coin. But when the Swiss lawyers did not even blink an eye as he suggested his Solomonic solution, the judge realized that they were ready to settle somewhere around his split-the-difference figure. This was rough justice indeed, and certainly no sophisticated process of calculation.

With that, Judge Korman decided that the time had come to draw both sides together in an informal setting. He invited them to a 7:00 P.M. dinner on August 10 at a historic Brooklyn restaurant, Gage & Tollner, ten minutes walk from the courthouse. Gage & Tollner occupies a handsome 1890s brownstone townhouse, with the original gaslights still flickering. Upstairs is just the kind of private room the judge wanted for intimacy. Although it is not unusual for judges to promote settlements, it was unusual for Judge Korman to invite such a large group for dinner in an informal atmosphere. It was also very wise.

The judge arranged for a large U-shaped table. He sat at the top, flanked at his left by the Swiss down one arm of the U and on his right by the plaintiffs' lawyers down the other arm. Everyone was punctual except Burt Neuborne, who arrived ten minutes late. Climbing the narrow and dimly lit stairs, he could see through the archway only to the head of the table, its two arms blocked from view by the narrow passageway. Instantly he thought of paintings depicting the Last Supper.

All the class-action lawyers were present, as well as Israel Singer, who had been hastily included at Hausfeld's request. Most of the lawyers, including most of the victims' Jewish attorneys, ordered lobster. Singer, strictly kosher, dined only on fruit and Coca-Cola.

Korman began by asking Hausfeld to repeat his historical presentation for the Swiss side. Hausfeld, whose unassuming presence belies a sharp and forceful tongue, summarized his material in twenty minutes and gave the judge and the Swiss lawyers copies of a summary entitled "Plaintiffs' Damages Calculation and Supporting Documentation." Hausfeld estimated that Jewish assets in Germany and its conquered territories amounted to $10 billion, almost all of which had been looted. He estimated that well over half of this wealth was movable and highly marketable, such as securities, foreign currency, gold and other precious metals, fine art, jewelry, and diamonds. In current dollars, he reckoned that the looted wealth eventually passing through the Swiss banks, together with slave labor profits, added up to $16.8 billion.

To emphasize that a trial would produce embarrassing information about the Swiss banks' wartime conduct, Hausfeld included some of the most scandalous documents declassified by the National Archives for my 1997 report on Nazi gold, such as the role of the Bär family bank in handling looted Nazi assets sent through Turkey.

The bank representatives sat stone-faced. Witten was genuinely unimpressed with Hausfeld's evidence because it was, in his view, old news, consisting of intelligence reports from the Operation Safehaven hunt for Nazi loot that had already been publicized. But he said nothing, abiding by Hausfeld's own ground rules against any cross-examination.

It was at this crucial moment that Judge Korman shocked everyone. In hopes of breaking the impasse, he announced he would throw out a settlement number for discussion. Korman had a good idea of my negotiating range from his separate talks with the parties. Still, to be certain, he asked what it was. Weiss and Hausfeld would not permit Korman to check with me by phone. So the judge said simply, "It's time for me to give you a figure." He offered two options: $1.05 billion plus whatever the Volcker audits would find in the dormant accounts, or a total of $1.25 billion which would include rough justice and an assumed number for Volcker's findings, whatever they might be when his audit was complete. These figures were not drawn from thin air. From his private conversations with the parties he knew that $1.25 billion was the bottom end of my original range, in which, like him, I had combined a Volcker figure with a rough justice number. The judge assumed from his contact with Volcker that the audit would find $200 million in dormant accounts. He simply deducted that figure from the $1.25 billion alternative to achieve his $1.05 billion option.

Yet all the lawyers were surprised. Despite their bravado, most of the class-action lawyers would have settled for less than $1 billion, and Witten for the Swiss said later that he "hoped it would be lower but feared it would be higher." But most of all, the lawyers recognized that, with the judge's offer, the case was over. The class-action lawyers dared not challenge the judge's compromise, and if the Swiss then decided to deploy their formidable legal resources, they could expect to suffer not only in Judge Korman's court but in the court of public opinion.

The judge adjourned the dinner at 10:00 P.M. and asked both sides to come to his chambers the next morning. He paid for his meal. Weiss and Witten split the balance, which meant Witten's smaller legal team was paying a larger share (at least Singer's adherence to dietary restrictions saved them money and another lawyer, Mel Urbach, had kept kosher, too).

When the victims' lawyers caucused after the dinner, they decided they would be better off taking the $1.05 billion and awaiting the Volcker audit for more. The lawyers for the Swiss made the opposite decision.

Completely reversing their position on separating the Volcker process to protect themselves against future accusations that they had avoided paying the true amount of dormant accounts, the Swiss preferred to settle for a flat sum of $1.25 billion, the bottom end of my original range. They feared that Volcker would be so thorough that the total would come to more than that, and they wanted to cut their losses.

The Swiss decided upon three conditions: There had to be an "all Switzerland" settlement covering not just the three banks but all Swiss industry and the Swiss National Bank; the banks could not be charged interest on the outstanding balance as it was paid off over three years; and the Swiss would receive credit for the $200 million Humanitarian Fund they had created before negotiations began. The lawyers went to Judge Korman's chambers the morning of August 11 convinced they had only to tie up the loose ends for the deal. It was not to be so simple. The whole day was spent around the judge's conference table in the Brooklyn federal courthouse.

In the time since the Gage & Tollner dinner, Israel Singer and Senator Al D'Amato had gotten their fingers in the deal. Immediately after the dinner, Singer debriefed D'Amato. To believe that any deal could be struck without D'Amato seizing some of the credit in an election year would be to expect that a highway could be opened, a bridge could be fixed, or an elderly Jewish voter could be assisted anywhere in New York State without D'Amato somehow putting his name on the government's largess.

D'Amato, smelling a deal, immediately injected himself into the negotiations in which he had never played a part. As important as his congressional hearings had been in 1996 in putting the Swiss bank affair on the public agenda, he had been completely out of my bargaining picture. In this most unusual of negotiations, something even more unusual was about to happen: D'Amato would suddenly try to make himself the deal maker in a negotiation being conducted by a federal judge. The idea of a politician suddenly barging into talks held under the auspices of a federal judge would be bizarre anywhere except in New York politics. It was possible only because of the senator's personal relationship with Judge Korman, going back to their early friendship and D'Amato's original agreement not to block Korman's judicial appointment. But it underscored the political nature of the whole affair. The lawsuits were little more than a platform for a political solution to the conflict, one in which I had already broken with precedent by interjecting the executive branch of the U.S. government.

D'Amato called the judge and said in his inimitable way, "You SOB, you didn't tell me you were going to make such a recommendation. I have been telling the victims they will never get more than $900 million." Korman was surprised to learn that D'Amato's number was more helpful to the Swiss than his.

At last all the parties agreed on the all-inclusive, all-Switzerland $1.25 billion figure, to be fully disbursed over three years. The judge had deliberately left the issue of interest for last. This was the classic stratagem of setting aside a minor issue until the end, when neither side would allow it to disrupt a major deal. But he had not reckoned on his friend D'Amato being a party to separate negotiations on interest. D'Amato seized on the interest issue in a way that caused even more confusion, anger, and bitterness than were already richly present. Sensing a victory with which he could be associated in an election year, D'Amato had quickly enlisted Israel Singer and Credit Suisse's Bob O'Brien in a private negotiation to forgive interest payments over the three-year payment period. Even this late in the negotiations, Singer and D'Amato thought they could cut a deal behind the backs of the lawyers, as both saw the WJRO and Bronfman as the victims' genuine plenipotentiaries.

Neither the judge nor the class-action lawyers were aware of the parallel discussions. The side deal came out only when the class-action lawyers started talking about interest, and the Swiss lawyers curtly dismissed the matter: "That's already agreed to," Witten said. "We resolved that with the World Jewish Congress." The class-action lawyers were furious to discover that any part of the deal could be concluded without their stamp of approval, and they did not consider themselves bound by any deal negotiated by Singer and D'Amato. Weiss said to D'Amato, "We have been arguing, and you have given up. If there is no interest, there is no deal." They demanded 8 percent, and then they staged a walkout. But D'Amato intercepted them before they could leave the courthouse. He wrapped his arm around Burt Neuborne and said, "Professor Neuborne, surely you aren't going to leave now over the issue of interest?"

When the judge called in the Swiss legal team, Roger Witten explained that he had persuaded the banks' CEOs to accept the terms negotiated with Singer and D'Amato, in the belief that Singer was speaking for the class-action lawyers. He could not go back to the CEOs again—a deal was a deal. By now the two legal teams were not on speaking terms, the victims' lawyers feeling betrayed by Singer and D'Amato, the Swiss feeling sandbagged by them.

Now it was the Swiss bank lawyers' turn to storm out of the judge's chambers; they went to the jury room. D'Amato burst in and pleaded with them not to blow the deal over a few million dollars in interest—"pocket change for you." Then he pounded the table and warned them, "Do you really want a boycott?" Witten replied, "Senator, that was a great speech, but you're giving it to the wrong audience. We relied upon you. Give that speech to Mel Weiss." D'Amato openly dismissed Weiss, who was a supporter of Representative Charles Schumer, his Democratic opponent in the November race for the Senate. "Why help him?" D'Amato said about Weiss. He waved his arms furiously like a windmill, telling them they were "crazy to crash the negotiations" over $34 million in interest that could buy them legal peace.

Undeterred, D'Amato countered with the suggestion that the interest could be at a below-market rate and would not need to begin immediately. Concerned that the impasse over interest could implode the negotiations, Judge Korman called the Swiss team into his office and added a recommendation to make the pill easier for the Swiss to swallow: Until the final payout, the money could be kept on deposit at one of the Swiss banks. The banks might actually break even or even make a profit on holding their own money. And so Witten made one last call to Switzerland and broke the bad news to the CEOs in the midst of their sacrosanct August vacations. To say the least, they were, as Witten put it, "unhappy" at the turn of events. But they felt trapped and agreed to negotiate on the basis of D'Amato's last proposal of a low rate.

D'Amato then went to an adjoining room, where the class-action lawyers were encamped. He pressed them for an interest rate formula that would be acceptable to the Swiss. He knew that, if the Swiss had to take one more blow, the deal could fall apart, so he put the onus on the victims' lawyers: "For $34 million are you going to fuck this up? You will pay more for legal fees—lay off!" He then proposed a rate of 3.78 percent. "One day my grandchildren will ask how you came to 3.78 percent," Swift said wryly. "I only wish I knew," D'Amato replied. "I picked it off the top of my head."

Later D'Amato insisted that he had simply taken the plaintiffs' demand of 8 percent and more or less split it in half. Actually, he had heard the figure from Mel Weiss, who had looked up the overnight Treasury funds rate in the *New York Times* while the wrangling was going on. With this number in his head, D'Amato shot out of the room and returned to the Swiss, who were still huddled in the jury room of the judge's court. These financially savvy Swiss bank lawyers found 3.78 percent a highly appealing rate and negotiated an agreement to pay interest only on the remaining balance of the last payment three years down the road, with the money remaining in a Swiss bank.

Suddenly, Mel Weiss burst into the jury room and told the Swiss side he had made a mistake. He had read the wrong column in the newspaper. The 90 day Treasury bill rate was actually 4.9 percent. At this point, D'Amato had a fit. Before his eyes a potentially sweet victory was reverting to a bitter dispute. Having once sold an agreement to the Swiss banks with no interest at all and now having sold a second one at a low rate, he would not tolerate another modification introducing market rates of interest. He let Weiss know it was too late to undo his mistake.

Witten then insisted on settling the case of the Swiss bank guard Christoph Meili that Swift and Fagan had brought against UBS in 1998 for "destroying his image." Everyone moaned. But Witten also wanted the Meili case wrapped up so that he could end every pending matter once and for all. Yet again the whirling dervish, Senator D'Amato, wheeled into action. Swift and Fagan had initially demanded $10 million to $15 million; UBS offered $100,000. D'Amato persuaded both sides to accept $1 million. Even Judge Korman remarked that "it seems like a lot" when D'Amato implored him to bless the settlement. Ultimately, Meili's $1 million settlement was tucked away in Swift's application for attorneys' fees, which were capped at 1.8 percent of the overall $1.25 billion settlement.

Bodily towed by D'Amato, representatives of the two sides returned to Judge Korman's chambers to signify their agreement. But Bob O'Brien of Credit Suisse insisted that the deal also receive my blessing on behalf of the U.S. government. D'Amato agreed that "we gotta check with Stuart." He called me from the judge's chambers on a speakerphone and said, "If you do not say yes, there will not be a settlement."

The call was not a surprise. That morning, Witten had telephoned me from New York as I was returning from a meeting with members of Congress, telling me a deal was imminent. He suggested I fly to New York and bask in the glory. The settlement was cast in the concepts I had developed and was for an amount I first had recommended. "You should be here to be part of it," he said. Bennett Freeman immediately urged me to take the next shuttle to New York to be present for the last act and curtain call, as I had been for all the other parts of the play. In retrospect I wish I had followed his advice.

But some combination of wounded pride in having been excluded from the last negotiations and a concern that injecting myself at this point might upset the dynamics of a successful negotiation led me to remain reluctantly in Washington. After all, unlike D'Amato, I was not running for reelection.

On the telephone I was cool and distant. I asked for a quick accounting of the agreement but expressed my hesitancy about committing the U.S. government to endorse it on the basis of a phone call. I frankly resented being pushed without seeing the agreement, by lawyers who had excluded me; by the Swiss banks who had rejected my concepts and figures, which they now accepted; and by D'Amato, who was belatedly seeking to associate himself with an agreement in which he had no prior involvement.

D'Amato applied his unique brand of muscular diplomacy. He boasted that he had "all the crazies in one box" and said, "Stu, without you pushing the ball and the judge we could not get there."

I told him I would have to consider the settlement. I quickly caucused with our team to get their opinion. D'Amato called me back within minutes, fighting to prevent a political victory from slipping through his hands. The abrasive side he shows when crossed came out: "Stu, don't look like you've undercut the agreement."

My last call in the early evening on August 12 was an unusual joint conference call. Judge Korman, D'Amato, Singer, Witten, and Hausfeld were all on the line, often talking simultaneously on the judge's speakerphone. Weiss had left the scene to go on a vacation. The judge opened by announcing that the parties had come to an agreement. He said to me, "We owe you a debt of gratitude. It couldn't have worked without you." He urged me to approve the settlement. Sensing the reluctance and agitation in my voice, he explained, "I wanted to speak to you earlier, but they wouldn't let me." Witten, Singer, and Hausfeld in turn urged me to accept the agreement, emphasizing that it was structured as I had proposed and that the amount was within my range. Hausfeld said, "We followed your advice, and we gave a little and got a little." Witten was more urgent and more dire: "If you say you are still not satisfied, it will kill the banks, and the deal will crater."

I could hardly be churlish and scuttle the agreement, especially given my continued frustration over the Swiss government's refusal to involve itself. The settlement number, $1.25 billion, was the very first I had suggested back on May 26, and combined a rough justice fund with a liquidated sum for the Volcker process, as I first proposed. I finally said that, if all the parties and the judge felt the deal was fair, the U.S. government would support it publicly and enthusiastically. I felt a sense of relief and satisfaction, tinged with the natural human emotion of wanting to be there for the finale toward which I had worked so hard.

When D'Amato saw the settlement coming together, he quickly summoned Estelle Sapir and the other key witnesses from his congressional hearings. He also called CNN and arranged a press conference outside the courthouse in Brooklyn with all the lawyers and, of course, Estelle (whose case had long since been settled, a legal detail that did not bother the senator). It would happen at 6:25 P.M. on August 12, 1998, when the light was good and viewers were watching at home.

On the way out of the judge's chambers to the press conference, D'Amato put his arm around Roger Witten as if they were lifelong friends. Over his irrepressible smile he whispered to Witten, "Remember when you get down to that press conference to thank Al D'Amato—not Korman, not Eizenstat, but D'Amato. I'm the only one running for Senate." Witten passed the senatorial instruction to O'Brien, who had to conduct business in New York and did as he was told.

I wanted to be certain the sanctions would now be lifted and that we would obtain a positive statement from the Swiss government. Hevesi canceled the sanctions the very next day. The Swiss were not so forthcoming. My staff and I wanted to issue a joint statement with the Swiss government. Ambassador Kunin felt that some kind of apology was important, including lessons for the future and a commitment to Holocaust education. But Ambassador Defago gave me the first hint of Swiss reluctance the following morning, telling me that his government needed to see the actual agreement; the Socialists and Christian Democrats felt positive, but the other two parties in the coalition were skeptical. Then the Federal Council issued a negative statement declaring that the settlement had been a matter for the private banks and that the government of Switzerland had not been involved. Ambassador Kunin found this "churlish" and "craven toward the Swiss right wing."

I called President Cotti to express disappointment that the Federal Council's initial reaction had been "lukewarm and frankly unhelpful," particularly their statement that "no obligation ensues for the Swiss Confederation from the settlement." I told him that the "ball is now in Switzerland's court, and I hope you will be more forthcoming; you now have a golden opportunity to move rapidly toward closure." I also assured him it would not be a prelude to new demands if the government would acknowledge "explicitly the negative as well as the positive aspects of Switzerland's wartime record." That, I informed him, would enable the United States to promise formally not to reopen the 1946 Washington Accord. Cotti told me of resistance from the political right and said a definitive statement could come only when the matter was finally settled. The bottom line was that we could expect little more from the Swiss government. And we got little indeed.

The ending was true to form in this strange episode in law, diplomacy, and raw politics. Except for the Volcker audits, conducted independently from the lawsuits, the evidentiary essence of the legal process that could have lent legitimacy to the massive settlement was utterly lacking. Not one shred of traditional legal discovery was made. Instead, external pressures and the intervention of the U.S. government compensated for the serious flaws in the legal cases.

Until November 2001, more than three years after the August 1998 agreement, not one cent of the massive settlement reached the victims, a damning commentary on the ability of the American judicial system to handle huge political matters with international consequences. As crucial as Judge Korman was to the settlement, even he admitted that the courts are too cumbersome for the efficient dispatch of cases with this kind of diplomatic and political weight: "This should have been done as a government-to-government agreement. Litigation was the least desirable way to deal with it."

At one level the judge was right. It would have been better to have had a governmental agreement rather than a class-action lawsuit in U.S. courts. But from start to finish we had no Swiss government partner. The Swiss government buried its head in the deep Alpine snow and hoped we could pull out a settlement. Even if we had had a willing partner, it is doubtful we could have imposed a government-to-government settlement on the parties. The United States so prides itself on the access its citizens have to the courts to handle a myriad of complaints other societies handle outside the judicial system, that legally cutting off that access would have been exceedingly difficult.

For sure, had the Swiss government been as engaged as the United States was, a settlement would have been reached without resorting to Judge Korman's last-ditch intervention. But as it was, the involvement of the U.S. government was indispensable.

The three-year delay for payouts resulted from a variety of factors. The agreement reached in Judge Korman's chambers had to be put into final legal text. All the Jewish organizations in the WJRO had to sign off, and this inexplicably took many months. Worldwide notices for potential beneficiaries had to be placed in newspapers around the world. Judge Korman had to have a class-action hearing on the fairness of the settlement and for the plan's final approval. The agreement was renegotiated to shift the cost of the Volcker claims process to the $1.25 billion fund.

The judge appointed Judah Gribetz, a well-known figure in New York legal and Jewish circles, as a special master to work out the allocation plan for the funds. Gribetz had the indefinable quality Judge Korman called *sachal* (Yiddish for wisdom). Still, some of the lawyers objected to his plan, which delayed the judge's approval. But eventually Gribetz worked out an acceptable system, allocating the bulk of the funds, $800 million, to pay claimants for actual deposited accounts discovered by the Volcker audits, with only $100 million set aside for looted assets and $1,000 per person for Jewish and non-Jewish slave laborers who worked either for Swiss-owned companies or for German companies that deposited their revenues with Swiss banks (115,000 people have so far been paid), and a small amount for refugees mistreated by Swiss officials. The judge's approval of the Gribetz plan showed the low opinion he held of the claims for looted assets and slave labor.

Then appeals by two lawyers who were not a part of our negotiations further delayed the distribution of money. One lawyer in Florida demanded some of the funds be used for health care for South Florida Holocaust survivors, until his case was finally dropped. Former attorney general Ramsey Clark filed a challenge on behalf of the Sinti-Roma (gypsy) community, contending they were shortchanged.

But one major reason for the delay showed the Swiss banks reverting to the old behavior that haunted them for so long—failing to fully face their past. Judge Korman insisted he would not release the Swiss banks from the class-action suits until the banks published the names of account holders with likely Holocaust relationships. Even after fifty years, they continued to resist, arguing over how many account holders to disclose.

The Volcker Committee process was a casualty of the settlement. Volcker sensed a hardening of Swiss attitudes after the settlement, telling me, "The Swiss banks then went into a hole and refused to cooperate for reasons I do not know." As soon as the bank chairmen returned from their August vacations in 1998, they told Volcker that his audit, whose cost was skyrocketing, was no longer so crucial and asked him to wind it up. The banks did not know their man. Volcker categorically refused and insisted on completing his task. He reminded them that from the start his objective and theirs had been to find the real numbers in the dormant accounts as a matter of historical accountability. Volcker argued that if the process were aborted now, people would doubt its outcome. Moreover, he knew that Judge Korman did not want merely to sprinkle money indiscriminately among Holocaust survivors but would insist on first restoring property to those families with identifiable accounts. This would be impossible without a complete audit. Indeed, Judge Korman told me, "I cannot just drop money over heavily Jewish areas."

It was Volcker who brought the matter to at least a minimum of historical certainty. He wanted to publish the names of all accounts that could plausibly be related to the Holocaust. The Swiss argued successfully for a tougher standard of a "possible or probable" connection. To the very end, there was acrimony over how many bank accounts should be made public. The banks began to restrict access to the information and records needed to publish the names, even to the files the auditors had segregated as likely Holocaust-related account holders. The Swiss also made it harder for claimants to identify accounts by refusing to centralize their records.

After three years and more than $200 million in auditors' costs for five international accounting firms, and an equal amount in internal costs to the banks, the Volcker Committee issued its final report on December 6, 1999. It represented the most extensive and expensive audit in history. Records were found for 4.1 million of the 6.8 million accounts opened in Swiss banks from 1933 to 1945, of which 2.25 million were audited and matched against Yad Vashem lists of Holocaust victims. Some 54,000 accounts had a "probable or possible" relationship to victims seeking to protect their money, securities, or valuables from the Nazis.

Deeply embarrassed by the Volcker auditors' initial list of 54,000 accounts, the banks disputed it, saying it included many duplications and erroneous names. The Swiss Bankers Association wanted only 5,000 accounts published. As in their negotiations with the U.S. government half a century earlier, the Swiss haggled to the last moment. Rather than burnishing their reputation after agreeing to the court settlement, spending enormous amounts of money on the Volcker audits, and opening their records, their last-ditch haggling left a bad image. The Swiss Federal Banking Commission said it needed four months to decide if it would accept the Volcker recommendations and, when it did, made implementation of the recommendations only voluntary. Volcker complained to Judge Korman to force the Swiss to honor his committee's recommendations. The judge's only leverage was his refusal to accept the settlement unless the Swiss banks were required to follow the Volcker report and there was a rational scheme for the distribution of funds, based on published lists. He later told me that the Swiss banks fought so tenaciously to limit the number of published accounts because they wanted to tell the Swiss public they had been "blackmailed to pay" such a large settlement, not because there were so many Holocaust accounts for which they had "destroyed records and stonewalled."

Lengthy negotiations ensued until concessions were made to the Swiss that, together with culling duplications from the list, more than halved the number of published names from 54,000 to 21,000. Nevertheless, Volcker's final report was a remarkable document, and what he achieved in finally publishing even 21,000 names was historic.

It is a measure of the depths to which their reputation had fallen that the Swiss banks welcomed Volcker's damning conclusions. For although the committee found "questionable and deceitful actions by some individual banks in the handling of accounts of victims," including withholding of information, inappropriate closing of accounts, "many cases of insensitivity to the efforts of victims or heirs of victims to claim dormant or closed accounts," and "a general lack of diligence—even active resistance—in response to earlier private and official inquiries about dormant accounts," it found no evidence of an active conspiracy.

Perhaps even more historic were the shocking discoveries in Switzerland's own independent Bergier Commission report, which came out in March 2002—revelations that went well beyond the findings in our 1997 Nazi gold report. No country before or since has commissioned such a critical examination of an important part of its own history as the Swiss did here. Professor Bergier and the international experts on his commission exploded the myth, subscribed to by the Volcker Committee, that there was no conspiracy to deprive Holocaust-era account holders of their money.

Bergier found that in May 1954 the big Swiss banks "coordinated their response to heirs so that the banks would have at their disposal a concerted mechanism for deflecting any kind of inquiry. They agreed not to provide further information on transactions dating back more than ten years under any circumstances, and to refer to the statutory obligation to keep files for only ten years, even if their records would have allowed them to provide the information." Moreover, Bergier bitingly reported that the Swiss banks not only adopted a "common procedure" to comply with German requests to hand over the assets of German and Austrian Jews to the Nazi treasury but also handed over the accounts of Polish Jews, sometimes over the objection of their own legal staff (as in the case of SBC) and even when the Reichsbank said they were not required to do so. Judge Korman called me immediately after he got a copy of the Bergier report and faxed me the key findings. We shared our mutual revulsion. "Devastating," he described them. To Judge Korman, Bergier's findings explained much of the Swiss banks' failure to assist account owners in identifying their assets. There was the factor of greed: Under Swiss law unclaimed accounts became the property of the banks. But they were also afraid they would be held liable for transferring accounts to the Reichsbank.

The missing link was the public acceptance of the settlement by the Swiss government itself. An opportunity arose after Ruth Dreifuss became the nation's first female and first Jewish president in 1999. When I learned that Vice President Al Gore was going to Davos, Switzerland, to participate in the World Economic Forum that January, I decided this seemed the right time to bring the Swiss government on board.

I had two preparatory meetings with President Dreifuss, a pleasant, round-faced, bespectacled woman of fifty-nine. She told me it was important to her to provide closure because she is a Jew and because she is a woman. "You were viewed by all participants as a fair arbitrator in a difficult situation," she told me, but she explained that Switzerland had been shocked by two things: first, class actions, which are "new in Europe," and second, the novel concept of "rough justice." She also surprised me by saying that "your useful help is seen in Switzerland with a question." Had I intervened as a government official or because of my private interests? Was I acting in a double role? I assured her everything I did came from my governmental responsibilities.

She told me that after her meeting with Vice President Gore she would make a statement only in her own name to Swiss television but that "the Federal Council knows what I'll say." I found it remarkable, even by Swiss standards, that the Federal Council still could not bring itself to endorse the settlement a year and a half later and had left the task to one lone, politically courageous person.

The Swiss public saw Vice President Gore's meeting with President Dreifuss as the equivalent of a peace agreement. There was a crush of press and cameras in the small lobby of the Moratani Hotel. I saw the occasion as the culmination of three and a half years of work. I took great satisfaction that it was ending on a positive note. President Dreifuss said with conviction that Switzerland had a "commitment to address our history in World War II." Although the threat to relations between Bern and Washington had been removed, the process would make the Swiss more aware of the problem of racism, she said.

Despite the settlement and the seemingly happy ending, few of the prominent figures in this drama came away with their careers much enhanced, and no victors emerged.

Christoph Meili, the courageous Swiss bank guard who reported the shredding of documents, is bitter, even with his $1 million settlement. He calls his lawyer Ed Fagan a crook for allegedly promising to take his case without a fee and then later making him sign a 25 percent contingency agreement to get the money. He believes that Jewish groups also used him to their advantage and treated him like a welfare case. To cap his indignity, he was arrested in Orange County, California, on September 22, 2001, for alleged abuse of his wife, Giuseppina. She bailed him out of jail, dropped the charges, and filed for divorce.

Fame has also been unkind to Ed Fagan. An unflattering front-page article in the *New York Times* indicated that he was under disciplinary investigation for mistreating clients. He admitted he was so swamped by inquiries from Holocaust survivors that he could not pursue his other business. "I've never in my life seen a piece like that on such an insignificant person," he told me. "Now who am *I*? I'm a lawyer."

Thomas Borer, head of the Swiss Holocaust task force, became the Swiss ambassador to Germany, but in April 2002 was recalled because of a publicized affair with a German beautician, Djamile Rowe. This came after his wife, the former Texas beauty queen, was photographed sitting in the lap of a rock star at a German discotheque. After his diplomatic career went up in flames, Rowe admitted that she had lied about the affair. Borer is now a Berlin-based business consultant.

Alan Hevesi, whose threats of sanctions did so much to bring the Swiss banks to their knees, finished fourth in the 2001 Democratic primary for mayor of New York City.

Al D'Amato's tactic of cultivating an ethnic image to attract New York's multicultural electorate eventually backfired. During the senatorial race of 1998 he dismissed his opponent, Representative Charles Schumer, as a "putzhead." D'Amato's use of this vulgar Yiddish-American epithet contributed to his defeat. Jewish voters deserted him en masse for Schumer, forgetting or simply ignoring D'Amato's seminal Senate hearings that brought the Swiss banks to public attention and his victory lap on the steps of the Brooklyn federal courthouse. A final indignity to D'Amato was a sarcastic postelection letter "congratulating" him on his "miserably failed reelection" from David Vogelsanger, who had been political affairs and press officer at the Swiss Embassy in Washington and had just been transferred to diplomatic oblivion in Bulgaria for other diplomatic indiscretions connected to the Swiss bank affair.

Saddest of all were the victims who waited so long to find their families' Swiss bank accounts and assets. There have been over 32,000 claims filed, and many families will finally recover. The average award for the first 250 families has been over $93,000. But for many others the passage of time and the destruction of records has erased evidence and hope. The remarkable woman who started it all, Greta Beer, eventually received $510 from the Humanitarian Fund, established by the Swiss Bankers Association during the early years of the bank crisis. She believes the banks destroyed records of the large account holders, including those of Siegfried Deligdisch, her father. The truth will never be known. Greta lives alone in subsidized housing in a Boston suburb, increasingly haunted by her father's account. She obtained small vindication early in 2001 when the Swiss banks published more than 20,000 wartime account holders following completion of the Volcker Committee's audits, including one for Bernhard Deligdisch, her late uncle and her father's business associate. But this will be of no direct benefit to her, only to Bernhard's heirs.

It is still too early to determine what the long-term impact will be on Switzerland of the Volcker bank audits, my Nazi gold report, the Swiss's own remarkably honest and self-critical Bergier report, and the class-action negotiations. Certainly the Swiss public has been bombarded with a whole new set of facts about the conduct of their government and their banks during and after World War II. The Bergier report went far beyond ours. It found multiple violations of Swiss neutrality by the acceptance of looted gold; the unregulated railway traffic, including Nazi war criminals in flight; the camouflaging of German business interests; and the use of some 11,000 forced laborers in Swiss-owned factories located in Nazi Germany. The Swiss Bank Corporation, whose merger with Union Bank of Switzerland was so controversial during our negotiations, was found to have violated its own country's laws by helping German firms trade in stolen securities. At the end of the war, Switzerland held far more German assets than U.S. negotiators realized, assets that remained to a large extent untouched, thanks to the obdurate and stalling Swiss negotiators. Millions were returned to their German owners, the Bergier report confirmed, rather than to the Allies, as promised in its 1946 agreement with the United States, and the banks "obstructed the return of securities from Jews and inhabitants of occupied countries."

The Swiss people's mythology about their role as the fearless wartime neutral has been challenged. Yet myths die hard. There is no doubt the Swiss people were virulently anti-Nazi during the war. There was virtually no public sympathy for Hitler. The Swiss were not responsible for the Holocaust. Their refugee policy was hardly worse than the United States', under far less duress. And they felt justly proud of preserving their democracy and their independence, when few in Europe enjoyed either. But their elites, in business and government, played a far more complicated game.

The confrontational nature of the Swiss bank affair will complicate the ability of average Swiss citizens to absorb the new realities thrust upon them and to learn from them. The effort to bring to account the bankers and other leaders of a past generation too often morphed, in the Swiss public's eyes, into an unfair attack on the country as a whole. Domestic hostility toward the United States and toward the World Jewish Congress and World Jewish Restitution Organization has still not fully abated. Hans Bär, the Swiss Jewish banker who played such an important role in trying to control the hurricane, thinks that the Swiss believe their banks were "ransomed in the United States." But at the same time he sadly concludes, "The Swiss do not seem to want to be reminded of the past; Switzerland still has a lot of anti-Semitism." Christoph Blocher, the right-wing billionaire populist, used the affair, along with other popular disenchantments, to make his People's Party the second most powerful in the Swiss Parliament.

Still, there are some signs that the whole affair has begun to have some salutary impact in Switzerland, particularly by helping to end the Swiss's splendid isolation, which left them so unprepared to deal with their bank crisis. To help repair the tainted reputation of their banks, the Swiss have now become active leaders in international anti-money-laundering efforts; they have been freezing secret accounts of dictators like the Nigerian strongman Sani Abacha and cooperating with the Bush administration's efforts to block assets of terrorists. In a 2002 referendum, the Swiss people narrowly approved their country's membership in the United Nations.

But the Swiss establishment has still not fully absorbed the hard lessons of what the country has gone through. The Swiss government to this day has distanced itself from the settlement. Switzerland's renowned newspaper, *Neue Zürcher Zeitung*, offered little help in educating public opinion. Its powerful editor, Hugo Bütler, strongly opposed the settlement and urged the banks to stand firm throughout my negotiations.

Ruth Dreifuss, who had the gumption to stand alone with Al Gore to finally embrace the settlement during her one-year term as Swiss president, wrote me a letter out of the blue on March 28, 2002, in her capacity as Swiss federal councillor for home affairs. She asked me to correct what she considered an erroneous statement I had made more than two years earlier to the House Banking Committee, shortly after her meeting with Vice President Gore. I had told Congress that Dreifuss—one of a long line of Swiss officials beginning with President Arnold Koller in March 1997—had assured us that the Swiss government remained committed to creating a massive Solidarity Foundation from the sale of $5 billion of its gold reserves in order to support a variety of worthy causes, from famine, drought, and natural disaster relief to genocide prevention, including Holocaust-related programs. She now wrote to tell me that this was not accurate and that "the Swiss Government did *not* anticipate that the future solidarity foundation would be used for payments to former victims of the Holocaust." She was "keen to clarify this point."

More recently, in the spring of 2002, the Swiss government froze military and other government contracts with Israel, in protest against the Israeli government's policies toward the Palestinians. The Swiss minister of the economy, Pascal Couchepin, told the Israeli ambassador to Switzerland, Igal Antebi, that, having been embarrassed by what had been done to them during the Swiss bank affair, it was now Switzerland's time to respond.

Swiss president Kasper Villeger followed up with a public statement in July 2002, saying that it would not be possible to make payments from the "Foundation for Solidarity"—proposed by his predecessor, Arnold Koller, in March 1997—to Holocaust victims or Jewish groups. This was meant to clear the political decks of lingering resentment from the Swiss bank affair and secure public approval of the foundation—now explicitly stripped of any Holocaust payments—in a fall 2002 national referendum. Villeger's spokesperson said, "The firm promises from former President Koller are no longer valid." The backsliding did no good. The Swiss public voted down the Solidarity Foundation. Wonders never cease with the Swiss.

# CHAPTER NINE

# The Barbarians of Culture

THE LOOTING of artworks is as old as war; the Roman plunder of the Temple of Jerusalem in 70 A.D., depicted in the Arch of Titus in Rome, was typical of warfare in the ancient world. Few visitors to the Louvre know that the cream of its Italian collection, including the Mona Lisa, was brought to France by Napoleon. Still fewer know that hundreds of paintings stolen from wealthy French Jews by the Nazis made their way to France's great national collections and remained there for decades.

But like the Holocaust itself, the efficiency, brutality, and scale of the Nazi art theft was unprecedented in history. Experts have estimated that as many as 600,000 paintings were stolen, of which more than 100,000 are still missing fifty years after the war. When furniture, china, rare books, coins, and items of the decorative arts are included, the numbers swell into the millions. There was nothing casual about this massive plunder of art. It was supervised by the Einsatzstab Reichsleiter Rosenberg (ERR), headed by Alfred Rosenberg, who in his spare time administered the Eastern European concentration camps.

One of the Holocaust's greatest ironies is that its most malevolent perpetrators fancied themselves a new cultural elite. What kind of mental gymnastics made it possible to combine a refined taste for art and a barbarian's lust for the blood of innocents? Hitler, an indifferent painter during his early years in Vienna, viewed the amassing of art as a necessary project in his creation of an Aryan master race. The cultural centerpiece of his Thousand Year Reich was to be the Führermuseum in his birthplace, Linz, Austria. Throughout the war, first Hans Posse, and then Hermann Voss,

Hitler's art curators, sent him photographs of the looted work from which some 8,000 pieces were prepared for the Linz collection. Hitler's taste was for the old masters; most modern works had long been rejected by the Nazis as "degenerate art" and disposed of through Switzerland, where some Swiss art dealers and banks made a killing on sales and commissions.

Hermann Göring, Hitler's right-hand man, had an even greater appetite for art and by the end of the war had filled each of his eight spacious residences with works stolen or purchased at prices discounted under duress. Otto Abetz, the German ambassador to France and a principal force behind the looting, reserved twenty-one paintings for his house and offices, including works by Braque, Degas, and Monet. Other Nazi art collectors included SS chief Heinrich Himmler, propaganda minister Joseph Goebbels, foreign minister Joachim von Ribbentrop, and Hitler's personal assistant, Martin Bormann. In France alone, more than 1 million cubic meters of personal belongings of Jewish families were sent to German families, including 8,000 pianos.

In the Soviet Union, the Nazis engaged in mass destruction of the cultural patrimony of people they regarded as *untermenschen* (subhumans). The Soviet prosecutor at Nuremberg accused the German invaders of destroying 427 of the 992 museums that fell into their hands. This wanton destruction would not go unavenged, as the Soviets in their turn systematically plundered huge amounts of Nazi art and historic German treasures, from masterpieces once owned by Jews to Heinrich Schliemann's golden discoveries at the site of ancient Troy in the nineteenth century. Stalin planned to exhibit these trophies at a supermuseum in Moscow, a plan bearing a chilling similarity to the Führermuseum, and also never carried out. Most of this booty remained hidden from the world for half a century. The looting on both sides continues to haunt the art world to this day.

During the war the Allies were not oblivious to what was going on. On January 5, 1943, they issued the London Declaration, calling on neutral nations not to trade in art looted by the Nazis. U.S. Army commanders agreed to include curators and other art historians in the conquering armies as "Monuments, Fine Arts, and Archives" officers. They provided an extraordinary service in preserving Europe's cultural heritage during the final days of the war. As the Allied armies crossed the German border, these "Monuments Men," as they were called, found a wealth of looted art and cultural objects that they dispatched to collecting points to be cataloged and eventually returned to their owners. President Truman ordered the looted objects to be repatriated by the military as quickly as possible, but the occupying armies had many more pressing tasks than locating the original owners or their heirs. Following international legal precedent, the U.S. and British commands returned the objects to their countries of origin and relied on each government to trace the owners and ultimately return the stolen property.

This reliance was often misplaced. For example, France collected more than 60,000 stolen objects, and during the four years following the end of the war, 45,000 of these were returned to their owners. But in 1949 the French dissolved the commission that performed this work, and of the remaining 15,000 pieces, 2,000 were placed in French museums, and 13,000 considered to be "heirless" were sold at auction.

The Soviet government refused to allow the Western Allies access to the territory they controlled to provide an account of the enormous seizure of art by the Red Army. The issue soon dropped from sight, as archives needed to trace stolen property were buried in Soviet repositories.

The wall of silence on art was breached mainly by four scholars I met during my work on art recovery:

- Jonathan Petropoulos, a Harvard graduate student who realized that there had been no scholarly treatment of art looting during World War II. His 1990 doctoral dissertation, *Art as Politics in the Third Reich*, was published in 1996.

- Lynn Nicholas, who was working at the National Gallery of Art in Washington as personal assistant to the director, J. Carter Brown, when she read the obituary of Rose Valland, the wartime curator of the Louvre. Valland had courageously spied for the Allies to keep track of the loot, copying the rubber stamps the Nazis put on their packages and figuring out the German numerical codes—all of which greatly facilitated the postwar recovery of stolen art. The account of Valland's work inspired Nicholas to begin research on her own award-winning 1994 book, *The Rape of Europa*, which describes the Nazis' massive looting of art.

- Konstantine Akinsha, whose 1995 book, *Beautiful Loot: The Soviet Plunder of Europe's Art Treasures*, documented the Red Army's "trophy art," taken from the Germans under the Soviet military administration of Germany and spirited away to the Soviet Union.

• Hector Feliciano, an American journalist based in Paris who documented in his polemical 1997 book, *The Lost Museum: The Nazi Conspiracy to Steal the World's Greatest Works of Art*, the 2,000 art objects that had been held since the early 1950s by French museums that had made little effort to find their owners.

The contributions of these four depended upon declassifying Allied war documents and accessing Eastern European government archives after the Cold War ended. At about the same time, the World Jewish Congress launched the Commission for Art Recovery in 1998 under the leadership of an experienced professional in tracing stolen art, Constance Lowenthal. An art historian, she specialized in art stolen or fraudulently taken from its owners, was a former executive director of the International Foundation for Art Research, and wrote a popular column for the *Wall Street Journal* called "Art Crime Update."

In January 1995 Professor Elizabeth Simpson of the Bard Graduate Center for Studies in the Decorative Arts organized a conference in New York on "The Spoils of War" that for the first time brought together German, American, and Russian experts on looted art. Given that the Russian delegation insisted that their "trophy art" was legitimate compensation for Russia's horrific wartime losses, the very fact that Irina Antonova, the director of Moscow's Pushkin Museum, would even attend the conference was an act of courage. She received a standing ovation.

The books by these four scholars and the Bard Conference were important milestones, but the issue had not yet come to the attention of governments and the general public. I used the London Conference on Nazi Gold, in December 1997, to stage a brief closing seminar on art, initially over the objections of our host government, the British, who wanted the conference focused strictly on looted Nazi gold.

At London, we needed an expert to introduce the topic. Hector Feliciano was our controversial choice. The French were upset at this selection because of his exposé on their country's looted art. But Feliciano made a powerful appeal for increased access to art archives in France, Russia, and elsewhere in Europe. He accused art dealers on both sides of the Atlantic of neglect or worse in documenting the ownership of the art transferred during the war. However discomfiting to his audience, his speech marked the first time these points had been publicly made before an international gathering of senior officials. It had its intended effect. Even the French delegation gave a surprisingly candid account of the number of objects seized by the Nazis, sold publicly during the war, and distributed to French museums.

At the end of the London conference, I announced a second conference, to be held in Washington, in which art and cultural property would be the chief focus. I had already obtained the approval of Miles Lerman, chair of the U.S. Holocaust Memorial Museum, for the museum to be the conference's cosponsor.

I got my first hint that the Russians might be serious about restoring looted art to its proper owners in March 1998, when a mutual friend, Willy Nagel, arranged a meeting for me in London with Yuri Fokine, the Russian ambassador to Britain. Fokine said that the Russians would indicate at the Washington conference their willingness to open their archives. This was the first crack in the walls they had built around their trophy art.

An utterly unexpected event soon put the question of looted art before the public in a most dramatic way and tested the normally cozy ties among museums and dealers in the international art world. The test case centered on *Portrait of Wally* and *Dead City III*, two paintings by the Austrian artist Egon Schiele on loan from Austria's Leopold Foundation to New York's Museum of Modern Art (MOMA) for a special exhibition. Acting on a complaint by two families claiming that the paintings had been stolen from their relatives by the Nazis, Robert Morgenthau, the Manhattan district attorney, subpoenaed the paintings in January 1998. Morgenthau is the son of Henry Morgenthau, the secretary of the treasury whose wartime appeal to save European Jews from annihilation finally moved Roosevelt.

But the legal issues that Robert Morgenthau confronted were far more tortuous than those his father faced, involving a complex ownership history and a formal loan agreement from the Austrians to MOMA. The New York Court of Appeals refused to uphold Morgenthau's subpoenas, basing its ruling on a New York law prohibiting the seizure of any work of fine art while on display in a New York museum by a nonresident exhibitor, here the Leopold Foundation of Austria. This law was designed to foster the free exchange of art for public display. It seemed the paintings were free to be returned to Austria, until the U.S. attorney's office argued that the paintings were subject to forfeiture under the National Stolen Property Act. *Dead City III* was returned when a U.S. court found insufficient evidence that it was stolen. But the more famous painting, *Portrait of Wally*, remains contested in federal court five years after Morgenthau's initial action.

The seizure of the Schiele paintings put American museums in a frightening dilemma. This was the first time that a civil claim for a painting seized by the Nazis had turned into a criminal case. Museum directors did not want to turn a blind eye to looted art, but if American prosecutors were ready to intervene in private disputes over ownership, it would become impossible for U.S. museums to borrow art for display from other countries. Ultimately, legitimate claims would also become more difficult to pursue because fear of seizure would drive looted paintings even deeper underground.

Although I had questions about Morgenthau's tactics and later the U.S. attorney's, I was reluctant to get involved. My senior position at the State Department, which I began in the summer of 1997, made it important that I not alienate Austria, and the politics of a case involving a Holocaust family made it particularly unattractive for me to oppose their claim. I already had my hands full with other Holocaust problems, but it was not easy to stay on the sidelines, because the Austrian government let me know how upset it was about Morgenthau's case. Austrian authorities told me they were willing to submit the issue of the Schiele paintings' ownership to an independent tribunal. Still, I felt the best posture was to let the case play itself out.

Meanwhile Philippe de Montebello, the longtime director of the Metropolitan Museum of Art in New York, was thrust into this unprecedented controversy by the House Banking Committee, chaired by Representative James Leach of Iowa, which held hearings on Holocaust assets in February 1998. Debonair, French born and educated, with a patrician bearing, de Montebello recalled as a child "keeping one step ahead of the Gestapo and the Vichy government, with a father who was serving in the Resistance." De Montebello took pains to distinguish between art museums that display their works in public and the Swiss banks, "which recently have been shown to have hoarded for half a century the spoils of war and genocide." Pressed by Chairman Leach, he promised that the Association of Art Museum Directors (AAMD) would present guidelines within four months for addressing the problem of looted artworks.

About 170 American art museums belong to the AAMD. Questions about looted Holocaust-era art had first arisen at the association's semiannual meeting of the previous June, as a reaction to the Feliciano and Nicholas books and press accounts of several families' claims against American museums accused of unknowingly displaying stolen art. When the issue formally came up on the next meeting's agenda, in January 1998, the Schiele heirs were in full cry, and the Washington conference was less than a year away. The AAMD created a Task Force on the Spoliation of Art During the Nazi/World War II Era (1933–45), with de Montebello as chair and the country's most powerful museum directors as members.

It was clear that the Washington conference would be no tea party. The Russians, despite my London meeting with Ambassador Fokine, had not made any move to open their archives, and we feared they would boycott it. I needed a full-time senior official to take charge of planning the conference, and I was fortunate that J. D. Bindenagel, who had served as number 2 in the U.S. embassy in Bonn, was between assignments. He worked on the Washington conference for an entire year, and much of its success resulted from his skill.

On June 9, 1998, my State Department team and I convened a day-long roundtable at the Holocaust Museum to reach a consensus among American art experts on goals for the Washington conference, to be held in November. Among the thirty people present were officials of the AAMD, lawyers, art historians who specialize in retrieving lost or looted art, and representatives of the Art Dealers Association. We emerged with the principal objective of internationalizing the guidelines that de Montebello presented to the AAMD on June 4. His task force had recommended that American art museums immediately start researching their collections for looted works; publish information in a centralized and publicly accessible database to assist war victims and their heirs; seek all possible information about the history of the ownership—"provenance" in the art world—of any work before acquiring it; refuse any works showing evidence of unlawful confiscation; seek warranties from sellers of valid title free of claims; and finally, resolve by mediation any claims against pieces in a museum's collection "in an equitable, appropriate, and mutually agreeable manner."

But organizing an international consensus based upon the AAMD principles proved much more difficult. In particular, the Netherlands, Germany, England, and France refused to endorse them, resenting the notion that

American principles should be imposed upon their museums. Bindenagel and I proceeded nevertheless to hold an organizing seminar for the Washington conference at the end of June. This was an unusual step. But we felt that the subject of art restitution was so new to most countries that, for the conference to have any chance of success in November, we needed to present what we knew about Nazi-looted art and give the contentious issues sure to arise a preliminary airing. We also wanted to build confidence among the Russians, who feared the conference would turn into an effort to divest them of their trophy art, and among the Germans, who feared it would lead to yet another excuse for more Holocaust reparations.

Earl "Rusty" Powell, director of the National Gallery in Washington, D.C., gave a compelling presentation of the AAMD guidelines, making a deeper impression than if the summary had come from the U.S. government. Ronald Lauder, then chair of New York's MOMA and formerly U.S. ambassador to Austria during part of the Waldheim era, reported that according to secret U.S. government documents, the Nazis had stolen one-quarter of Europe's total wartime stock of art and that only about half had been returned to their owners or their heirs, with the rest in museums or private collections. Michael Kurtz of the U.S. National Archives, presenting a history of looted art, cited military archives revealing that a staggering 50 million artworks of all kinds were placed in 1,400 repositories in the U.S. occupation zone of Germany and ultimately returned to the country of origin.

Although these presentations helped the delegations focus on the dimensions of the problem, we could not avoid contention. David Gross of the European Jewish Congress stressed the huge amounts of looted art in Russia. The Greek delegation demanded that art confiscated by the Nazis from the thriving Jewish community of Salonika and then seized by the Red Army be returned to the small surviving Jewish community in that city. Sybil Milton of the U.S. Holocaust Museum shocked everyone with the disclosure that 55,000 works of art created in concentration camps had never been found.

But it was the Russian delegation, whose attendance was in doubt until the last minute, that we were most anxious to hear. To my great relief the Russians supported the idea of the Washington conference. But they said restitution was a delicate and complicated matter, lacking either an international or Russian legal basis. What they next said seemed to confirm the worst German fears about the conference: They wanted the Germans to provide new compensation for Russian citizens for their suffering at Nazi hands. I then had to reassure the Germans this would not be a topic for the Washington conference.

The seminar proved important in raising the long-suppressed issue of looted art, promoting the new AAMD guidelines as a possible basis for international agreement, and engaging the Russians in a discussion. But when Bindenagel went to Europe for follow-up consultations, the Europeans still would not sign onto the AAMD guidelines. So our planning team repackaged them by drafting ten principles that looked new and different but kept the AAMD's essential points, as well as a paper outlining best practices in dealing with art looted by the Nazis. These proposals were distributed to all delegations a few weeks before the conference; they were neither immediately accepted nor summarily rejected.

I believed that if we could persuade one country to take the lead, others might be shamed into taking action. Austria seemed like a good candidate. Because of its tainted past dating from its willing incorporation into the German Reich in 1938, Austria could make a useful symbol, if Vienna was willing to step forward. Moreover, Austria would hold the rotating presidency of the European Union during the second half of 1998, and whatever it did would receive special attention. I had to travel to Vienna to plan the regular summit between the United States and the EU, so I added art restitution to my agenda.

I was encouraged by Paul Grosz, head of the small Austrian Jewish community, but he stressed the need for a low-key approach to avoid an anti-Semitic backlash: "We don't want a Swiss situation in Austria, as Austrians and as Jews." The key was Elisabeth Gehrer, a tall, imposing woman, who as minister of education and culture had jurisdiction over Austria's glorious state museums. She immediately took command of our meeting. She made clear she wanted the Schiele dispute resolved and realized that a defensive attitude would not help. Citing an Austrian government report just completed on art confiscated during the Nazi era, she declared that Austria wanted to be "big and generous," but because the art objects belonged to the state, a new law would have to be passed to allow their return to any owners who could be found. Art with no living heirs would remain in public museums, but objects that had not been returned to victims or heirs, for what she delicately called "technical reasons," would now be identified and restituted.

When I left the meeting, I was elated. If the Austrians passed their new art law, it could serve as a model for the Washington conference. Our State Department team also received an encouraging sign from France in early November, when the Foreign Ministry published a catalog of 333 stolen paintings and posted it on the Internet in an attempt to locate the works' original owners.

Early in the morning of November 30, the opening day of the Washington conference, I met with Bindenagel, Bennett Freeman of my staff, and Judge Abner Mikva, whom we had picked as conference chair because of his reputation for judicial fairness and political integrity as a former member of Congress and retired federal judge. The Austrian Parliament had approved the new art law that same day, so we were cautiously optimistic. During the four days of the conference we would hold plenary sessions and smaller breakout sessions on Nazi-confiscated art; Holocaust-era insurance claims; communal property restitution; archives, books, and the role of historical commissions; and Holocaust education, remembrance, and research. Few of these topics had ever merited international attention before. And the opening ceremony had special meaning for me, as it was held in the U.S. Holocaust Memorial Museum, the very building I helped initiate with a simple memorandum to President Carter more than twenty years earlier.

I was deeply moved by Elie Wiesel's opening speech urging us not to lose sight of "conscience, morality, and memory" as we focused on restitution. But no contribution to the start of the working sessions at the State Department the next morning was more important than Secretary Madeleine Albright's keynote address. Surprisingly, she turned to her own story in a way she had not done in public before. She referred to the "long list of names on the wall of the Pinkas Synagogue in Prague, among them those of my grandparents, Olga and Arnost Korbel and Ruzene Speiglova." Then she continued: "I think of the blood that is in my family veins. Does it matter what kind of blood it is? It shouldn't; it is just blood that does its job. But it mattered to Hitler, and that matters to us all; because that is why six million Jews died. We must never allow these distinctions to obscure the common humanity that binds us all as people."

It was just at that time that Secretary Albright was also trying to prod President Clinton into military action to stop the murder of Kosovar Albanians in the Balkans and move the United States' NATO allies from their passivity. I know from our conversations that her own experiences during World War II, some of which she shared in her keynote speech, were powerful factors in bringing her to what I believe was her finest hour, persuading President Clinton to intervene in Kosovo.

The conference concentrated on each type of stolen asset, including communal property. But how it dealt with looted art would be the measure of the conference's success. I had asked Representative James Leach to chair the art sessions and to help persuade the delegates to adopt the draft principles. The opening presentations at the conference were made by Jonathan Petropoulos, Konstantine Akinsha, and Lynn Nicholas, who described the Nazi thefts as "the greatest displacement of works of art in history."

At the art session the emotional highlight was a presentation by Colonel Seymour Pomerenze, one of the few surviving Monuments Men, who directed the depot at Offenbach in a former warehouse of I. G. Farben (the manufacturer of the gas used in the extermination camps). He recalled his first impression of the "sea of crates and books. . . . I thought, what a horrible mess! What could I do with all these materials?" The contents ranged from European fine art to books from Yeshivas obliterated in Poland. He cited a diary entry by a fellow officer, Captain Isaac Bencowitz, expressing his feelings about the boxes of looted books: "There was something sad and mournful about these volumes, . . . as if they were whispering a tale of yearning and hope since obliterated." If this did not move the delegates, little else could.

We finally got the response we hoped for as Austria, the Netherlands, Germany, the Czech Republic, Switzerland, Sweden, Greece, and Hungary described the efforts underway to catalog confiscated art in their state museums. The Dutch reported that they had identified four thousand works in their state collections that they now were anxious to return to their rightful owners. The Austrians made a similarly impressive presentation. Thrown on the defensive by the open debate, the Russians described legislation that reaffirmed their right to keep trophy art from Germany as compensation for war losses but would permit an eighteen-month claims period for individuals or religious institutions whose art was stolen by the Nazis for racial or political reasons. Valeriy Kulishov, chief of the Office of Restitution in Russia's Ministry of Culture, reminded the delegates of the 20 million Soviet civilians, including 2 million Soviet Jews, who perished in the war. He also made the frank admission that during the Cold War an "atmosphere of secrecy . . . surrounded and still surrounds the repositories of Russian museums where so-called 'trophy art' is kept." Kulishov promised the conference that Russia would support the draft principles and "do all we can to find art pieces and return them to the countries where they were looted."

Despite intense lobbying by my team and I, including Representative Leach, substantial opposition to adopting the AAMD-based principles remained in France, Germany, Italy, and Switzerland, as Bindenagel found when he polled the delegations beginning at 7:00 A.M. on December 3, the last day of the conference. I tried to negotiate a last-minute compromise with the heads of the French, German, and Swiss delegations, because I knew that the conference would be judged a failure if we could not even agree to a set of general principles on how to address the issue of looted art. The Europeans were especially upset at one of Congressman Leach's recommendations, that each country should enact national legislation to implement the principles. They worried that the proposed principles would override their judicial processes, which differed from Anglo-Saxon law. In sum, they still did not want the appearance of American principles being imposed on them.

With the closing session only a few hours away, it was too late to rewrite each principle to suit every country. So, to give the key countries political cover, I made one last attempt and suggested what in diplomatic terms is called a chapeau—literally, a hat. Under my proposal a new introductory paragraph to our principles would now state that the Washington conference recognized that countries with different legal systems could "act within the context of their own laws." That did it. The European negotiators indicated they could accept this. We could keep the principles intact, but they would not be binding. As we went to the closing plenary session, I did not dare put the principles to a formal vote of all forty-four countries. So Judge Mikva and I devised another diplomatic device. Mikva, as conference chair, declared them adopted by consensus. No nation objected.

I was elated by what we achieved: important moral authority in five areas. First, the principles called on museums, governments, commercial galleries, and auction houses to cooperate in tracing looted art through more stringent research into the provenance of every item. Second, given the difficulty of producing evidence of ownership, the art community was asked to permit leeway in accepting claims on stolen art during the Hitler era. Third, there would be an international effort to publish information about provenance. Fourth, a system of conflict resolution would be established to prevent art claims from turning into protracted legal battles. Fifth—and least definite—attempts would be made to find a fair solution when owners of looted works could not be found.

Since none of these principles was legally binding, one may legitimately ask whether anything had really changed. What the conference did was provide international attention and legitimacy to the return of looted Nazi art. Once the imprimatur of the forty-four countries including the United States—the world's largest single art market—was placed on what became known as the Washington Principles, art recovery could no longer be ignored. We effectively internationalized the AAMD principles. "The art world will never be the same," Philippe de Montebello whispered to me as the conference closed. To the conference itself, he was equally direct: "On the issue of the spoliation of art in the World War II/Nazi era, the genie is, at last, out of the bottle, and no resistance, apathy, or silence can ever fit it back inside again."

The Washington Principles changed the way the art world did business. Every home owner is familiar with the procedure of tracing title to a house back to its first owner to ensure no claim is likely to arise. The art world did not operate that way. Buyers simply relied on sellers' assurances. As Lynn Nicholas explained to me, dealing in art is highly secretive because executors of estates usually do not want sales known and investors often buy art to avoid taxes. "And they also sell it," she said, "in a roundabout way without wanting to be identified. It's never been titled in any formal way. Part of the fun for collectors is the mystery and the intrigue. It's always been that kind of business—international, uncontrolled, secretive."

But in the years since the conference, as de Montebello later pointed out to me, "this has changed drastically; the whole psychology has changed. Art dealers, galleries, museums now check the ownership of paintings from Europe to determine if there are gaps from the World War II era which might indicate the painting had been confiscated. And if so, they are posting the information on Web sites." Jonathan Petropoulos said that, although the work he and other scholars had done provided the "kindling wood," the Washington Principles provided the "sparks that set off the remarkable conflagration" about Nazi-looted art.

One early sign of this impact came at my closing press briefing at the Washington conference. Unexpectedly, the Russians asked if they could participate and present documentation indicating that several paintings in their possession had been traced to Holocaust victims. In dramatic fashion Victor Petrakov of the Department for Protection of Cultural Objects gave me the documents at the news conference and pledged support for the Washington Principles.

Major American museums now take the AAMD and Washington Principles seriously, spending money and allocating staff to research provenance to detect whether paintings have been looted. In 1999 the International Council of Museums called on its members to follow the Washington Principles. Austria has reviewed the collections of all federal museums and returned more than 250 artworks to the Rothschild family and more than 2000 to others. In December 1999 the German Ministry of Culture issued a statement signed by all German museums entitled "On the Tracing and Return of Nazi-Confiscated Art, Especially from Jewish Property," promising that the German government would exert its influence to return confiscated art to former owners or their heirs. The provenance of all museum collections is being examined, and suspect works are posted on the Internet at Germany's Lost Art Database. The Germans have also broadened their definition of looted art, and claimants no longer have to prove that sales were forced.

Sweden established a commission to locate art as well as other assets brought into the country before and during World War II, placed newspaper advertisements, and asked the country's Jewish leaders for information about the community's losses. France is completing research into the provenance of more than 2,000 works returned from Germany after the war. Italy has published a catalog of art treasures lost during the war, including those from the collections of Holocaust victims.

I recommended that President Clinton create an advisory commission on Holocaust assets to study looted assets that made their way to the United States. The commission was chaired by Edgar Bronfman. The art subcommittee, on which I sat, headed by William Singer of Chicago, heard the directors of several great museums detail their efforts to identify and return Nazi-looted art. De Montebello reported that after the Washington conference his museum had found Nazi-era gaps in the ownership records of 393 of its 2,700 European paintings. Although this does not mean that all 393 paintings were looted, it indicates the increased care taken by American museums. At the National Gallery, Frans Synder's *Still Life with Fruit and Game,* donated in 1990 by a New York art dealer who was a Jewish refugee from Nazi Germany, was discovered by the museum's researcher to have been confiscated from Edgar Stern, a prominent French Jewish art collector. It was returned to his heirs at the end of 2000.

Three months after the Washington conference, Lawrence Wheeler, director of the North Carolina Museum of Art, received a letter from Constance Lowenthal claiming that one of the prizes of its modest collection, *Madonna and Child in a Landscape* by Lucas Cranach the Elder, was not the museum's rightful property. It had been donated by Marianne Khuner of Beverly Hills, California, in 1964. Lowenthal's research showed the painting had been part of the collection of Philippe Von Gomperz, a Viennese Jewish industrialist arrested by the Gestapo in Prague after the German invasion. He was forced to sign over his property to the Nazis in exchange for safe passage to Switzerland for himself and his sister. The Cranach painting, subsequently sold to the Nazi governor of Vienna, eventually found its way into Khuner's collection. Wheeler and his chief curator, John Coffey, stressed the painting's centrality to their collection. More to the point, Coffey told me, "There is no way we'd ever be able to afford a Cranach of that quality."

Less than a year after receiving Lowenthal's letter, Wheeler was able to confirm that the Cranach Madonna had indeed been stolen from Von Gomperz. The proof was a photograph of the painting in the archives of Vienna's Kunsthistorisches Museum, giving its provenance and showing it to be one of those taken to Hitler for review in 1943. On that evidence, the North Carolina museum returned the painting to Von Gomperz's heirs—two grandnieces, Marianne and Cornelia Hainisch—who had it appraised by Sotheby's at a value up to $1.2 million.

The museum wrote to the sisters that it could not afford to match the auction house's estimate but offered all the money it had—about $600,000, half Sotheby's top estimate. The museum promised to tell the painting's story in the gallery and pointed out that, if the Cranach disappeared into a private collection or even was sold to another museum, the painting would lose any real contact with Phillip Von Gomperz. Members of the North Carolina Jewish community who were patrons of the museum were also mobilized to write the Hainisch sisters, telling them how much it mattered to them to have care of the painting, given its history. The sisters, retired schoolteachers in their eighties living in Vienna, were moved by the appeals but also somewhat perplexed. Much to the surprise of all concerned, they were not Jewish, an earlier generation of the family having converted to Christianity.

The Hainisch sisters appreciated the museum's pledge and sold back the painting for the proffered $600,000. Their gracious letter of acceptance was, Coffey said, "one of the great moments of my career." The painting remains in the museum's collection, accompanied by its Nazi-era history for public enlightenment, and will be part of a traveling exhibition on Nazi art pillage.

Elaine Rosenberg is the daughter-in-law of Paul Rosenberg, a leading prewar Parisian art dealer who escaped to New York in 1940. She has made it her life's work to recoup the stock of Impressionist and post-Impressionist paintings her father-in-law was unable to save from the Nazis, who stored them at the Jeu de Paume museum. Paul Rosenberg successfully moved some works to the United States at the height of the German U-boat attacks. Others, which were being taken by the Nazis to Germany by train as the tide of battle turned, were liberated en route by a Free French Army unit commanded by none other than Paul's son Alexandre, Elaine's husband.

Two years after the promulgation of the Washington Principles, Elaine told me in her Manhattan office how they had helped her obtain the cooperation of museum officials. Museums now consult her research into the provenance of paintings. Her tireless work has been rewarded by the return of a 1904 Monet from his water-lily series that had made its way through the French museum system to Caen, and a 1928 Matisse odalisque that had been innocently donated to the Seattle Art Museum by wealthy American collectors. The return of the Matisse was little short of miraculous.

Elaine's daughter, Elizabeth, on vacation in the Catskills, had found in her copy of Hector Feliciano's book, *The Lost Museum,* a photograph of her grandfather Paul's missing Matisse. A New York photographer, Bing Wright, in the next cabin, flipped through it and exclaimed, "I know that painting; my grandparents had it on their wall." It turned out that Prentice and Virginia Bloedel, Wright's grandparents, had purchased it from the Knoeller Gallery in New York City, which in turn had bought it from the Jeu de Paume gallery; in 1991 the Bloedels had donated it to the Seattle Art Museum. Elaine and Elizabeth contacted the museum and claimed the odalisque, which had a number on its back, 5795, the very number Paul Rosenberg's gallery gave it when he bought the painting in 1928. The museum returned the painting to Elaine Rosenberg the following year.

The Washington Principles have also helped people like Willi Korte, an American art researcher, and Washington lawyer Tom Kline, both professionals in the recovery of stolen art, particularly in Europe. Korte recalled that even as late as the 1990s, "if you had gone to any European museum and said, "This is my grandfather's painting which was taken from his home before he fled or before he was deported, they would have laughed you out of town. You wouldn't have had any particular legal recourse." He cited the case of Max Silverberg, a German Jewish industrialist and a passionate collector of Impressionists. His collection was seized by the Nazis, and fifty works were sold in a 1935 auction in Berlin, eventually finding their way to private individuals and museums in Germany. When his family reclaimed the collection, the German government argued that the paintings had not been stolen but sold. This impasse continued until the adoption of the Washington Principles. Within months, the National Gallery in Berlin decided to return a Van Gogh drawing without any major litigation. It was later sold at auction for $8.5 million and is currently in New York's MOMA. Paintings in Switzerland and even a Pissarro from the Israel Museum in Jerusalem were found to be looted and returned to their owners. The Washington Principles made possible what was for more than fifty years out of reach.

. . .

LIKE MOST stories from real life, many of those concerning Nazi-looted art do not have Hollywood endings. Most of the looted art will never be returned—not because the European or American museums lack the will to implement the Washington Principles but because the owners and heirs were killed by the Nazis. Most will remain in French, German, and Austrian museums because no one is left to claim them. Major private collections do not feel bound by the Washington Principles.

The issue of heirless Nazi-looted art is particularly difficult and one we did not directly address through the Washington Principles. At the Vilnius International Forum on Holocaust-Era Looted Cultural Assets, in Lithuania in October 2000, Colette Avital, Israel's consul general in New York, insisted that her country was the only legitimate heir of what was once Jewish property. I found myself caught once again in a crossfire of claims between local Jews, national governments, the World Jewish Restitution Organization, and the state of Israel. Israeli representatives framed the

CHAPTER TEN

## Remembering
## Dora-Mittelbau

I N 1943, when the Nazis first envisioned the V-2 missile as a weapon to win the war by terrorizing the civilian population of London, they needed to site the missile's production facilities underground, safe from Allied bombing. The factories were built into dome-shaped hills adjacent to the town of Nordhausen, near Hanover in central Germany. Thousands of slave laborers were transferred from the Buchenwald concentration camp nearby to tunnels already dug by I. G. Farben to store oil, at a site called Dora-Mittelbau. They dug the tunnels in twelve-hour shifts, seven days a week, boring holes in rock for the placement of dynamite and carrying off debris by hand. Forced to live in these tunnels, they never saw sunlight and slept on clumps of straw in wooden bunks four tiers high. Their sleep was interrupted by explosions that poured clouds of dust and showers of stone over them. There was no drinking water, sanitary facilities, fresh air, or ventilation.

Dora-Mittelbau quickly became a living grave: dysentery, typhus, and tuberculosis took a heavy toll. Twice a day the bodies of the dead were removed, their tattooed numbers listed by the camp's statistics office, and heaped in a wire enclosure until wagons came to take them out. It was estimated that, each day, 1 percent of the workers died and were replaced by other slave laborers. The SS general at the camp, SS-Brigadenführer Hans Kammler, turned aside comments about the beastly conditions with this remark: "Never mind the human victims. The work must proceed and be finished in the shortest possible time."

In the autumn of 1999 Germany's chancellor, Gerhard Schröder, who had been in office less than a year, visited the tunnels of Dora-Mittelbau. He viewed the cages in which the workers had been kept and heard survivors describe their hideous conditions. He was accompanied by an aged and ailing Dutchman who had survived because his job had been to count the dead. Schröder and his wife, Doris, supported the man from either side as they walked the tunnels. Although Schröder had been to several concentration camps during his public career and had heard the names of child victims read out at the candlelit Holocaust memorial at Yad Vashem in Jerusalem, it was this visit to Dora-Mittelbau, so close to the capital of his home state of Lower Saxony, that gave him a sense of the reality of tyranny. The visit, he told me, "was like a kick in the head."

Following his September 1998 election, Schröder's "Red-Green" coalition of Social Democrats and Greens had pledged in its governing agreement to provide justice for slave and forced laborers, an issue no postwar chancellor had been willing to confront because of its political sensitivity. But Schröder's visit to Dora-Mittelbau encouraged him to act on his government's promise.

.     .     .

DURING World War II Nazi Germany forcibly employed about 10 million people. Some were deported from their countries following German occupation to be laborers in German industry and agriculture. Others were forcibly relocated within their own countries to work for German firms in occupied territories. This massive draft of labor, unprecedented in scope and purpose, freed up working-age German men to fight while keeping the economy running. It enabled Germany, with a wartime population of 79 million (including Austria and the Sudetenland), to induct a staggering total of 17 million men into its armed forces. This was over 40 percent of its entire male population, even taking into account children and the elderly.

There were two types of involuntary laborers. Those we came to call slave laborers had been confined in concentration camps and ghettos, like those moved from Buchenwald to the Dora-Mittelbau pit. They were worked to death, and the Nazis saw this as simply another form of extermination. Slightly more than half the slave laborers were Jewish, the rest mostly Poles and Russians.

Forced laborers, almost exclusively non-Jewish workers from Eastern

Europe, worked in everything from armaments factories to German farms and even in the postal service. Their living conditions were harsh but better than those of slave laborers because they were considered assets of the state. They were often paid minimal salaries and lived with their families in lightly guarded camps.

Both slave and forced workers toiled for private German industry, for government enterprises like the railway, and for a vast network of SS-controlled companies, like Hermann Göring Werke, headed by Paul Pleiger, Göring's friend, which became a huge industrial complex in mining and machinery.

One of the most chilling documents I have ever seen was a memorandum estimating the profits the SS made on slave laborers. Reckoning that the average slave laborer survived for nine months, the SS calculated that it made a profit of 1,431 reichsmarks on each worker. To this was added what the SS called "the proceeds from the rational utilization of cadavers: gold from teeth, clothing, valuables and cash." Total profits from each laborer were therefore set at "1,631 marks, plus proceeds from utilization of bones and ashes."

None of these laborers had ever been compensated for their coerced work through any of the postwar programs negotiated by the German government, the Israeli government, and the Claims Conference, the New York-based group through which pension and other payments went to Jewish Holocaust survivors. In the fifty-plus years since the war's end, the German government had paid more than 100 billion deutsche marks (DM) to Jewish and some non-Jewish victims of Nazi persecution, for their general loss of liberty and damage to their health. But they explicitly excluded payments for slave and forced labor, which they believed to be reparations under international law. In a 1953 agreement such claims had been deferred until "the final settlement of the problem of reparation"—which never occurred. Moreover, millions of non-Jewish forced workers, trapped for two generations behind the Iron Curtain, had never received any compensation whatever from Germany, deepening their resentment against an increasingly prosperous Germany and fanning anti-Semitic feelings—nowhere more than in Poland, which lost some 1.9 million non-Jewish citizens to Nazi tyranny, as well as 85 percent of its 3.25 million Polish Jews.

Public discussion in Germany about compensating these laborers had been going on since the early 1980s, and it had been part of the platform of the small Green Party for most of that time. A subcommittee of the Bundestag, Germany's parliament, examined it in 1989. But Chancellor Helmut Kohl, who supported health and pension programs for Jewish Holocaust survivors and property restitution in the former East Germany after reunification, steadfastly refused to open up German industry and government to the claims of non-Jewish workers in Eastern Europe. He argued that Eastern European agricultural workers had helped with the German harvest for generations so their employment at low wages during wartime was nothing unusual. He also felt that Germany itself had never been compensated for the 500,000 German soldiers who had been deported after World War II to forced labor camps in the Soviet Union, about half of whom died, or for the 12 million to 14 million German civilians expelled between 1944 and 1947 from their homes in formerly German territories in Poland, Czechoslovakia, and parts of Russia, some 2 million of whom died of cold or disease or at the hands of Soviet soldiers.

In the early 1990s, after the fall of the Berlin Wall, as a reward for the countries' support of German reunification, Germany paid 1.5 billion marks to new reconciliation foundations in Belarus, the Czech Republic, Poland, Russia, and Ukraine, which in turn made payments through humanitarian organizations to those of their citizens who had been victimized by the Nazis. Some of the money, however, was siphoned into overseas bank accounts by former Communist officials, leaving the Eastern Europeans unrequited and the Germans with a negative view of the whole exercise. In any case, the amounts were tiny when compared to the 100 billion DM ($60 billion) that Germany had paid largely to Jewish Holocaust survivors over the previous forty years.

By the mid-1990s, approximately 250,000 former slave laborers were still alive. There was no hard count of the number of surviving forced laborers, but there were thought to be more than 1 million. What was indisputable was that most of those left alive were in their seventies and eighties and were dying at a rate of approximately 1 percent per month.

As my State Department team and I were working on the Swiss bank negotiations, many of the same American class-action lawyers—Mel Weiss, Michael Hausfeld, Robert Swift, Ed Fagan—saw an irresistibly vulnerable new target: German companies that had benefited from slave and forced labor and profited from the theft of Jewish property. On March 4, 1998, Weiss and Hausfeld filed a class-action suit, on behalf of Jewish and non-

Jewish victims, in federal court in Newark, New Jersey, against the Ford Motor Company and its German subsidiary Ford Werke for their use of slave and forced labor from Belgium, Italy, Russia, and Ukraine to make trucks for the German Army. In June Fagan and Swift sued Deutsche Bank and Dresdner Bank for profiting from Jewish property stolen and "Aryanized" by the Nazis, for dealing in victim gold, and for financing the construction of Auschwitz. Other lawyers soon piled on, eventually bringing some fifty cases in federal and state courts from New York to California against more than a dozen German companies that now were doing business in the United States, among them such manufacturing giants as Volkswagen, Thyssen-Krupp, Siemens, BASF, and Bayer; the insurance conglomerate Allianz; and the two banks, Deutsche and Dresdner.

The suits could not have come at a worse time for these firms, since many had recently invested heavily in the American market. Daimler-Benz took over Chrysler in May 1998, and Deutsche Bank was in the process of acquiring Bankers Trust, the eighth largest bank in the United States. Volkswagen was about to introduce its new Beetle to the American market, where it had been a symbol of cheap and unfettered transport for baby boomers in the 1960s. Allianz, which was in danger of losing its California business license, was the parent company of Fireman's Fund, which employed about 4,000 people in California, including some 2,500 at its headquarters in Novato. The last thing the German companies needed now was a plastering in the American media similar to what the Swiss banks had received.

The Germans had another reason to be upset. Many of the companies believed that they had already fulfilled their obligations. I would later be repeatedly reminded by representatives of the German firms that in 1959 Krupp had reached an agreement with the Claims Conference, brokered by U.S. high commissioner for Germany John J. McCloy, to pay 5,000 marks to each of its 4,000 surviving Jewish slave laborers in exchange for a waiver from each worker of any future claims. The Claims Conference had also agreed to refuse assistance to slave labor claimants, help defend Krupp against additional claims, and even indemnify Krupp for any further payments they were required to make.

Krupp was not the only German company to enter into such an agreement. Between 1958 and 1966, six others, including I. G. Farben, Daimler-Benz, and Siemens paid more than 75 million marks to the Claims Conference, which made pledges similar to those it gave to Krupp. Much later Volkswagen (VW) reached an agreement with the Claims Conference to fund social projects for survivors in Ukraine, Israel, and Poland. In September 1998, after the filing of the lawsuits, VW created a compensation fund of 20 million marks to pay 10,000 marks per person to 20,000 workers it exploited during the war. Siemens announced a fund of 25 million marks for the same purpose. None of these measures stopped the class-action lawyers from filing billion-dollar claims, nor did they prevent the Claims Conference from ignoring its earlier commitments and trying to exact more from these and other companies.

In August 1998 representatives of twelve major companies met at the offices of the Federation of German Industries to develop a strategy that would avoid a fiasco comparable to what happened to the Swiss banks. Two of the leading officials who attended were Manfred Gentz, chief financial officer of DaimlerChrysler, and Michael Janssen, executive vice president of Degussa, the company that smelted victim gold into bars for the Reichsbank. Although their lawyers—Roger Witten and Robert Kimmit from Wilmer, Cutler, & Pickering (the same law firm that had represented the Swiss banks)—assured them that the cases were without merit and could be won in the U.S. courts, Gentz, Janssen, and their colleagues quickly realized that these cases were unique among class actions because of the German connection to the Holocaust and the emotions this aroused in the American Jewish community. They knew that though they might win in U.S. courts, they could lose in the court of public opinion in the largest marketplace in the world. They wanted to dispose of the cases as quickly and cheaply as possible to remove a cloud from their ability to do business in the United States—but without admitting legal liability, without any continuing oversight by U.S. courts, and without fear they could be sued in the future.

The companies also had a sense of moral responsibility, like many of the Germans born during or after the war. Many of Germany's actions have sprung from their desire to demonstrate to themselves as much as the world at large that they have learned the bitter lessons of the Hitler era and deserve to be treated as a normal nation again. In postwar Germany, Holocaust denial is a criminal offense, and Germany's payment of massive benefits to individual Holocaust victims was without precedent in the annals of war.

Gentz, tall and slender, taut, with angular features and silver-white hair that belied his relative youth, was born in Berlin in 1943, at the height of the war. His father, a Nazi Party member, was assigned to the Ministry of Inter-

A synagogue in Chelm, Poland, which was converted by the Nazis into a granary during World War II. In the 1990s I worked to restore synagogues and other communal property to the Jewish communities of Eastern Europe.

Sacks of looted Nazi gold discovered at the end of the war by American troops in the Merkers Salt Mine. The Germans used looted gold from victims and occupied nations to purchase the raw materials from neutral nations that supported their war effort, employing the Swiss National Bank to convert it into hard currency.

The infamous "J" stamp proposed by the Swiss government to the Third Reich to identify and block entry of Jewish refugees fleeing from Nazi Germany.

The family of Greta Deligdisch Beer, second from left, whose story about dormant Holocaust-era Swiss bank accounts first vaulted the issue to the attention of American politicians and the world. Greta's father, Siegfried Deligdisch, established a Swiss bank account to protect his assets from the Nazis, but after the war the Swiss banks made it almost impossible for Greta and thousands like her to find their families' accounts.

Hans Bär, head of the Swiss Jewish family-owned Bank Julius Bär. He played a constructive role in helping to handle the crisis, understanding the perspective of both sides.

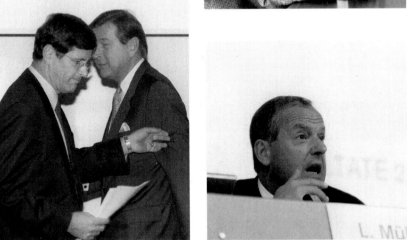

Mathis Cabiallavetta (Union Bank of Switzerland), Marcel Ospel (Swiss Bank Corporation), and Lukas Muehlemann (Credit Suisse) were caught between competing pressures from American class action lawyers and Jewish organizations, and an angry Swiss public and distant Swiss government.

Ambassador Thomas Borer, the young diplomat appointed by the Swiss government to head a task force to handle the Swiss bank controversy, testifying before the U.S. Congress in December 1996, as I am looking on. While Borer was an effective representative for his government, he ultimately became a lightning rod for the anger of American politicians and Jewish organizations.

Christoph Meili, the young bank guard at the Zurich headquarters of the Union Bank of Switzerland, who found World War II bank documents about to be shredded, and became a famous international whistleblower by going public. For his courageous act, he lost his job and became a pariah in his own country.

At the London Conference on Nazi Gold in December 1997, I met with British Foreign Minister Robin Cook and Edgar Bronfman, president of the World Jewish Congress. Bronfman, the billionaire head of Seagrams, was the driving force in exposing the Swiss banks' misconduct during and after World War II.

Michael Hausfeld, an experienced class-action lawyer, organized a competing team of attorneys to the Fagan-Swift group. Mild-mannered in appearance, he was a ferocious and difficult advocate, but knew in the end when to cut a deal.

Edward Fagan, left, the most controversial American class-action lawyer, with Robert Swift and Michael Witti, members of the team he assembled for the Swiss, German, and Austrian negotiations. Fagan signed up the most victims for lawsuits, but his publicity stunts often stirred up animosity among the other parties.

Alfonse D'Amato, the colorful and controversial U.S. Senator from New York, announced the settlement of the Swiss bank negotiations on the steps of the federal courthouse in Brooklyn in August 1998. D'Amato's congressional hearings shined a critical spotlight on the Swiss banks' behavior, but he had played only a last-minute role in the class-action negotiations.

Alan Hevesi, Comptroller of the City of New York, controlled billions of dollars of municipal pension funds, and organized hundreds of state and local financial officers across the United States to threaten sanctions against the Swiss banks if they did not settle the class-action suits against them.

Judge Edward Korman of the U.S. District Court for the Eastern District of New York. Korman's direct intervention helped settle the Swiss bank cases and completed the negotiations I had begun.

General Dwight D. Eisenhower in May 1945 inspecting looted art treasures, hidden by the Nazis in a salt mine, along with General Omar N. Bradley and Lieutenant General George S. Patton, Jr.

Adolf Hitler in his Berlin bunker, examining the model of the Führer-museum for the best of the looted art taken by the SS, to be built in his hometown of Linz, Austria.

Forced laborers at underground Dora-Mittelbau facility building the V2 rocket to terrorize England. The Third Reich used some 10 million slave and forced laborers, Jewish and non-Jewish, from the nations they conquered to support the German economy and free their industrial and agricultural workers to fight on the war front.

One of a series of full-page newspaper advertisements that appeared in October 1999, organized by class-action lawyer Mel Weiss and sponsored by a number of Jewish organizations, to put pressure on German companies to pay billions of dollars to settle the suits against them. Other ads specifically took on Bayer, Daimler-Benz, and Ford.

At the White House on December 15, 1999, President Bill Clinton announces the 10 billion DM settlement I had brokered to cover all claims against German companies arising out of World War II.

German Chancellor Gerhard Schröder (center) and Count Otto Lambsdorff, Germany's chief government negotiator, joined me in Berlin on December 17, 1999, to celebrate the announcement of the German settlement. Looking on are members of the negotiating teams, including (far right) Manfred Gentz, chief financial officer of DaimlerChrysler and top representative of German industry; (far left) John Kornblum, the U.S. Ambassador to Germany. Little did we know that another seven months of tough negotiations still lay ahead.

A rare picture of unity at final signing ceremony on July 17, 1999, in Berlin. Among the people shown are Burt Neuborne (second from left), who was the bridge between the conflicting legal camps; John Kornblum (fourth from left), the U.S. Ambassador to Germany; myself (fifth from left); Otto Lambsdorff (sixth from left); Mel Weiss (center, with beard); Manfred Gentz of DaimlerChrysler (fifth from right), German industry's tough chief negotiator; Israel Singer of the World Jewish Congress (fourth from right); and J. D. Bindenagel (far right), head of the State Department's Office of Holocaust Issues.

The celebration in Vienna on October 24, 2000, of a 6 billion schilling agreement covering 150,000 surviving slave and forced laborers from Eastern Europe. With me are Maria Schaumayer, the special Austrian negotiator, and Austrian Chancellor Wolfgang Schuessel.

The roundup of foreign-born French Jews on May 14, 1941, by French police on the streets of Paris. On that date some 5,000 Jews between the ages of eighteen and forty were deported to internment camps in France, many of whom were sent to their deaths at Auschwitz.

Holocaust survivor Kurt Ladner signs the final settlement agreement on property claims with Austria at the State Department in Washington on January 17, 2001, as Gideon Taylor, the head of the Claims Conference, Israel Singer, and I look on.

nal Affairs. In the last months of the war he joined the German Army. Captured by the Russians, he was sent to the Soviet Union and died in a labor camp. Gentz's mother raised three sons, and they all discussed the Nazi crimes "very openly, very frankly," in terms of Germany's moral responsibility for the terrible wrongs committed. While pursuing his legal studies, Gentz visited Israel. He came to understand "the historical and moral responsibility of all Germans" for the war's crimes and even the war itself. And he shared his views with his wife and children, later taking them on trips to Israel, as well.

In 1986 Daimler-Benz voluntarily published a history of the firm during the Nazi period, including the fact that it was the first German company to use forced labor. Gentz, who was in charge of the project, brought survivors to the company's headquarters in Stuttgart to tell their stories. Instead of compensating the former forced laborers directly, Gentz preferred to help all survivors by supporting hospitals, psychiatric institutions, the Red Cross, and institutions in Eastern Europe, where the great majority lived. Daimler raised 30 million marks for this purpose and also erected a memorial to its forced laborers in front of the company's museum.

Michael Janssen, the other key member of the German firms' negotiating team, was also born during the war and, like many German professionals of his age, later studied in the United States. He did graduate work at Georgetown Law School under a professor who had fled Nazi Germany, then spent eighteen years in the German Foreign Service before joining Degussa. His interest in the surviving laborers grew out of his experiences during the Gulf War. Degussa legally exported vacuum pumps to Iraq during the 1980s. They could have been used to enrich uranium in Iraq's nuclear program, which Janssen realized could imperil Israel, where Degussa also had customers. As a sign of solidarity, Janssen and Degussa's CEO went to Israel during the height of the Gulf War. Both were evacuated from their hotel during a Scud missile attack. On his return, Janssen initiated a review of Degussa's export policy toward Iraq, developing internal regulations that were more restrictive than German law.

In 1996 he commissioned the American historian Peter Hayes, who had written a history of I. G. Farben, to look into Degussa's role in the Nazi war machine. With full access to the company's files, Hayes readily discovered that in its Frankfurt plant, Degussa had smelted gold from the teeth of Holocaust victims on the order of the Reichsbank. Janssen initially could not believe that the company's management knew the source of the gold. But he told me he heard from a former female employee that packages from the Reichsbank were clearly labeled as having originated in ghettos and extermination camps. In extant letters, Degussa employees asked when the next deliveries would be coming from these locations.

Janssen asked himself why this self-examination had not occurred until half a century after the horrible events. His explanation to me: "The generation of managers after the war was more or less the same as during the war. For them to look back would be looking back at their own failures and mistakes. The second generation after the war came into power through the first generation. They were still in very close contact with them. The third or fourth generation of managers felt much freer, they were farther away from what happened."

These new leaders of the German economy wanted to make a public demonstration of their sense of responsibility, improve the survivors' twilight years, help prevent the rise of totalitarian movements, and most important, put the issue behind them once and for all. They did not want to be sued for what they thought had been closed by the postwar agreements with the Claims Conference. They called their goal "legal peace."

At their August meeting, Gentz suggested as an alternative to the court cases that a German foundation be established, funded in equal parts to pay claims and to have a forward-looking component that would support projects on tolerance, combat anti-Semitism, and teach the lessons of the Holocaust. The claims money would not go simply to the remaining thousands of surviving workers of the dozen or so German companies being sued in American courts but to *all* surviving wartime workers for German firms, defunct or not. Gentz envisioned all of German industry contributing, even companies created after the war. This would eventually involve sums far larger than the officers of the companies themselves ever imagined.

But they knew they would need their own government's help and the United States' to ensure that their companies would not be harassed by an American legal system with rules far different than their own. As they saw it, the German firms were being subjected to a civil version of the Nuremberg war crimes trials, and they had no desire to negotiate with class-action lawyers whom they loathed for dragging them into court and who would insist on legal fees at the expense of victims. But when they asked Chancellor Kohl to help, he refused. It was slightly more than a month before the national elections, and the issue was too hot for him to handle. All that changed, however, after Kohl was voted out of office on September 28, 1998, and Schröder's Social Democrat–Green coalition succeeded him, with the mandate to pay compensation to these exploited laborers.

Even before being sworn in as chancellor, Schröder invited the CEOs of the defendant companies to a meeting in Hanover to discuss the pending suits. They poured out their fears. The auto companies were worried about consumer boycotts, the insurance companies feared that state insurance commissioners would restrict their operations, Deutsche Bank that its merger with Bankers Trust would be scuttled by New York authorities in the same way the Swiss UBS-SBC merger had almost been stopped. Siemens was planning a major expansion in the United States. All envisioned sustained controversy and negative publicity. Klaus Liesen of Volkswagen, on whose board Schröder had served, told the chancellor-elect of threats to publicize a picture of the company's founder with Adolf Hitler admiring the prototype Beetle in the 1930s. Schröder reassured the business barons that he would work with them and share both costs and problems. They all knew that the key to success was to engage the U.S. government. With some naïveté, born partly of hope, partly of fear, they believed the U.S. government could solve their problem by entering into an executive agreement with the German government to cut off all pending and future lawsuits and funnel all labor claims to a new German foundation.

Germany clearly was not Switzerland. Most important, the new generation of Germans did not hold a lofty, self-righteous view of themselves. Many had already made deeply personal efforts to understand and come to terms with their country's past, and a younger generation was now guiding the nation's destiny. Also unlike the Swiss, the postwar governments of the Federal Republic of Germany had tried to ensure that the nation made amends for the "unspeakable crimes"—in the historic phrase of its first chancellor, Konrad Adenauer—that had been committed in its name. Finally, even when politics prevented Kohl's Christian Democratic Party from responding to new issues like those of the conscripted workers, other parties were open to discussion and negotiation. All this meant that, when I became involved as the U.S. government's point man, I found sympathetic interlocutors on the German side.

I received my first feeler from the German government in September 1998, before the German elections, in the form of a written message from

Hans Von Ploetz, a senior official in the Foreign Ministry. I knew him from my days in Brussels, when he had been Germany's ambassador to NATO. Von Ploetz told me that the Germans were "grateful for your sobering and moderating role" in the preparation of the Washington conference on looted art and now hoped that a similar attitude would prevail in dealing with the class-action suits against the German companies. He stressed that if the suits led to threats of sanctions it would risk a backlash, "given the way Germany has handled the Holocaust issues over the years." He was clearly testing the waters to see if I would be interested in getting involved.

I was not the only U.S. government official engaged. Following Schröder's election, the U.S. ambassador to Germany, John Kornblum, found a receptive ear from the new chancellor. Kornblum had devoted a major part of his distinguished diplomatic career to strengthening the alliance between Washington and Bonn. He had served as the German desk officer at the State Department in the 1960s, and after the fall of Communism, he had worked with Israel Singer, the Claims Conference, and the German government to make Holocaust survivors in East Germany eligible for the same health and pension payments that had been available to survivors in West Germany. Shortly before Schröder's inauguration as chancellor, he and Kornblum discussed German industry's emerging problem on a flight to Washington for a meeting with President Bill Clinton. Kornblum told Schröder any plan needed a dynamic element, "a bridge to the future" that would live long after the survivors themselves had died. Schröder liked the idea, and it squared with the concept that Gentz independently had discussed with his colleagues in industry.

What emerged from Gentz's and Kornblum's suggestions was an idea for two funds of equal amounts. One, designated "Remembrance and Responsibility," would make payments to survivors. A separate "Future Fund" would be a permanent endowment, the income from which would support projects to promote understanding and social justice and to keep alive the memory of the threat posed by totalitarianism. There could also be funds for care of the elderly, health services, scholarships, and programs for victims' heirs. The Germans' goal was to persuade the U.S. government to accept this two-fund idea as an appropriate discharge of the German firms' responsibility and to help them obtain legal peace from class-action lawsuits in U.S. courts.

It was also my goal to give the German private firms legal peace from future suits, but only if they paid a fair price to those they had injured so grievously five decades earlier. To accomplish this dual goal, I was determined to avoid the problems that had bedeviled the Swiss negotiations and required a federal judge to complete the agreement I had come so close to reaching. This time I was going to organize the negotiations. If the U.S. government was again to get directly involved in helping resolve private lawsuits, I was determined that the responsible foreign government, not just private companies, would have to be directly involved and directly engaged through a senior official who would be my counterpart. I would not deal only with warring private parties on both sides, as in the Swiss cases. I was also determined from the outset, as I had finally achieved in the Swiss negotiations, to have the class-action lawyers and the Claims Conference form a cohesive negotiating unit. They had to trust me to work out the best deal possible; I could not have them running behind my back to a judge. And last, the Germans had to be committed to stay the course and not simply put down their final offer and walk away, as the Swiss banks had done.

I got my first wish, a credible German government counterpart. The new government's point man was Bodo Hombach, Schröder's chief of staff and an experienced politician who had been his campaign manager. Especially relevant, he had chaired the German-Israeli Association, long worked with Israel, and was close friends of prominent Israelis. My first encounter with this giant of a man was on December 14, 1998, when he and Ambassador Kornblum visited me at my State Department office. At six feet three inches in height and more than 250 pounds, Hombach could have been a defensive end in the National Football League. I joked to myself that, if this negotiation were to descend to arm wrestling, I would be a sure loser with my slender six-foot frame.

But I quickly found that whatever intimidation his girth created was dispelled by his mirth. He had a ready smile, a largeness of spirit to match his physical size, and the warmth and buoyancy of a natural politician, who bantered easily with his defeated opponent, Helmut Kohl, an even heftier man of over three hundred pounds. "I told him no, Mr. Chancellor, I don't have the same weight, I am thirty kilos [about sixty pounds] less than you." Kohl, who used to have eating contests with the voracious Bill Clinton, challenged Hombach to a lunch; Bodo laughed, he told me, and backed down.

Hombach emphasized that Germany wanted not only to settle the slave labor claims but all the other claims against German companies, including those against the banks and insurance companies, who were accused of profiting from the confiscation of Jewish assets and paying only a fraction of the life insurance policies they had written. A satisfactory settlement depended on their deep pockets. Rolf Breuer, the powerful chairman of Deutsche Bank, which held shares in many of Germany's biggest corporations, had been the prime CEO mover behind the German foundation proposed by Gentz, so his bank and other financial institutions could hardly be excluded either.

Hombach officially asked me to work with the German government and industry to resolve the class-action suits, and I readily agreed, so long as the class-action lawyers did, too. I realized this would be the last major negotiation with the Germans about World War II. Since I had become totally immersed in the Swiss negotiations, involving a small neutral nation, it was clear from the outset that, as a top State Department official, I could do no less to help Germany, a NATO ally responsible for a third of the GDP of Western Europe, resolve its legal dilemma. I did not even seek White House clearance. Secretary of State Albright supported me, and that was enough.

I recognized from the start that, because of postwar Germany's willingness to face its past, the talks would be very different from those with the Swiss. But I never imagined the emotions these negotiations would raise, nor their complexity and bitterness. The German settlement would turn out to be five times larger than the Swiss, include eight governments, and involve countless trips across the Atlantic.

Here I was dealing with the legal successors of Nazi Germany itself. The lawsuits opened deep wounds still unhealed five decades after World War II, and unleashed long-suppressed emotions. The former Communist nations of Eastern Europe felt passionately that the suffering of their citizens had never been adequately recognized or compensated, whereas Germany had paid billions to the Jews. It was as if the entire Swiss episode had merely set the scene for this German one. And the lawsuits led to a novel legal approach by the U.S. government, one not employed on the Swiss settlement, to help resolve lawsuits brought by private individuals against private German companies.

Throughout the difficult months to follow, German companies wanted it both ways: insisting they were making a purely moral gesture for which they had no legal liability, while persistently demanding ironclad protection against future lawsuits; trying to cover a narrow group of beneficiaries through their foundation, while insisting on the broadest legal protection against claims. These contradictions compromised the high moral impulses that guided the initial efforts of companies that had prospered like few others in the world during postwar decades. But their bottom line was not morality or historical accountability. Corporations are not social welfare institutions. They are responsible to their shareholders to achieve the highest possible rate of return. They wanted to dispose of the class-action suits as cheaply and expeditiously as they could, so they could have unfettered access to the American marketplace without the dark cloud of Nazi history hovering over them.

Otto von Bismarck, the chancellor who united the German states into one country in the nineteenth century, once remarked that the public should not witness either the making of sausages or laws. Certainly the same can be said of the German negotiations.

.    .    .

BODO HOMBACH envisioned a speedy negotiation between the German government and industry on one side and the U.S. government on the other, excluding the lawyers and the governments of Eastern Europe. I took precisely the opposite of this crimped view, recalling the political wisdom of Lyndon B. Johnson, the first president I served, as a junior member of his White House staff. Israel Singer had met Johnson in a confrontational setting, as an antiwar protester, but I drew a very different lesson from Johnson's preference to bring his political rivals inside his tent "pissing out" rather than outside his tent "pissing in." For me, his vulgar wisdom pointed to the profound truth that, in a negotiation, a lasting result is more likely to emerge by including everyone with a stake in the outcome rather than by freezing out people who may be left resentful. It is a way of neutralizing adversaries.

From the start, I tried to convince the Germans that to have an enduring agreement all stakeholders needed to be included—the class-action lawyers, Eastern European countries whose forced workers had never been paid, the state of Israel, and the Claims Conference, which represented the interests of the Jewish slave laborers. This made for a messy and more complex negotiation, and there would be times when the difficulties of balancing the competing interests made me question my own judgment. But in the end I knew it would lead to a more satisfying result.

The first issue that might have circumscribed the talks was deceptively simple. It involved the non-Jewish forced laborers and agricultural workers. Hombach, having visited Israel and won its government's support for the foundation, insisted to me that the foundation had to focus on "the singular notion of the Holocaust; this is where we have a particular historical obligation." Conceding that it might cause consternation among Germany's eastern neighbors to play down the plight of their non-Jewish forced laborers, he insisted their problem was simply a "wage differential" that was a consequence of war—far different from the plight of the slave laborers, who had been worked to death. Taking this to its logical conclusion, he refused to compensate those Eastern Europeans who had been dragooned to work on German farms. For generations, Hombach argued, Poles, Czechs, and others had come to Germany voluntarily to earn money bringing in the harvest. Even Ambassador Kornblum's Ukrainian grandfather had come to Germany to work the land, Hombach said, and Kornblum had told him that his grandfather ranked his time as a forced laborer during World War II among the "best times of my life, as I escaped Stalinist terror."

I cringed at Hombach's insensitivity but gradually began to understand if not accept his strong feelings, which he assured me reflected those of ordinary Germans. He cited the contrasting experience of Manfred Gentz's own father, one of the over 500,000 German soldiers deported after the war to the Soviet Union as forced laborers.

Yet if the negotiations were to succeed, I could not ignore the stream of Eastern European representatives, led by Polish officials, who came to me demanding a seat at the table for their forced industrial and agricultural workers. Jerzy Kozminski, the Polish ambassador to Washington, told me that more than 2 million Poles had been deported to work in Germany, one-quarter to one-half of whom survived the war. Half the deportees were Polish peasants taken from their farms to produce food for Germans instead of for their own families and people. Kozminski said they deserved to be treated the same as forced laborers in industry, though he conceded there could be higher payments for slave laborers—many of whom, he stressed, were non-Jewish Poles.

It was a hard sell to Hombach. The Poles' deep feelings against Germany were fully reciprocated by the Germans. Hombach argued that the huge German estates confiscated in Poland after the war could be used to pay the victims. But he finally came around because of arguments from geography and realpolitik. I warned him that warm relations with formerly Communist neighbors were in Germany's own long-term interest, especially if Poland and others, still resentful about their wartime treatment, were eventually to join the European Union. He also confided to me that Polish officials warned him that the German government was "fomenting anti-Semitism" by helping only the Jewish survivors. Hombach reluctantly concluded that there was no alternative to including the Eastern Europeans but warned that we "need to tiptoe carefully."

If Hombach was fearful of opening a Pandora's box of claims from Eastern Europe, he was downright disdainful of the class-action lawyers. Ed Fagan, up to his old tricks to raise public sympathy for higher payments and legal fees, was parading around Germany holding press conferences with Holocaust victims as props, denouncing Degussa as "badness personified," the German banks as "conspirators, collaborators, and money launderers," and the German government for failing to meet its obligation to victims. Hombach called this a "scorched earth policy," as he resisted meeting with Fagan and the other class-action lawyers. Nevertheless I told Hombach that, although the Claims Conference, the state of Israel, and the Eastern European governments could give Germany political peace, only the class-action lawyers held the keys to his other goal—legal peace in U.S. courts. My job was to find the formula that would convince the class-action lawyers to use those keys to settle their cases and simultaneously assure the Germans they would not be sued again in the future.

I realized that I would have to convince Chancellor Schröder in person of the Clinton administration's commitment to resolve the class-actions through inclusive, broad-based negotiations. I flew to Bonn and, accompanied by Ambassador Kornblum, met the chancellor in his spartan office on January 27, 1999. On the way there, I reflected on how different I felt than on my first crossing into Germany as a student back in the summer of 1963. On that trip, I was all too cognizant that only two decades earlier I would have been arrested and killed simply for being Jewish. Now I was a welcome guest at the German chancellery building, situated on carefully manicured grounds abutting the Rhine River, as a senior U.S. government official and guest of the country's highest elected leader.

Schröder is a broad-chested man standing about six feet tall, with thick, dark hair and sharp features. In his office was a photograph of his father in a Wehrmacht uniform, a reminder that World War II was not far away. Schröder conveys an air of certitude. He speaks no English, and we communicated through a translator. I came at a difficult political time for the chancellor. The left wing of his Social Democratic Party, led by his finance minister, Oscar Lafontaine, was balking at the spending cuts he was seeking to stem the tide of red in the government's budget. But he was completely engaged in our issue, and like most politicians who reach the top, he was able to wall off his other problems and focus on the matter before him. From this first meeting I felt he would use his political chips to achieve a fair settlement of the matters before us, and over the next eighteen months we would develop a relationship of confidence and trust.

Like Hombach, who joined us in our meeting, Schröder told me he wanted to exclude the class-action lawyers from the talks, leaving to German industry and our two governments alone, he argued, the task of settling current and future claims by U.S. citizens—conveniently ignoring the claims of those who lived in Eastern Europe and Israel. "You will need to force me physically into a meeting with them," Hombach added, referring to the lawyers. "I want to satisfy victims' claims, not lawyers' fees," Schröder said.

I once again explained why there was no choice but to deal with the lawyers. The U.S. government could not snap its fingers and make the lawsuits disappear. Without the consent of Congress, which would be next to impossible to achieve, the U.S. president had no constitutional power to enter into an executive agreement with the German chancellor to cut off access to U.S. courts by Holocaust claimants and require them to pursue these claims through a German foundation. Only the lawyers could seek to have the cases dismissed, if they were satisfied with the settlement. Moreover, without the Claims Conference, the Israeli government, and the Eastern European countries in the room, Germany would never get the political controversy behind it. The chancellor reluctantly agreed to my strategy of including all the stakeholders in our negotiations.

Hombach then, again, made a distinction between Jewish laborers whose work was designed to lead to their deaths and the non-Jewish workers from Eastern Europe, whose circumstances were far different. Schröder said, "It would cause enormous problems for Germany if you treat the others the same, some of whom were even given holidays." I could see that bringing in the Eastern Europeans' claims was going to be extremely difficult.

Afterward, in Hombach's spacious office, down the hall from the chancellor's, Hombach and I had our first meeting about money. Standing alone in front of his desk, he told me in confidence that German industry was thinking of a foundation of 1.7 billion marks (about $850 million) to settle the lawsuits and to fund future-oriented projects. "No one knows; don't tell anyone," he almost whispered.

Here I made a mistake. I nodded my head up and down, acknowledging my pledge of confidentiality. But Hombach took it as my agreement to settle for this amount, which I not only considered a pittance but knew the lawyers and Claims Conference would never accept as coming from all of German industry, banks, and insurance companies. It was only two-thirds of what three Swiss banks had paid for their legal exoneration and would have to be spread over a far greater number of claimants. It would have left them with only a few hundred dollars each. But I did not say this. It was not the last of our misunderstandings.

Even though the chancellor had given me a reluctant approval for a meeting between Hombach and the lawyers, it took several calls to get them together in my State Department conference room on February 8. With resignation, Hombach said he had been warned against the lawyers by the chancellor and the companies, who believed they were greedy and unreliable. He would see them only because he trusted me. But he wanted to "avoid the impression I am negotiating with the lawyers; this would go on for years and cost a lot of money." Never were truer words spoken.

Once the meeting began, though, Hombach was eloquent and compelling in describing the German companies' desire to establish a fund in a "fair and swift and expeditious" manner to avoid extended litigation involving elderly victims. He stressed there was "no parallel to the Swiss model," because Germany accepted its continuing moral responsibility, extending from the private companies to the state-owned enterprises, for those who had slipped through all the prior compensation programs. If German companies knew they could be protected from future lawsuits through an administrative process to pay victims quickly, the negotiations could gather momentum. The higher the degree of legal protection, the more the companies would be willing to contribute to the foundation. "No one," he warned the lawyers, "wants to pay twice."

At my urging, the lawyers were on their best behavior. Michael Hausfeld led off by agreeing to quick action. Grateful for this first opportunity to deal directly with the Germans, he promised, "we can meld your concept with ours." Mel Weiss was also conciliatory—at least by his standards—in acknowledging that Germany had come forward with the idea of a fund to compensate the victims. But he said that Hombach had to understand that these claims had lain dormant for fifty years, and only the pressure of litigation had gotten private industry's attention. A fund established and administered by the German government alone, he declared, was anathema and just as unacceptable as the Humanitarian Fund when proposed by the Swiss.

To Weiss, only continuing supervision by a U.S. judge could assure that the German foundation would operate properly. Yet this was precisely the type of class-action settlement the German companies told me from the outset they would never enter. They saw American court supervision of the German foundation as a breach of German sovereignty; an admission of legal guilt for actions for which they felt, at most, only a moral responsibility; and a precedent for subjecting them to liability in U.S. courts for other claims. Hombach reassured the lawyers that the foundation would not be under exclusive German control. Its board would be composed of persons of high repute from different countries, and the government would be flexible on its structure. "I am not a Prussian," he joked. "I am a Rhinelander," meaning he was flexible. Everyone burst out laughing and the meeting adjourned.

Then I turned to Eastern Europe, where pressure for inclusion in the talks was increasing. Ukrainian demonstrators at the German Embassy in Kiev demanded that some half million of their forced workers be given just compensation. Our embassies in Eastern Europe were reporting tensions over a spreading rumor that negotiations would include only the German government, German industry, the U.S. government, and American Jewish groups. This tension was conveyed to me when I met the Polish chancellery minister, Wieslaw Walendziak, who repeated the history of Poles being "exploited on farms" in wartime Germany. "My mother's father was starved to death," he said emotionally. He pointed out that only 1 percent of Germany's postwar reparations had been paid to Poles, even though they were second only to the Jews in the number persecuted. "I agree on a differentiation between Jews and forced laborers," he said, but this was precisely the kind of complex problem that had to be discussed in a negotiation including Poland.

When I called Hombach, he grumbled: "This is difficult to stomach, but I will follow your advice." I was helped in convincing Hombach to include the Poles and other Eastern Europeans by an unlikely source: Israel Singer, of the World Jewish Congress and Claims Conference. Here Singer was wearing his Claims Conference hat rather than the WJRO's, because all matters involving Germany were handled since the 1952 Luxembourg agreement by the Claims Conference. Singer recognized from the start that excluding the Eastern Europeans from our negotiations would fan anti-Semitism. At least he would find the post-Communist Poles more reasonable than their notoriously nationalist Roman Catholic cardinal, Jozef Glemp. Hombach told me that when he had explained to Glemp Germany's special obligation to Holocaust victims, the cardinal shrugged him off with the startling remark, "The Jews killed Jesus, and this has always been their fate."

Now I had accomplished my first major objective: For better or worse, everyone would be inside one tent. But it was hardly one happy big top.

.    .    .

I HAD URGED Hombach and Gentz in the strongest terms not to spring any surprises lest they undermine the confidence essential to a successful negotiation. Yet that is exactly what they did, to my great consternation. On February 16, without warning, Schröder and sixteen German business leaders announced a "German Initiative" to compensate wartime laborers through a new foundation called "Remembrance, Responsibility and the Future," initially financed by German companies. Schröder made it clear that a key purpose was to "counter lawsuits, particularly class-action suits, and to remove the bases of the campaign being led against German industry and our country."

However high-minded, the announcement provoked a furious reaction from the lawyers, who saw it as an effort to impose a settlement and cut them out. Weiss reverted to type, warning that he would again turn to New York City comptroller Alan Hevesi for sanctions, as he had done during the Swiss negotiations. His face red with rage at the unilateral announcement of the foundation, he bellowed, "We will not let the Germans shove something down the throats of the survivors."

I promised to do all I could to stop the Germans from moving ahead on their foundation without first submitting it to negotiations that included the lawyers. But I also asked the lawyers to avoid public attacks against the Germans and each other, as well as threats of sanctions. This was particularly timely because Deutsche Bank had just announced its intention to acquire Bankers Trust and bail out this venerable American institution from the consequences of its exposure when the Russian and other foreign markets collapsed in 1998. I could foresee a replay of the UBS-SBC merger during our Swiss negotiations, because Deutsche Bank's chairman Rolf Breuer had staked his reputation on the merger and was also a principal force behind the German Initiative. If the first was blocked, the second would be in mortal danger.

Just as Deutsche Bank was about to file its application to U.S. bank regulators, I received an unexpected call from Breuer himself that helped personalize the exposure felt by German business. With evident pain in his voice, Breuer told me that Deutsche Bank had commissioned a study of its own wartime activities by Professor Gerald Feldman of the University of California at Berkeley. To his astonishment, Breuer learned that the bank's branch in Silesia had financed the German construction companies that built Auschwitz and the I. G. Farben complex there, including the crematoria. If this was not bad enough, the bank's Berlin branch had been guilty of expropriating ("Aryanizing") Jewish property, auctioning it off, and transferring the proceeds to the Gestapo. It had also liquidated small accounts of its Jewish customers and added the money to the bank's profits. Although the amounts were marginal, Breuer said he had no intention of hiding the facts.

I told him I respected his willingness to delve into the past and publish the results and that this would not deter me from trying to ensure that the merger was considered by federal and state banking officials purely on its merits. His relief was audible in his voice. I quickly called Israel Singer of the World Jewish Congress, which, along with Mel Weiss, had been behind the threat of sanctions against the Swiss. This time Singer took the opposite tack because, as he said, "we are dead if they lose the merger." Singer realized that Deutsche Bank was central to any settlement, would help fund it, and through its cross-shareholdings in other large German companies, would convince others to follow its lead. As chairman of the Claims Conference negotiating committee, Singer had recently concluded agreements with the Germans to add 78,000 new lifetime pensions for survivors from the former East Germany, as well as the return of large amounts of property there. The last thing he wanted was to antagonize the Germans. Still, I had to scurry to block Mel Weiss from promoting sanctions that would have scuttled both the merger and our negotiations. Robert Kimmit, the Germans' American lawyer and former U.S. ambassador to Germany, told me it enhanced my credibility with his clients that I made this effort to hold the more aggressive lawyers at bay.

That cleared the way to organize the negotiations in my big tent. During the next several months, my staff and I produced several organizational charts for the negotiations; we called them "wiring diagrams." There would be separate working groups on labor, insurance, and banking, each including representatives of all of the parties and governments. Another working group on legal closure, what we called the "legal think tank," was limited to the class-action lawyers, the German corporate lawyers, and the U.S. and German governments.

To bridge the gap between the class-action lawyers' demand for separate funds for each type of claim—labor, insurance, banking—and the Germans' idea of a single fund to cap their liability for all conceivable war-related claims, I proposed a solution to Hombach through a graphic metaphor. I had remembered how President Roosevelt sold the Lend-Lease program in 1941, to aid Great Britain at its time of maximum peril, by evoking a person lending a neighbor a garden hose to put out a fire in his house. My concept was of a house with a roof. There would be a single overall settlement fund that the Germans sought in order to put a ceiling on their liability. The house would have separate doors through which claims would be brought for coerced labor, insurance, bank Aryanization, and all other Nazi-era injuries caused by German companies, as the class-action lawyers wanted. Each door would lead to a room representing a specific subcap but within a total we would negotiate. The Future Fund the German companies wanted would also be within the one big roofed house.

Hombach broke into his broad warm smile. He liked the concept, with one caveat: There could be no room set aside for Eastern European agricultural workers. I told him he would need to find one for them too. He grimaced but told me, "Thanks, Stu, you have become a pilot for me through difficult waters; we are on the same wavelength."

Just when it seemed I was getting all the players into the tent, a new one arrived. Former senator Al D'Amato, fresh from his election defeat, called to say he was feeling ignored. He had been appointed special master by federal judge Shirley Wohl Kram, of the Southern District of New York, for the class-action cases against the German banks and insisted on being included in my negotiations. Given his reputation from the Swiss negotiations, this involved another hard sell to Hombach. But I went back to my basic playbook. No one would be excluded who had the power to throw a monkey wrench into our desired outcome. Again Hombach reluctantly agreed, and D'Amato and his talented aide, Viet Dinh (now a senior Justice Department official in the Bush administration), flitted in and out of our negotiations. Meanwhile I instructed the class-action lawyers that, if they wanted to participate—and the entire negotiation had been structured so they could—they would have to organize themselves into a single team. They would have to make peace with each other and with Israel Singer so they could speak with one voice.

Through the late winter and early spring of 1999, I heard their often infantile, ego-driven maneuvers, quarrels, and manipulations, peppered with accusatory words like "scandalous," "double-crossed," "poisonous," "evil," and worse. The lawyers jockeyed for precedence on the basis of how many victims they claimed to have signed up as clients. Singer became apoplectic when he learned that Hausfeld was representing not only individual Jewish victims in his class-action suits but the Polish government as well, which had very different interests. Hausfeld returned the animus, saying that for Singer "truth is a random event." Although I helped achieve an uneasy truce between them over Hausfeld's new Polish connection, their mutual enmity would continue through the length of the negotiations.

At last, five months after I was enlisted by the Germans, we had settled on the shape of the table, agreed on the composition of the working groups, and developed an understanding of how the German foundation would operate. I had coaxed all the parties under one roof for better or worse, but it was a tense gathering. As late as a dinner the night before our first major negotiating session in Washington on May 12, Gentz was complaining that the German and U.S. governments were cutting German industry out of the loop. Finally Hombach put his foot down, saying to Gentz that they needed to trust me "to guide us through the procedure" and that, if German industry "wants politicians involved, you need to accept the rules of the game." This was the most satisfying point of the meal.

But the week before that dinner, another roof had suddenly, and unexpectedly, fallen in on me. On the morning of Friday, May 7, I received an unusual call from Treasury Secretary Robert Rubin asking to meet with me. I told him my day was packed. How about later in the week? With his famously courteous insistence he said it had to be right away. I quickly juggled my schedule and proposed 11:00 A.M. in his office. No, it would be in the office of White House Chief of Staff John Podesta, he said, compounding the mystery.

When we met, Rubin, one of the most successful treasury secretaries since Alexander Hamilton, told me he had decided that it was time for him to leave government. He and the president had agreed that his deputy, Lawrence Summers, would move up to Rubin's cabinet place, and they all wanted me to move over from the State Department to succeed Summers as number 2 at Treasury. Rubin insisted that I could not mention this to anyone else in the government, not even to my boss, Secretary of State Madeleine Albright, for fear that word of his departure would leak and upset financial markets. I protested that the markets would learn soon enough and that it was unfair to Albright, but to no avail.

Although I had diplomatic experience with international commerce and trade, finance was not my strong point. But I soon learned that the reason for this lateral move was to add an experienced hand for Summers, to compliment his titanic brilliance and perceived brashness, and as President Clinton personally told me, to "heal the rift between Treasury and State" that had opened in their opposing views on how to cure the Asian financial crisis in 1997 and 1998. It took me several days of soul searching, discussions with Fran and our sons, Jay and Brian, and meetings with Summers, Podesta, and National Security Adviser Sandy Berger to decide to take the job. I loved the State Department and working with Secretary Albright. But this was too good an offer to turn down, and if the president wanted me to take it, I could hardly say no. But as part of the deal, I demanded and received a guarantee that I could carry my Holocaust portfolio with me, just as I had in all my jobs since being ambassador to the European Union. To his credit, Summers supported me in my Holocaust tasks from the day I entered the Treasury to the very moment the administration ended, even when it laid additional burdens on him. He was a prince to work for, and we never had a moment's disagreement.

My other condition for taking the job was more personal and more painful. I insisted on receiving the blessing of Madeleine Albright, my trusted friend, boss, and mentor, who had given me great responsibilities for international economic policy. At first, like Rubin, the managers of the Clinton White House refused to let me tell her. They wanted to present her with a fait accompli. I told them it was intolerable to sit across a table from her, knowing but deliberately withholding something of great import to the running of her department. Finally Podesta called her a scant day before the official announcement. The day before the start of my German talks, Albright called me to meet with her about what she dryly described as a "not particularly pleasant discussion with Podesta."

With trepidation, I went to her Georgetown townhouse that night at 10:35 P.M., where we had often gathered to work on past presidential campaigns. Echoing a cry of anguish at being told at the last moment, her first reaction was "They're shits at the White House." But we both concluded that I had no choice but to take the job because we both served the president and had to bend to his wishes. We would of course remain friends— and we have. She nevertheless told me, "I'm not happy, but I can't stand in your way." She graciously agreed to permit her own State Department staff in the Office of Holocaust Issues, headed by Ambassador J. D. Bindenagel, to continue reporting to me on Holocaust matters. Given the historic rivalry between the State and Treasury Departments on everything including the time of day, this extraordinary gesture demonstrated her own deep commitment to what I was doing. But she could not shake off the way she had been kept out of the loop by the people closest to the president, for whom, as with all other White House staffs, loyalty usually preceded principle. As she said to me angrily, she could be trusted with nuclear secrets but not with Rubin's departure from the administration.

# CHAPTER ELEVEN

ༀ

# As Old as the Pyramids

A s Bodo Hombach and I looked down from the podium at the first plenary negotiating session in the cavernous Loy Henderson Auditorium in the State Department, I knew we were beginning the last German negotiation on the unfinished business of World War II. Arrayed around the square table were successors to the German state and industry that had wreaked havoc a half century earlier; representatives of many of the Eastern European countries the Germans had vanquished; the Claims Conference and class-action lawyers, each feeling they were the legitimate representatives of millions of individuals who had been murdered, maimed, and robbed; the state of Israel, born in part out of the tears of the Holocaust; and the U.S. government, which had expended so much to win the war but so little for its civilian victims. Hombach had wisely included German parliamentarians from all four parties, which would later prove critical in winning swift Bundestag approval for the deal we finally struck.

The majesty of the moment was temporarily shattered by Michael Hausfeld's sour complaint that we had allowed Ed Fagan into the session. I ignored Hausfeld and joined Hombach in welcoming everyone. The first plenary session, like the dozen or so that followed over more than a year, were occasions to make set speeches with maximum demands. The real negotiations took place in small meetings outside the formal sessions, with the plenaries nevertheless bestowing on all parties a sense of involvement.

Gentz's opening statement set the tone for German industry during the balance of the negotiations, a mixture of candor and morality with cold pragmatism. Although fluent in English, Gentz addressed the plenary in German, accepting the "historic responsibility" of German firms having been integrated into the Nazi regime and relying on force to recruit workers. He described industry's proposals as a "humanitarian gesture for those hurt by German companies" and stressed the importance of achieving legal peace.

Horst Kohler, general counsel of Deutsche Bank, chose to sharply criticize the class-action settlement in the Swiss cases for its lengthy delay in paying victims and the large sums paid to the lawyers. Kohler's statement, factually incorrect about the lawyers—Weiss and Hausfeld had actually worked pro bono—seemed deliberately provocative and struck its mark at once.

Mel Weiss chose to be his natural, combative self. "You can't have it both ways," he told the gathering, "saying you are making a moral gesture provided there is legal closure." A humanitarian gesture, he added, should not be tied to questions of legal certainty. Hausfeld also shot back at Kohler, "There will be no legal closure if you dictate to us with arrogant positions." But Burt Neuborne, always the peacemaker, said the lawyers were trying to help the Germans close the book on the war. He advised the gathering to learn from everyone's mistakes with the Swiss by not just focusing on money but deciding how to allocate it before going to court for approval. When Fagan got up to speak, I hardly knew what to expect. But his remarks about achieving a positive result reflected his usual tactic of mixing outrageous statements before the television cameras with sweet reason inside the negotiating room.

What gave this plenary a special dignity were the words from those who could not have been heard during the war or, for that matter, immediately after it ended: the survivors. Ben Meed, Roman Kent, Noah Flug, and Karl Brozik, Holocaust survivors all, elevated the talks above the matters that occupied the lawyers. Meed, who evaded the Warsaw ghetto roundup and escaped to the United States, where he founded the American Gathering of Holocaust Survivors with Roman Kent, asked for a moment of silence in honor of the 6 million dead. In awe of his surroundings, he said, "Fifty years ago I couldn't be in the State Department."

Meed, Kent, and the other survivors were like the Germans in one critical respect—they had a passionate dislike for the class-action lawyers. Kent, with whom I had developed a special bond because of our Atlanta connection, had already warned me that the survivors would prevent the lawyers from getting their hands on the settlement money.

Russia, Belarus, Ukraine, Poland, and the Czech Republic were together at a major negotiation on World War II issues for the first time. They were the five countries with whom Germany had created reconciliation foundations following German reunification. The Eastern Europeans had a common message that they too had suffered and now wanted to be involved, not just informed of, decisions made in their name. Even so, the Germans had not yet accepted them as members of the working groups in which much of the hard bargaining would occur. Hombach admonished them against "exaggerated expectations."

In the six weeks before the next plenary session, in Bonn on June 22, 1999, I needed to begin resolving the major problems: the number of those eligible for payments from the German foundation; the ratio of payments for slave laborers to those for forced laborers; participation of the Eastern Europeans in the working groups; conflict within the lawyers' camp and between it and Singer; and a mechanism for achieving legal closure that would be acceptable to U.S. jurisprudence, the U.S. and German governments, the German companies, and the class-action lawyers. I insisted that we not address the issue of money until we had made more progress on these issues.

I believed that success required consensus among Singer, Hausfeld, and Weiss. But I also felt that all roads to settlement would lead through Weiss, whose prestige among the class-action lawyers was highest and who was also the toughest negotiator. I needed to rebuild my ties to Weiss, which had been frayed during the Swiss negotiations. I was pleased that he said he wanted to clear the air, adding that he was sorry he had questioned my objectivity at the end of the Swiss negotiations and felt that I had contributed critically to achieve a successful outcome.

Developing the same relationship with Gentz and his colleagues was more difficult. They always viewed me as an ally of the plaintiffs' attorneys, when in fact I fought the class-action lawyers as much as I fought the German businessmen. I later learned that the Germans' own in-house lawyers, general counsels like Deutsche Bank's Kohler, would have preferred to duke it out in court with the Americans instead of reaching the political settlement preferred by their bosses. Lawyers are lawyers the world over. Kohler, a short, pleasant, sandy-haired man, became one of the most important figures on the German negotiating team and one of its toughest hard-liners. Yet he remained mystified by Weiss's truculent attitude, which he summarized as "you want closure, you pay."

Kohler argued that his bank had already paid after the war for trading in looted gold and had returned confiscated property, except where it had been impossible behind the Iron Curtain. Payment in the East, especially for forced labor, was a sore subject with all Germans. Hombach reminded me that Germany had paid compensation to Poland in 1991; reparations there and elsewhere in Eastern Europe had often merely lined the pockets of corrupt government bureaucrats, he argued, so why negotiate with them again on forced labor? "The German mindset is ready to address the singular atrocities of the Holocaust, but forced labor is as old as time—for example, the building of the Pyramids," he said.

But German feelings went deeper. Hombach time and again reverted to the experience of German soldiers being carted off as slave laborers to the Soviet Union. So the notion of paying these same countries, including the Russians, for their forced labor in Germany was a difficult pill for the Germans to take. Hombach was still not willing to involve the Eastern Europeans in all facets of the negotiations.

.    .    .

IN GOVERNMENT, few things are more debilitating than leaks to the press. Although the press lives off inside information about decisions not yet fully formed, it can poison negotiations when one side goes public to preempt the other's arguments in hopes of subverting them. Such a leak almost aborted our negotiations.

When Gentz and I met on June 8, he laid out a troubling set of criteria that would severely limit the number of workers who could ever hope to be paid. In fact, his proposal was certain to ring every alarm bell with the plaintiffs' attorneys, the Claims Conference, and the Eastern Europeans. Far from an expansive moral initiative, it had a crimped notion of who should be paid by the German foundation while insisting on the most expansive bar to any future claims against Germany industry—legal peace.

As Gentz described it, only forced and slave laborers who were now needy would be permitted to recover monetary compensation, for there was "no moral obligation if they are not needy." His colleague, Michael Janssen of Degussa, said that German industry did not want to pay Holocaust survivors who were now medical doctors. When I explained that the purpose was to pay people for their hardship in the past, regardless of their success since the war, Gentz replied, "Why should we pay for suffering sixty years ago?" In addition, Gentz insisted that the German companies would cover only people who had been deported into the Third Reich's 1937 borders and who were confined in guarded camps, neatly cutting out Austria and the Sudetenland and excluding the forced workers relocated within their own countries to work for the Germans. His rationale: "We want to give money to those who lived under the worst conditions, so this means those deported and who lived in prisonlike conditions." To further limit their costs, the German initiative would pay only those who had worked six months or more. Nor would they cover the hundreds of thousands of laborers who were forced to work for government companies, like the railway or post office, or for SS companies, and certainly not agricultural workers. If these were to be paid at all, it would have to come from the German government, Gentz argued, not German industry.

As if all of this were not enough, Gentz added that, in any settlement, German companies should be able to offset not only those payments that individual German companies had already made to their own surviving workers but, more significant, the payments the German government had made over the past fifty years to Holocaust survivors. Although this was sure to enrage the Claims Conference, which had negotiated those payments, Gentz did not stop there. He had something just as provocative for the Eastern Europeans. The companies wanted the victims paid on a scale according to where they now lived—less for those in Eastern Europe (where most of the survivors lived) than those in the United States, Western Europe, or Israel. As Gentz put it indelicately, 5,000 German marks would not mean much to "a rich Jew in New York" but would make a great deal of difference to a Ukrainian pensioner. To cap the indignities, the plan did nothing to cover insurance or banking claims, although Gentz and Hombach had insisted that Deutsche Bank and Dresdner Bank had to be fully protected from future lawsuits, since they would be major funders of the German foundation.

This proposal was a prescription for disaster. I told Gentz it would be totally unacceptable to the victims and to the U.S. government. A six-month requirement would unfairly exclude a substantial portion of slave laborers who happened to work for a shorter period of time; conditions were so atrocious that all slave laborers deserved some payment. Eastern Europeans, who had waited so long for some justice, would be outraged to find their payments lower than those who had not only prospered in the West but in many cases had already received Holocaust payments from the Germans. Payments could not simply be welfare for the needy, I said, but moral restitution regardless of current circumstance. And the Germans could not have it both ways. They were seeking the U.S. government's blessing for the foundation as the exclusive and final remedy for claimants, yet they were so narrowly defining eligibility that hundreds of thousands would be left without any remedy at all, either in a U.S. court or through the foundation.

I barely finished my critique of their plan when Gentz dropped an even bigger bombshell. His paper containing these points had been leaked to the German press and would appear the next morning. He regretted the leak and did not know who was responsible, but it was a reality. I had been disturbed that the Germans acted without warning in announcing their general initiative with Chancellor Schröder on February 16. Now, despite my constant admonitions to avoid surprises, they were doing so again by publicly filling in the details, without negotiation. I had to restrain my fury at a second preemptive act.

To compound the problem, Gentz and his colleagues intended to hold a formal press conference to announce the leaked plan. It was one thing to have a leak; I had dealt with these for years in government. But a press conference would validate the worst thoughts of the victims' side—that this was no accident but a conscious effort by German industry to impose their plan unilaterally. We furiously worked to head off the press briefing, but in vain. We drafted a proposed statement for Gentz to release to explain away the leak, but he refused to return Ambassador Kornblum's telephone calls. Even German industry's American lawyer, Robert Kimmit, failed to get the press conference canceled. Roger Witten, another of his lawyers, admitted that Gentz was being "hardheaded" about going forward. But go forward he did, right into a storm.

The trust among all the parties that I had carefully nurtured for several months collapsed in a day. The class-action lawyers exploded. The press conference was held on the eve of the first working-group session of the "legal think tank," the goal of which was to find ways to provide German industry with legal peace from future suits, and the lawyers felt betrayed. They called the German action obnoxious, a lack of good faith, a disastrous mistake. Weiss, in particular, was chagrined. He had brought Harvard law professor Arthur Miller down for the session to help devise creative ways to achieve legal peace for the Germans. He said angrily that he had been willing to overlook statements in the German press attacking the lawyers as shylocks, but the effort to "unilaterally thrust your plan down our throats" was too much. Ignoring my pleas that the Germans had made a transatlantic trip for the session, he led a walkout with Hausfeld and several of the others.

I spent several days coaxing the walkouts back to the bargaining table in time for our June 22 plenary in Bonn. But it took two months, until the end of August, to deal with the fundamental flaws in the unilateral German plan. Time and again, in meetings, conference calls, and plenary sessions I rallied the Claims Conference, the Eastern Europeans, and even the German companies' own American lawyers to resolve all of the concerns about the German proposal. It was like extracting impacted teeth, one by one. Perhaps the best line came from the Claims Conference team's Roman Kent about Gentz's notion of offsetting German industry's obligations with their government's Holocaust payments: "You don't want us to offset our Marshall Plan payments to you!"

But in the end it was an appeal to Gentz's pocketbook that prevailed. Although it took time for German industry to accept the notion, I was able to convince Gentz and his colleagues that they could not have the all-encompassing legal peace they desired against future claims unless all victims had the potential of being paid by the German foundation. I received assistance from an unexpected front. Robert Kimmit came up with the creative idea of a "catchall" category to cover all potential claimants who did not neatly fit into the definitions of slave and forced laborers and other claimants. Under Kimmit's concept anyone who had been wronged by German industry during the war—even if not specifically defined as an eligible claimant under the labor, insurance, or banking categories—could receive some payment from the German foundation. Kimmit helped convince Gentz that, without the potential of any claimant having a recovery through the German foundation, the U.S. government could not be expected to help dismiss the claimants' class-action suits to recover through the U.S. courts.

By the time of our August 24–26 plenary session in Bonn, I had defanged almost all of the problems arising from the June-leaked proposal and we had created what in diplomatic parlance is called a "bracketed text" from the German firms' document, the areas of consensus on how the German foundation would operate, with brackets around those areas still in disagreement. This became our bible for much of the remainder of the negotiation.

During the time I was dealing with the leaked plan, an unexpected event occurred that could have threatened the talks but, in the end, helped ensure their success. On June 30 Bodo Hombach told me he was resigning his position as head of the chancellor's office and as my counterpart in order to become the head of the Stability Pact for Southeast Europe, assisting economic development in the war-torn Balkans. This came as a shock and a disappointment. On a personal level, I had bonded with the big, gregarious politician, whose heart was so clearly in the right place in dealing with Germany's special responsibility for the Holocaust and who was at the chancellor's right hand.

I learned later that, as with so much in politics, there was more to his departure than met the eye. The chancellor's legislative program was foundering in the Bundestag, and Hombach had become the scapegoat. There was also adverse press publicity over the financing of Hombach's second home. I knew I would miss him, but I was more anxious about who his successor would be.

I need not have worried. By the middle of July, Count Otto Lambsdorff, a wise elder statesman and former leader of the centrist Free Democratic Party, a traditional balance wheel in postwar German politics, was chosen as the chancellor's personal representative. I had known Lambsdorff since the Carter administration, when he was Germany's economic minister, and we had kept in touch after he left office in 1984. Fortuitously, during one of my first trips to Bonn for these negotiations, never thinking he would be involved, I met him in his tiny office to discuss the new German Initiative and to give him my perspective.

His title of Count was Russian—one of his ancestors had served as a general in the court of Tsar Nicholas I—and as a young man he had volunteered for the Wehrmacht just two weeks before Germany surrendered, had been wounded, and now still walked with a cane. Lambsdorff, one of the "good Germans" the Allied occupation authorities found so rare after the war, became a lawyer and a judge, was elected to the Bundestag, and was, at the age of seventy-three, in political semiretirement as honorary chair of his party. He had close ties to German business and a long history of working for friendly relations with the United States. He also had the advantage of being at the end of a distinguished career, unworried about stepping on the toes of either German industry or Schröder's government. I was touched by how he came out of a comfortable retirement to answer his country's call, crossing the ocean a dozen times and pushing himself to the limits at his age. His deeply lined face, furrowed brow, and broad forehead, along with his optimism and wisdom, seemed a metaphor for Germany's difficult passage from pariah state to respected democracy.

I found solace in talking with Count Lambsdorff, who reassured me that we would conclude a deal because it was in the "political, moral, and historical interest of German and American relations." A breakdown, he warned, could lead to trade and economic disruption from possible sanctions and consumer boycotts, and by giving German companies a bad name. So "we are condemned to succeed," he said. He had a fine political sensibility, counseling us, for example, to avoid the term "final payment" in our bracketed text lest it evoke Hitler's "final solution." Lambsdorff promised to work full time, while Hombach had been stretched with other obligations as minister of the chancellery. But he also had a sense of urgency because of another kind of time pressure: The average age of the surviving laborers was eighty, and 10 percent died annually. He told me he wanted to give money to people while they were still alive to see and use it.

"Stu, someone needed to do this job," he said when we held our first meeting in my office in the Treasury. He spoke with the clarity I had long admired in him. Germans had a "moral obligation, that is the starting point." Slave laborers should have first priority. The "solution must be financially bearable." And "I know we cannot get 100 percent legal certainty," but there must be sufficient legal peace for German industry.

Lambsdorff added a gravitas to the talks that was badly needed. Such an experienced, candid, and patient negotiator was the ideal choice to pick up at the intensely prickly point where Hombach had been forced to leave off, and he came none too soon. We still had several major issues to resolve. One involved whether workers forcibly employed by SS companies and on German farms would be able to recover from the German foundation. Another was money: How much should each slave or forced worker receive and what would be the sum total of the German foundation for insurance, banking, and other claims? And last was how to provide the legal peace the German companies demanded as the condition for any payments.

The refusal of German industry to cover SS and agricultural workers— as Gentz put it, they had the "highest resistance" to paying workers never employed at all by private industry—quickly became a deal breaker. If they were to be covered, the German government would have to do so since the SS companies were state-owned during the war. Yet Singer was insistent that any agreement had to cover SS workers, who often worked inter- changeably for private and government-owned companies. The Poles, Ukrainians, and Russians felt just as strongly about agricultural workers.

Lambsdorff and I both recognized that the only solution to the SS worker issue was to have the German government establish a public foun- dation parallel to the private-sector German foundation in order to cover SS workers, public employees, and others who might fall through the cracks. Within a few weeks of starting, Lambsdorff told me in principle that the chancellor had agreed to such a government fund.

Coverage of agricultural workers, however, was more complicated and emotional for the Germans. I found it one of the few moral blind spots for the Germans, and for Lambsdorff. Otherwise so sensitive to the nuances of the Holocaust, Lambsdorff did not see how agricultural workers could be covered. "Some were happy to be on German farms rather than in their own countries," he insisted. He remembered that, "when I was twelve or thirteen [before the war], I saw them. It was traditional for Poles and Ukrainian workers to come to Germany for the harvests and they still do so today." For the chancellor it was politically impossible to directly cover them, Lambs- dorff told me. This was a political red line he would not cross.

Neither Lambsdorff nor the chancellor could see the difference between voluntary and coerced agricultural work. But the Eastern Europeans, par- ticularly the Poles, certainly did. They made it clear that they would balk at any settlement that excluded agricultural workers, who were around half their total forced labor group. This issue, more than any other, evoked bit- ter feelings between the Poles and Germans during the talks. What to do between two irreconcilable positions?

Our team and I developed a solution. The most efficient delivery system for the German foundation labor funds in Eastern Europe was the existing reconciliation foundations that the Germans had created in the early 1990s to pay those victims of Nazism who had been living behind the Iron Curtain. Why not allocate a lump sum to each of these foundations based upon an estimate of the number of surviving laborers and give them the choice of covering agricultural as well as industrial workers? In this way the Germans would not have to admit agricultural workers were being covered, and the Eastern Europeans could show their publics that they would be protected. After weeks of hard bargaining, this compromise won the day.

Now we faced the money issue. The class-action lawyers had been willing to follow my advice and postpone the discussion of money until we resolved most of the issues about the structure and eligibility requirements for the German foundation. But with the progress we had made by August, the class-action lawyers grew restless and would wait no longer. I warned them that the Germans would be unable to provide any public response to their financial demands because the CEOs would not be meeting with the chancellor until September 6, after the sacrosanct August vacation in Germany. But the lawyers insisted on going forward anyway. The August 24–26 plenary session would be the first occasion to get down to what they saw all along as the real business: How much money were the Germans willing to pay to buy their legal peace?

We knew that the Nazis had conscripted about 10 million workers. But how many were still alive to be paid? The Claims Conference had good records for Jewish survivors, but for forced laborers it was anyone's guess.

We were saved by the work of Professor Lutz Niethammer, a German historian and close friend of Bodo Hombach, who asked him to serve as an informal adviser. From a variety of sources Niethammer estimated that there were between 1.2 million and 1.5 million laborers still alive—around 1 million forced laborers, mostly non-Jews from Eastern Europe, and some 200,000 slave laborers, slightly more than half of whom were Jewish. We had already reached a consensus that slave laborers were to be paid several times more than forced laborers but had not settled on how much more.

But Michael Hausfeld was not satisfied. With no forewarning he hired the Washington-based firm of Robert Nathan & Associates, who, predictably, found almost twice the number of surviving laborers, 2.3 million. This was not a mere academic exercise. The higher the number of anticipated claimants, the higher the capped amount of the German foundation would have to be to accommodate them.

I warned Hausfeld that inflated numbers would put us on a collision course with the Germans. Israel Singer was also livid. He said that Hausfeld was traveling to Eastern Europe signing up forced laborers by the hour and had jacked up the number of survivors through the guise of the Nathan study. "They've gone mad. I think they want to blow this up," he concluded.

The dispute over the number of surviving workers was resolved only when I got Hausfeld to agree to be bound by the consensus of experts at a conference Niethammer organized in Florence. The final estimates were close to Niethammer's original numbers: 1.5 million workers still alive—242,000 slave laborers (182,000 of whom had worked for private German industry and 60,000 for Reich-controlled institutions), 670,000 forced industrial workers, and 590,000 agricultural workers.

The plaintiffs' attorneys also had exaggerated expectations of how much they could get from the Germans. Late in June, Robert Swift and Ed Fagan told me privately that a settlement would not work unless it was in the double-digit billions of dollars. Mel Weiss had begun telling the German press that he would settle for nothing less than $30 billion, about 60 billion DM.

I met Weiss on August 19, urging him to temper his first demand to the Germans at the Bonn plenary. Instead, Weiss told me he was hiring a PR firm to dramatize the wartime behavior of German firms and would demand a staggering 74 billion marks, about $37 billion. "Pain is part of the process" for the German companies, he said. I told him these figures would end our talks on the spot and that by using a PR firm he was acting as he had accused Fagan of doing in the Swiss cases. He said I was beginning to persuade him. I was soon to see how very little.

Against these numbers stood German industry's still secret offer of only 1.7 billion marks—less than 1 billion dollars. I realized there were going to be limits to how much German industry would go above this figure. One advantage of convincing the chancellor to pay compensation to the SS workers and other public sector laborers was that it gave me another pot of money to add to the private sector's.

I gave what I believed would be Weiss's numbers to the Germans at dinner the night before the August plenary in Bonn. Lambsdorff warned me that, if these exaggerated demands got out, they "will turn the German public around immediately"—which up to now had been critical of the German companies for not doing more. Gentz's reaction was similarly gloomy: "Secretary Eizenstat, it is highly improbable we can surpass 1 or 2 billion DM and impossible to achieve even 4 billion DM," let alone the kind of numbers Weiss was throwing around. Gentz warned that, if Weiss was serious, the German companies would prefer to take their chances in court. He said that Hombach believed that I had agreed to accept the 1.7 billion DM offer, given to me in confidence in January. I replied that I had done nothing of the sort but agreed that Weiss's numbers were way out of line with reality.

Gentz had far less capacity than Lambsdorff for what Germans call *Fingerspitzengefühl*—literally, feeling at the end of one's fingers and, figuratively, a sense of how another person perceives your words and actions. It took all my willpower to remain silent when Gentz finished by reminding me that any payments ultimately came at the expense of "our shareholders, many of whom are Jewish." I wrote in the margin of my legal pad, "unbelievable." Lest this be a chance remark, he repeated a moment later that "a lot of the shareholders are Jewish, and we take from them to pay the victims."

At the plenary session at the German Foreign Ministry the next day, Weiss's "concession" to my pleas for moderation was to demand $30 billion (60 billion DM) instead of $37 billion. The German side blanched. Although I had prepared them at the dinner the night before, it was still a shock to hear the figure formally presented. In deference to Weiss's standing among the plaintiffs' lawyers, no one contradicted him, but I knew that he did not speak for a united victims' front. Indeed, Singer was as appalled as the Germans.

Singer dealt with the Germans differently from the Swiss. The Claims Conference had carefully cultivated its relationship with the German government during almost half a century of massive reparations payments. Singer had once joshed that Hombach was "our friend who lays the golden eggs." Although his friend may have gone, he had no intention of permitting the class-action lawyers to strangle the German goose. Still, the chair of the Claims Conference, Rabbi Israel Miller, a gentle and warm person who conveyed a spiritual quality and had devoted his life to helping Holocaust survivors, warned me, "The lawyers are painting the Jewish groups into a corner with outrageous demands. It is hard for us to be seen as accepting less than they want."

Now that we had gotten down to talking money, I realized the sides were so far apart that the talks were at risk of imploding. During a break, I told Weiss that he had to see Gentz one-on-one and reassure him that this was only an opening demand and that he was willing to settle for less. He agreed, and they went off to a small room off the main hall. Gentz later told me this helped save the talks. But I needed to do more. I needed to distance the U.S. government from Weiss's highly inflated demand.

It was time to take a risk. With Ambassador Kornblum and J. D. Bindenagel, I met with Gentz, Janssen from Degussa, and Lambsdorff in a small, cramped, windowless rectangular conference room right off the main hall of the Foreign Ministry. The Germans were in a foul mood. I decided to offer a U.S. government number. I had talked about it with my staff, but it was as much instinct as anything. I felt that, psychologically, the victims' side would need a double-digit billion DM settlement but that to have any chance to get the Germans to this level would mean the lowest possible double-digit figure. So I looked squarely at Gentz, Janssen, and Lambsdorff and told them that I would recommend a 10 billion DM settlement. I would work to get the victims' side down to this level and expected the Germans to come up to it.

Gentz said immediately that 10 billion DM was "impossible to achieve." Gravely he intoned: "Secretary Eizenstat, you are standing in front of the ruins of what we have done"; the gulf between the two sides was as "wide as the Atlantic Ocean." I stood firm and then informed the plaintiffs' attorneys and the Claims Conference of my compromise figure. The Israelis and the Claims Conference were immediately sympathetic, but as Bobby Brown from Israeli prime minister Barak's office put it, "the plaintiffs' attorneys will say it is a sell-out."

Still, despite all the waves, our boat had not sunk. Gentz had refrained from walking out over Weiss's outrageous demand. The lawyers had stuck with the talks even though the Germans had offered no number except their old one of 1.7 billion DM, preferring to wait until their CEOs met with the chancellor on September 6. We had reached agreement on most of the outstanding issues regarding eligibility for the German foundation. And Lambsdorff had gotten the chancellor's agreement to submit a bill to the Bundestag in September to establish a companion federal foundation reimbursing victims not covered by industry.

We were all bone tired from three days of nonstop negotiating, but our work was far from done. As I flew back to Washington, I was already trying to think about how to get the two sides into the same 10-billion-DM ballpark. With the chancellor and the captains of German industry set to meet on September 6, just a fortnight away, it was time to deploy the main weapon in my arsenal, the president of the United States.

# CHAPTER TWELVE

# Ten Billion Marks

A s DEPUTY secretary of the treasury I attended early-morning White House staff meetings, along with Secretary Larry Summers, in the spacious West Wing office of Chief of Staff John Podesta, just down the narrow hallway from the Oval Office. Larry and I were the only ones from a Cabinet department permitted to attend. These meetings provided unparalleled access to the strongest levers of government, including the president. But I had to use this access sparingly because so many senior government officials vie to have the president support their projects. I was about to join the fray for the first time.

At the meeting on Monday, August 30, 1999, I told Jim Steinberg, the deputy national security adviser, that I needed a letter from Clinton to Schröder in time to influence the chancellor for his September 6 meeting with the German business leaders. Our team drafted the letter, and it was approved and sent that Thursday. The speedy turnaround was a reflection of the president's personal interest and the support the White House Staff extended to me in the midst of the myriad issues they faced. In the letter, the president complimented Schröder by saying that "history will remember your government and those involved in the initiative for contributing to justice in the lifetime of survivors." He also noted the German Initiative's agreement on our key principles and recognized the significant progress in achieving legal peace. But the real purpose of the letter was to goad the chancellor to recognize that at his September 6 meeting "a substantial commitment by German companies and the German government will be required."

I also applied pressure from another direction. I gained support for my 10-billion-mark proposal from Israel Singer, who had Edgar Bronfman call Schröder to urge industry to raise its meager contribution of 1.7 billion marks. Ambassador Kornblum also called Schröder's top foreign policy adviser, Michael Steiner, who replied that the chancellor would not let us fail.

The Clinton letter had its intended effect on Schröder's meeting with the industrialists. The chancellor responded to the president shortly after the meeting, saying, "I am convinced that the companies would be ready and in a position to come up with substantial financial contributions and to win over additional companies to participate in the foundation." But he cautioned the president that "I cannot tell at this point whether the financial dimension mentioned by Mr. Eizenstat [10 billion DM] may be reached."

Two weeks after their meeting with Schröder, the German CEOs agreed at a contentious internal meeting to follow Schröder's and Clinton's admonitions to be more forthcoming with their pocketbooks, more than doubling their offer from 1.7 billion DM to 4 billion DM. And for the first time, the chancellor proposed 2 billion DM in government funds from a proposed new Federal Foundation, for a total of 6 billion DM.

As welcome as this sizeable increase was, I knew it was not close to what was needed to settle the cases. Not only that, it occasioned one of the most difficult episodes in the talks. Gentz and Lambsdorff told me that soon after I made my 10 billion DM proposal to the Germans, Ambassador Kornblum, without my knowledge, indicated to Rolf Breuer of Deutsche Bank that the United States would actually settle for between 7 billion and 8 billion DM. This had been the number against which they thought they were working when they caucused following the chancellor's meeting.

I was stunned. I told them I had not changed my mind and Kornblum had no authority to reduce my 10 billion DM number. I immediately put Kornblum on a conference call with them. He became defensive and said that he had only meant that the private sector should offer 7 billion to 8 billion DM. Breuer called the next day to tell me that Kornblum had in fact specifically assured him the 7 billion to 8 billion was a total number, including the German government's contribution.

After I read him the riot act, Kornblum was chagrined and profusely apologized for getting involved in the negotiations. I let it drop and never mentioned it again. Ambassador Kornblum had been enormously helpful, and I did not intend to let this error obscure his contributions. But the damage was done. Gentz complained bitterly of the "heavy misunderstanding" under which he had convinced German industry to increase its contribution to 4 billion DM. With jaw clinched so tightly it seemed his words could not escape, he said to Kornblum in accented but perfect English, "You were there when Secretary Eizenstat put 10 billion down, and when you then do 7 to 8 billion one day later, you can understand our misunderstanding." Gentz remained distrustful of us from that time forward, saying that if he could not take the word of the U.S. ambassador, whom could he trust? Privately, I believed that he was using the unhappy episode as a bargaining tool, but we certainly gave him a lot with which to work.

At about the same time, another thunderbolt struck. On September 15, to the consternation of the class-action lawyers, two U.S. judges strengthened the German companies' position immeasurably. With unexpected speed, judges Joseph A. Greenaway and Dickinson R. Debevoise, both of the federal district court in New Jersey, separately granted the German companies' motion to dismiss the suits. Judge Debevoise dismissed the cases against Degussa and Siemens, which had been sued for taking victims' gold and for using forced labor. The court said it was bound to defer to the postwar treaties governing reparations claims. Later that same day, Judge Greenaway dismissed the class-action suit initiated by Mel Weiss against Ford Motor Company, which sought compensation for forced labor at Ford's Cologne plant during the war. "Courts," Greenaway held, "may not pass judgment upon the political negotiations of the Executive Branch and the international community." In essence, the judges found that the cases presented political questions that had traditionally been handled by the German and U.S. governments as reparations matters and were covered by postwar treaties that could not be judged by the judicial branch. Judge Greenaway also found the suits barred by the passage of time.

These rulings immediately changed the landscape of the talks. The plaintiffs' lawyers of course filed appeals, but the bravado surrounding their demands now rang hollow. Indeed, the question arose whether the German companies would even want to keep talking. Hausfeld immediately warned his colleagues that they needed to avoid posturing. Israel Singer called me to say with satisfaction that the lawyers were no longer in the driver's seat and that "this is your ball game now." I saw these decisions as a mixed blessing but more positive than negative. Although I feared the Germans might

lose interest in reaching my 10 billion DM target, they would help me bring
Weiss and company back from the world of unrealistic dreams to bitter realities, which had been my biggest task.

The judges' decisions nevertheless put me in a difficult spot. Until now,
I had been able to keep the U.S. government out of the legal issues surrounding the class-action cases. But my legal advisers, David Anderson, a
senior attorney in the Civil Division of the Department of Justice, and
Ronald Bettauer, assistant legal adviser for international claims and investment disputes at the State Department, strongly disagreed with the rulings,
arguing that the postwar agreements concerning Germany did not bar the
suits against German companies. But David Anderson wanted to file a U.S.
government brief on the postwar treaties that would have the effect of supporting the plaintiffs' lawyers' position. I refused, knowing that, in the eyes
of the Germans, this would surely end my role as an objective interlocutor.
But to be sure the Germans did not get overconfident with their legal victory, I tried to keep them guessing by telling them that, although the U.S.
government would stay neutral, our lawyers disagreed with the judges'
interpretations of the postwar treaties.

But I misread the political situation. The day after the decisions, Gentz
called to reassure me that German industry had no intention of bailing out
of the talks. In fact, as many as thirty-five companies were ready to contribute, and "not just peanuts," he said. I asked myself why Gentz was willing to pursue the talks with the firms' legal position so strong. The answer
I came up with was that the Germans had never given much credence to the
legal case against them. What they really wanted was to remove the threat
of economic sanctions, boycotts, and other recriminations the Swiss banks
had faced and that would haunt them even if they were victorious in court.
These were cases they could not afford to win.

The judicial decisions altered the dynamics of the negotiations. Mel
Weiss admitted that the two decisions justified a lower settlement figure.
Unfortunately they also shifted his tactics toward greater confrontation. He
decided that if he could not win in the courtroom, he would take his case to
the court of public opinion. To him this meant political pressure, just as it
had against the Swiss. He told me he was going to start a $250,000 adver-
tising campaign in the United States against huge companies like Bayer and
Ford. One ad would threaten a huge "headache" for Bayer, the aspirin
maker, if it refused to pay—a clear invitation to a boycott without actually

saying so. Another would show Henry Ford receiving an award from Nazi officials, along with a photograph of forced laborers at the Ford plant during the war. Weiss also persuaded Charles Schumer, the newly elected U.S. senator from New York, to sponsor legislation to reverse the effect of the two court decisions. I tried unsuccessfully to convince Weiss and Schumer that this would only harden German industry's position. Full-page ads ran in major papers around the country.

When Lambsdorff formally presented the 6 billion DM offer at the October 7 plenary at the State Department, he pointed out that the Schröder government was putting up one-third of the money at a time of severe cuts elsewhere in the budget and that it was important to decide quickly, since "help must go to the living and not those in tombs." From my constant harping on the need for 10 billion DM, Lambsdorff realized he had to offer hope for more funds. So when he presented it to the plaintiffs' attorneys, he left open the possibility of going higher by saying this was Germany's best offer "at this point." Everyone caught the phrase. Gentz angrily responded to Lambsdorff's hint, saying that the companies were making purely voluntary donations and "don't entertain hopes that German industry can do more."

This was no comfort to the plaintiffs' attorneys. Weiss expressed "profound disappointment at a paltry amount," well below my 10 billion DM figure and a tenth of his opening demand. He called it a disgrace at a time when Deutsche Bank had just paid $3.5 billion to acquire Bankers Trust. Divided among some 1.5 million laborers, it would amount to only 4,000 DM per worker, or about $2,000. Even this overstated the amount, since the German money would also have to be spread to cover insurance and banking claims and the Future Fund German industry so fervently desired. Weiss accused German industry of treating this as "a mere business proposition, just another lawsuit." But I was relieved by his next words: "We won't leave the table, as we don't want to be blamed if this breaks up."

Afterward I spoke to the principal negotiators in small groups to keep everyone on the reservation. Bobby Brown, representing the Israeli government, said Weiss's negative advertising and Fagan's parading of survivors in public was hurting Jerusalem's friendly relations with Bonn. "We don't want to be dragged into a public fight with them on Holocaust issues," he said. But this made little impact on the lawyers. Gentz was also unmoved. Although admitting that German industry had been "wrapped up" with the

Third Reich, he said that 6 billion DM was reasonable. The numbers "won't be higher in four weeks or six months; we can't go any higher; there is no chance to bring the numbers up for our side." And the more the lawyers attacked the German companies, the fewer firms he could enlist to contribute, he asserted. Turning to Weiss, he said, "You will bear responsibility" if the German companies quit the German Initiative. "I don't want to be blamed every day by the U.S.," Gentz exclaimed in frustration.

It was clear that Gentz was serious. I could expect little more to close the gap from the German private sector. The German government would have to do more if I were to have any chance of reaching the 10 billion DM target.

My team and I worked on a new proposal. I suggested to Lambsdorff that the Germans merge the German private sector foundation with the Federal Foundation the chancellor had pledged to create, not for bureaucratic efficiency but because I believed it would encourage the German government to match the private sector's contribution. Lambsdorff liked the idea and a few days later said he had convinced the chancellor to accept a single foundation.

He in turn suggested that we offer a joint U.S.-German proposal for 8 billion. I knew how difficult it was for him to continually go back for more money, but I told him that I had to stick to my 10 billion DM figure. "Stu, 10 billion is absolutely impossible," he responded with a deep sigh.

The only possible step forward was for President Clinton to write another letter to Schröder. Obtaining a presidential letter to a foreign head of government is usually difficult on any topic. Getting a second one is even more so because the White House Staff wants to avoid debasing the coin of the presidential word. But when I asked for another, Chief of Staff Podesta and the National Security Council quickly obtained it, another instance of the support I always received from President Clinton and those around him. Getting this second letter was possible both because of my daily interaction with Podesta, National Security Adviser Sandy Berger, and the senior White House staff, who respected my mission and wanted it to succeed, and because the president had, with his initial letter, invested his prestige in obtaining a positive outcome.

This second letter, dated November 13, recognized that the plaintiffs' lawyers had significantly modified their demands and that all sides had agreed on "an effective mechanism to achieve legal closure." Then he put the arm on Schröder by saying that I was acting as his personal representative in insisting that the Germans contribute a total of at least 10 billion marks. This meant, the president wrote, that there needed to be "a significant increase in the contributions from German companies beyond their opening offer of four billion D-marks" and a willingness by the German government to "increase its two billion D-mark contribution, even if spread over two fiscal years," this last being my idea to ease their budget crunch at a time when the chancellor was cutting popular domestic programs. To make clear his personal interest, Clinton wrote a postscript in his own hand, "I hope we can work this out together."

The letter had a direct impact. Lambsdorff told me he believed the government would increase its contribution from 2 billion to 3 billion DM and the chancellor would also pressure industry to make one last increase, from 4 billion to 5 billion DM, for a total of 8 billion DM. But if I could not bring the plaintiffs' lawyers to settle for 8 billion, he warned, "it does not make sense to continue."

I received an unexpected visit that gave me a private window into the chancellor's thinking. Without Lambsdorff's knowledge, Schröder sent a personal emissary, Klaus Gretschmann, his director general for economic and financial affairs, to sound me out on the following question: If the chancellor could put together the 10 billion DM package I had proposed, could I get the victims' side to accept it, regardless of how it was split between industry and the government? I could only say I hoped so and would work hard to get the class-action lawyers, Singer, and the Eastern Europeans to accept this as a final compromise. I told him they were interested in the bottom line and I was certain they would not care how German industry and government divided the contributions.

Tempers were on edge when the parties met in Bonn for the mid-November plenary. Fagan immediately released to the press a totally implausible demand of 180 billion DM, which served only to shock the Germans and further sour the atmosphere. Singer warned me that such antics, to which he added Schumer's bill and Weiss's advertisements, were stirring up anti-Semitism and painting Jews into a corner, for it appeared, he said, that "the Jews are driving the talks," instead of the U.S. and German governments. In classic Singer imagery, he bemoaned the predicament of being "attached to the lawyers like Siamese twins that grew and stayed attached!"

To try to air our differences in an informal setting the night before the main plenary session, the Germans arranged for a dinner with all the parties in a small Bonn restaurant that they took over for the evening. But when, during the dinner, Gentz suggested for the first time a willingness to negotiate in a range between 6 billion and 10 billion DM, Hausfeld dismissively shot it down. Gentz's emotional dam broke. He spewed out his frustration at the "aggressive American legal system" and demanded to know from Hausfeld "who is your constituency?"—the implication being that he was not genuinely representing the best interests of survivors. Then Lambsdorff lost his usual aplomb, noting that if these talks failed over excessive demands, it would strengthen right-wing politicians already on the rise in Europe—Christoph Blocher in Switzerland and Jörg Haider in Austria— a veiled reference to anti-Semitism as a weapon by European populists. The dinner ended in acrimony. There was no peace pipe for dessert.

But this turn of events gave me an idea. Each side should propose a range that included 10 billion DM, for the Germans the high end, for the victims' side the low end. From there, I believed I could negotiate a way to reach that figure.

At an early-morning meeting at the German Foreign Ministry, things turned from bad to worse. Gentz, understandably upset at the dinner's outcome, refused to offer even 8 billion DM until Lambsdorff, turning red with anger, pulled him aside to admonish him. While Lambsdorff was working Gentz over, I went to the Claims Conference's holding room. Singer remarked pungently that "Gentz and Hausfeld were teammates from hell last night." But he quickly said that he had the blessing of Israeli prime minister Ehud Barak to settle within 6 billion to 10 billion DM, at least if insurance claims could be handled separately and above any final figure. He had no intention of being labeled a blackmailer by the Germans.

Now I went to the lion's den, the plaintiffs' lawyers' holding room. Hausfeld said they would agree to reduce their demand from 25 billion to 17 billion DM. I rejected it. They made a frantic call to Weiss at his home in New York. When I was called back into their room, Hausfeld asked: "How about negotiating in a range of 10 billion to 17 billion?" I told them the top end was still too high. Neuborne and Hausfeld then lowered their range to 10 billion to 15 billion but asked for my commitment to fight for the high end. I told them I would do my best.

I now had two ranges—one from the Germans at 6 billion to 10 billion marks, to which Lambsdorff had gotten Gentz to agree, and the other from the victims and their lawyers at 10 billion to 15 billion marks—that touched at 10 billion DM. The parties knew I was driving them in precisely this direction. But Lambsdorff was uncharacteristically downbeat; 8 billion, he said, was Germany's maximum.

When the plenary began, it was as if the storm of the past thirty-six hours had simply blown away. Perhaps everyone now knew the others' bottom line. Perhaps it was the historical significance of the moment. This would be the last major international negotiation before the Foreign Ministry left Germany's Cold War capital, Bonn, for the new capital of a reunified Germany, what Chancellor Schröder liked to call the "Berlin Republic." Indeed, the halls and offices were full of packing cases for the move.

On his best behavior, Hausfeld stated each side's ranges and proposed that negotiations should commence within them. Neuborne said that for the first time he could see the outlines of a settlement. Lambsdorff and Gentz began making noises about agreement and complimenting me for my work in providing legal peace, which was the most difficult issue other than money.

Lambsdorff and I then flew to Berlin to discuss another aspect of a settlement, a public apology to the slave and forced workers by German president Johannes Rau. Postwar Germany has had a history of outspoken presidents like Roman Herzog and Richard von Weizsäcker who have helped the nation confront its past—perhaps to balance the historic scandal of Hitler being legally chosen as chancellor by the president of the Weimar Republic, Field Marshal Paul von Hindenburg. Rau, a longtime active Social Democrat like Schröder, was raised in a strict Protestant family and was very active in the church. A silver-haired man of seventy-one with a broad face and a grandfatherly smile, he had a lifelong commitment to reconciliation with Jews and had made over thirty trips to Israel, receiving honorary degrees from three Israeli universities.

I was slightly unnerved by the request I was going to make and awestruck by the magnificent setting in which I would make it, the president's residence, the eighteenth-century Bellevue Palace. With its sweeping entry through high barred gates and long curved driveway, opulent appointments, and a large lawn in the back, it was a sharp contrast to the old Bonn Foreign Ministry building we had left behind. Once inside, I summarized for Rau the current state of our negotiations and then told him that President Clinton had been personally engaged by sending two letters to the chancellor. Rau could play an important role in promoting a settlement, I said, by urging the government to raise its contribution from 3 billion to 5 billion marks, matching the new contribution level of the private sector, and by considering a public apology for Germany's mistreatment of conscripted workers. Rau had been briefed by Lambsdorff and said, without hesitation, he was prepared to do everything I had asked.

I had three more stops to make before returning to Washington. First I went to see Mannfred Overhaus, the state secretary of the Finance Ministry, which occupied the massive building that housed Herman Göring's Air Ministry during the war. Overhaus's job was that of any finance ministry official in any country, which is to spend as little of the public's money as possible, and he told me 3 billion marks was the government's limit.

My next stop was to see former chancellor Helmut Kohl, who had presided over Germany's reunification and was the longest serving chancellor in German history. He was still a leading figure in the Bundestag and in the Christian Democratic Party. After greeting me warmly in an office as small as this massive man was large, he said that it was "ridiculous the huge banks can't do more" and that he would support us. Given his refusal to agree to address the issue of forced labor during his lengthy chancellorship, this was a useful concession.

For final inspiration before heading home, I stopped briefly at the new Jewish Museum in Berlin, still under construction and headed by an American, Michael Blumenthal, my colleague in the Carter administration when he was secretary of the Treasury. It is a remarkable, jarring building, like a shattered star, with no straight lines, asymmetrical walls, sloping walkways—a tribute to the Jewish contribution to German life over the centuries. Its chilling triangular Holocaust room, with huge metal door that slams shut behind you, only one dim light, and an opening to the elements near the high ceiling, gave me a claustrophobic feeling of dread. It was a reminder of why I was in Germany.

But neither sentiment nor Rau's willingness to issue an apology would conclude these negotiations. I needed the victims' side to settle for their absolute minimum of 10 billion marks and the German government to move from its "absolute maximum" by another 2 billion.

Once again I would need my heaviest artillery, the president of the United States. I learned that Clinton, Schröder, and Prime Minister Tony

Blair of Britain were meeting on Sunday, November 21, in Florence for a "third way" conference on how they had moved their parties into the political center and back to power. Antony Blinken, the National Security Council's top European assistant, readily agreed to put the problem on Clinton's private agenda with Schröder and briefed me later on what happened.

Clinton told Schröder that both sides were close but had to do a little more; perhaps the extra money could be budgeted over two or three years. Schröder pleaded budget stringency. Undaunted, Clinton came back and pointed out what a success it would be for both sides to put the past behind them. Schröder said he wanted to avoid an impasse that had left such ill will in Switzerland. But now the German companies reckoned it was cheaper to go to court than to pay more, and pressing them for more would raise an anti-Semitic backlash. Blinken reported to me the grim news that, "It was as close to a no as you can get, although he didn't slam the door shut."

In a gloomy letter of December 1, Schröder reminded the president that he had already followed the president's recommendation in his November 13 letter and increased the German offer from 6 billion to 8 billion DM. But, he said bluntly and seemingly conclusively, there "was no scope for any further increases." He closed with a dire warning. If the German offer of 8 billion DM was again declined, the foundation would probably collapse with "wholly unpredictable results of such a failure for German-American relations." This was an explicit warning that a failure of the talks not only would have a negative impact on German companies doing business in the United States but might cause broader divisions between the two close allies.

The Germans suspected that even if they agreed to settle at 10 billion, it would be only a temporary way station to some higher demand. So I needed to line up the victims' side quickly to agree to a deal for 10 billion DM and confirm for the Germans that it would really settle the wartime claims once and for all. I had been working for several weeks on the Eastern Europeans to lower their sights and accept my 10 billion DM figure, and here Poland was the key.

On November 15, I met with Bronislaw Geremek, the Polish foreign minister. To me he represented the best in post-Communist Poland. Tall, lean, slightly stooped, he had a dignity and a sorrowful demeanor that reflected the fact that he was an Auschwitz survivor of Jewish descent. After reassuring him that Poland's 200,000 surviving agricultural workers would be covered, I admonished him not to demand more from the Germans than they would bear. Poland would surely be joining Germany as a member of the European Union within a few years, I stressed, and the Poles should not allow these negotiations to poison what was already a historically difficult relationship. I was delighted and relieved when he told me, "I am ready for a flexible solution," and would endorse my 10 billion DM figure.

In intensive meetings and telephone calls between November 24 and December 3, the class-action attorneys agreed to drop their range to 10 billion to 11 billion DM. Weiss recognized that he had milked his public pressure for as much as it was worth, asked Senator Schumer to call off his legislative push, and stopped his anti-German ads. He told me, "I am torn up inside on this, and one thing I believe is they are getting away with murder." He implored me not to praise the German companies—"Just say it is the best you can get from them." Nevertheless, the lawyers tried to squeeze out the last drop and held out for the top of their new range, at 11 billion DM.

I then engaged in what I could only call creative accounting. I persuaded Lambsdorff and Gentz to add the interest that would be earned on the money while we were getting the cases dismissed and setting up the foundation, that would now be one joint private sector–federal government organization. They ended up agreeing to pay at least 100 million DM in interest. But most ambitious was my idea to create a "mirror image" fund for the dozens of American companies whose big German subsidiaries had employed slave labor. According to a 1943 Treasury Department list, the more celebrated names included Ford, General Motors, Gillette, IBM, and Kodak, among many others.

I got off to a fast start on December 3, when I met with John Rintamaki, Ford's group vice president and chief of staff. An energetic, upbeat person, he got right to the point. Strikingly frank, he volunteered that Henry Ford, the company's founder, was a notorious anti-Semite who had been publicly recognized by Hitler for his work in Germany. He made no attempt to deny that the Nazis had employed forced and slave laborers in Ford's plants and promised to help recruit American companies with a goal of raising half a billion dollars. He said his task would be easier if we could create a charitable organization so the corporate contributions would qualify as tax deductions.

Craig Johnstone, head of the international division of the U.S. Chamber of Commerce and a former State Department colleague, made it easier for the companies to contribute without appearing to admit wartime guilt by persuading the Chamber of Commerce to approve a humanitarian fund that its corporate membership could use for everything from hurricane to Holocaust relief. We jointly launched it with fanfare at a news conference at the chamber's Washington, D.C., headquarters.

But the money never arrived. Despite several more meetings with Rintamaki, who made a genuine effort to convince other firms to join, it was a dry hole. In December 2001, two years after my first meeting with Rintamaki and well after the end of the Clinton administration, one of Rintamaki's aides told me that the Ford Motor Company would contribute $2 million. No other American company ever gave a nickel to the chamber fund, relying upon their German subsidiaries to pay instead into the German Foundation.

All my creative accounting still could not bridge the gap, with the Germans stuck at 8 billion and the lawyers at 11 billion. I called for a full-court press, with Secretary Albright, Secretary Summers, Sandy Berger, and John Podesta all contacting their German counterparts. But the only significant response from these efforts was Ambassador Kornblum reporting to me that Schröder feared too high a settlement could arouse Germany's far right.

While the Germans dithered, outside pressures were at work. CalPERS, the California Public Employees' Retirement System, which is not only the world's largest but one of the most active in corporate governance, sent letters to twenty-five German companies in its portfolio implying it might dump its holdings of their stocks if the class-action suits were not settled. At the same time, the American Jewish Committee took full-page advertisements in major newspapers listing 275 German companies that had used slave and forced labor during the war. Still there was no immediate response.

The next week, December 6–13, was especially intense. Everything seemed to be coming apart. Lambsdorff said that representatives of Allianz had been "treated like convicted criminals" at a hearing before the California Insurance Commission and had been forced into contributing to a new California humanitarian fund. Hausfeld was backsliding, now talking of 12 billion marks, which in turn put pressure on Weiss not to look soft. Weiss boasted to me that the Germans "won't walk away from 12 billion DM; we will batter them. They'll come back to the table like the Swiss."

Unaware of the backtracking on the lawyers' side, Lambsdorff told me that, whatever Schröder might be saying about sticking to 8 billion marks, if I could organize a unified front from the victims for a settlement of 10 billion marks, the chancellor would rethink his position. That would be no easy task with that fractious coalition. Singer said that he, Weiss, Neuborne, Swift, and Fagan could accept 10 billion, but Hausfeld was the holdout.

I went back to Hausfeld and urged him to be a statesman. He now held the agreement in his hands, I said. After a long pause, he said, "Okay." But getting to 10 billion marks was still not so simple. A few days later, Hausfeld, Weiss, and Neuborne marched into my office and announced they had reached a consensus. Hausfeld crowed proudly that they all would settle at 10.5 billion DM plus the additional costs of administering the foundation. I blew up at them, practically shouting, "You're going to screw it all up over 500 million." They asked to rethink the matter and marched out.

Neuborne and Hausfeld called later in the day to explain that they needed the extra 500 million DM to satisfy all the competing demands. I told them to forget it. Here again, Neuborne was a constructive influence, convincing Hausfeld to give in. Hausfeld then backed away, agreeing to 10 billion if I could raise an additional fund from the American corporations. I foolishly said I hoped I could raise the equivalent of another 1 billion DM, or a half billion U.S. dollars, the figure Rintamaki had given me.

They took this as a commitment but agreed to settle with the Germans now and hope I could raise the rest later. But one remaining misunderstanding would surface only later. The class-action lawyers, Singer, and I (and my team) all assumed that valid insurance policies would be paid over and above the 10 billion marks. The Germans understood everything was within the 10 billion figure, including insurance. But at this point neither side was aware of the looming dispute.

I telephoned Lambsdorff at 9:00 A.M. on Sunday, December 12. Now that I had a firm figure of 10 billion DM from the lawyers, he could take it to the chancellor. At 5:00 P.M.—11:00 P.M. in Germany—Lambsdorff called. He said that Schröder wanted a letter from Clinton confirming the lawyers' agreement accepting 10 billion DM and guaranteeing to end all legal action. It was even harder to contain my own elation when Sandy Berger called just before 9:00 P.M. to confirm the deal. "Stu, this is an enormous accomplishment. I don't know how you got the Germans over the 8 billion. This is something you'll carry with you for the rest of your life. It's just terrific." I thanked him but told him we would need to get the president's letter out immediately. I would draft it, and he promised to get it moving the next day.

The deal was not sealed until we sent the president's letter and received an official reply. We did something rarely if ever done with a presidential letter to a foreign head of government, breaking even more diplomatic traditions. We negotiated it with the Washington lawyers for the German companies—Lloyd Cutler and his partners, Roger Witten and Robert Kimmit. Until they agreed to the language for the legal peace the Germans insisted upon, Schröder would object to any increased contribution from the German government.

We had tried unsuccessfully for months to persuade Gentz and his colleagues that their best protection against future suits was a traditional class-action settlement overseen by a federal judge. Even their own lawyer, Roger Witten, told our team that it was "striking not just to Stu but to me that the German companies refused the surest route to legal peace, from class-action releases." But the Germans feared that a traditional class-action settlement would be an admission of guilt that would only create a precedent for even more lawsuits. No amount of argument could convince them otherwise. We needed a hybrid solution.

Now our "legal think tank" came through, as we negotiated several documents with the Germans in an attempt to protect them from being dragged back into court. The most important was entitled "The Elements of the Statement of Interest," in which we agreed on the elements of what the U.S. government would argue in U.S. courts to help dismiss lawsuits against German companies. There was no precedent in American history for such a legal negotiation by the U.S. government with private companies and for intervening this way in present and future private lawsuits.

President Clinton's earlier letters to Schröder had granted concession after concession to give the Germans more reassurance of legal peace, each one of which I had to extract in tough negotiations not only with the Germans but our own Justice Department, which was uneasy about this novel posture by the U.S. government. We had received explicit assurances from Gentz and Lambsdorff in our November 16–17 negotiating round of their satisfaction with the legal peace we were providing. Lambsdorff even applauded me for working "indefatigably to achieve legal closure, and we are all grateful."

In what I thought was a conclusive December 9 negotiation with Roger

Witten, I made the last concession I believed possible. We strengthened the statement of interest so that the U.S. government would affirmatively state that dismissal of lawsuits was consistent with our foreign policy interests. Witten is a careful lawyer, so his reaction was music to my ears and what I had waited months to hear: "Bingo! That does it for me and all the American lawyers and for the German businessmen." Lambsdorff also said firmly that this "solves the problem of closure" for him and Gentz.

I rushed to incorporate our verbal agreement into the president's letter of December 13. Our team and I negotiated every sentence with Witten and his partners and with the Justice Department, whose officials were prepared to make only a foreign policy argument in court but not to prejudge the legal outcome. The president's letter told the chancellor that we had obtained a firm commitment from all the victims' representatives to settle at 10 billion marks and recited the language of legal closure that I had so carefully negotiated with the German-industry lawyers. Schröder responded by letter the next day, accepting the settlement and the terms of legal peace for "all payments for former Nazi slave and forced laborers, damage to property, as well as for the Future Fund." He closed by thanking the president, Lambsdorff, and me.

Disagreements about the letters broke out even before the ink was dry. One was over legal fees. Hausfeld argued that the fees for the lawyers had to be over and above the 10 billion. The Germans balked—10 billion was 10 billion. My solution was to bury the legal fees in the amount we allocated for administrative fees. For once, Hausfeld was positive. "God bless you, and thank you for not forgetting us," he said. Singer added, "We thank you and the Jewish people thank you."

# CHAPTER THIRTEEN

# A Strange Ending

WITH PRESIDENT CLINTON's personal thanks still ringing in my ears as he announced our 10 billion DM settlement on the South Lawn of the White House, I returned to Berlin for the signing ceremony on December 17, 1999, one of the most satisfying days of my life. The plenary session was held before a crush of press in the large conference center at Berlin's Grand Hyatt Hotel. Count Lambsdorff, German foreign minister Joschka Fischer, Secretary Albright, and I sat at the head of a mammoth set of rectangular tables. A huge space separated us from the Eastern Europeans, Israelis, the representatives of the Claims Conference, German business, and the class-action lawyers, who were arrayed all around. That distance was a metaphor for what was to come.

Lambsdorff told his fellow Germans it was fair for them to be paying half the cost, because the Nazi state had sponsored the deportation and criminal employment for which Germany now was belatedly making amends. He gave the class-action lawyers their due by conceding that without their suits "we wouldn't have started." There could be no appropriate price for what happened, he said, but the 10 billion DM amount was "dignified, fair, and appropriate."

Gentz, the hard-bitten negotiator for German industry, was the most expansive, accepting moral responsibility and issuing a pledge that German companies would open their archives to "shed light on the dark pages of history," a demand of the plaintiffs' attorneys. He appealed to all German companies to contribute to the fund as an act of solidarity, whether or not they had used coerced labor.

At the joint news conference that followed, it was Schröder who took the bark off the past with a bluntness rare for leaders addressing their own citizens. He hoped this would be a fitting end to a "bloody century [when] Germany inflicted suffering on the world and perpetrated the Holocaust, a scar that cannot be healed." Germans could only hope to alleviate some of the pain, and legal closure would matter less than historical significance. Schröder, Lambsdorff, and I clasped each other's hands outside the press center, with all the parties standing behind us, to cement our agreement.

The event that capped a very special day was Rau's public apology before the cameras at his presidential residence. He "begged forgiveness" on behalf of the German people for the mistreatment of slave and forced laborers. Even the class-action lawyers were moved. Roman Kent, the Holocaust survivor from the Claims Conference, was so taken by Rau's sentiments that he spontaneously leaped from the audience to the president's microphone and cried, "This is what we wanted to hear."

The glow of the day quickly wore off. Soon it was as if nothing had been settled. I would never have imagined that more than half a year would be required to reach an actual settlement, beginning with negotiating—or more precisely, bickering over—the distribution of the money. As the Germans say, "*Der Teufel ist im Detail*" (the devil is in the detail).

·     ·     ·

I LEARNED that we had paid a stiff price for pressing the Germans to merge the private and public foundations into one. Although it helped persuade Schröder to pay half the bill, the German Finance Ministry took over drafting the legislation establishing the foundation, putting in charge a shy career official, Otto Loeffler, who had been responsible for implementing Germany's remaining postwar compensation programs.

Loeffler's drafting took place in bureaucratic isolation from industry or diplomacy, and many of our hard-earned compromises went out the window. Ambassador Kornblum described this as the narrow German mode of the *Beamte*, the civil servant deliberately insulated from wider considerations and oblivious to the political consequences of his actions, the arrogant isolation of the bureaucracy dating back to the proud Prussian civil service of the nineteenth century. Even the German firms were upset. Their attorney, Robert Kimmit, a former U.S. ambassador to Germany, complained that the German government was "proceeding as if this was just another piece of legislation where we're not involved." When Gentz raised complaints, the bureaucrats "blew him off," in Kimmit's words.

This exposed the contrast between Germany and the United States in the relationship between business and government. Big business in Germany is much more reluctant to lobby government on specific issues than in the United States—and often is ignored when it does so.

Kornblum advised me to take matters to the political level to head off the "headless horsemen, a car without a driver. I don't know how to stop it." At my request, Lambsdorff agreed to delay having the government forward the monstrosity to the Bundestag for passage. Better to get it right. He found it "embarrassing, after Berlin, to have these problems."

It took weeks of painstaking calls and meetings to revise Loeffler's draft bill, and another spate of letters from Albright, Summers, Berger, and Podesta—who himself added a handwritten postscript stressing the urgency of bringing the draft legislation into line with our previous agreements. In addition, I testified before the Domestic Affairs Committee of the Bundestag, a rare appearance for a government official before another country's legislative body. I recognized the Bundestag's sovereign right to legislate but noted the need to capture all of the nuances of our compromises in their legislation. The Bundestag never fully got it right. What was passed in the end largely incorporated our agreement but departed in areas like attorneys' fees. Lambsdorff and I had to supplement the bill with a series of side letters to reassure the class-action lawyers and Claims Conference that the new foundation created by the Bundestag would honor our hard-earned compromises.

.    .    .

BUT THE problems with the draft legislation paled by comparison with the three-month torment of deciding how to allocate the 10 billion DM. Whatever semblance of unity there had been among the Eastern Europeans, plaintiffs' attorneys, and Claims Conference in persuading the Germans to pay the maximum possible broke into open warfare as they tried to divide the pie. The process brought out the worst in everyone. In fact, new labor claimants popped up, with the Romani (gypsy) community and the Jehovah's Witnesses presenting to me compelling evidence of slave labor conditions similar to those of Jewish concentration camp inmates.

Everyone agreed that we should avoid repeating the mistake of the Swiss negotiations, where the parties agreed on a lump sum settlement of $1.25 billion but left it up to the court to allocate the funds. This was a primary reason for the three-year delay in getting money to victims. We would have to negotiate the division of the 10 billion DM ourselves, but no one could have imagined how difficult this would be.

There were essentially three categories of claims that had to be satisfied. First were those of conscripted workers. The issue of how much should be allocated to each pitted the Eastern Europeans against the Claims Conference. Second was banking and insurance. Here the principal battle engaged the class-action lawyers, who fought for individual claimants seeking damages for Aryanized assets and unpaid life insurance policies, and the Claims Conference, which sought a large humanitarian fund to help Holocaust victims in general, since most of the claimant families had been killed by the Nazis. And third was the Future Fund, so important to the German companies because it would identify them with projects of tolerance and help them raise funds from German companies not implicated in World War II.

Initially Lambsdorff and I hoped to sit back and let the other parties fight it out. But it soon became clear that this would tear the agreement apart. The first and most critical issue was how much of the 10 billion marks should go to the laborers; next was how that amount would be divided between slave laborers and forced laborers. Everything else would flow from there. The Eastern Europeans demanded that fully 90 percent of the 10 billion marks should be allocated for laborers. This left little for insurance and banking claims, which were entirely Jewish oriented, or for the Future Fund. After only one day of discussion at the February 1 plenary session, the Germans plunked down their own detailed scheme, yet again without any consultation: allocating 7.7 billion marks for workers; 1 billion for the Future Fund; 1 billion for banking, property, and insurance settlements; and the rest for administration. I could barely contain my frustration at their lack of coordination with me.

The key was to persuade the Eastern Europeans to scale down their 90 percent demand for laborers, and central to that was again Poland, the country with the best organized and most vocal delegation and the one with the greatest sense of grievance against the Germans. It was no simple task to soften up Foreign Minister Bronislaw Geremek when we met at the Polish Embassy in Washington, on February 9, 2000. Removing his glasses from his weathered face, this Auschwitz survivor looked me in the eyes and said, "I was a slave laborer in a German machine shop." He did not need to remind me that the Poles—Jews and non-Jews alike—had received virtually nothing over the decades from the Germans.

On February 16, the night before the next plenary session, I decided to put the antagonists together in the large conference room in the U.S. Embassy in Berlin. I hoped that directly confronting one another's pain would produce in each a shared recognition of the need to compromise. It was an evening heavy with the history of pent-up emotions. Polish deputy foreign minister Jerzy Kranz opposed humanitarian programs run by the Claims Conference and more money for Jewish property claims because Eastern Europeans had gotten "far less than the Jewish victims" over the past five decades. Roman Kent emotionally objected: "This is not a fight with the Eastern Europeans; both peoples suffered, and it is obscene to fight over it." For all of the tensions, the meeting had a positive impact, an epiphany, as each side heard the others' grievances.

The plenary session itself had a historic twist because it was the first major international meeting at the new Foreign Ministry in Berlin. Perhaps it was the setting or, more likely, the recognition that there were only so many ways to carve up this 10 billion DM turkey, but the parties tried to be civil while nevertheless pursuing their maximum demands. Singer called for a "new spirit of Berlin so we do not fight each other as gladiators." But the thin veneer of civility masked deep feelings.

For two months, through several formal plenary sessions in Berlin and Washington and scores of calls and small meetings, I struggled to come up with a formula that would suit everyone. This was a zero-sum game. Every deutsche mark we allocated to one category was a deutsche mark taken away from another worthy claimant. The bargaining over how to slice up the pie, with limitless permutations, became so complex that our State Department specialist, Jody Manning, had to keep track of all the competing demands on a computer spreadsheet.

Tempers flared. Ed Fagan said that the disagreement among the lawyers was outrageous: "The Germans are watching us behave like vultures over a dead piece of meat." Mel Weiss insultingly suggested that the funds for Eastern Europe would be drained off to government officials. The normally unflappable elder statesman Lambsdorff said, "It is unbelievable that we can agree to 10 billion DM and not agree how to divide it up. No one group can take so much that there is not enough left for others. Where do you want us to go, for God's sake?"

My job was clear. The only way to bring everyone together was for me to persuade Lambsdorff to forge a joint proposal and ram it down everyone's throats. Even the lawyers were ready. "Someone needs to break the tie, and we trust you to do it," Neuborne told me. So Lambsdorff and I set a "make or break" session for Berlin for March 22–23. We had to put an end to the haggling or let everyone know the entire enterprise would collapse.

Before this session, Lambsdorff and I agreed on what we called the Joint Chairmen's Proposal. This required heavy lifting for Lambsdorff, who had to move Gentz and his industry colleagues off their February 1 proposal. It called for 8.1 billion DM for labor, divided among the Claims Conference, the five Eastern European nations, and claimants living in the rest of the world. The Eastern Europeans had demanded their forced laborers receive half of what slave laborers, mostly Jewish, received. Singer and the Claims Conference wanted closer to a four-to-one ratio. Lambsdorff and I compromised on a three-to-one ratio—slave laborers would each receive up to 15,000 DM and forced workers up to 5,000 DM, depending upon the number of actual surviving claimants. There was 1 billion DM for property claims, banking, and insurance, which in turn was subdivided between a claims and a humanitarian component, with the humanitarian getting the majority. The Future Fund, for which Gentz had insisted on 1 billion DM, was reduced, much to his great displeasure, to 700 million. And 200 million DM would go for the administrative costs of running the German foundation and for legal fees for the class-action lawyers. This became the final agreement, but not before there was more blood on the floor.

The old adage that to make an omelette you have to break some eggs was never truer. I had to reach two secret deals in order to seal the agreement. The first was with the Poles, the strongest holdouts for a huge allocation for laborers. For weeks they refused to budge in demanding 9 billion of the 10 billion DM for laborers, leading me to tell them to "have a nice life—we'll go on without you." Now I needed a different approach. On March 22 in Berlin I asked to see the Polish delegation alone. I told them that I recognized the unrequited injustices they had suffered since the war and offered to add to the amount allocated to Poland another $10 million (20 million DM) that would not show up in the official allocation. It would come from the $25 million Congress had appropriated to the Nazi Persecutee Relief

Fund following the 1997 London gold conference. I swore them to secrecy. Ministers Jerzy Widzyk and Jerzy Kranz were clearly moved by the gesture. Within a few hours they had gotten all the other Eastern Europeans to accept the Joint Chairmen's Proposal.

The second private deal was with Singer, Gideon Taylor, and the Claims Conference at a four-hour session that stretched from late in the night of March 22 until 2:45 A.M. Gentz, Lambsdorff, and our team were present. It was fitting that Singer, a superb negotiator, should be among the last pieces of the puzzle to fall into place. In order to build up the amount allocated to the five Eastern European countries, I had persuaded Singer to agree to allow them amounts for their Jewish slave labor survivors as well as for their non-Jewish forced laborers. For Singer this was a difficult concession. Many of the elderly survivors in the Claims Conference delegation distrusted the Eastern Europeans as anti-Semites who would never allow their Jewish citizens to get a fair share of the money. But Singer was a statesman. If he refused to allow the Eastern Europeans to control funding for all of their victims it could lead to deep resentment and increased anti-Semitism, especially since Singer had become convinced over the course of our lengthy negotiations that close to half the slave laborers were non-Jews, subject to the same brutalities as the Jews. He "took hell" from the Jewish survivors, but Singer kept his agreement with me. Just before meeting with me, he informed the Polish delegation of his decision.

But Singer made two midnight demands as a price. One was to give the Claims Conference a loose, "dual key" oversight over the lists of people the Eastern Europeans would pay, to assure funds were not diverted away from Jewish survivors. The second was harder to swallow, especially for the Germans. Singer and Taylor argued that there were some 8,000 Jewish slave laborers who lived in other parts of the world not represented in our talks, and they wanted the Claims Conference to control the money for them. They also wanted to be given enough money to pay the 28,000 Jewish forced laborers in this category the full 5,000 DM each. It meant that a third of the funds we had set aside for this group—we called it "Rest of the World"—would go to them. Gentz and Lambsdorff were appalled. So was I, telling Singer bluntly that his position threatened the talks and could create the very anti-Semitic backlash he had been trying to avert. Singer responded angrily that he could not compromise further. With the visibly reluctant consent of the Germans, I agreed to a secret footnote in the German legislation to give these Jewish laborers an additional amount of 260 million DM, or $130 million. This effectively meant less for non-Jewish forced laborers, primarily in Western Europe and the United States. I reluctantly gave in to this demand because I believed Singer might have aborted the deal on the spot. It was too risky at this stage to call his bluff. But I remain embarrassed at the concession.

With only a few hours' rest following the grueling session with Singer, we began what was the most bitter and intense negotiation of the entire saga with Germany, the one to break the back of the dispute over insurance. Insurance had hung over us like a dark cloud throughout the negotiations. The dilemma was how to square two separate processes: our negotiations with Allianz and other German insurance companies as part of the broad German Initiative, and those headed by former Secretary of State Lawrence Eagleburger with five major European insurers, of which Allianz was the only German member.

My first contact with the German private sector had been not over slave and forced labor but over insurance, when I met before the German elections with Henning Schulte-Noelle, the tall, austere chairman of Allianz, in my State Department office in August 1998. He took pains to point out that Allianz and other German insurers were different from Swiss banks. They had paid thousands of beneficiaries under postwar German restitution laws. Nevertheless, Allianz was signing a memorandum of understanding (MOU) with the Claims Conference and some forty state insurance commissioners in the United States to create the International Commission on Holocaust-Era Insurance Claims (ICHEIC).

Under the agreement, Allianz and four other European insurance giants, AXA of France, Winterthur and Zurich of Switzerland, and Generali of Italy, would agree to open their files and pay any remaining World War II claims. In exchange, the state insurance commissioners would grant them "safe harbor" protection from sanctions. As was the case with the Volcker Commission for the Swiss banks, Israel Singer and the World Jewish Congress were also represented. I appointed J. D. Bindenagel as our U.S. government representative to ICHEIC.

At the request of the leaders of the National Association of Insurance Commissioners, Glenn Pomeroy of North Dakota and Neil Levin of New York (who would later be killed in the September 11 World Trade Center tragedy), I was asked to encourage Eagleburger to chair the commission. I thought he was a great choice. Even though we belonged to different political parties, my respect and affection for him dated to my days in the Carter White House, when he was the U.S. ambassador to Yugoslavia. He was then as now blunt, irreverent, gruff, irascible, and brilliant. Now, twenty years later and close to seventy, Eagleburger was in deteriorating health. He was heavy, with a bad hip, and he walked painfully with a cane. A chain smoker, he suffered from chronic asthma, alternately puffing on a cigarette and inhaling an aerator.

He agreed to accept the chairmanship and later told me it was the worst decision of his life. He said that negotiating with the Soviets at the height of the Cold War was easier than trying to convince the European insurers and Singer's Claims Conference to agree. There was incessant internal bickering over every issue—how to value policies from prewar days, which lists of policyholders should be opened, the costs to be borne in processing claims, the ICHEIC claims process itself. Eagleburger had difficulty getting the companies, particularly Allianz, to fulfill the terms of the MOU. Allianz's chief negotiator, Herbert Hansmeyer, the head of its North American division, was an unrelenting bulldog of a negotiator. And ICHEIC's administrative failings led to few claims paid and large costs. All took a toll on Eagleburger's already tenuous health. But he held on out of a sense of duty, frequently threatening to resign and actually doing so for twenty-four hours in February 2002 to try to bring sense to the warring parties.

The fear Schulte-Noelle had gravely expressed to me in the summer of 1998, that Allianz would end up paying twice, once to ICHEIC and again to the class-action lawyers, continued to bedevil me. Unless I could resolve this issue, we could not complete our deal with Germany, which insisted that all World War II claims had to be resolved before it would pay the 10 billion DM settlement.

I tried for over a year to find a solution, but Eagleburger wanted nothing to do with my negotiations—reminding me of Paul Volcker in the Swiss negotiations—primarily because of his deep disdain for the class-action lawyers, whom he called "parasites." He wanted none of the insurance money to be diverted into their pockets. It took all my pushing to persuade him finally to meet with them. But he made it clear he came only under duress, and the meeting in the Treasury conference room tingled with animosity, prompting Weiss to blurt out, "If this breaks up over insurance, I'll be happy."

Beyond personalities, there were major substantive differences. The Germans disingenuously argued that in agreeing to their last-second addition to President Clinton's December 13 letter, which specifically mentioned insurance companies, we had agreed that all insurance claims had to come within the 10 billion DM cap rather than in addition to it, as our team, the class-action lawyers, and the Claims Conference had been led to believe. We understood Hansmeyer to frequently assure us that of course they would honor any legitimate insurance claims, without being bound by an artificial ceiling for all other claims.

To crack this huge nut, on the morning of March 23 I put all the parties together in one conference room off the main hall of the newly renovated Foreign Ministry building in Berlin. Appropriately, the building had been an extension to the wartime Reichsbank, where the Nazis had planned the war's financing. I told everyone to consider the doors locked until we reached an agreement. We went nonstop for five hours, punctuated with bitter statements like Hansmeyer's warning of fraud because "Jewish groups will stir people up" to make questionable insurance claims in the former Communist countries.

When we came up for air, we had an agreement. Claims against German companies would be handled consistently with ICHEIC principles. The amount set aside for insurance humanitarian funds, where there were no living beneficiaries, would flow to ICHEIC. In case there were more claimants than anticipated, a reserve of an additional 100 million DM would be created within the Future Fund. Everyone had to compromise and did, particularly the victims' side, which swallowed the bitter pill of including insurance claims inside the 10 billion DM ceiling. Eagleburger had to agree to Allianz's demand that it contribute only once, to the German Foundation, and not also to ICHEIC. Lambsdorff assured us that with this deal all of the other German insurance companies would join ICHEIC. "They will come; don't push them publicly," he told me. "They will join. I am absolutely sure." They never have to this day.

When we moved to the formal plenary it was all done, secret deals and all. I was bone tired but elated. Everything now seemed in place. We had the 10 billion DM. We had agreed on how to divide it down to the last pfennig. And we had been assured that the Germans were satisfied with legal peace. I even worked through a last-minute demand by the German Foreign Ministry to foreclose suits by American POWs, eventually persuading the Pentagon and the Germans to agree to keep the current uncertain status quo about their right to sue Germany. There was only one discordant note. As we were all about to depart, Gentz suddenly said that, although he was pleased about our success in dividing up the 10 billion DM, "I am less happy there is still no resolution on legal closure." I did not understand what he was talking about.

I had presumed that the legal peace issue had been settled by the December exchange of letters between Clinton and Schröder. It was as if we were starting from scratch. This was no misunderstanding. It was a deliberate effort to reopen a closed book and a direct affront to the president and our team, who had painstakingly negotiated every word with the German companies' lawyers. Industry's last-minute maneuvers to obtain even more than was agreed by their own elected national leader removed for me much of the moral dimension of German industry's original initiative.

The last-minute dispute started innocently enough with Witten's request at the end of April for a further assurance that the German Foundation "should be regarded as the exclusive remedy for all claims against German companies arising out of the Nazi era." But it soon became obvious that German industry wanted more than semantic changes. They insisted upon a definitive commitment by the United States to support some legal ground for the dismissal of future suits, rather than simply stating that dismissal was in our foreign policy interests, as we had agreed. Lloyd Cutler repeated ad nauseam in meeting after meeting that "the U.S. needs to support one or more legal grounds for dismissal." This tested to the limit my long positive relationship with my distinguished former Carter White House colleague. The Germans and their lawyers knew full well from months of explanation that we would not take a formal legal position barring U.S. citizens from their own courts, and the president's letter they helped draft had reflected this. "I don't disagree we have been over this in the president's letter," Witten admitted, but nevertheless there "is an obsession on our side," he said, that there had to be a legal basis for dismissal coming from the U.S. government, not just a foreign policy statement.

We held fast, and the Germans tried one ploy after another to get us to bite. Then Cutler and his partners made a strategic mistake that came close to losing more than a year's worth of work on a historic agreement. Cutler tried an end run to Seth Waxman, his old friend, who was now the solicitor general of the United States. The solicitor general's office is unique, for its occupant—the government's chief advocate before the Supreme Court—is not only a member of the executive branch but also an officer of the court. As soon as he heard Cutler's arguments and the German lawyers', Waxman, who had not been previously engaged in our talks, decided that I had already given away too much and that the Germans were trying to shoehorn our nation's foreign policy interests into the corpus of the law. Waxman was also aghast that, at his initial meeting at the Justice Department with German industry, one of the lawyers from Germany said that they wanted a "final solution" to their legal problems, insensitively evoking Hitler's Final Solution. To this day, Waxman refers to this meeting as the "final solution" meeting.

Gentz insisted that no money would be paid to a single victim until all of the fifty pending cases were dismissed, even those in state courts. One headstrong judge could halt all payments by simply allowing a suit to proceed. Waxman's temperature level began to reach the boiling point. He correctly felt that the Germans were overreaching. They "are setting us up for failure," he said—and he was intent on refusing them any further concessions. Waxman, fearing that I would go too far to accommodate them, even wrote me a stern letter standing up for the Justice Department's right to answer a judge's questions about the U.S. government's view of legal issues in the German cases, even if the result was that cases brought against German companies would not be dismissed.

The Germans had needlessly opened a can of worms. Before bringing in Waxman, Justice seemed content to be neutral on any legal argument by either side. Now Waxman wanted to affirmatively rebut those German arguments with which he disagreed, such as Germany's contention that postwar agreements barred suits against German companies. Otherwise, Waxman argued, U.S. judges would be "suspicious" that the Justice Department had compromised its independent judgment.

Intending to placate Waxman, I made a major mistake. I disregarded the basic diplomatic maxim that, to achieve agreement, studied ambiguity is often better than excessive legal precision. He persuaded me to sign a May 18 letter to Lambsdorff emphasizing the Justice Department's position that our statement of interest represented only a policy position and not a legal position; and moreover that if the Germans continued to insist that our own negotiations, the fifty-five years of governmental cooperation on Holocaust matters, or the postwar treaties themselves were legal bars to future lawsuits against them, "we will need to make clear our position to the contrary."

Just as the Germans had thrown down the legal gauntlet to us, we were throwing it back in their faces. The letter provoked a furious reaction. Gentz complained that it was one thing for the United States to stay silent but another to actively oppose their legal arguments.

To resolve the standoff, I went to Berlin on June 1 for an all-day session that lasted until almost 1:00 A.M. at the DaimlerChrysler center, the only building on the famous Potsdamerplatz left standing by American bombardment during the war. This proved a metaphor for the meeting's unsuccessful outcome: The Germans remained unshaken. In the margins of my yellow legal pad I wrote, "Tension is like waiting for a baby in the delivery room." But there would be no baby born this long night. Lambsdorff was for the first time visibly uneasy about where we were headed. He privately lamented to me that what he called "legal ayatollahs" whom "we have never seen in our negotiations are sabotaging this." These were the German companies' lawyers based in Germany and their American trial lawyers who were itching to try the cases if our negotiations failed.

I was going to have to turn to politics once again. Before going to bed I made one last call to Tony Blinken, who was traveling with President Clinton in Germany. Tony had briefed the president about the impasse between the Germans and the Justice Department. He told me that the president's reaction was that the Department of Justice was being "hard over [a favorite phrase at the Clinton White House, meaning unyielding], given what Stu has done." The president would raise the matter with Schröder when they met, before the president was to receive the Charlemagne Award in Aachen on June 2. The last thing the president needed was a negative story about our negotiations. In effect we were negotiating in Germany simultaneously at both my level and that of the heads of government. Tony also reminded me of something easy to forget in the heat of bargaining: "The last step is always the hardest in any negotiation."

This proved to be correct. Negotiations with both the Germans and— equally difficult—within the U.S. government occupied almost every waking hour for the next week. Waxman developed a creative formulation that said the Justice Department would favor dismissing the suits "on any valid legal ground." For the first time, proposed language evoked something less than contempt from the Germans. But Waxman continued to insist that he would argue against the German interpretation of the postwar treaties if asked by the U.S. Supreme Court, unless the President himself committed to be silent.

This led me back to the White House, where irresolvable differences between agencies are brokered—and we were at that point now. Waxman and I met with National Security Adviser Sandy Berger, who was both a foreign policy expert and an experienced lawyer with a great capacity to find compromises. What followed was like an intense, two-hour oral argument before a judge. After hearing us out in his spacious West Wing office, Berger said that "the president wants to get this done for foreign policy and humanitarian reasons—old people are dying." Moreover, relations with Germany were going through a rough patch on other issues, like capital punishment and cooperation in the Balkans. Waxman argued that a commitment never to oppose the government's view of its own treaties would undermine his department's credibility with the courts.

Berger shifted to a political level: The German foreign minister had warned him that the slave labor negotiations were straining our relations by bringing to the fore old World War II issues, like the treatment of POWs, with which I had struggled. Sandy urged Waxman not to put the president in the position of facing the stark alternatives of either rolling the Justice Department and earning its ire or accepting their position and aborting our deal. Waxman bent slightly with an exquisite double negative, promising that Justice "will not take a position that there are no legal grounds for dismissal."

But he was tenacious in defending his independence and credibility—suppose the solicitor general refused to respond to a request from the Supreme Court for a government opinion on the treaties? Yes, said Berger, but "there are risks all around if this agreement craters." The magic word "itself" saved the day. I suggested saying that, although we would not foreswear taking a contrary legal position to the Germans, we would not take a legal position "which would itself preclude dismissal of these cases." This meant we would not assert a position that would prevent a dismissal of future cases against the Germans.

"A hole in one," said Waxman, "beautiful as a negotiating position." A double negative again. But he still refused to foreswear in writing taking a negative position in court to the Germans or to revoke my May 18 letter to them, as the Germans were insisting.

I felt at loose ends, so I borrowed a page from the Cuban missile crisis, which was resolved only after John F. Kennedy received two different letters from Nikita Khrushchev and simply ignored the second because the first, far less bellicose, told him what he wanted to hear. I now proposed the opposite. We would ignore my May 18 letter and supersede it with one from Berger and the president's legal counsel, Beth Nolan, who were more definitive voices than I.

We then began what became the final negotiation with the Germans over legal closure on June 12, meeting at the Treasury in the large main conference room opposite the suite that contained my office and that of Secretary Summers. The room has a huge, beautiful gold clock on the far wall, and as the minutes ticked away we all knew this was the last chance at an agreement. Waxman assured the Germans that his department had no intention of volunteering its view in future cases against the German companies but would go no further.

Lambsdorff said he was "depressed that legal arguments are being made while 1 million survivors wait for justice." But he cleverly grasped at the double negative that had emerged from the Berger meeting: Double negatives, he noted, normally are interpreted as a yes. David Ogden of the Justice Department picked up the ball: "It is at worst neutral, as you initially wanted, and at best is supportive of you on one or more legal grounds." Realizing we were starting to see some thaw, I provided a draft letter to supersede our previous proposals. It promised that we would do nothing to keep present and future cases alive and stated that it "will be the enduring and high interest of the United States to support efforts to achieve dismissal of all World War II–era cases"; that the Justice Department "will affirmatively recommend dismissal on any valid legal ground"; and "that the U.S. would take no legal position which would itself preclude dismissal of these cases, and will, in fact, enumerate the real, legal hurdles plaintiffs face."

At this point I was summoned to the White House for a meeting with President Clinton on another matter and asked the Germans to review our proposal. I made it clear that this was truly our last offer. At the end of our meeting President Clinton pulled me aside. In the Cabinet Room, with his back to the Rose Garden, he said, "I understand the Justice Department is being unreasonable. Can I help? Aren't they part of the executive branch? They are taking a ridiculous position!" I explained that we would know within a few hours if the Germans would accept our last offer. If we failed, I would need him again, both with the Germans and our own Department of Justice.

When I returned to my office, my team started drafting two public statements there: one for failure, one for success. Lambsdorff then asked to see me alone. He confided that the German companies were "seeking more than they ever bargained for." I certainly agreed with that!

At 6:00 P.M. the Germans let us know they had called their CEOs and talked with their German lawyers and were ready to return to the Treasury conference room. I was as tense as I could ever remember. With the utter silence of uncertainty flooding the room, Gentz began by apologizing for taking so long but said he had to persuade the German litigation specialists that we had come a long way to achieve "an acceptable degree of legal peace." Then the punch line: "I agree to your proposal, with one addition." My spirits rose and sank in one second; we could not restart the bargaining process. Gentz wanted to elaborate on our promise to recommend dismissing the suits on any valid legal ground with the phrase that any such ground, "under the United States system of jurisprudence, is for the U.S. courts to determine." This seemed harmless to me, and I turned to the solicitor general. Waxman nodded his acceptance and went further by declaring that it is "in our interest to work with you in a friendly and cooperative way." Tension and uncertainty turned to relief and exhilaration.

We overcame the final hurdle by adding a sentence to the Berger-Nolan letter, which was sent to Michael Steiner, the chancellor's national security assistant, on June 16. That sentence said that their letter "clarifies the exchange of correspondence between the parties and states the final position of the Administration on legal closure." This effectively expunged my May 18 letter as inoperative—exactly the way I had planned to resolve my mini-Cuban missile crisis.

My spirits were further lifted the next day when my old friend Lambsdorff called before leaving for Germany. "We finally did this together, the last stumbling block has been removed," he said. Knowing how concerned we were about the problems that had strung out the Swiss payments, he reminded me, it would be up to him to certify legal closure to the German Bundestag so payments could start. He had no intention of waiting years for the last state court to dismiss a suit, as Gentz had demanded, but promised to give the signal when all the federal cases were dismissed. I had come to relish his largeness of spirit, and I told him we would never have succeeded without his willingness time and again to convince both the chancellor and his own business community of the importance of a settlement. He had been indispensable.

.    .    .

WHEN I LANDED in Berlin in the early morning of July 17, I went straight to the hotel where our team had spent several days putting the final documents in order. Finally, I had reason to be satisfied. After eighteen months, the marathon negotiations were finally completed. In a few hours' time, a historic ceremony would take place in an especially appropriate setting. This would be the first major international agreement to be concluded and signed in the new German foreign ministry.

But just as I came into the hotel lobby, I was met by a barrage of almost incomprehensible news. The German lawyers wanted to include the Berger-Nolan letter in the body of the executive agreement between our two countries. We refused and put it in the preamble, making it clear the letter could be taken into account in interpreting the agreement. Worse, several of the American lawyers, led by Ed Fagan, suddenly announced that they would refuse to sign. This would sabotage all our work and be a source of great embarrassment in front of the huge press contingent that was already assembling.

I reached Fagan on a cell phone at his hotel, only later learning that he was also under contract with ABC-TV and wearing a hidden microphone, a record low even for this classic publicity hound. The tape was later aired. Disingenuously claiming he had not realized he was in Berlin for a signing ceremony, he asked for more than a half dozen changes. I told him I would consider them but could not make changes now. Then he got to the point, which was to ensure that he got a fair share of the attorneys' fees. I alternately berated and beseeched him, reminding him I had always treated him honorably—like a *mensch,* I said in our mutual vernacular—when everyone else was ostracizing him. Finally he agreed when I assured him that I would advise Ken Feinberg and former attorney general Nicholas Katzenbach, the arbitrators dividing up the legal fees, that he had made important contributions to the settlement—as indeed he had.

Fagan was not the only holdout. His colleague Bob Swift had not even shown up in Berlin. I had to frantically reach him in Hawaii, pleading that he not undercut all we had done together. I also had to coax Michael Witti, a German plaintiffs' lawyer aligned with Fagan and Swift, home in a sickbed, to sign. Both finally agreed.

With a great relief at having salvaged the agreement, I met the German delegation in their holding room off the main hallway of the Foreign Ministry, expecting congratulations. Instead I was met with a stunning invective few American officials have ever heard from a negotiator in a friendly country, particularly one from the private sector.

All the weight Gentz had carried for his colleagues finally broke over him like one giant tidal wave. What for me was a triumphant moment was for Gentz a moment of great frustration. Soon after I sat down at the table, Gentz launched into a broadside, accusing the United States of reneging on all of the commitments we had made involving legal peace at our marathon June 12 negotiating session in Washington. He then listed a litany of seven separate instances in which he contended we had failed to keep our commitments. These included not making the Nolan-Berger letter, which had sealed our agreement on legal peace, part of the formal executive agreement between Germany and the United States; failing to permit the German side to negotiate the final text of the statement of interest that we would file to facilitate the dismissal of current and future cases; and not seeing key documents.

My team and I considered Gentz's complaints to be totally without foundation. In each of the seven instances, his version of what was promised was simply incorrect, or wishful thinking, or both. We were completely transparent in sharing documents and had a clear understanding with Lambsdorff about the terms of our agreement.

But Gentz's greatest concern was over the timing of German industry's requirement to pay its 5 billion DM share of the 10 billion DM settlement. To avoid delay, I had suggested a certain date, like January 1, 2001. The Germans had rejected my suggestion, and in a major concession to them, I had reluctantly agreed that no payments would be required until all cases were dismissed. Yet, remarkably, Gentz asserted out of the blue that, even after all cases were dismissed, German industry would still not transfer the full 5 billion DM to the German Foundation. Rather, the firms would pay only "as needed" by the foundation for specific payments to victims, and not before. In effect, he wanted the German companies to keep the money in their own accounts for years, reserving the benefits of holding the money for themselves rather than for the victims. It is difficult to conceive of a more outrageous statement, one less in keeping with the spirit of the agreement we were about to sign.

Twice during his outburst, Gentz brushed aside the entreaties of his own foreign minister, Joschka Fischer, who darted into the room to warn him that the cameras were ready and the audience in the vast main hall outside was growing restless. Gentz concluded his bill of particulars against the U.S. government by a final insult. He was "heavily disappointed," he said, and far from the partnership we had promised on June 12 to secure legal peace, there had been "really a dictatorship of the U.S."

Up to that point I had kept my cool. But this was intolerable. The Justice Department's Buchholz remembered later that the temperature in the room seemed to increase ten degrees. I told Gentz, "You should be embarrassed to say that," adding that it was "a sad commentary to work for eighteen months and then have you use the term 'dictatorship.'" I told him angrily that I had not asked for this assignment but had been asked by his government to work on finding a solution to the lawsuits against them. His statement, I went on, "impugns not only us but also the Federal Republic of Germany." I pointedly reminded Gentz that the United States had no history of dictatorship, the implication being clear.

Lambsdorff, trying to calm things down, said, "I would not use the phrase 'dictatorship.'" Gentz reasserted that over the past four weeks, the Americans had decided everything and "didn't talk with us or take into consideration our argument." His only retreat was to suggest that he was only talking about an "economic dictatorship," an unusual statement to come from the chief financial officer of DaimlerChrysler, the newly merged German-American automaker. He grudgingly admitted that he had no choice now but to sign our settlement publicly. But later in the evening, at a dinner for the two delegations, when he had to sign one last document ensuring that the German Foundation would honor our agreement on legal fees, he simply could not bring himself to do it. In disgust, he said the lawyers were getting too much money and "I can't defend it," even though we had agreed that legal fees would be only slightly more than 1 percent of the overall settlement. Turning tartly to his American lawyer, he instructed Roger Witten, "You sign for German industry, not me."

Gentz's behavior epitomized the tensions of our long negotiation to make German companies face their responsibility to the last remaining victims of Nazi tyranny, whom they so grievously injured over fifty years before. But Gentz's final outburst could not detract from the magnitude of what Germany had done. Even though for mixed motives, German industry as a whole finally accepted accountability for their unsavory contributions to the Third Reich—the civil side of Nuremberg's criminal liability. They agreed to pay all surviving coerced laborers, even those for companies that no longer exist. And in an era when political leaders rarely display courage, Chancellor Schröder deserves a chapter in John F. Kennedy's *Profiles in Courage*. He not only pressed German industry to do the right thing but led his own taxpayers to contribute another 5 billion DM on top of their massive Holocaust reparations payments, at a time when he was proposing massive spending cuts in popular social programs. I concluded my negotiations holding a firm conviction that postwar Germany is entitled to full acceptance as a "normal" nation, with a well-ingrained set of democratic values.

# CHAPTER FOURTEEN

# Unser Wien

THE BIBLE says that the sins of the father should not be visited upon the son. But just how much do present generations owe the victims of the past when part of their prosperity is based on their country having enslaved and robbed them? Nowhere in Europe was this question more pointed and more unresolved than in Austria. The nation fought alongside Nazi Germany but long managed to escape its past with the help of an ironic witticism straight from a Viennese coffeehouse: "Austria has managed to convince itself and the world that Beethoven was an Austrian and Hitler was a German." As for the Germans it will always be a matter for debate whether Germany's atonement has been sufficient for its sins, or ever can be. But indisputably, atone Germany has, starting with its first postwar chancellor, Konrad Adenauer, who acknowledged German guilt for the Holocaust and began payments to survivors that now total over 100 billion DM (over $60 billion). To this day the debate engages German writers, artists, intellectuals, and politicians. Not so in Austria, which ignored the complications of its wartime collaboration with Hitler's Reich until it was finally forced by outside forces to look inward.

Germany and Austria have been bound at the hip during much of the twentieth century, so it was little surprise that Austria would next be in the crosshairs of the class-action lawyers. Both countries nursed wounds and grievances from their defeat in World War I. Whereas Germany was strapped with burdensome reparations, Austria lost its huge, cosmopolitan empire and became a rump country. Both were devastated by the Great Depression. Pro-Nazi sentiment soared in Austria during the 1930s, and those pressures together with Hitler's demands pushed the two German-speaking nations together. They became one when the Wehrmacht marched across the border at dawn on March 12, 1938, the day before there was to be a plebiscite, called by Austria's courageous Chancellor Kurt von Schuschnigg, on Austria's independence. Instead, Hitler signed a law incorporating his native land into the German Reich. The vote for *Anschluss* (literally, "connection") between the two was held on April 13 and was a mere formality, winning approval by the totalitarian figure of 99.7 percent.

Anti-Semitic savagery not seen since the Middle Ages was unleashed spontaneously on the sophisticated Jewish community of Vienna. Its swiftness and ferocity surpassed even what had happened in Germany, where Nazi rule had stripped Jews of their freedoms through measures of gradually increasing severity. I got a firsthand view from Kurt Ladner, an Austrian Holocaust survivor. As a boy he recalled the stunning transformation, over the first weekend following the invasion, from a country that tolerated Jews to a nation of hatred. His next-door neighbor, who only months before had allowed him to take chocolate from their Christmas tree, opened his window and shouted at him, "*Heil* Hitler! Kill all the Jews."

Without even a pretense of legality, sweeping orders were issued for the quick confiscation of Jewish property and businesses, frequently without compensation. Austrians themselves still call this the period of "wild Aryanization." Nearly 7,000 Jewish businesses were liquidated between March and June 1938. Jewish dwellings were seized to alleviate Vienna's housing shortage and to reward Austrians who had served the Nazi movement. Jewish religious and cultural institutions—synagogues, schools, hospitals, even the capital's famous Hakoah Sports Club, on whose soccer team Kurt Ladner was a star athlete as a boy—were confiscated or destroyed.

In May 1938 the infamous Nuremberg laws were extended to Austria, dismissing Jews from public service, forbidding them to practice their professions, and banning them from public parks. In August the Central Office for Jewish Emigration was created, its deputy director a nondescript Austrian-born SS officer named Adolf Eichmann. On November 9, 1938, in what became known in Austria and Germany as Kristallnacht, some fifty synagogues were burned and over 4,000 Jewish-owned businesses were looted in Vienna alone. By the end of 1939, 126,000 of Austria's 185,000 Jews had fled. Exit taxes were imposed, which many Jews paid by cashing in their life insurance policies. Many also were pressured to relinquish their property to an Emigration Fund before they were handed their passports. Apartment dwellers and shopkeepers who conducted their lives or businesses under the shelter of long leases, which in normal times could be bought and sold like property, were simply dispossessed. The remaining 60,000 Austrian Jews were killed in Nazi death camps. By the autumn of 1944, 65,000 Hungarian Jews swelled the corps of 700,000 forced laborers on Austrian soil.

Austrians played a disproportionately large role in the Third Reich. Although they represented only 8 percent of the combined German-Austrian population, Austrians made up 14 percent of the SS, and 40 percent of the killing force in Auschwitz. Austrians also joined the Nazi party at the same rate as Germans did.

Hitler's Austrian accomplices were nevertheless encouraged by the Allied powers to style themselves as Hitler's "first victims," a phrase their own leaders, including Chancellor Wolfgang Schuessel, were still using half a century later. Their delusion was fostered from the autumn of 1943, when the foreign ministers of the United States, Great Britain, and the Soviet Union, meeting in Moscow to map strategies for defeating and occupying Germany, promised Austria postwar independence and exoneration. A declaration of November 1 calling the *Anschluss* null and void and Austria "the first victim of Hitlerite aggression" was issued without fanfare or explanation. Although the Allied declaration concluded by "reminding" Austria of its "responsibility which it cannot evade for participating in the war on Hitler's side," this qualifying phrase was lost in the fog. The Allied declaration failed utterly in its purpose of stiffening Austrian resistance to Hitler. But it played a critical role in shaping the country's collective postwar psyche, in effect treating Austria as a liberated, not defeated, nation.

Austria was permitted to denazify itself, which meant that all but the most fervent former Nazis were integrated into positions of power and Austrians avoided guilt for Nazi atrocities. They began distinguishing themselves by wearing Tyrolean and Styrian peasant hats, speaking German with a Viennese dialect, and glorifying Austrian soldiers at war memorials and Austrian victims at concentration camps, with little mention of the Jews.

Under Allied coaxing, between 1946 and 1949 Austria passed seven laws to restore Nazi-seized property to Jews. But these were full of loopholes, with inadequate worldwide notice and short claims periods, and were applied by Austrian courts with a notable lack of sympathy. During the framing of the 1955 State Treaty that granted Austria its independence as a neutral barrier against the Soviet bloc in the Cold War, it was only intense pressure from the U.S. government and from Jewish and American labor groups that produced language obligating Austria to compensate Holocaust victims for their property or to return it.

It was not until the 1980s that Austria was forced to take a harder look at its wartime record. Kurt Waldheim, an Austrian who had served two terms as United Nations secretary general, was chosen by the mainstream conservative People's Party as its nominee for president. He campaigned as "the man the world trusts." Although admitting he had served briefly in the German Army during World War II, Waldheim claimed that he had been injured on the Russian front in 1941 and spent the rest of the war quietly completing his law studies in Vienna. This turned out to be a complete fabrication.

In the midst of the presidential campaign, the World Jewish Congress, through an enterprising young lawyer, Eli Rosenbaum—who would later become head of the Nazi-hunting Office of Special Investigations in the U.S. Department of Justice, where he would work on the 1997 Nazi-gold report—disclosed that, based upon an official Waffen SS photograph from 1943, Waldheim had met with an infamous SS general at the airstrip in Podgorica, Yugoslavia, the site at just that time of a huge slaughter of Yugoslavian Jews. Further evidence disclosed that he served at Salonika, Greece, the site of the mass deportation of Greek Jews. Notwithstanding the sensational disclosures and the international furor, Waldheim dismissed the accusations and won the presidency by a comfortable margin. But world opinion was not as forgiving as the Austrian electorate. Waldheim became the first head of state ever placed on the U.S. "watch list" of undesirable aliens, which precluded him from entering the United States.

The Waldheim affair was a painful episode for many Austrians, but it was also a watershed for the country. In 1987 the Austrian cardinal Franz König gave a speech implying that as Christians and as Austrians his fellow citizens shared responsibility for the Holocaust. In 1990 Chancellor Franz Vranitzky established a fund for Jewish victims who had been children in 1938 and were ineligible for prior programs. In 1991 he took the most dramatic step by acknowledging Austria's culpability for Nazi persecution and its moral responsibility for assistance to Jewish victims. In 1995, in commemoration of the fiftieth anniversary of Austria's Second Republic, the National Fund for the Victims of National Socialism was created to make payments of 70,000 schillings (about $4,500) to Austrian Holocaust survivors; to support Jewish museums, synagogues, hospitals, old-age homes, counseling services, and educational efforts to combat anti-Semitism; and to develop a comprehensive list of Austrian Holocaust victims. Design and construction of a Holocaust memorial in Vienna's Judenplatz was also initiated; it would be unveiled in October 2000.

But so little property of major importance had been returned over the years that two authors, Tina Walzer and Stephan Templ, published a guide in 2002 to the many Viennese tourist sites once owned in whole or part by Jews, sardonically taking its title from the city's official tourist newsletter, *Unser Wien*—Our Vienna. The confiscated properties included prime hotels, famous restaurants, and many elegant cafes. It was clear the nation had not adequately addressed its mass confiscation of Jewish property and its wartime use of forced and slave labor.

Once again it was the class-action lawyers who forced the issue into the open. On October 16, 1998, Ed Fagan and Bob Swift filed the first of several class-actions against Austrian companies in U.S. court in Brooklyn. Now that Germany was resolving similar demands from conscripted workers, the time was ripe for making Austria pay. Fagan warmed to the task by telling an Austrian news conference that Austrian companies employing slave laborers were "dishonest pimps for the Nazis! They made money, they made ammunition, bunkers, and weapons, and they have prolonged the war, thus allowing further millions of people being killed." The same cast of characters, the "usual suspects" I dealt with on Switzerland and Germany— Michael Hausfeld, Mel Weiss, and company—soon filed their own suits, both for forced labor and for Austria's failure to return property confiscated by the Nazis.

Recognizing the costs of litigation and the potential damage to their reputations, Austrian companies pressed their government to work out a solution through diplomatic negotiation. Having the example of the Swiss and Germans before them, Austrian corporations and government officials alike were determined not to engage in lengthy negotiations that would expose them to bad publicity or, worse, sanctions in the United States. As a first step, on September 29, 1998, just before Fagan filed suit, the Austrian government established a historical commission headed by Clemens Jabloner, president of the Austrian Administrative Court, to investigate the status of Austria's postwar restitution and reparations program.

A year later the Austrian government found a more compelling political reason for seeking resolution of the claims of Jewish survivors. In the parliamentary elections of October 1999, the Social Democrats received 33 percent of the vote, which ordinarily would have been enough for them to form a coalition government with the second-place party, the conservative People's Party, which had won 27 percent. But negotiations between the two collapsed after three months, prompting Wolfgang Schuessel, the leader of the People's Party, to take a gamble on winning the chancellorship for himself by making a pact with Jörg Haider, the governor of Carinthia province and the leader of the aggressively nationalist Freedom Party, which had received 27 percent of the vote.

Schuessel's strategy worked—he was able to form a working coalition with Haider's party—but it provoked a diplomatic firestorm. Preaching a message of xenophobia and prejudice that played to his constituency's worst fears, Haider struck many in Europe and the United States as a throwback to an earlier, uglier time in Austria's history. A handsome demagogic populist and ultranationalist, he had addressed gatherings of SS veterans and other Nazis during the campaign, often sliding in an apologia for Nazi crimes and praise for the German armed forces. His party's electoral successes were built on an anti-immigrant cry of "Austria for the Austrians." Although Haider never directly opposed returning confiscated Jewish property—he himself resided on a 3,800-acre family estate once owned by Jews and purchased at a knockdown price during the war by his great-uncle—he argued that the 3 million ethnic Germans who had been expelled from the Czech Sudetenland after the war, many of whom lived in Austria, should have their confiscated property returned, as well. He falsely accused the leader of the Austrian Jewish community, Ariel Muzicant, of fabricating anti-Semitic letters to build up sympathy and then, in a nasty pun on his name, the same as a popular Austrian detergent, asked how someone named Ariel could be so dirty.

Led by the Socialist government in France, the member states of the European Union imposed unprecedented sanctions on one of its own member states. They were largely symbolic—the other EU countries limited their bilateral ties with Austria and cold-shouldered Chancellor Schuessel at meetings of EU heads of government, but Austria continued to participate in regular European Union meetings. Still, they stung Austrian pride.

With Austria forced into diplomatic isolation by its EU partners,

Schuessel needed to demonstrate to the world his sensitivity to Holocaust issues by tackling the forced labor issue the class-action suits had thrust into prominence. The presence of Haider's party in the government presented a dilemma for the Clinton administration. The European diplomatic boycott of Vienna may have been more symbolic than real, but could Washington be seen to do less by maintaining normal diplomatic relations with Austria? Israel's decision to withdraw its ambassador to Austria and sever diplomatic relations put the administration in a further bind. Secretary of State Albright was looking for a solution, diplomatically expressing concern by recalling the United States' ambassador, Kathryn Hall, for consultations, while telling me in private that she had known Schuessel for years and respected him.

This was a view shared by my friend and former Brussels colleague Dietrich von Kyaw, Germany's ambassador to the EU and a friend of Schuessel. Yet not everyone was so understanding. The Austrian-born U.S. ambassador to France, Felix Rohatyn, told me that he could never forget that Austrian Nazis forced his grandparents to clean the streets of Vienna with a toothbrush before killing them. To Rohatyn, Schuessel was the real villain for giving Haider respectability by taking his party into the government. Richard Holbrooke, who had brought me into the issue of Holocaust reparations and now was the United States' UN ambassador, favored stringent isolation but realistically questioned how long it could last.

On February 4, 2000, the administration reached an internal compromise, a "restricted contacts" policy under which each proposed meeting with the Schuessel government would be judged on its importance to U.S. interests, but with no contact permitted with Haider or with any Freedom Party members in the government. With the Austrian class-action suits spurring me to take on my accustomed role as mediator, Secretary Albright permitted me to have unfettered negotiations with the Schuessel government, even including Freedom Party ministers, if necessary to my success. But it would surely make it difficult for me to draw on other senior U.S. officials to press their Austrian counterparts, as I had done at key points in the German negotiations.

Fortunately, a remarkable person, Maria Schaumayer, appeared as my negotiating partner. She, like Count Lambsdorff, would prove to be one of the most able people with whom I dealt in all of the Holocaust-related negotiations. A former president of the Austrian Central Bank and one of her country's most distinguished citizens (she had turned down an offer from Schuessel to serve as chancellor herself), she had been persuaded by Schuessel to come out of retirement and serve as his special representative to lead the negotiations in order to establish what the Austrians called a new "Reconciliation, Peace and Cooperation" fund for surviving forced laborers. She told me she was answering a call to duty and thanking the Republic of Austria one more time for having offered her "such great opportunities in life."

There was also a personal factor to her willingness to enter what she knew would be a contentious arena. She was eight years old when the Nazis swept across Austria in 1938. Her father had opposed Hitler and was arrested by the Gestapo immediately after the *Anschluss*, then released and rearrested. His property was sold, and he was deprived of his livelihood. As a young girl living near the Hungarian border, she saw the great currents of the war—the German invasion and retreat, then the advance of the Soviet Army. But one haunting image stuck with her more than any other: the forced march of Hungarian Jewish slave laborers in the bitterly cold winter of 1944–45. She confided to me that it was not until she heard a historian's presentation on the plight of Hungarian Jews more than half a century later that she realized what she had seen as a child.

With her neatly groomed gray hair, sparkling eyes, effervescent smile, and upbeat manner, Maria Schaumayer could have passed for anyone's grandmother. But she was unlike any grandmother I knew. Crisp and confident in a country of wartime shadows, she had long experience at the top levels of public service. From our first meeting in my office at the Treasury Department on March 20, 2000, she made it clear that she wanted no repeat of the haggling we had had with the Germans over who would participate in the negotiations. The Eastern European governments, the plaintiffs' attorneys, the Jewish groups—all would be included, she emphatically said. Nor would she struggle like the Germans over the status of agricultural workers; a substantial portion of Austria's forced laborers had worked on farms, and she promised that they would be covered.

But Maria, as she insisted I call her, firmly drew one boundary. She said that her mandate extended only to slave and forced labor issues, which were to be kept strictly separate from the much more complex and contentious problem of looted property.

This separation would cause me the greatest difficulty in my negotiations. The plaintiffs' lawyers wanted the issues joined to gain leverage, but this was hardly a mere tactical matter for the Austrians. The labor claims were of primary interest to the nations of Eastern Europe that had supplied most of the workers; today these nations were Austria's diplomatic and economic partners. By contrast, most of the property claims were held by Jews who had fled Austria before the war and were scattered across Europe, Israel, and the United States.

I began to work on a double track, as I sought some way to satisfy the plaintiffs' lawyers' insistence on combining the labor and property talks and Austria's equally firm determination to keep them separate. On the labor question our negotiations moved with dispatch. Schaumayer had mastered the details of our German agreements and was determined to improve upon them. She told me that the government planned to put a law through Parliament by the end of the spring session, with money flowing by July. I received a copy of this draft law only a little more than a month after our first meeting.

I never had to negotiate with the private sector on any of the crucial labor issues, as I did in Germany, but only with Maria. This greatly eased my burden. She presented clear criteria for beneficiaries and tried to be as inclusive as possible. Only the slave laborers from Austria's Mauthausen concentration camp, who worked at the giant Herman Göring Werke nearby, would be excluded. She noted that they were already covered under the terms of the German negotiations and would be compensated by the German Foundation. But surviving Hungarian Jews who had worked on German military fortifications in Austria would be treated as slave laborers and receive the maximum payment from Austria, even though they did not live in concentration camps.

Nor was she content simply to mimic the German standards for eligibility; children who lived in labor camps and women who were forced to undergo abortions would be compensated, as well. The Austrian fund would be capitalized by the government and the private sector in roughly equal shares. The Austrians would also pay on a per-capita level slightly improved over the Germans'. The Germans agreed only to pay "up to" 15,000 DM and 5,000 DM for slave and forced laborers, respectively—perhaps less if there were more claimants than we expected given the 10-billion-DM cap. Austria would guarantee its claimants the equivalent in Austrian schillings of the maximum, regardless of the number of surviving workers.

A few days after she presented the impressive draft law, I learned how much the Austrians were prepared to pay, though the news came through an unconventional but characteristically direct channel that Schaumayer used with political skill. Invited to appear on the state broadcasting station's news program, *Pressestunde* (Newshour), Maria announced that the Austrian fund for laborers would be capped at 6 billion schillings ($400 million). She had never discussed this figure with me, with the plaintiffs' attorneys, with Austrian industry, or even with her own negotiating team. We were all equally surprised. Initially I saw this as an irritating replay of the unilateral announcements I had come to expect from the Germans. But the figure was so generous that few could argue with it, since everyone agreed it provided more than enough money to meet her per-capita pledge and then some, with even the most optimistic forecast of the number of surviving claimants.

She later explained that, although she had often discussed the general dimensions of the fund with her team, they had never decided upon a specific figure. She acted on a hunch. If she put out a generous figure that she could defend in good conscience to satisfy claimants and the U.S. government, she would simultaneously use it to calm the Austrian public riled by the unrealistic demands that Ed Fagan had made a few weeks earlier—a labor fund of 60 billion schillings and a property fund of 80 billion. She quickly won the support of the four major political parties for the 6 billion schilling fund. She then invited me to cochair a conference for representatives of the principal sources of conscripted Austrian workers—Belarus, the Czech Republic, Hungary, Poland, Russia, and Ukraine. I accepted, but only on the condition that Austria agree to address the Nazi-era property claims promptly. After checking with Chancellor Schuessel, she accepted my terms.

On May 16 we met in the magnificent Hofburg Palace of the Hapsburg emperors, whose enormous chandeliers, beautiful friezes, high ceilings, and sparkling white walls made it an improbable place to discuss the horrors of World War II. We went over many of the familiar issues with Eastern Europeans and, thanks to Maria Schaumayer, we were able to work out such complex and emotional matters as levels and standards for compensation. Between the morning and afternoon sessions, we enjoyed a sumptuous buffet lunch—noteworthy because it was the first strictly kosher lunch ever served in the Hofburg Palace, prepared by the caterer for the Israeli Embassy in Vienna. I could only smile at what Empress Maria

Theresa might have thought about having her magnificent palace used for a kosher meal.

.      .      .

MY NEXT challenge was to find a way to use the momentum and goodwill of the labor discussions, where everyone was satisfied with the emerging agreement, to address the more difficult property claims. I had pledged to Maria Schaumayer to keep the labor and property negotiations separate, but the plaintiffs' lawyers were hanging tough in keeping the two parts of their cases tied by an invisible umbilical cord. They refused to withdraw their labor cases until their property cases were also settled, fearing that the Austrians would abandon the Jewish property claims as soon as the politically potent labor claims were resolved. I argued that they needed to trust Chancellor Schuessel and asked them how, in good conscience, they could use their property cases to deny some 150,000 aging former laborers—their own clients—a long-awaited and deserved payment? But they were unmoved. The labor agreement would have to wait.

The only way I could conceive of moving forward was for the Austrians to appoint a separate special envoy for property to convince the plaintiffs' attorneys that their property claims would not be left high and dry if the labor claims were settled. It would also solve a problem for the Claims Conference, which had gotten itself into a box. Because the state of Israel had completely severed diplomatic relations with Austria over the Schuessel-Haider coalition deal, the Claims Conference believed it could not deal with the chancellor. Israel Singer, of both the World Jewish Congress and Claims Conference, distrusted Schuessel anyway for his pact with Haider. Singer and Gideon Taylor pleaded with me for some kind of political fig leaf to cover their participation in these important negotiations.

Happily Austria's president was no longer Kurt Waldheim, who left office in 1992. In fact, his successor, Thomas Klestil, had a great sensitivity to Holocaust issues. A striking, big-framed man with a dignity and generosity of spirit to match, he had delivered before the Israeli Knesset in 1994 an emotional apology for Austria's role in the war. Austria's president, like Germany's, is not a member of the government and brings a moral stature to any difficult issue he or she addresses. I met Klestil at his magnificent office in the former residence of the Hapsburg emperors. Knowing I would need it at some point, I began by asking if he would issue an apology for Austria's mistreatment of Jews in general and forced laborers in particular as Rau had done. Klestil immediately agreed.

Building on this, I told him frankly I needed his help to find a way for the Claims Conference to join our talks. Otherwise, it would sabotage them from the outside. I asked if he could in some way, without offending the chancellor, be involved in the appointment of a special envoy for the property negotiations.

Choosing an envoy and determining his relationship to Schuessel and Klestil was more difficult. Klestil explained that under the Austrian constitution the president could not appoint a representative. He candidly explained his poor relationship with Schuessel. He told me that he had recently sat stone-faced at a ceremony marking the hundred-day anniversary of the new coalition government. Not only had Klestil opposed putting Haider's Freedom Party in the government, but before approving the coalition, he had taken the unprecedented step of demanding that both governing parties sign a declaration he had drafted committing them to observe democratic norms. He joked to me that "we are not [Schuessel's] favorite children." I suggested an alternative—a special envoy appointed by the chancellor but reporting to the president as well. That might work, he said, because the president had the constitutional right to receive regular reports from the government's appointees.

It took me weeks to forge a compromise on this unusual appointment along the lines I had proposed to Klestil. On the government side, at the end of May, just after meeting with Klestil, I met with Schuessel's foreign minister, Benita Ferrero-Waldner. As I was the first senior U.S. government official to meet with her, she unloaded a stream of invective against Ed Fagan for his "insulting comments"; against the Austrian Jewish community, which refused to meet with her; and against Israel Singer—"it is like blackmail with Singer." She deeply resented being treated "like we are a Nazi country and a Nazi people."

Fortunately, Schuessel was considerably more constructive. Given the different opinions about him in our own administration, and as the first senior official from the Clinton administration to meet him as chancellor, I was anxious to take his measure. I soon became a fan of his, validating Secretary Albright's confidence. Although Schuessel was a very tough negotiator who held his cards close to his chest, I would soon come to trust him as a person of his word. His spartan office was in sharp contrast to the opulent palace in which I had met President Klestil the day before. There were few of the trappings of power one associates with a head of government—no flags, no pictures with the powerful. His large office was furnished with unexceptionable modern furniture, including black leather chairs in a semicircle around a low coffee table, and a few modern paintings on the wall. Despite his slight build, his energy, intelligence, and intensity made him a significant presence. Although I certainly did not approve of his bringing Haider's Freedom Party into government, I had been in politics long enough to know that the thirst for power at the top all too often produces unpalatable relationships. Schuessel's explanation to me was the classic argument of the self-confident politician: He believed he could reinforce the Freedom Party's moderates by giving them a taste of power and thus isolate them from their radical wing. (Time has proven him correct.)

Schuessel said proudly that the old Social Democratic coalition never could have achieved the four-party agreement he had delivered for parliamentary support of the conscripted workers' settlement. He now was prepared to address the problem of confiscated properties. Having obtained the Freedom Party's agreement on labor payments from its representative, Vice Chancellor Susanne Riess-Passer, he would need something for the property deal because "I owe her." He insisted that she join him at the press conference announcing the special envoy who would handle the Austrian side of the negotiations. I said it was fine with me but I simply could not meet with her at the early stage in the negotiations. They named as the envoy Ernst Sucharipa, the dean of the Austrian Diplomatic Academy.

I was struck by the difference in the tone of my next meetings, with Hannah Lessing and Ariel Muzicant. Lessing, head of the Austrian National Fund, had already dispensed over $180 million to 27,000 Austrian Holocaust survivors since 1995. Young, vivacious, tough, and smart, she always wore a Jewish star prominently around her neck. She had the confidence of both the Austrian government and the Austrian Jewish community. But she said that, with Haider's party in power, the Jews felt as if the 1930s had returned.

Muzicant, the leader of the small Austrian Jewish community, was more apocalyptic. A slightly paunchy, balding man whose warm and earnest manner masked a steely determination to secure the future of Austrian Jewry, he was born in Israel, moved to Vienna as a child with his parents in

1956, and grew wealthy in real estate. He regarded Austrian society as riddled with anti-Semitism and was angry that former Austrian SS officers were receiving better social benefits than Jewish concentration camp survivors. The Austrian government, he believed, would respond only to pressure. He also compared the present to the prewar period, except the Jews' fear now was psychological, not physical.

Muzicant gave me an early taste of the bitter battles that loomed ahead on restitution. He had no patience for the American lawyers and implored me to "stop Fagan from raving." He distrusted the motives of the Claims Conference. Muzicant wanted money from the Austrian government for schools, old-age homes, and hospitals, because the only Jewish communal properties returned to date had been synagogues, often in need of expensive repair. He was, significantly, supporting the small Austrian Jewish community out of his own pocket. Years of frustration at dealing with the Austrian government had made him suspicious, doubly so of Schuessel for his alliance with Haider's party. His bitter denunciations of Schuessel so poisoned the atmosphere that the chancellor refused to talk with him.

But it was my job to get the parties together. Building on my Swiss and German experiences, I knew that I needed to convince Chancellor Schuessel to include all parties in our negotiations, including the class-action lawyers and Ariel Muzicant. Fundamentally, I had to find a face-saving way for both sides to put the labor negotiations to bed and immediately begin paying aging forced workers, while reassuring the victims' side that Austria was serious about addressing deficiencies in its postwar property restitution. I had to create trust where none existed. I also put all parties on notice that we did not have the "luxury" of the long, tortuous negotiations with Germany. It was already May 2000, and the end of the Clinton administration was fast approaching.

# CHAPTER FIFTEEN

# Bridge over Troubled Water

I BEGAN discussing with the Austrian negotiators the idea of a bridge between the labor and property cases, to end the impasse on dismissing the labor cases. Everyone agreed that there was one type of property that had never been subject to previous Austrian restitution: long-term leases on apartments and businesses, which can run from a score to several hundred years. Ninety-five percent of prewar Viennese lived in such leaseholds, which in normal times could be bought and sold like real property, leaving undisturbed the ownership—and the income stream—of the underlying land, owned by upper-class entrepreneurs. When the lease expired, the landowners usually renewed it at whatever rent the market would bear. Such leases are common in Europe; in the United States they are rare. Within a year of the 1938 *Anschluss*, two-thirds of the 60,000 Jewish family apartments held on long-term leases in Vienna alone were "Aryanized" by the Nazis.

Since it was impossible now to put thousands of Jews back into their old apartments or shops, I started discussing with all the parties a sum of money as compensation. It would also serve as a sign of good faith, a down payment I called it, to the suspicious Claims Conference and plaintiffs' lawyers that, after settling the labor cases, the government would not renege on its pledge to deal with property claims. Singer suggested I negotiate a sum with the Austrians that would be divided into individual payments to each of the 21,000 Austrian Holocaust survivors—a few still in Austria, most living abroad. The government would also agree to contribute to the settlement of other property issues where the Jabloner historical commission found past restitution programs were inadequate. But the commission was not due to report until 2002. Singer and the Israeli government agreed to this arrangement, but the plaintiffs' lawyers still refused to delink their labor cases.

The Austrian special property envoy, Ernst Sucharipa, had both academic and government experience, but he was more sympathetic toward a property deal than the chancellor. He was warm and friendly but seemed a bit nervous in our sessions. I soon learned why. Although raised as a Catholic, two of his grandparents were Jewish. A member of the opposition Social Democrats, he was a good friend of President Klestil but had no personal relationship with Schuessel, who kept him on a very short leash. Sucharipa did not have the stature of Maria Schaumayer to make decisions and then sell them to the chancellor. He was also working on an issue made far more politically sensitive by a public fear that restitution really meant returning properties actually occupied by Austrians to the Jews.

But even after the government sent word to me through Sucharipa early in July that it might be ready to make an immediate payment of $150 million without waiting for the Jabloner commission report, positions only hardened. Singer said Austria still was not acting properly and "we need to let them have it; they need a wake-up call." He complained that Sucharipa, though a good man, was "an empty bag" without a clear mandate from the chancellor. He was ready to once again give Austria what he called the "Waldheim treatment" that the World Jewish Congress had staged a decade earlier—complete ostracism. Singer, who tried to be diplomatic with the Germans, refused to deal at all with the Austrian government because of Schuessel's pact with Haider's Freedom Party, because of Israel's refusal to have normal diplomatic ties with the Austrians, and for an intensely personal reason. In 1938, shortly after the Anschluss, his father had been one of thousands of Jews forced to clean the streets of Vienna, with jeering crowds watching.

Unaware of this enmity, Sucharipa sent me Austria's property proposal for immediate payments to the leaseholders, including claims for their furniture and personal effects, plus a further examination of gaps in past restitution to be filled by payments from a proposed General Settlement Fund. I knew this would be insufficient for the plaintiffs' attorneys because it specifically excluded banking and insurance claims, social security programs for elderly survivors, return of artworks, and the activities of the Dorotheum, the Vienna state auction house through which almost all the Aryanized property was sold during the war. Austria was prepared to examine these other property issues but only in the future, on the basis of the Jabloner report in 2002.

When Hans Winkler and Martin Eichtinger, Austrian officials who had been working with Maria Schaumayer, visited me on July 21 to finalize the labor agreement, I warned them that Sucharipa's proposals had to be broadened to cover all property claims, with a timetable for settling them. After they left, our team decided to develop our own counterproposal to break the impasse. It included a larger fund covering all property claims and an independent panel of three assessors to review the claims. To thread the needle between the plaintiffs' lawyers, who insisted on being able to reopen all past restitution cases, and the Austrian government, which wanted none challenged, I suggested that property claims could be allowed where there were "gaps and deficiencies" in postwar Austrian restitution laws.

This found favor with the lawyers, the Claims Conference, and even the Austrians—with one giant caveat. Sucharipa told me on September 14 that Schuessel was adamant that the government's $150 million would not be a down payment but would be the final payment. Any additional money for other property claims would have to come from the private sector, which up to now had shown no interest in contributing to a property settlement.

I told Sucharipa that he would have to do better if he hoped to persuade the lawyers and that, if he could not, I was prepared to cancel our meetings as a waste of everyone's time. Although personally sympathetic, Sucharipa told me he was under very strict instructions from Schuessel not to deviate from his original offer. Sucharipa admitted this was a "major shift" in his mandate, but he was stuck with it. The chancellor's word was final. Equally frustrating, the chancellor had vetoed Sucharipa's agreement to conclude the property talks by the end of the year.

As expected, Sucharipa's offer fell before the lawyers like dead wood. It severely undermined the fragile trust I had begun to build between the victims' side and the Austrians. I had to move quickly. On the spot I decided I needed to meet alone with the plaintiffs' attorneys and the Claims Conference and try to reach an agreement with them that I could present to the Austrians. The only way to keep the talks alive was to brandish before the lawyers and Singer a series of legal and political sticks and carrots.

I reminded them that time was not on their side. It was now September 15, 2000, less than two months from the U.S. presidential election, and there was no certainty that Al Gore or George W. Bush would keep up the pressure on the Austrians. Moreover, three days earlier, the Europeans had unconditionally lifted their diplomatic sanctions against Austria, relieving pressure on the Schuessel government to demonstrate that it was no longer the pariah of Europe. I reminded the lawyers that they had never won a Holocaust-era case in court and, if they insisted on reopening all the old property restitution cases that Austrian courts had previously ruled on, they would do so without my support. I also told them I was under pressure from the Eastern European governments complaining bitterly that the lawyers' property claims were unnecessarily delaying payments to their elderly forced laborers.

After three hours of heated debate, the lawyers agreed to a framework I could give to Sucharipa to take back to Vienna. Its principal features were similar to what I had initially presented to the Austrians and what the chancellor had so substantially altered. It included the $7,000-per-person payment Singer demanded for leased apartments and businesses, and a deadline of the end of the year 2000 for concluding negotiations on all property issues, including those that belonged to the Austrian Jewish community. A representative of Austria's private companies would have to join the negotiations with the aim of obtaining a contribution to the General Settlement Fund. Most difficult for the plaintiffs' side, I got them to agree that the fund could deal only with cases decided under prior Austrian restitution law in "specifically defined circumstances," which would limit the opportunities for ingenious lawyers to have the fund cover old property cases that had been long since closed.

I then stressed to Sucharipa before he left for Vienna that time was running out. "You are preaching to the converted," he replied, having talked with the chancellor overnight and found him unyielding. Nevertheless I told him the new text I had hammered out with the plaintiffs' attorneys and Singer had to be the basis for proceeding on both the labor and property negotiations, or our negotiations would collapse. This was not a threat; it was reality.

I had to change the chancellor's position by ratcheting up the political pressure. So on September 16 I had Secretary of State Albright call Chancellor Schuessel in Vienna, with me on the line. She urged him to be flexible in addressing property issues or we would never get the labor cases dismissed. He was initially defensive, saying he thought Sucharipa had delivered "all that you wanted" and that he had already agreed to $150 million to settle the apartment leases, which had clearly never been covered by postwar restitution laws. He was not willing to add to the money from the privatization of state-owned assets, an idea I had floated, but indicated a willingness to press the Dorotheum to contribute. Still, he said it was not possible to conclude the property talks by the end of 2000.

When Secretary Albright continued to press him, the chancellor changed tunes. "Let Stu come to Vienna," and we can discuss it all, he said. But it was clear that, as a savvy negotiator, he had a price. He told us that, with the EU having lifted its sanctions, "now the U.S. is the only country in the world which treats us with a special status." What he wanted was full normalization of relations. This resonated with Secretary Albright, who told me just before our call to Schuessel that the U.S. ambassador to Austria, Kathryn Hall, was reporting from Vienna anti-United States sentiment in the Austrian public, with the EU sanctions lifted and our "limited contacts" policy still in place.

So I was dispatched by Secretary Albright to Vienna on October 5 to resolve the impasse. Everything would depend upon my negotiation with the chancellor—the future of the still unborn labor agreement, whether property talks would ever begin, and our diplomatic relationship with Austria itself.

The chancellor knew how to play for high political stakes. He insisted on framing the negotiations in the context of U.S.-Austrian economic relations as well as our political relationship. He had Hans Winkler, the Foreign Ministry's legal adviser, remind me that U.S. firms were bidding for a major helicopter sale to the Austrian military and, if an American company got the contract, the government would need to justify it by announcing that diplomatic relations had returned to normal. I realized how politically charged this could become in the American Jewish community only a month before U.S. presidential elections, so before embarking I checked with Sandy Berger to cover my political bases at the White House. He told me to ensure I had political protection for any deal by obtaining the approval of Singer and the Claims Conference to anything I negotiated.

Then followed marathon negotiations. With the chancellor unshakable on not contributing another schilling from the federal treasury, I had to get the Austrian private sector engaged. I started in the afternoon of October 5 in Vienna by meeting Herbert Pichler, a senior member of the Austrian Chamber of Commerce. Although Austrian businesses had contributed about two-fifths of the money for the labor fund, with the Austrian government picking up the rest, they had remained on the sidelines and were clearly unhappy about being thrust by Schuessel into the property negotiations. After all, as Pichler pointed out, many of Austria's major industrial companies were owned by German companies that had already settled in the German negotiations. Moreover, the prosperous Austrian banks had made a separate settlement in a case brought by Bob Swift before federal judge Shirley Wohl Kram of the Southern District of New York. The banks could not be expected to contribute yet again in our negotiations, he said. Still, Pichler, a quiet, intense man, said that the Austrian firms were "seriously willing to contribute to dealing with the burdens of the past."

I was ushered into the chancellor's office a little after 5:00 P.M. on the same day for what would turn out to be a session lasting seven hours. Schuessel came out to greet me warmly and said we should talk alone, leaving his team and mine in his outer office for the first several hours. This would be my most intensive negotiation with a head of government during all the years of my Holocaust pursuits.

My experience with presidents, prime ministers, and chancellors is that they almost never engage in detailed substantive negotiations, and certainly not without their aides. If Jimmy Carter was a conspicuous exception to this rule in fashioning the Camp David Accords, Schuessel was another, underscoring both his knowledge of the subject and its extreme political sensitivity. He began by telling me that he was born in 1945, the war's final year, to a mother who had hidden from Allied bombs while carrying him. This gave him a special desire to deal with the problems of Austria's past. But when he complained about the linkage of the labor and property talks, I simply told him that, whether we liked it or not, the attorneys would refuse to dismiss their labor suits until we agreed on a process for settling the property claims.

We then got down to negotiating paragraph by paragraph a framework document our team had prepared. This became an odd triangular negotiation. In a bizarre twist founded in American political realities, and reinforced by Sandy Berger's admonition to be certain that Israel Singer approved any deal, I frequently used the speaker phone in Schuessel's office to call Israel Singer and Gideon Taylor of the Claims Conference in New York to gain their assent to changes the chancellor and I were negotiating.

Since they still refused to talk to the chancellor directly because of his coalition agreement with Jörg Haider, I became their go-between as the chancellor waited and listened. Schuessel often looked stunned as Singer, Taylor, and I engaged in animated conversations that occasionally turned into shouting matches of a kind that were not part of his office routine.

Singer and Taylor's price for blessing a labor settlement that was almost exclusively for non-Jewish forced laborers was a $150 million payment to some 21,000 surviving Austrian Jews—$7,000 per person—who had lost their apartments, businesses, and personal belongings when they fled Austria after the 1938 *Anschluss*. They also insisted upon an ironclad commitment to deal with other property claims not adequately covered by past Austrian restitution programs.

After several hours we were joined by the teams from both sides, and they worked on the important details. Schuessel took me onto the small balcony outside his spacious if austere office to view the magnificent panorama of floodlit Baroque Viennese palaces that now were mainly government ministries and museums; it was a refreshing break. By 11:00 P.M. we were all ravenously hungry but dared not ask for anything. The chancellor saved us. As if we were pulling an all-nighter at the Clinton White House, Schuessel sent out for pizza from his favorite Italian restaurant, Ninfida. Because I keep kosher and watch my calories, I asked for a cheese sandwich. The closest I came was a plain cheese pizza. By midnight we were gobbling it down, the chancellor too, standing in his adjoining conference room and discussing final points while he ate. Pizza never tasted better. We called these talks the "pizza negotiations."

The bridge between the labor and property cases that we so laboriously constructed on the night of October 5 was formally known as the "Framework Concerning Austrian Negotiations Regarding Austrian Nazi Era Property/Aryanization Issues." My legal team was using the chancellor's secretary's computer in his outer office to prepare the final text, checking language as they went along with Singer and Taylor by telephone in New York. As it turned out, this furious transatlantic typing exercise produced misunderstandings with the Claims Conference on whether confiscated jewelry was to be covered by the $150 million payment and the status of heirs. They insisted this was not a petty concern but represented a valuable item that should be paid for separately. We had to resolve it over the weekend after we returned to Washington, finally persuading them to agree to include it within the $150 million amount, as Schuessel insisted.

The chancellor and I announced our agreement well after midnight to the waiting press corps outside his office. By 12:45 A.M. we faxed the framework agreement back to the plaintiffs' attorneys in the United States, and I met with several who had come to Vienna. I got their blessing, except for Deborah Sturman, Mel Weiss's colleague, who had to be assured that Singer approved of the deal.

Singer and Taylor reluctantly agreed to allow the $150 million to cover three categories of survivors' claims: the apartment and business leases, stolen movable property such as furniture, and valuables such as jewelry. The recovery of stolen art was kept separate. Schuessel wanted that to be the end of it but conceded that the rights of heirs and other broader property questions would have to be resolved in further negotiations.

To satisfy the plaintiffs' lawyers and Singer, I persuaded the chancellor that the negotiations over the size and structure of the General Settlement Fund for property claims would address "potential gaps and deficiencies in prior Austrian restitution programs" and would begin on the very same day the labor agreement was signed. Schuessel agreed to make every effort to finish them by the end of the year, a deadline that slipped only a few weeks, to the final days of the Clinton administration in mid-January. But in a bitter pill for the plaintiffs' attorneys and Claims Conference to swallow, previously decided restitution cases would not be reopened, except under "specifically defined circumstances" that we would negotiate.

I had even won an important concession for Muzicant, the leader of the Austrian Jewish community: The negotiations would also address the return of Jewish communal property in government hands. As I was departing for Washington, Muzicant was in the VIP lounge of the Vienna Airport to thank me with a big bear hug for the agreement we had reached in our negotiating marathon.

But I soon learned that even this did not satisfy him. On the eve of the October 24 date we set for signing the labor agreement and immediately commencing the property negotiations, suddenly a new lawsuit was filed in New York, asserting additional Austrian labor and property claims. The case had been brought by Jay Fialkoff, a lawyer who had not participated in our talks, and it soon became all too clear that Muzicant was behind the suit in the belief that it would give him greater leverage in the property negotiations. From that day forward I came to the reluctant conclusion that I could not rely upon him. What he accomplished was a further delay in paying 150,000 surviving forced laborers in Eastern Europe while poisoning the complex talks on property.

The Austrian labor agreement was signed on October 24, 2000, following a last-second side letter agreement I reached to have the Austrian labor fund pay the Claims Conference an additional $15 million for Jewish slave laborers at Mauthausen and the Dachau subcamps in Austria, in case there was a shortfall in payments to them from the German Foundation. The signing ceremony was moving, with Schuessel and Schaumayer publicly acknowledging the agreement as an essential part of Austria's belated confrontation with its own past. As we had done in Berlin, when we went to the Bellevue Palace for President Rau's apology, so here we went to the Hofburg Palace for a statement by President Klestil of Austria.

Because the Austrians had not faced their past as had the Germans, Klestil's statement had even more impact. "We Austrians are finally looking in the eye of the historical truth—indeed the entire truth," he said. "All too often we have spoken about Austria as the first country that lost its freedom and independence to National Socialism, and all too seldom about the fact that many of the most malicious executioners of the National Socialists' dictatorship were Austrians." Then, with Austrian survivors like Kurt Ladner present, he said, "In the name of the Republic of Austria, I bow with deep sorrow before the victims of that time. . . . At the end of the twentieth century we are finally making an effort to overcome the last barriers on the way to a better future, and this is based on a shared commitment to the principle 'Never Again.'" This was not as strong as the draft statement I had been led to believe he would deliver, with a more explicit apology. But it was nevertheless a step forward.

At the conclusion of the reception, President Klestil took me for a short private tour of the Hofburg Palace, including the regal old office of Emperor Franz Josef, the ruler of the vast Austro-Hungarian Empire before World War I. I could not help but reflect to myself how far modern-day Austria had fallen from its pinnacle. Now we were about to begin tough negotiations on confiscated property that would be an early test of how far Austria had come in facing its past.

By 9:30 P.M. of the same day, as the Austrians promised, we began our property negotiations with what amounted to a seminar on Austria's postwar property restitution, led by Bailer Galanda, a history professor at the University of Vienna, and Laurie Cohen, a historian working with the Claims Conference. Dr. Galanda's presentation was refreshingly candid and, together with Cohen's work, gave us a better picture of the gaps and deficiencies in Austria's postwar restitution programs.

From 1946 to 1949 under the postwar Allied occupation, Austria enacted seven laws to restore property seized during the Nazi era, laws that Schuessel's generation felt were adequate. In fact, each one had been given prior approval by the Allied High Command. In a 1959 agreement with the newly independent nation, the U.S. government committed itself not to support the pursuit of Nazi-era property claims against Austria, and in 1961 the Claims Conference also forswore further claims. My team and I were doing just the opposite and had to walk on eggshells to avoid even the appearance of backing away from the United States' forty-year-old commitment.

The historical record the two experts presented was not pretty. Besides the huge lacuna of the long-term leases we had just filled with our $150 million deal, there was another glaring omission in prior Austrian restitution efforts. Of the 34,780 Jewish businesses registered with the Nazis in 1938, only 4,300, almost all large and valuable enterprises, were Aryanized and, after the war, either returned or compensated for to their owners. The great bulk, some 30,000 small businesses, mostly shops, had been completely destroyed with no compensation having ever been paid. This needed to be rectified. Moreover, the Dorotheum earned 12 million Reichsmarks in profits between 1941 and 1944 from Aryanized property.

Unresolved as well was how to make good on the 181 million Reichsmarks in exit or "flight" taxes paid by those escaping Austria and another 147 million Reichsmarks in special, onerous property taxes. These taxes were so glaring that after the presentations, Sucharipa whispered to me that the Austrian government should pony up more money to the General Settlement Fund.

All this and more was put to us by Galanda and Cohen. Perhaps most egregious were the judgments of some Austrian courts in deciding property claims after the war. They required the original Jewish owner to repay the current occupant the forced sales price he had been required to take, adjusted upward for inflation, thus enriching the Aryanizers twice. I was touched by the response from Herbert Pichler of the Austrian Chamber of Commerce: "These talks have had a great impression on me. It is hard for my generation to understand and appreciate the extent of the suffering."

Before leaving Vienna, I sought advice from Simon Wiesenthal, Vienna's famous Nazi hunter, who was now ninety-one years old but still mentally sharp. While I was inspired by his life's work, he gave me little solace for the three-month sprint that lay ahead. He warned me that, however laudable our property negotiations, they would only stoke anti-Semitism because the overwhelming number of beneficiaries would not be the actual survivors like himself but their heirs, almost all of whom lived outside Austria.

As I left Vienna and prepared for our mid-November round of talks after the U.S. presidential election, two events created unneeded high waves in an already turbulent sea. On November 9, the anniversary of Kristallnacht, Chancellor Schuessel nearly caused a meltdown in our property talks by giving an incendiary interview to the *Jerusalem Post* in which he coupled a call for Israel's ambassador to return to Vienna, now that European Union restrictions had been lifted, with a recitation of Austria's "first victim" status during the war. He emphasized in other public statements immediately following that he would not allow the opponents of modern-day Austria to paint it as the successor to the perpetrators of Nazi horrors.

The Claims Conference and the Israelis were bouncing off the walls. Singer said he was "horrified" and told me that he was now going to see New York City comptroller Alan Hevesi about potential financial sanctions against the Austrians. He urged that the November round of negotiations be canceled. I refused and calmed their feelings. Muzicant boycotted the session but made a decision that caused far more damage.

Muzicant irreparably split the Jewish side by picking as his representative Charles Moerdler, the silk-smooth Wall Street lawyer and experienced litigator who had convinced Judge Kram to accept a controversial $40 million settlement against his Austrian bank clients, over the vehement objection of the Claims Conference, which believed the Austrian banks had gotten off too cheaply. Now Moerdler had flipped sides and was representing Muzicant against the Austrians. Muzicant stubbornly defended his selection of Moerdler, telling me, "I don't want a Jewish war, but I can't be kept out of the negotiations." Moerdler made several productive but theatrical interventions during these meetings, describing the extent of the damage to Jewish communal property but raising the ire of the plaintiffs' attorneys. They saw him as an unwanted competitor with an unctuous personality and accused him to his face of having a conflict of interest because he had represented the Austrian banks before Judge Kram. After one shouting match between the lawyers and Moerdler at the State Department, I cited to Moerdler a favorite Biblical passage to summarize the views of the other lawyers toward him. Isaac, blind in his old age and deceived by his youngest son, Jacob, into giving him the blessing normally accorded to Jacob's older brother Esau, says, "The voice is the voice of Jacob, but the hands are the hands of Esau." I privately asked him to withdraw from representing Muzicant's groups, but he refused. Over the objections of the other lawyers, I reluctantly allowed him to continue to participate in our negotiations. It was a goodwill gesture not returned, and I came to rue my decision.

The split between the Austrian Jewish community (the Israelitische Kultusgemeinde, or IKG) and the Claims Conference involved a conflict more fundamental than Moerdler's role. The Claims Conference represented Austrian Holocaust survivors who had fled, and its primary goal was to recompense these elderly people abroad before they died. The IKG represented the Jewish community of Austria, numbering about 9,000, only about 1,000 of whom were Holocaust survivors. Muzicant argued that the small Jewish community was on the verge of bankruptcy because it had received only a token compensation for the loss of some fifty synagogues, schools, and social facilities transferred to the Austrian federal and provincial governments following the war, and for the more than six hundred associations, foundations, and benevolent funds dissolved in Vienna alone between 1938 and 1945. The IKG argued that the losses amounted to some 500 million of today's dollars. They wanted a lump sum payment as compensation and the return of any remaining Jewish properties in the government's hands.

I sympathized with Muzicant's aim, but as I frequently reminded him and Moerdler, the purpose of our negotiations was to dismiss the lawsuits involving private property and labor claims and thus allow long-overdue compensation to elderly individuals and the heirs of those who once owned property. However meritorious the claims, Jewish communal property was not a part of the lawsuits. Although I tried mightily, and largely succeeded, in accommodating many of their goals, I could not permit Muzicant and Moerdler to hijack the negotiations. Even so, they came perilously close.

To cut through the arguments over what further gaps and deficiencies existed in past Austrian restitution laws, such as the claim that there had been inadequate worldwide notice and abbreviated claims periods, we decided to structure the General Settlement Fund from the top down. We did not have the luxury of time to debate all the gaps and deficiencies in past Austrian law. We would first decide upon a capped amount and then divide it among the categories according to the amount of proof presented by the claimants. There would be "hard" and "soft" claims, the latter a sort of "rough justice" concept for claims with little evidence, similar to the arrangements I had worked out for Switzerland and Germany.

But with the American presidential election still unresolved at the end of November and the certainty that I would be forced to leave office if the Republican candidate, George W. Bush, became president, I did not have time to work both sides down from a steep initial figure. Michael Hausfeld had demanded $800 million, but I told him that this was far too high. He admitted that this was simply an arbitrary figure, with little backup; he had simply doubled the $400 million awarded to the laborers. But Hausfeld's figure made it clear that, in addition to the $150 million I had already gotten for apartments, I would need at least another $200 million from the Austrians to be in the ballpark.

With normal relations restored quietly after their meeting of November 8 (conveniently after the U.S. presidential election), Schuessel and his foreign minister, Benita Ferrero-Waldner, told Secretary of State Albright that, as a goodwill gesture, Austria had decided to purchase American-made Sikorsky helicopters. She thanked him and immediately turned to my negotiations, telling the chancellor that his leadership would be necessary to increase the property figure above $150 million. Schuessel pledged another $100 million from the state-owned Dorotheum and from private Austrian companies in Pichler's Austrian Chamber of Commerce. But he warned, "I have limits." Albright also ended with a warning. She said that I was an important asset and that given the uncertain outcome of the presidential election, the chancellor should take full advantage of my services while I was still in office by coming up with more money for the stolen property.

As we approached our deadline, I met privately with Schuessel in his office on November 30, and he again waxed personal. He told me his parents were divorced when he was only three years old, and he did not learn until he was sixteen and the leader of the Catholic Youth Movement that his father had been a member of the Nazi Party, a revelation that led to a lifelong estrangement. By this time I had met or spoken at length with him nearly a dozen times. I believed that he truly wanted a solution and that he was acting with courage in a political environment that was far more difficult than Schröder's in Germany. His grasp of detail was impressive, and it was clear he was making decisions personally because he himself would have to absorb the political shock waves. But even at this late stage his offer of another $100 million, almost all from the private sector, did not come close to the $200 million I believed to be the bare minimum that the plaintiffs' attorneys, the Claims Conference, and Muzicant might accept.

The chancellor was gauging Austria's debt by using our German settlement of 10 billion marks ($5 billion) as a benchmark. Given that the German economy was ten times the size of Austria's, he felt his country would be paying its full dues with a labor settlement of $400 million and a property settlement of $150 million, to which he had already agreed in our "pizza negotiations." Repeatedly comparing Austria's figures to Germany's, he ignored Germany's cumulative payments to Holocaust survivors of more than $60 billion over the previous half century; Austria's restitution amounted to only a tiny fraction of this.

He then revealed a new position. He said he had worked very hard on raising an additional $140 million—$50 million from the banks and insurance companies, $20 million from the Dorotheum, $50 million from the Austrian central bank, and $20 million from the Chamber of Commerce. As an important gesture to Muzicant, he would also agree to a three-person panel to decide on the ownership of any Jewish communal property still in the government's hands. But the government itself could not raise another schilling.

Although he said "it would be a pity if there was no agreement," he warned that, if the government itself paid anything more, "the parliament would throw me out of office." In fact, he asserted, even if this new $140 million private-sector contribution he had organized leaked out prematurely to the Austrian papers, he would be a political corpse. I had to make a judgment. Was this just good bargaining, or were his political pressures so severe he really could not contribute more from the public treasury? I decided it was not posturing. But then what?

We were miles apart. I had told all the class-action lawyers their demands were excessive and I would not support them, from Hausfeld's $800 million to ones from plaintiffs' attorneys Robert Swift, Steve Whinston, Randy Schoenberg, and from Moerdler in the 1 billion to 2 billion dollar range. Schuessel was so far from this ballpark that I told him it would be better for both of us to keep the $140 million offer quiet at the formal negotiating session about to begin. He agreed. This was a calculated risk. Although I was willing to try to reduce the victims' demands, the plaintiffs' lawyers were likely to walk out of the talks if they knew the small size of the

Austrian offer. Yet they would also be angry at receiving no figure at all in the afternoon plenary session. I believed the balance of risks tilted toward no offer, giving me more time to find ways to raise the Austrian offer.

The plenary session on November 30 was unproductive. Fagan caused a momentary blowup at an early-morning news conference, calling into question our labor agreement and the government's good faith on property issues. But Fagan's antics were hardly the problem. The lawyers kept raising the ante in public instead of lowering it. As we agreed, Ernst Sucharipa refused to give a number, saying that the government was still trying to finalize its offer. This made the plaintiffs' lawyers red hot with fury, as I knew it would. They had traveled all the way to Austria to get nothing, leading them to question Austria's commitment to the whole process.

Then an unexpected event occurred that changed the whole direction of the negotiations. A rump group of the plaintiffs' lawyers, led by Bob Swift and Ed Fagan, approached my team at the Kreisky Center around midnight. We faced them with stale half-eaten sandwiches strewn on the table of our delegation room, a metaphor for our downbeat feelings. I began by stressing that time was not on our side with the hourglass running out on the Clinton administration's term.

Swift realized something needed to be done quickly and proposed an approach that ultimately worked. To make it apparent that they had achieved a larger settlement from the Austrians than was actually the case, he said the final figure had to "straddle $1 billion," but the numbers could be pumped up by aggregating everything the Austrians had done, present or past. This group of lawyers was effectively cutting their own demand roughly in half and augmenting the size of the settlement with contributions Austria had already made.

Now I felt I had something. When the lawyers left, I started jotting down figures on my trademark yellow legal pad with our team. I reached $880 million by adding the $400 million labor amount, the $150 million for the leases in our "pizza negotiations," and the $140 million in fresh money Schuessel had just promised, then throwing in $40 million from Judge Kram's bank settlement and another $150 million that Hannah Lessing's National Fund had distributed since 1995. It was creative accounting that would make even Arthur Andersen blink. But if that would reach a bottom line acceptable to all, so be it.

On the flight back to Washington, I thought about the battle ahead. I had six weeks left in office and had to close an enormous financial gap, to say nothing of wrangling over details of how the money would be parceled out. If the Austrians could not present a reasonable opening offer at our next meeting on December 20–21 in Washington, I was convinced that the talks would break down. With Bill Clinton's term of office due to expire on January 20, we would simply run out of time.

I could not be certain whether the time element worked for or against me. Did Schuessel want to play for time and hope that the next administration would have less interest in pressing Austria for a solution, or did he genuinely want to resolve it, therefore needing my help? The results of the presidential election were still in the courts. Sucharipa gave a hint in a press interview on December 3: "Either we come to an agreement in time around the holiday period, or we have to wait for the next Administration. In which case we will lose time and also probably Eizenstat, a very valuable and constructive negotiator."

Realizing that the chancellor was not bluffing when he refused to add more public money, I had to find ways to make the package more attractive to the Claims Conference, Muzicant, and the rest of the plaintiffs' lawyers. I urged the Austrians to try to improve other parts of the package if Schuessel could not go higher.

Back in October, the Claims Conference had come to me with a proposal to apply Austrian pension benefits to Holocaust survivors who had been driven from the country by the Nazis. At first I told them that the idea did not fit with property restitution. By December, as I grew desperate to find ways to increase the total Austrian pot, I was starting to think differently. Singer and Taylor told me they could accept a smaller settlement fund in exchange for larger pensions for Holocaust survivors. I searched for other bits and pieces that would satisfy each of the plaintiffs' attorneys without crossing the fiscal line drawn by Schuessel. These included recovery of land for the Hakoah Sports Club, a project on which Muzicant had spent eighteen frustrating years; government support for the restoration and maintenance of the Jewish cemeteries, which was important to several of the lawyers; and a subsidy for a Holocaust education program at the annual seminar in Salzburg, a special pet idea of Mel Weiss.

I packaged them up with the rest of our creative accounting into a $1 billion package and sent them to Schuessel to consider in making his counteroffer for our December 20–21 negotiating round. In a telephone call I then offered the sweetener of a public statement of praise by President Clinton, along with a warning that, if the talks failed, the victims' side had told me they would try to isolate Austria and complicate his government's ambitious efforts to privatize many of Austria's state-owned companies. Singer could create such a cloud over Austria that American investors might shy away from bidding for these government-owned corporations. At first he was unyielding, but just before I put down the phone, he hinted at an additional $50 million from the private sector.

When the Austrian package arrived, it included most of my bits and pieces and a tantalizingly unspecified additional cash offer for property claims. On December 21, at our plenary negotiations, Sucharipa laid out their comprehensive proposal with improved social benefits worth $65 million over ten years, a land swap and commitment to rebuild the Hakoah Sports Club, additional support for the maintenance of Jewish cemeteries across Austria, an arbitration panel for Jewish communal property still in government hands, the $140 million the chancellor had privately promised me plus another $10 million he added, and an unspecified amount of extra money we called the "X" factor, which I knew to be $50 million. Sucharipa tied it together into a package worth, by his reckoning, $1 billion. As I had urged them to do, the Austrians were playing Swift's game. However dubious the arithmetic, it helped keep the victims' side at the table.

After George W. Bush was confirmed by the U.S. Supreme Court on December 12 as the next president, the possibility arose that one side or the other might decide to hang tough and hope for a better deal from the Republicans. Indeed, I heard that Moerdler, himself a Republican, was telling Ariel Muzicant and the Austrian Jewish community not to settle, because they would get a better deal from the new Republican administration than from me, though on what logic I could not divine. Muzicant told me that, if the present deal was the best he could get from the Austrians, he would tell them to "go to hell."

To cut off a possible end run, I moved quickly with the help of the incoming Secretary of State, Colin Powell, during a general transition briefing I gave to him at the State Department. I asked to be allowed to tell all sides that he wanted the talks finished on our watch and not spill over into his. He promptly and graciously agreed, and he also accepted my recommendation to continue the State Department's Office of Holocaust Issues. Powell's New York City origins—aside from being the first African-

American Secretary of State in U.S. history, he also speaks and understands some Yiddish—made him sensitive to these issues.

The briefing also had an unintended benefit. When I later bumped into Powell in the State Department corridors, shoulder to shoulder with secretary of defense–designate Donald Rumsfeld, he said with a smile that he had "dropped in" unannounced to a meeting of some of the lawyers in the Austrian negotiations during the last hours of our talks. I laughed and told him I appreciated this tangible show of support.

During the Austrian end game in January, my long, adrenaline-fed work sessions were interspersed with moments of pure exhaustion. For every concession I obtained, Muzicant and Moerdler asked for more. We even agreed to their insistence on Austrian maintenance of "known and unknown" cemeteries, musing at the notion of supporting "unknown" cemeteries. Muzicant expected the government to pay lump sums for dissolved Jewish associations and all properties that could not be returned. But equally difficult was obtaining commitments from the Austrian government.

In my last face-to-face negotiation with Schuessel on January 10, he agreed to increase the original package of additional social benefits for Holocaust survivors from $65 million up to a maximum of $112 million over ten years. He also showed flexibility on the return of property, agreeing to appeal directly to mayors and governors to return any confiscated property in their hands. Schuessel further promised a parliamentary resolution assuring that the government would carry out the arbitration panel's property claims decisions, broaden Jewish communal property to be returned to include cultural and religious books, and adopt a more liberal standard for reopening unjust property settlements of the past. In what he and I thought was one last concession, he reluctantly agreed to raise another $10 million from the private sector for the General Settlement Fund, bringing it up to a total of $210 million.

Gaining each of these points was like pulling teeth until there were none left, or so I thought. Even Muzicant thanked the U.S. and Austrian teams for the good work, and well he should have. I also persuaded the chancellor to agree that the Jabloner commission would give priority to identifying assets owned by the Austrian Jewish community. The chancellor had walked the last mile to achieve a deal.

On January 16, a scant four days before the end of the administration, marathon negotiations began in the State Department. I kept the parties apart until we were close to a deal, shuttling from one holding room to another.

Two last-minute glitches arose. One was insurance. As in the German talks, insurance was the last big nut to crack. It surfaced late, when we had run out of money to deal with it. In 1938 Austrian Jews held over 20,000 life insurance policies, with a cash surrender value of 50 million Reichsmarks ($25 million) and a face value of 2 billion Reichsmarks ($1 billion). Nearly 80 percent of the policyholders had to cash them out to pay for the flight taxes that were their ticket to safety, losing the protection for their heirs when they died.

When the Nazis confiscated the remaining policies, they demanded only the cash surrender value, not the larger face value, because the latter would have required the Nazis to furnish death certificates, a strange legal vestige in a lawless society that would have forced them to admit to mass murder. Even the insurance compensation actually returned to survivors, after the Germans repaid the postwar Austrian government, was in dispute. The Austrian Insurance Association insisted that its members had done all they needed to do by paying surviving victims their cash surrender values under a 1958 law.

But an expert from the Jabloner commission confronted the Austrian insurers with their own shameful historical record. The survivors actually received only about 5 percent of the 1938 cash surrender value, with no accounting for the passage of time. The Austrians insisted that insurance claims be covered within the $210 million General Settlement Fund amount, whereas the victims argued that they should be over and above the capped sum—exactly the dispute with Allianz in our German negotiations. I recommended using interest on the $210 million to pay for insurance, and that settled it.

By 6:45 P.M. that day, we had made enough progress to get everyone together. We worked past midnight to iron out all the differences in what was now a four-page draft joint statement by all the parties, with sixteen pages of annexes. As I left for home for a few hours' sleep, Eric Rosand, my talented young State Department lawyer, worked on a final text and e-mailed and faxed copies to the class-action lawyers and the Claims Conference at 5:00 A.M. on January 17.

I telephoned Schuessel in Vienna at 7:10 A.M. I was almost embarrassed to have to ask him for one last concession—to return confiscated property that had ended up in the government's hands *after* rather than during the war. It should not matter when or how it came into the government's possession, I argued; it did not belong to the government anyway. There was a pause that seemed to last an eternity. He said, "Stu, is this your last request? If I agree, will we have a final deal?" With no hesitation I replied yes to both questions. He said, "All right, I agree." I breathed a great sigh of relief.

There was no time to waste. We incorporated the last-minute agreement by Schuessel, and by noon I felt that everybody was ready to sign, even Muzicant. I estimated that, if all the parts of the package were put together, we had a grand total of $1.1 billion dollars, with more to come from communal property. Claims for stolen art could be pursued separately, as well. We had come a long way from Austria's original insistence that it had already done all that was required on property restitution.

We organized a lunch to celebrate in the large, chandeliered Benjamin Franklin Room on the top floor of the State Department. It is as close as any room in official Washington to European splendor, and from its long balcony are some of the capital's best panoramic views. In a short toast, Bob Swift said that our agreement helped cap a movement unique to the 1990s in which victims of human rights violations received compensation. At my personal request Muzicant had agreed to give a positive statement. Holding a glass, he stood and said the agreement could be seen as a glass half-empty or half-full, and he saw it as half-full. From him, that qualified as a ringing endorsement.

In good spirits we left to go downstairs to sign the agreement. I saw Muzicant and Moerdler in animated conversation outside the Ben Franklin Room. Muzicant sheepishly came over to say he would not sign the agreement because it did not give his IKG organization direct cash payments to sustain Austria's struggling Jewish community. I was stunned. I told him he had just blessed the agreement and reminded him how hard I had fought for the Austrian Jewish community and how much I had achieved for them. I implored him to ignore the advice from Moerdler, who was observing us almost gleefully, with a smirk. Winkler and Sucharipa were witnessing the increasingly heated conversation from across the room, and I asked them to sign even if Muzicant refused. They could not. Schuessel had instructed them, adamantly, not to sign any agreement that did not also carry the signature of the head of Austria's Jewish community.

Within seconds I received another blow. Steve Whinston and Mel Urbach, lawyers who represented the Wien community in Brooklyn, said with no forewarning that they also would not sign. Their clients considered themselves the successors to the Orthodox Jewish community of prewar Vienna and would not cede to Muzicant's IKG the exclusive right to pursue Jewish communal property claims. What irony! Muzicant was balking because he felt the IKG did not get enough, whereas Whinston and Urbach were balking because they felt the IKG got too much. I pledged on the spot to give them a side letter confirming that other Jewish communities would be able to file property claims. They said they would first have to show their clients my letter.

Muzicant, Moerdler, and other representatives of the Austrian Jewish community now huddled again in a reception area outside the Loy Henderson Auditorium, where the signing was to take place. I burst in and talked directly with Muzicant, trying to ignore Moerdler. I again urgently stressed that his failure to sign would undermine all the work we had done together and throw away all the progress we had made for Austrian Holocaust survivors and for the IKG. He then made one last demand that leasehold interests in Jewish communal property should also be covered by the arbitration claims process. I replied that the best I could do would be to write to Schuessel on his behalf. Moerdler shot back that this was not a binding legal obligation. I could see Muzicant was wavering. I begged him to come into the auditorium and sign. I entered the auditorium not knowing what he would do.

All eyes were on Muzicant, who was caught between terrible pressure from his own lawyers and his own desire not to create a scandal by refusing to sign. I was greatly relieved to see him approach the podium. Again he gave me a bear hug. But he would only initial the agreement rather than signing his full name, noting below his initials, "See my letter of January 17, 2001." This letter, which he had scribbled just minutes before, said, "I have initialed the [agreement] to indicate that, subject to review and discussion, as needed, essential concepts of the proposal are acceptable in principle. Thank you for your tireless and unprecedented efforts on our behalf."

I did not know how to read his letter, since he had not achieved his principal objective of a cash payment to sustain the IKG. But this was enough to get Sucharipa and Winkler to sign for the Austrian government. To reassure the Austrians, I wrote them the next day stating that the U.S. position was that all those who had either signed or initialed the agreement were full parties to it.

Three images that day, following Muzicant's reluctant signature, helped make all the effort worthwhile. Ambassador Sucharipa, an unassuming man who did heroic work to get his government to bite the bullet on property restitution, said, "We have to live up to our past"—the fact that Austrians were perpetrators, onlookers, and victims. Kurt Ladner, the former boy soccer star of the Hakoah Sports Club, which would be rebuilt under our agreement, signed with a glow of unabashed joy. And Randy Schoenberg, one of the class-action lawyers, signed with tears flowing down his cheeks as he said that he would be able to pursue the recovery of a painting of the modern Austrian master Gustav Klimt, confiscated by the Nazis from his famous grandfather, the composer Arnold Schoenberg, who had died in Los Angeles always dreaming of recovering it.

❦

# CHAPTER SIXTEEN

# The French Exception

I HAD ONLY forty-eight hours left. In that short amount of time, George W. Bush would officially take his place as the forty-third president of the United States. Around the capital, parties were being held, boxes packed, and Democratic political appointees were planning their lives in the private sector. But I was impervious to all around me. My team and I were racing against the clock to complete not only the agreement with the Austrians but one with the French as well.

The essence of the short, intense French negotiations was a profound cultural divide between the democratic peoples on either side of the Atlantic, a clash of cultures between two perfectly legitimate but utterly different ways of regarding the state, public administration, individual rights, privacy, and of rendering justice to the victims of one of history's greatest crimes.

For half a century, the French had cast only sideways glances at their wartime behavior. But the history of World War II in France is like no other country's. Nazi Germany invaded France on May 10, 1940, and quickly overran the French defenses. Five weeks later, on June 14, the French government surrendered. Rather than occupy the entire country, the Nazis allowed Marshal Henri-Philippe Pétain, France's World War I hero, to set up a collaborationist government in the resort town of Vichy, which was given control of nearly two-fifths of French territory.

Although there was an active French Resistance and a government in exile under Charles de Gaulle, France was the only defeated Western European country that had a formal collaboration with the Nazis. One would think that in unoccupied France, the traditions of liberty, equality, and fraternity would have provided a safe haven for Jews fleeing from the East. But no other country in Western Europe so actively consorted with the Nazis and so enthusiastically supported their measures against Jews. A virulent strain of indigenous anti-Semitism in the Vichy regime turned France into a country of persecution rather than protection.

This French vassal state quickly imposed the panoply of Nazi racial laws to appease its masters and keep them out of Vichy territory. Jewish businesses, apartments, art, and bank accounts were ruthlessly confiscated by the Vichy authorities. Supposedly in response to the killing of several German officers by the French Resistance, German officials levied a huge fine of 1 billion French francs on the Jewish community. The Jewish community pleaded unsuccessfully with the French banks to lend them the sum on a short-term basis, and in the end took funds from several hundred of the largest Jewish accounts. In November 1942, when Allied forces invaded North Africa, the Germans occupied the rest of France, although the Vichy government continued to administer its areas for lack of German manpower.

It would later be estimated that between 6.5 billion and 7 billion francs of Jewish property were expropriated by the Vichy authorities, as well as more than 80,000 bank accounts.

But the special targets of the Vichy government were the foreign-born Jews who had emigrated to France in the 1920s and 1930s. Although two-thirds of the French-born Jews were saved from deportation to Auschwitz, not so the Jews from Eastern Europe—Jews like Rose Helène Spreiregen, whom I met by chance at the wedding of a mutual friend. Hers was a typical story, but one she broke a silence of fifty-five years to tell me.

Born to Polish parents in Paris during the early 1930s, Rose Helène was in the capital with her mother and grandmother when the Germans occupied the city in June 1940. The Vichy French, she said, were "always trying to be one step ahead of the Germans." Her uncle, Samuel Bester, and her cousins were among 3,700 foreign Jews rounded up by the police in May 1941. They were taken to the Drancy concentration camp outside Paris and from there to Auschwitz in June 1942. While Rose Helène's mother, Rivka Bester, was seeking safe passage for Rose Helène to unoccupied France, Rivka was betrayed, arrested on July 25, 1942, and sent to Drancy. She volunteered to accompany a trainload of orphaned children to Auschwitz. Upon arrival, the children and their brave chaperone were gassed.

For the next year, Rose Helène and her grandmother hid in the family apartment in Paris. During roundups they often slept in the laundry of a courageous French couple, Paul and Yvonne Martin. Rose Helène recalls that the tension was unbearable—"we were in constant fear." As the Germans closed in, she and her grandmother obtained false papers from the Resistance. Discarding her yellow Jewish star, which she remembered having to remove and sew back on every time she washed her dress, they were escorted to the train station by Paul Martin for a trip to Voiron in the south of France, where her aunt, Ellen Bester, was living. When guards inspected the train, Rose Helène used her fluent French to convince them that her grandmother, who spoke only Yiddish, was too sick to speak. She lived out the war in Voiron, where they hid their Jewish identity from the pro-Nazi French *milice* (militia). And she was one of the lucky ones.

The French preferred to forget their wartime history, but that began to change on July 16, 1995, when Jacques Chirac, the first postwar president with no World War II baggage, publicly and unequivocally accepted responsibility for the Vichy government's nefarious actions. The recent trials of Klaus Barbie and other Vichy French collaborators had awakened Chirac and his postwar generation to the sordid side of France's wartime history. "Yes, the criminal folly of the occupier was seconded by the French, by the French state," Chirac courageously declared. He accepted that the deportation of Jews to their deaths, the looting of Jewish apartments, and the seizure of art and bank accounts had been actions of the French state and not just of its Nazi occupiers. His acceptance of the nation's responsibility for the actions of Vichy France was utterly contrary to the denials of his predecessors, from Charles de Gaulle to Chirac's political archenemy François Mitterrand, whose lifelong friendship with the notorious chief of the Vichy police, Rene Bousquet, had just been made public.

The setting for Chirac's speech was both sobering and appropriate. Chirac spoke on the fifty-third anniversary of the notorious roundup of 13,000 Jews, about 8,000 of them women and children, at an indoor sports stadium in Paris known as the Velodrome d'Hiver. From there they were deported to death camps. He offered his apology to a major Jewish organization, the Sons and Daughters of Jewish Deportees from France, which was headed by Serge Klarsfeld, a Nazi-hunting activist and Holocaust survivor who was also the president's friend. Upon assuming the state's historical responsibility for such crimes, Chirac agreed to reexamine the country's past through a new government institution.

At Chirac's direction and after more than a year of discussions with France's Jewish leaders, Prime Minister Alain Juppé announced the creation of the Study Mission on the Spoliation of Jews in France. He made the announcement before the Conseil Representatif des Institutions Juives de France (CRIF), the central Jewish organization, at a Holocaust commemoration in January 1997. He deliberately chose as chair of the task force a non-Jew, Jean Matteoli, a distinguished magistrate who had been a Resistance fighter during the war. Adolphe Steg, a French Holocaust survivor jailed by the Vichy regime, and distinguished professor of medicine who was also a former president of the CRIF, was named deputy director. It came to be called the Matteoli Commission, and was composed of historians, diplomats, lawyers, academics, and magistrates.

Steg was in charge of research, and he told me, "This is not a Jewish affair; it concerns the whole country." The task force's purpose was "first and foremost to shed light on a twofold historical process, that is to say the spoliation and looting undergone on the property of the Jews of France during the occupations, and the restitution and compensation which they did or did not obtain," he added. When I first met Matteoli and Steg in Paris on May 4, 1999, long before I contemplated becoming involved in any class-action suits, they asked me to review the commission's mandate and sought my blessing on behalf of the U.S. government, which I willingly and publicly gave. They kept me closely informed of their work.

After two and a half years of investigation, the Matteoli Commission published its final report on April 17, 2000, detailing Vichy's crimes, including its vast confiscation of property. The report identified but did not publish, because of privacy concerns, approximately 64,000 names on 80,000 bank accounts that presumably belonged to Holocaust victims. By this time, Juppé had been succeeded in an election for prime minister by the Socialist Lionel Jospin. Jospin quickly affirmed his commitment to the commission in a letter to Matteoli and set in motion a number of initiatives in the formal bureaucratic manner peculiar to France's proud elite administrative corps.

Jospin issued a decree creating a second commission to calculate financial damage to individual claimants who had not already received reparations. Pierre Drai, a Jew from Algeria who had served as chief judge of France's highest court of appeal, headed the "Commission for the Compensation of Victims of Spoliation Resulting from Anti-Semitic Legislation in Force During the Occupation." (Official French nomenclature is nothing if not precise.) The Drai Commission, whose members were drawn from law, finance, and the universities, would handle claims on a case-by-case basis for material damage to Holocaust victims or to their heirs. These included looted apartments and businesses, unpaid insurance policies, and bank accounts or other assets blocked by French banks. There was no ceiling on payments, but the Drai Commission had no legal power to enforce its decisions; it was essentially intended to be a mediation body.

Under heavy lobbying from Klarsfeld and his organization, Jospin agreed to create a fund that would pay either a lump sum or a monthly pension to French Jews orphaned during the war, like Rose Helène Spreiregen. Finally, the Matteoli Commission recommended the creation of a Shoah foundation to fund projects related to the Holocaust. It became the largest charitable organization in France's history, with an initial endowment of 2.5 billion francs (about $375 million), contributed by French banks and insurance companies, the French central bank, and the French government.

The French had reason to be satisfied with their actions. They had taken remarkable administrative steps on their own to face their past. But these did not fit the mold of the adversarial American legal system. The French were chagrined that this was not enough to satisfy the American lawyers who had filed three class-action suits against France's major banks— Société Général, Crédit Lyonnais, BNP Paribas, Crédit Commercial, and Chase Manhattan's French branch—charging they had failed to return looted assets and bank accounts. The first case had been filed in New York on December 17, 1997, on behalf of heirs of French citizens who were now U.S. citizens; the second a year later, on December 23, 1998, by non-U.S. citizens—when the official French search for justice was already underway with the full political support of the mainstream parties of both right and left and the French Jewish community. The third was filed by the same lawyers in California state court.

The cases started almost by chance when a French Holocaust survivor, Anna Zeitenberg, met a lawyer at a cocktail party early in 1997 and asked rather offhandedly whether the French banks could be sued like the Swiss banks. The case ended up in the hands of Ken McCallion, who specialized in class-action suits, and Richard Weisberg, a professor at Cardozo Law School and the author of the book *Vichy Law and the Holocaust in France*. McCallion then contacted Harriet Tamen, an international banking attorney with a quarter century of experience at Chase Manhattan, Citibank, and Crédit Lyonnais who spoke fluent French, to strengthen his legal team. In due course other veteran attorneys, including Michael Hausfeld, were brought in. To increase the number of claimants, the legal team advertised for French survivors and their heirs. The Simon Wiesenthal Center in Los Angeles and Paris helped with historical research to identify and contact claimants for the class actions and provided office space for the lawyers in its Paris headquarters.

The lawyers left no stone unturned, finding heart-wrenching stories in the unlikeliest of places. In Paris one day, Tamen, lunching with her good friend Anne Marie Benisti, asked her luncheon companion to "humor me" and ask her Algerian Jewish father about his wartime finances. Anne Marie called back, almost hysterical, to report that she had learned for the first time that two of her father's bank accounts had been expropriated by Société Général and Crédit Lyonnais and sent to Germany. "I was prosperous before the war, and I had to start all over again. Finally someone is doing something," the father told his daughter. Benisti became the lead plaintiff in one of the lawsuits.

But with their government at last deeply engaged, the French Jewish community resisted joining in this American legal battle, concerned that the fight for restitution in U.S. courts would overshadow the historical responsibility to which France had already admitted. Henri Hajdenberg, president of the CRIF, emphasized this point to me repeatedly. He argued that it was "not worth fighting for 2 billion French francs, even 2 billion dollars," if the financial gain undermined the historical and moral foundation of the official French government movement to redress the wrongs of the past. Jewish leaders like Hajdenberg, Theo Klein, and Serge Klarsfeld trusted their highly centralized government institutions, staffed by the best trained civil servants in the world, more than the distant U.S. judicial system, to provide justice to French Jews.

The French banks reacted to the class-action complaints with what McCallion called a "scorched earth policy," adamantly resisting discovery, rejecting the American allegations, and filing motions to dismiss the cases. They felt especially confident after the two similar class-action suits against German companies were dismissed in September 1999. But on August 30, 2000, Judge Sterling Johnson shocked the French banking community by refusing to dismiss the American lawsuits. It turned out that just before

Jewish assets were frozen in 1941, the French Bank Association asked its members to list their Jewish account holders, which to Judge Johnson implied a conspiracy between the French banks and the Nazi occupiers to deprive French Jews of their assets. He gave short shrift to the Matteoli and Drai Commissions as satisfactory vehicles to achieve a comprehensive remedy to the victims.

Tamen correctly described Johnson's opinion as the strongest ever issued in a Holocaust case, and the first time in all the Holocaust litigations that a U.S. judge had permitted a case to go forward toward trial by denying a motion to dismiss. Johnson then ordered the discovery stage to start immediately, which meant that the plaintiffs' lawyers could begin delving into the banks' wartime archives for material to use in a trial. Needless to say, this prospect enthralled Harriet Tamen, Ken McCallion, and the other class-action lawyers. The French banks quickly realized that their interests would best be served by negotiating a settlement.

Within a fortnight, Jaques Andreani, a former French ambassador to the United States and now an ambassador-at-large for Holocaust issues, appeared in my office at the Treasury to discuss the class-action suits. At seventy-one, Andreani had a distinguished diplomatic career and had gained the confidence of top French officials and political leaders. He was to be for the upcoming French negotiations what Count Lambsdorff was to the German ones and Maria Schaumayer to the Austrian cases. Like them he had come out of a comfortable retirement to take on a tough and thankless assignment. He was dedicated to justice for French victims of the Holocaust and to insuring that the class actions did not worsen Franco-American relations, which had been his longtime passion.

The ambassador stressed the "seriousness, dedication, and thoroughness" with which France was examining its wartime history and cited the 80,000 bank accounts identified by the Matteoli Commission. Unfortunately, Andreani told me, French privacy laws prevented publication of the lists. But Prime Minister Jospin was on the verge of issuing an executive order to transfer the list of accounts from the Matteoli Commission to the Drai Commission for use in processing claims. French Jewish organizations and the World Jewish Congress would be allowed to consult the lists and contact families. Although Andreani realized that in the United States this might be seen as a lack of transparency, in France it was considered a successful compromise with much stricter privacy laws than those in the United States.

The ambassador assured me that France planned to go ahead with these projects irrespective of the lawsuits. He bitterly assailed Judge Johnson's ruling for failing to understand how the Drai Commission process fully protected the interests of survivors and warned of grave political implications, since the American legal system was ignoring the elaborate steps being taken by the French government. That left the two systems, the Drai process in France and the American judicial procedure, in direct conflict. Not only did Andreani question the right of a U.S. court to involve itself in a dispute that involved only French banks and French citizens, but he pointed out that French laws prohibited foreign courts from compelling French entities to disclose information in the course of a lawsuit. Thus, he warned, the French government might simply instruct the banks to refuse to participate in the suits. (This was just the kind of impasse that Judge Korman had foreseen when he prevented the class-action suits against the Swiss banks from going ahead and held out for a negotiated settlement.)

When I hashed this over with our team, we noted that Andreani had never asked us to intervene. No one knew where this was headed. We did not have to wait long to find out.

On November 1, 2000, less than a week before the presidential election, the ambassador returned to my office. Initially, he again lauded the work of the Drai process, the simplicity of its procedures when no documentation was available because of the passage of time, and the absence of any limit on awards. He then announced with satisfaction that Simone Veil, a leading political figure in France and a Jewish survivor of Auschwitz, would head the new Foundation for the Memory of the Shoah, set to open on the first of the year. French banks, including those being sued in the American courts, had contributed about $100 million to the foundation.

Some thirty minutes into the meeting, I wondered whether this was going to be another lengthy recitation of French accomplishments, with no action item for me. But Ambassador Andreani finally got to the point. To ensure an amicable settlement and avoid "a conflict of relations with France," Andreani made a formal request for me and the U.S. government to intervene and help negotiate a solution to the class action.

His timing could not have been worse. The United States was only a week away from presidential elections, and it was clear that there would be a postelection session of Congress that would demand a significant amount of my time. Our Austrian negotiations were at a difficult point, and not all of the German cases had been resolved so that money could start flowing to the former slave laborers.

I was also hesitant to get involved because the French are notoriously difficult negotiators, as I had learned during my ambassadorial tour in Brussels. Whether the subject was U.S. economic sanctions against European countries investing in Cuba and Iran, or freer trade at the Uruguay Round, our biggest hurdle was usually the French. Their diplomats are imbued with a strong sense of national pride, history, and sovereignty, and they often adopt a contrarian position even with their allies, as a way of elevating their own standing. I knew they would zealously protect the Drai claims process from U.S. interference. At the same time, I knew that a messy trial would upset our relations with a close, if prickly, political and economic ally in Europe. More important, a settlement was in the best interest of the survivors, for whom a prompt resolution would mean restitution in their lifetime.

In anticipation that Andreani would ask for our help, I had already queried my overworked team whether they could handle one last project. David Anderson, the Justice Department attorney in our German negotiations, ruefully said, "Well, okay, if we can get at least one trip to Paris!" Everyone laughed, and it was settled. If all of the parties wanted us, then we would mediate, one last time, to help resolve a set of World War II wrongs.

When I told Andreani that we accepted his invitation, there was a visible sense of relief on his face. "It is positive that you are willing to help," he said. But he quickly pointed out that neither the Swiss model nor the German model was applicable, because France had already made "a significant effort to come to terms with this tragic period." I knew I had my work cut out for me. Given French pride in what they had set in motion, the trick would be to find a solution that kept the essence of the French model intact, with the Drai claims process at its heart, while also accommodating the demands of the victims' lawyers.

The landscape I faced in the French negotiations was far different from what I had experienced with the Swiss, Germans, and Austrians: no pressure here from Congress, from Israel Singer, or from Alan Hevesi. Adolphe Steg's forceful testimony before the House Banking Committee convinced Chairman James Leach that the French could be trusted to do justice, their own way, for Holocaust victims. Steg, along with Henri Hajdenberg, the CRIF president, made it clear to Singer that the French Jewish community could handle things themselves, without American Jewish interference. In the end, Singer and the World Jewish Congress quietly settled for one seat on the Shoah Foundation. As for Hevesi, he was convinced, after meeting with Steg in New York and with Prime Minister Jospin and the Matteoli Commission in Paris, to sheathe his sanctions sword and let the French get about their work. This left the class-action lawyers with no external pressure to help them.

As I embarked on this last negotiation, my mind turned to a meeting three years earlier with Felix Rohatyn, the U.S. ambassador to France. I had first come to know Felix in the 1970s, when we were working on the financial bailout of New York City, he as a New York investment banker and I as the head of domestic policy in the Carter White House. The story Felix told me in 1997 shocked me. Felix was born in Vienna to a Polish Jewish family, and the Rohatyns escaped the Nazis by way of Paris and Casablanca. During the war, Vichy officials confiscated his family's property and converted their Paris home into a residence for Otto Abetz, the German ambassador to France. Years later, having returned to Paris as U.S. ambassador, Rohatyn was talking to Prime Minister Alain Juppé after the establishment of the Matteoli Commission. Juppé remarked that if Rohatyn had stayed in France he "would be a Frenchman today." To which Felix replied, "Mr. Prime Minister, if I had stayed in France, I would be dead today."

The negotiations started on a difficult footing. My team met first with the class-action lawyers on November 21, 2000. It soon became evident that Harriet Tamen was the most knowledgeable and the most unyielding, the most passionate and embittered about the recent French efforts at restitution, which she deemed woefully inadequate. An intense person with a sharp mind, bristling with kinetic energy, and hair cropped so short it created an accurate impression of toughness, she was counterbalanced by Michael Hausfeld, who had been the hawk against the Swiss. Now a veteran of three difficult negotiations, he wanted to settle the French case quickly and creatively. He also realized the danger of leaving these negotiations unfinished when the Clinton administration left office. Although the outcome of the presidential election was still in the balance, he sensed that a Bush administration would lack the expertise, and perhaps the interest, that we had built up over six years in resolving Holocaust issues. And without the government as a catalyst, the lawyers and their clients would face a long and uncertain course in the courts.

I immediately stressed to the lawyers that we would have to recognize the unique French situation by treating their official Matteoli research and Drai claims process with respect. The Matteoli report emphasized that more than 92 percent of the money in blocked accounts had been returned to the banks, but there was no evidence of how much had been returned to the account holders. Documentation was lacking for about one-quarter of the blocked accounts, and the commission estimated that only about 11 percent of those accounts belonged to Holocaust-related depositors. It was for this reason that the French banks had pledged to pay into the Foundation for the Memory of the Shoah some $100 million. I told the lawyers that the orphans fund allowed individuals to choose a one-time payment of 180,000 French francs—about $25,000—or a monthly stipend. Last, I told them about the Shoah foundation, which would start with around $375 million from public and private funds, and explained the distinguished stature of its president, Simone Veil, in French public life as a former minister of health and president of the European Parliament. None of this could be ignored.

The American lawyers had a very jaundiced view of what the French had taken pride in creating. They argued that the Drai process was not designed nor intended to deal with individual claims such as those of their clients, that it lacked transparency, that its decisions were made without standards and representation, and that its recommendations were not legally binding on the banks. The American legal team also alleged that the Matteoli Commission simply missed between 20,000 and 35,000 people with potential claims (although it would never substantiate this claim).

Hausfeld promptly laid out a completely different procedure for settlement. He proposed an entirely new foundation outside of the Drai Commission to distribute money to victims and heirs.

Bluntly, I told Hausfeld and his colleagues that the French would never accept a plan that essentially rejected their own work. Instead, we needed to form a marriage of American ideas with the French organizations that were already hard at work. This was the real test of the negotiations.

At this point, I got my first direct exposure to Tamen's bitter feelings towards the French. She distrusted the findings of the Matteoli Commission and attacked the entire Drai settlement process for not establishing uniform public standards, for making only nonbinding recommendations, for procedures not subject to public scrutiny or appeal, and for not paying claims to those who had already received compensation from the postwar

French or German governments. Tamen was supported by McCallion, who noted that two international banks had already settled on behalf of their French affiliates, Barclays for $3.6 million and J. P. Morgan for $2.75 million, demonstrating the force of the cases.

I left the meeting aware that I faced an uphill battle. To determine where we stood with the other side, my team and I met three days later with Fred Davis, Owen Pell, and Philip Bechtel, the attorneys for the French banks. They were far less belligerent than their Swiss and German counterparts, in part because Judge Johnson had not dismissed their opponents' case and they knew they might have to face the embarrassing procedure of discovery and ultimately a trial. But they stoutly defended the French government's procedures, which had been established almost a year before the first lawsuit was filed.

They assured me that the banks had pledged to Prime Minister Jospin that they would follow the Drai Commission's claims recommendations, though they were willing to consider more transparency and better international notice to claimants. Most important, they stressed, the CRIF, the central French Jewish organization, had accepted the French government's program with only minor exceptions.

With no time to lose, I brought the two sides together for the first time on November 29. Ambassador Andreani opened the meeting with a litany of France's actions under Chirac's new policy and stressed that the French budget contained an open-ended line to pay all Drai recommendations. Claire Andrieu, the attractive, youthful executive director of the Matteoli Commission, presented herself with such obvious integrity, earnestness, and sympathy for the victims, to whom she had devoted the past three years of her life, that she thoroughly disarmed the class-action lawyers. Steg also emphasized the seriousness of purpose of the commission's work.

Thrown on the defensive, Hausfeld countered that, "no matter how laudable the approach," the French procedures could not accurately measure the compensation due the victims. He and the other lawyers held out for a "rough justice" payment on the Swiss model, ensuring that the banks disgorged all their Holocaust profits. Harriet Tamen insultingly said that the claimants simply could not trust the Drai settlement process.

Andreani reacted sharply, stressing that the French banks would pay the Drai claims on a case-by-case basis and had in effect disgorged any profits from unclaimed accounts through their payments to the Shoah foundation.

The French bluntly rejected the notion of payments to a rough justice fund; they found it "abhorrent" for Jewish survivors to recover funds based solely on their religious affiliation and not on hard evidence that they or their families had personally lost assets in French banks.

This exchange defined the most contentious issue for the remainder of the negotiations. I stepped in and suggested that Simone Veil's Shoah foundation might have two windows—one for projects of tolerance and the other for claims that did not meet the Drai standards. Then I turned for support to the French Jewish community, through Hajdenberg, on a telephone hookup from Paris. He supported his own government to the hilt and announced the full trust of France's Jewish community in the Drai procedures, administered by Lucien Kalfon, a respected senior civil servant, who was himself Jewish. It was clear that Hajdenberg resented American intervention in what he believed was France's own business.

Andreani had the last word. He politely noted that, although I had presented some creative ideas, the Shoah foundation would focus solely on projects to promote tolerance, and a rough justice fund was out of the question.

With the parties fully engaged, I now could see three major obstacles to an agreement. First, I had to convince the American lawyers that the Drai process could be trusted, at least if we built in some improvements such as the right to an internal appeal and more transparency. I then had to persuade the French, despite their protestations, to accept some kind of rough justice fund to make small per-capita payments to claimants who had no direct proof of bank accounts but who would be willing to sign an affidavit that they had a good faith belief their relatives had such an account. The American lawyers had to show the judge and their clients that the French banks would pay something beyond what they were already committed to pay under the Drai process—otherwise they could not justify settling the cases and getting their legal fees. Finally, I would need to broker a figure for that new fund that would satisfy both sides.

To accomplish these goals and to make the class-action lawyers comfortable with the French model, I invited Lucien Kalfon of the Drai Commission to meet the American lawyers in Washington. He graciously accepted on only a few days' notice, and on December 5 we met in Secretary Summers's stately conference room, directly across from my office. Twenty-three people were present, including Kalfon, Andreani, the class-action lawyers, the bank lawyers, and David Buchholz of the Justice Department, who drafted a paper designed to serve as the basis for a settlement. Six more participated in the meeting via a conference call.

Kalfon began by responding in detail to Harriet Tamen's concerns, emphasizing the careful steps taken toward restitution and stressing that the ten people on the Drai Commission who made the final decisions included judges of the Supreme Court, state counselors from France's highest financial body, university professors, and business leaders. He said that previous reparations payments would not cancel out claims by the survivors for pain and suffering. He also reassured McCallion and Tamen that the banks had pledged to Prime Minister Jospin to respect any findings by the Drai Commission. So it was more than simply a mediation body.

Finally, Kalfon fully recognized the clash of cultures implied by the American demand for publication of all 64,000 names on the 80,000 accounts. In the United States transparency is crucial, whereas the French set a higher value on privacy, and Kalfon demonstrated this by noting that the French Jewish organizations had agreed that the lists should not be published. In France, as in many relatively homogeneous European countries, Jews still feel themselves to be outsiders in varying degrees and have no desire to draw attention to themselves, a quite different view from that held by the proud immigrant groups in the United States' pluralistic society. Kalfon nevertheless recognized the need to be conciliatory. He said that Holocaust groups and the American lawyers could receive permission from the prime minister to view the list. This was a significant concession.

I distributed Dave Buchholz's paper, which adapted the French procedures to incorporate the American concerns. In it we accepted the Drai process to pay all specific claims—"hard claims," with some evidence of a bank account—in full but asked for a written commitment from the French banks to pay according to the commission's recommendations, along with an escrow fund to ensure that the money would be there. We also devised a mechanism that eventually proved crucial in forging a compromise: a second account, in addition to Drai's, to pay lump sums to people who could not meet even the Drai Commission's relaxed rules of evidence—"soft claims," we called them. Claims without proof would need only an affidavit of material losses and proof of French residence during the war. To sweeten this bitter pill for the banks, we proposed that the money would come out of the sum they had already pledged to the Shoah foundation.

I was greatly relieved by the response. Several lawyers praised the paper as a "constructive" start. Clearly Kalfon's trip had been well worth it.

But when I met with my staff on December 12, the optimism had fallen away. The State Department's J. D. Bindenagel reported that the French would not change their settlement process and had rejected the notion that the Shoah foundation could pay claimants whose claims failed before the Drai Commission.

We were also facing a truly insurmountable barrier, the Christmas holiday week. To get a running start in the New Year—when we would have only about three weeks left before Inauguration Day to settle this and other cases—Andreani, the French lawyers, and the American class-action team received from us on December 24, instead of a holiday card, a new set of settlement principles. They kept the essence of Dave Buchholz's approach but had the French banks rather than the Shoah foundation pay into the proposed rough justice, or soft claims, fund.

A day after the New Year, Tamen was leading the fight for a $1 billion payment by the banks, whereas Hausfeld and McCallion were pushing for a more reasonable compromise. In two days, I warned Hausfeld, the French would be meeting to develop their response to the December 24 draft. By that time, the American lawyers needed to form a unified front for the difficult decisions ahead.

Within twenty-four hours Hausfeld had persuaded all of them to negotiate on the basis of our December 24 principles. I telephoned Andreani on January 3 and asked if the French would negotiate on the same basis. Because I would soon be leaving office, I warned him that I did not have time for protracted negotiations, and though I appreciated all the French efforts, it was the American lawyers who would ultimately have to agree to end the litigation.

I gave Andreani something close to an ultimatum. If these issues were "simply insurmountable barriers for the French government to overcome, then I believe we will be unable to reach an agreement, and I would question the value of my coming to France next week," I said. Like any good diplomat, Andreani refused to yield his country's main point, its opposition to some kind of rough justice guaranteed-minimum payment to those with no direct proof of accounts.

But we continued to discuss ways to reach a middle ground. Rob Gianfranceschi of the U.S. Embassy in Paris, who was listening in on the call and had mastered the details of the French program, reminded Andreani that, in addition to the three levels of evidence the Drai Commission required to process claims ("proof," "presumptions," and "indicators," each flexible and requiring progressively less proof), there was a fourth category under the Drai process. This last category permitted payment on a claimant's "intimate personal conviction," a wonderful and expressive French phrase. Rob pointed out that this category was very similar to the rough justice demand of the class-action lawyers in requiring little or no documentation. Even the banks had paid some claims in this Drai category.

This impressed Andreani. It meant that we were keeping with the spirit of France's own invention. Andreani expressed his appreciation for my efforts and our imagination and, as he rang off, promised to do "the utmost to favor a settlement." At last we were making progress.

As the days left to the Clinton administration grew fewer, the parties focused on the need to settle. On January 4 I reconnected with Andreani, who informed me that the French government committee viewed our settlement principles favorably but still rejected the idea of lump-sum payments for soft claims. The French concern was legitimate. If they agreed to such payments for the relatively small number of claims against the banks, they would feel compelled to do so for the far larger number of claims for apartments, businesses, and insurance policies.

But when I spoke with the bank attorneys later that day, they were ready to put money on the table for the new rough justice fund, despite continued French government resistance. For the first time, I decided to press the plaintiffs' attorneys for settlement numbers. I praised them for suggesting important improvements to the Drai process. Yet I also warned them that the French government had rejected their idea of uniform per-capita payments for the soft claims in the new fund. It ran counter to the French idea that justice should be individualized on a case-by-case basis. Furthermore, the Matteoli Commission historians believed that only a small number, perhaps 1,000 to 1,500 accounts, were missing from their report, nothing like the figure twenty times higher that Tamen and McCallion were alleging.

With pulse quickening, on Sunday evening, January 7, 2001, I boarded a flight to Paris for what would be my final foreign assignment. As I landed, I knew I had a chance to go out with a flash and finish both the French and Austrian negotiations, or go out with a thud by finishing neither.

My team and I landed at 8:30 A.M. on Monday morning, January 8, with only three listless hours of sleep on the airplane. It was going to be a long day and an even longer night, one not filled with Parisian revelry.

Our first appointment was with Pierre Drai. His headquarters were located in a spare but handsome nineteenth-century house with elegant high doors and ceilings and fine wall moldings. Drai, one of France's most respected judges, was sincere and frank. He admitted the difficulties of inventing and organizing a process unique to France, based upon "equity and fairness, not law." He also reported that to date only 135 out of the 6,200 claims had been lodged against banks; the rest were for looted apartments and businesses, which were not a part of the class-action suits and were outside our negotiations.

My job was to convince Drai to change his claims process to the satisfaction of the plaintiffs' lawyers. He was basically agreeable but, like his French government compatriots, balked at the idea of a rough justice per-capita amount for individual claimants with no proof of bank accounts, because he found it an advantage for each claimant to receive an individual review of his or her case.

Once again, we had reached a profound cultural gap. It was the French who were on the side of individual judgments and the Americans on the side of uniformity in the name of equality and efficiency. The American lawyers had a point that the only way for families to identify their accounts was to publish the names of the account holders—which offended French notions of privacy. These fundamentally different ways of viewing what both sides agreed was a historical injustice would present the most difficult gap to bridge in the marathon session we had planned for the afternoon and evening.

Before our negotiations began, Hajdenberg, Andreani, and Matteoli joined us for a working lunch at the Foreign Ministry. But for me, the most prominent person in attendance was Simone Veil, the newly selected chair of the Shoah foundation. Besides having a long and distinguished history of public service in France, she is an Auschwitz survivor. Now a stately, dignified woman in her seventies, she added a personal perspective to the French opposition to rough justice, lump-sum payments.

"I know what you have done for compensation for these unfortunate events in Europe," she began to tell me. "I was deported at the age of sixteen along with my parents and my brother; they never came back." For orphans like her, Veil said, "we didn't know if our families had bank assets." On the contrary, many of them incorrectly believed that their parents had great riches. And that was why she believed that claimants should provide evidence in order to receive compensation rather than have a right to recover with no proof. I explained the need for a rough justice concept for people who could not produce proof of bank accounts after all these decades, but who nevertheless had reason to believe their families had assets in French banks. I felt uncomfortable arguing this point with a French icon who was herself directly touched by the crimes of Vichy France, and she was unmoved by my argument.

At 3:00 P.M. I had a half-hour meeting with Prime Minister Lionel Jospin at his office in the elegant Hotel de Matignon on the Left Bank. Jospin is a tall, sturdy, pleasant man, with wavy white hair and not a great deal of charisma but a quiet charm, seriousness, and directness that I found refreshing. He spoke English well and welcomed me warmly. "My role is not to negotiate," Jospin stressed, and he recounted his government's work while thanking me for my efforts to resolve the legal conflict. He added, "I am a little disappointed with the class actions because they have caused difficulty between our two countries and with the French Jewish community, whose philosophy is different."

I explained the main points of contention. He conceded that the process they had created could be more transparent and better publicized, but he opposed "another system [the United States] telling us how to act." He urged me to try to resolve the dilemma—"today."

At 3:30 P.M., our marathon negotiating session began, with Andreani once again reciting France's accomplishments and unhelpfully blasting the American lawyers for their lack of flexibility and for distrusting the processes the French government had put in place to bring justice to victims. I had asked Henri Hajdenberg to speak, believing that his support for his own government might help bend the lawyers and the representatives of the Wiesenthal Center in France, who had joined the talks. This turned out to be a serious misjudgment on my part.

Hajdenberg did little to soften the lawyers' hearts. He blamed them for inflaming the problem by trying to substitute their ideas for those of France's own Jewish community. "We are not in Poland or Switzerland, and the French Jewish community can defend its rights. The government of France has heard our cry," he said, and what French Jews now wanted was "historical accountability, not bank accounts." I silently sympathized with his position that the French had taken major steps to deal with their past. But I had to keep these sentiments to myself. By now, the lawyers were visibly upset, and I was, too, since this was hardly the way to get our negotiations going. Tactically, asking Hajdenberg to speak was a mistake on my part, and as quickly as possible I moved to the business at hand.

The main obstacle remained the distinction between hard claims, backed by evidence, and soft claims, backed by little more than memory, hope, and deprivation. To overcome this, David Anderson of the Justice Department suggested an idea I had endorsed that proved critical to the ultimate resolution. All claims would be presented to the Drai Commission, with or without proof. Those claims without proof that could demonstrate an "intimate personal connection"—the Drai Commission's own term—to indicate that the family once had an account would be referred to the proposed rough justice fund for a flat per-capita payment, as long as the Drai Commission found no blatant bad faith. The assumption was that the vast majority of the claims in this category would be turned over to the rough justice fund for payment. This would preserve the centrality of the Drai process but give the plaintiffs the new fund they demanded. At last Andreani agreed to cover both categories except, he said, "where there is manifest bad faith."

I rushed next door to the plaintiffs' lawyers. McCallion said, "It would be a tragedy if we can't design a settlement," and the plaintiffs' attorneys accepted our settlement principles. To guarantee payment of the hard claims, the lawyers put a $100 million price tag on an escrow account for the Drai Commission. For the soft claims they demanded a set amount for each claimant from a rough justice fund, with 20 percent of the fund set aside for the Wiesenthal Center to help find claimants. I quickly discouraged this idea since the French Jewish establishment had little respect for the Wiesenthal Center. But we were getting down to business.

Back on the French side, Fred Davis, one of the lawyers for the French banks, said that $100 million was far higher than they were willing to pay and suggested a $10 million escrow account for hard claims. But in a major breakthrough, the attorney for Société Général, Christian Schriecke, interjected that the French banks would consider a minimum payment for soft claims out of a victims fund, like the rough justice fund we had suggested, for soft claims with little proof, administered by a nongovernmental organization. The amount could be no higher than the minimum paid for hard claims by the Drai Commission, and he recommended $1,000.

An agreement now seemed within my grasp. I began shuttling back and forth between the two sides, each time narrowing the gap ever so slightly.

All in all, I had six separate meetings with the American team and seven with the French lawyers. There is a rhythm to international negotiations, which usually drag on for months until each side has a will to finish and knows it can live with the settlement that is beginning to form. I sensed we were at one of those points, and although the French were hosting the talks, I virtually usurped the role of chair, insisting that no one could go home until we had come close to an agreement. But at last, fatigue was overtaking us, and I was afraid progress was slipping. I asked everyone to sleep on my suggestion of a compromise $50 million renewable escrow account for hard claims paid through the Drai Commission and a separate $18 million rough justice fund. By the time I called the session to a close, we had met until well past 2:00 A.M. on Tuesday, January 9.

No one got much sleep. I kept going on sheer adrenaline, knowing that as soon as these negotiations were over, I would have to fly to Austria to finish a different round of talks.

The holdout among the class-action lawyers was Harriet Tamen, who was pressing for more money. Because of the six-hour time difference between Paris and New York, McCallion had been unable to reach Hausfeld to have him talk Tamen into accepting a settlement. When we resumed at 8:45 A.M. on Tuesday, the class-action lawyers rejected my figure of $18 million but said that they were willing to consider $25 million. Although I would have preferred to have them agree to the lower figure, I recognized that we had succeeded in creating a bridge between the Drai process and the plaintiffs' demands, and we had narrowed the monetary differences. Harriet Tamen, the hawk, had been somber but quiet while the $25 million proposal was being floated, a sign that the pressure of her colleagues had begun to work. I left Paris for Vienna, satisfied that we had broken the back of these negotiations.

Face-to-face discussions often leave many questions unanswered; agreements unravel when more closely examined on paper. Upon my return to Washington on Thursday, January 11, Pell and Davis, two of the French bank attorneys, walked into my office with a six-page list of issues still to be resolved. I told the lawyers that, however persuasive, their paper represented a step backward at a very late date. They responded that they were flexible. Since I had only nine days left in office, I would soon find out how flexible.

Michael Hausfeld came to me on Monday, January 15, with parameters for the final negotiations: $25 million for the rough justice fund "to put this to bed and to bring us peace with Harriet," he said, and $5,000 for each soft claim.

Thus began a final sprint after years of running a successful marathon—three days of intensive, back-to-back negotiations with the Austrians and the French that continued almost round the clock. I was already physically and emotionally exhausted. A new grandson born on my birthday, January 15, along with farewell receptions at the Treasury, had kept my heart full while my mind was busy working out settlement details. My effects were already being boxed up for a forced evacuation from my office. I had a transition meeting there with George W. Bush's choice as Secretary of the Treasury, Paul O'Neill, the former chairman of Alcoa, whom I had known for years. There was a surreal quality to what felt like a hostile corporate takeover in the midst of my last-gasp negotiations.

We started with the Austrians on Tuesday morning, January 16, worked through the night and into Wednesday, took a short break and then worked on the French discussions through Wednesday night and into Thursday morning. There was no more time for posturing; we did not want to see the curtain come down on the administration with a failure in the last act of the drama.

When we had all gathered on Wednesday night, Andreani made a huge concession. The French would agree to a fixed per-capita sum to be paid automatically from a rough justice fund to claimants filing an affidavit in good faith that they or their family had an account, even if they were not on the historical list of 80,000 accounts and there was no other evidence—if they were initially processed through the Drai Commission. Hausfeld and McCallion accepted this but asked that the U.S. government oversee the Drai process to ensure fair compensation. That was stepping too hard on French sensibilities. Andreani flatly refused and I agreed with him.

To speed up things, I asked the two parties to separate into adjoining conference rooms on the State Department's main floor, while I shuttled back and forth, trying to find a middle ground. Both sides accepted my proposal of a $50 million revolving escrow fund for hard claims. I proposed to split the difference between what the banks called their "last and final offer" of $20 million for the rough justice fund and the lawyers' demand for $25 million. That would come to $22.5 million, and we would set a ceiling of up to $3,000 for each per-capita payment, more than twice the French offer but well below the American lawyers' demand of $5,000. When the French adamantly defended their $1,000 limit on individual payments by citing the same ceiling for the Swiss slave laborers, I disarmed them by saying, "If you want to pay $1.25 billion like the Swiss banks, then $1,000 is okay." Although it was nearly midnight, the class-action lawyers were frantically making phone calls on the pay phones in the State Department hallway to obtain sign-offs from their colleagues and clients. I also had to obtain one final sign-off from Harriet Tamen, who remained resistant to compromise.

When I walked to the class-action lawyers' conference room next door, it was 12:30 A.M. I had negotiated through the second successive night, first to complete the Austrian negotiations and now this. Forty-eight hours was all I had left before George W. Bush's inauguration. I told the lawyers that they had to reciprocate with a display of flexibility. Their numbers edged closer toward my middle ground. At about 1:15 A.M. I felt we were close enough to call it a night and decided to reconvene at 9:00 A.M.

When I met with the French team on Thursday morning, January 18, they presented some major compromises. Schriecke of Société Général said that it would be easier for the banks to accept the higher proposal for per-capita payments in a two-stage process. Since we did not know how many claims would be filed, there would be an initial payment of $1,500. If money was still left in the $22.5 million fund, the initial payment would be increased to a maximum of $2,950 for each claimant. If anything was left over after that, it would go to the Shoah foundation. As a further bow to the Americans and the Wiesenthal Center, the Shoah foundation would distribute money to organizations both inside and outside France.

Andreani then told me that each claimant could pick a representative to observe the Drai proceedings in confidence. The class-action lawyers did not seem to realize that the rules of the Drai process had always permitted the claimants' representatives to attend the hearings. I made this a big selling point to the American lawyers. Here was a perfect opportunity to involve the Wiesenthal Center, I said, to which McCallion responded, "This is a tremendous breakthrough." I could only smile to myself.

After a few more rounds of shuttle diplomacy, the final package was set. In the end, the French banks agreed to pay $22.5 million for the rough justice fund, with soft-claims payments capped at $3,000 per person. The Wiesenthal Center would be paid $500,000 out of the interest from the rough justice fund to cover its expenses in accessing the names on the bank accounts and facilitating claims. The Drai Commission would issue a general report on the size and disposition of its caseload but release no names publicly, to preserve French notions of privacy. In confidence, it would report the results of each individual case only to the U.S. government. In a bow to the lawyers, I persuaded the French that the Drai Commission report could be viewed by the plaintiffs' lawyers at the State Department so long as it was not reproduced, either by them or by the Wiesenthal Center.

Around noon, before anyone had second thoughts, I invited everyone to a signing ceremony in the seventh floor State Department Treaty Room, elegantly decorated with historic Americana and with paintings of past secretaries of state all around. With all the signatures on the dotted line, I felt an overwhelming combination of weariness, relief, and satisfaction.

Andreani assured me that the French government was pleased that we had preserved the original French structure. Harriet Tamen, forever the holdout, was not so content, confiding later that signing the settlement was "the biggest mistake" of her life. But the rest of the class-action lawyers were relieved not to have to endure a protracted battle in court. They were content that they had helped bring the French financial institutions into the ambit of human rights by holding them legally accountable for collaborating in the genocide and theft of their proud nation's Jewish population.

We had found a way to preserve French honor and to respect France's belated efforts to come to terms with its Vichy past, while grafting American-style justice onto French institutions.

CONCLUSION

*ᴗᴖ*

# A Final Accounting
# for World War II

A S THE CHANCE for a moment's reflection finally came at the close of
the Clinton administration on January 20, 2001, I asked myself
whether it had been worth following this difficult and often tortuous path through four different and challenging positions in three government agencies. The answer was not simple.

I was painfully aware how imperfect our efforts were in providing justice
to Hitler's victims. Obviously it was too late for those who were killed during the war or died in the years afterward. There were also real costs to our
enterprise. Critics, even in the Jewish community, charged that the emphasis on material restitution overshadowed the human tragedy of the Holocaust. Others railed against what they saw as an insidious "Holocaust
industry" of lawyers and Jewish organizations profiting at the expense of
victims.

Our negotiations were not idealized exercises in moral expiation or giant
civics lessons. They were difficult, emotional, confrontational clashes over
billions of dollars, wounded national pride, and efforts at belated justice,
involving cataclysmic events that had taken place more than fifty years
before. Those required to pay had played no direct part in the horrific
crimes.

The huge settlement that Swiss, German, Austrian, and French banks,
insurance companies, and industrial enterprises made on their class-action
cases after fifty years of postwar amnesia were not concluded because of a
sudden tinge of conscience by a new generation of corporate leadership.
They did what corporations are supposed to do: They acted in the best

interests of their shareholders. The costs of fighting cases that they might have won in a court of law had become too steep to sustain in the court of public opinion and in the enormous, profitable U.S. marketplace, where they were operating and hoped to expand.

In the boisterous politics of the United States, the clash of interests produces policy. This occurred in our negotiations. The lawsuits were simply a vehicle for a titanic political struggle, which was messy, sometimes unseemly, and constantly frustrating.

Undeniably, the political and economic pressures placed on European companies to contribute to our settlements caused resentment. Herbert Hansmeyer, the head of North American activities for the German insurer Allianz and one of the chief negotiators in the German cases, characterized our hard-earned settlement as "an act of public appeasement," saying "I cannot become very emotional about insurance claims that are sixty years old." Edwald Kist, chairman of the Dutch insurer ING Group, told me recently that the World Jewish Congress and state insurance commissioners in the United States did not serve the best interests of the Dutch Jewish community with their pressure tactics.

What is more serious, anti-Semitic sentiments increased, most notably in Switzerland, where they have been successfully mined by Christoph Blocher, the right-wing politician who has vaulted his People's Party into the second largest political group in the Swiss Parliament. By exaggerating Jewish pressure on Switzerland ("The Jews are only interested in money," he said in a 1997 speech at the height of the Swiss bank controversy), by casting Switzerland in the role of aggrieved victim of American bullying, by threatening to take the proposed Solidarity Fund to a public referendum and certain defeat, this billionaire-turned-populist cowed the Swiss political establishment into a sullen silence, stoked the smoldering embers of anti-Semitism, and reinforced right-wing sentiments throughout Europe. A cartoon in the Swiss press at the height of my negotiations spoke for far too many. Under the caption *"Helvetia unter Druck"* ("Switzerland under pressure") is a Jew holding a press, crushing mother Switzerland into disgorging gold.

There were also disappointments and mistakes. I regret the divisions my foreword to the 1997 Nazi gold report caused in Switzerland. In discussing the wartime role of Switzerland and its consequences to the Allied war effort, I substituted candor for diplomacy. Although the report spoke the truth, a conviction I hold even more strongly today, it is also undeniable that more cautious language could have conveyed the same ideas, perhaps with less political fallout. But this will never be known. The Swiss press was spoiling for a fight and consciously distorted my references to the clash between morality and neutrality and the prolongation of the war, to make it appear that the comments were aimed solely at Switzerland, when they unmistakably were addressed to all the neutrals.

My bitter experience with the Swiss negotiations, in which the Swiss government refused to be a negotiating partner, taught me a lesson that I never forgot in joining the German, Austrian, and French talks. I would never again risk the prestige of the U.S. government in trying to settle class-action lawsuits against foreign companies, unless their governments were willing to become directly engaged. Otherwise, I would be left once more to the caprice of unruly private interests, without the broad view that governments bring to the table. I knew that the intervention of the United States in private lawsuits can be justified only in the most unusual circumstances—when there are strong foreign policy interests and when the victims include U.S. citizens—but I learned the hard way that it is essential that the foreign government be willing to share the burden of achieving a settlement. If the resolution of such lawsuits is not important to the host government, then neither should it be to the U.S. government. Fortunately, the governments of Germany, Austria, and France, in contrast to that of Switzerland, recognized that the reputation of their private companies reflected on their nations' reputations. Without their assistance, I could never have been successful.

Another disappointment grew out of the inadequacies of the American legal system as a place to resolve complex political issues. U.S. courts are not the best places to resolve profound historical and political questions. Procedures are too cumbersome, the rules of evidence too exacting. Third parties, recalcitrant opponents, or obdurate judges can hold up payments to needy people for an unconscionable period of time. One federal judge held up payments to elderly forced laborers for half a year in the German case and longer in the Austrian cases. There was a three-year delay in payments in the Swiss case, even under the wise guidance of Judge Edward Korman. The insurance issues in our German negotiations lingered for over two years after our settlement, until an agreement was reached in October 2002 with ICHEIC, the Claims Conference, and Allianz, but virtually no policies have been paid, largely because the German insurers have taken unreasonable positions on key issues I considered settled by our negotiations. Yet it cannot be doubted that, without the suits, the pressures they generated, and the involvement of the U.S. government they occasioned, the massive settlements would never have occurred.

And I regret not pressing my own government hard enough to put property restitution higher on the agenda in dealing with the new democracies of Eastern Europe. During the first two years on this project I was based in Europe and lacked easy access to the power centers in Washington. By the time I returned to the capital, the major negotiations dominated my time, along with my regular responsibilities. Still, I wish I had done more.

Worse was the lack of engagement of the state of Israel in this enterprise. The Israeli government stayed on the sidelines when I was slogging through Eastern Europe trying to return Jewish communal property to the Jewish communities reawakened after the Cold War, when its involvement would have been helpful in stirring action by the new democracies of the old Communist bloc. They were engaged only at a secondary level, if at all, in the major negotiations I conducted.

I told Israeli prime ministers Benjamin Netanyahu and Ehud Barak, as well as Israel's ambassadors in the Eastern European countries, that I found it ironic that the U.S. government took a greater interest in the return of Jewish communal properties than the Jewish state did. But the Israeli government was content to leave the heavy lifting to the United States and to a nongovernmental agency, the World Jewish Restitution Organization (WJRO), just as fifty years earlier they had delegated negotiations of Holocaust reparations with Germany to another private group, the Claims Conference. Part of the reason was not to complicate their political relations with the newly liberated Eastern European nations with such a controversial issue. But there was a more profound reason.

Plain and simple, the Israeli state since its founding has been based upon the powerful Zionist idea that the real home for the world's Jews is Israel, the place to which the exiles should return 2,000 years after the destruction of the Second Temple by the Romans. The concept of *aliyah*, literally "going up," was not only a philosophical ideal. Israeli governments have always sought as many immigrants as possible in order to build a demographic defense against their overwhelmingly more populous Arab neighbors and to provide a skilled labor force to power the Israeli economy. From the countries of the former Soviet Union, over 900,000 immigrants have arrived in Israel since the fall of the Berlin Wall, with another 25,000 from other Eastern European nations. Although Israel's Jewish Agency provides support to post–Cold War Jewish communities that remain in Eastern Europe, the bulk of their funding comes from American-based organizations like the American Joint Distribution Committee, the American Jewish Committee, and the World Jewish Congress (WJC). The Israeli government is not eager for these communities to dig deep roots in their countries; they want them in Israel instead.

.   .   .

BY ANY FAIR measure, I do believe we achieved practical, political, and moral successes far outweighing the costs and disappointments, and far greater than could have been imagined when I began this enterprise in 1995. We galvanized the world's attention on the overlooked issue of looted Holocaust-era assets, and we provided a final, if incomplete, financial accounting for the crimes of World War II. For the first time in the annals of warfare, systematic compensation was sought and achieved for individual civilian victims for injuries sustained by private companies as well as by governments—for everything from forced labor to lost property rights arising from bank accounts, insurance policies, artworks, and other physical property. This will provide a benchmark for future battles.

On the ground, Jewish and non-Jewish communities are getting back the physical infrastructure—schools, houses of worship, community centers, hospitals, and cemeteries—that will permit religious life to bloom on soil stained by blood and parched by Communism. The small remaining Jewish communities will have to struggle to survive. But survive they will, given the determination that has taken them this far, albeit never again as the major centers of Jewish learning, religion, and culture they once were.

Thousands of families will finally be able to locate their Swiss and French bank accounts. Over 30,000 Swiss bank claims have been lodged, and the 250 so far validated are averaging over $93,000 each. Money is flowing from all of the major settlements. Already almost 1 million forced and slave laborers have been paid from the German and Austrian foundations. Personal property is being reconnected to families. Art museums throughout the world are researching their collections to determine whether they hold any pieces that were looted by the Nazis. Thousands of pieces of art have been listed on Web sites, hundreds are being returned, and the 1998 Washington Principles are facilitating claims by families to retrieve the lost works of art that hold great emotional and financial value for them.

No one will become wealthy from the slave and forced labor payments, but over 1 million surviving victims of Nazi barbarity—the vast majority of whom are non-Jews from Eastern Europe—will find their declining years less harsh. More broadly, the money means they were not forgotten by the world. Paulina Zingereine, a Lithuanian Jew and former slave laborer in the Kaunas ghetto and Stutthoff concentration camp, told me poignantly, "The Soviet regime denied us justice. We were treated as anonymous Soviet citizens. We now receive financial compensation. But more important, we are now recognized as equals in the world of survivors."

For those who doubted the capacity of the U.S. government to do things right, this was a shining example of a governmental success at minimum cost, with agencies cooperating with few traditional turf concerns and with the White House, including the president, engaged. The federal government accomplished its twin political goals of helping victims of Nazi aggression while maintaining close diplomatic relations with Germany, Austria, France, and the nations of Eastern Europe, though not with Switzerland. Even there the rift is slowly healing with time, facilitated by the high-level U.S.-Swiss economic commission I put in place to soothe Swiss feelings. The successful negotiations removed a cloud over these nations and their companies, which would have created further political tensions and potentially harmed their business interests. By helping nations face their responsibilities for the past, I hope this experience will make them more tolerant and self-confident in the future.

But achieving these dual goals required a constant balancing act. The foreign governments and the victims' representatives each suspected our American team favored the other. We had to replace suspicion with trust. There was an added pressure for me, dedicated as I was to helping achieve justice for the victims of World War II by dint of my own background, to always place the U.S. government's broader interests at the forefront, never losing my objectivity in overcoming challenges from all sides.

No doubt the moral dimensions of our work often got clouded in the fog of rhetoric, recrimination, and threats of sanctions. As I first learned in the Carter White House in the 1970s, the Holocaust remains a highly combustible issue. It must be handled with greater care than some parties to our negotiations appreciated. Bullying at times went beyond the bounds of propriety.

But the critics of our work have gone too far. There is no "Holocaust industry." Three of the key class-action lawyers, Michael Hausfeld, Mel Weiss, and Burt Neuborne, took no fees at all in the Swiss negotiations, working, as lawyers say, pro bono, or "for the public good." Judge Korman's award of legal fees to the other lawyers will be less than 1 percent of the settlement, and even that will be paid out of interest. In all our negotiations, legal fees averaged only slightly above 1 percent of the total of some $8 billion recovered, spread out over dozens of lawyers. Even this caused an outcry, especially among Europeans unfamiliar with the American system of contingency fees. Pro bono donation of legal services ended with the Swiss cases. In the German cases, there were fifty-two different law firms that divided up $54 million in legal fees out of the 10-billion-DM ($5 billion) settlement, the biggest single fee, $6.5 million, going to Mel Weiss's firm, with the average fee being a little over $1 million. The twenty-eight law firms in the Austrian case divided up $4.7 million, the largest being to Michael Hausfeld's firm, of $1.7 million, and the average being $170,000.

All of this is a pittance compared to fees in a victorious mass injury case, which can range from 15 to over 30 percent, or come to nothing if they lose. In the recent $200 billion tobacco settlement, the Mississippi law firm of Ness, Motley, Loadholt, Richardson & Poole will receive at least $1 billion. In the Dalkon Shield case, for faulty design of female contraceptives by the pharmaceutical manufacturer A. H. Robins, lawyers collected over $90 million in legal fees. The asbestos settlements bankrupted companies like Johns-Manville while providing eye-popping fees to the lawyers.

The Holocaust cases were a part of the broader excesses of the class-action system the United States uses to resolve mass injury cases, which is spinning out of control and exerting a drag on the U.S. economy. There is a crying need for reform, but this is no reason for special indictment of the Holocaust settlements.

Financial compensation remains our accepted way of dealing with civil wrongs, especially when the United States lacks the social safety net of Europe. The victims of the twentieth century's worst barbarities deserved no less a right to recover than other victims, and a unique combination of legal, political, and diplomatic intervention provided it—even though each individual victim will receive far less than victims of civil torts for the lifelong physical and psychological injuries they will carry to their graves. Abraham Foxman, the executive director of the Anti-Defamation League, himself a hidden child in Poland during the war, has struggled with the propriety of monetizing the Holocaust and has agonized about the "last sound bite of the century" on the Holocaust focusing on money and assets. But he finally concluded: "After all, it's important to have an accounting and accountability. Not only for the victims, not only for the loss, but as a message for the future, in that it's important for people to know that if you do evil, if you rob, if you steal, you're going to pay a price." I could not say it better.

There were successes at a moral level as well, supplied by the moving statements of remorse by German president Rau and Austrian president Klestil; payment by German and Austrian companies to far more forced workers than they would ever have been legally liable to cover; the German Future Fund and French Shoah foundation to promote tolerance, Holocaust memory, and the lessons of wholesale injustice; and the French government's efforts to repay confiscated property well before the threat of lawsuits.

Most satisfying for me was leading an enterprise fully backed by the United States government to help remove, in a modest way, some of the moral stain on the record of the Roosevelt administration, which fought the war so valiantly but abandoned the refugees to Hitler's grim fate, and on the record of later presidents who allowed the victims' plight to be pushed aside in favor of other priorities.

.        .        .

I BELIEVE the most lasting legacy of the effort I led was simply the emergence of the truth—truth about the dimensions of the massive theft of property, the methods used by the Nazis to sustain their war effort with looted gold and millions of coerced laborers, the unredressed injustices to millions. Historical facts can be suppressed, but eventually they bubble to the surface. What started as a tiny trickle from long-buried U.S. archives became a torrent of information that helps provide a final accounting for World War II. Beyond the immediate impact of the settlements, there are long-term implications of our efforts to bring justice to the victims of World War II in the fashion we did. I believe this will resonate for years in

Europe and the United States and, I hope, in other places where genocide has occurred. Memories of the genocide of World War II are sinfully short, as we have seen in Rwanda and in the former Yugoslavia. But that is why we searched for something more enduring than money and restitution of property, as important as these were to the individual victims. More permanent memory through education was our answer.

That is why we put into place structures to have the Holocaust seared into the conscience of future generations, so they understand the disaster that befalls mankind when intolerance goes unchecked, when racial and religious bias becomes a basis for government policy, and when well-meaning people and good countries stay on the sidelines while human rights are violated.

At our encouragement, twenty-one countries, from Argentina and Brazil to Latvia and Lithuania, have established some twenty-eight historical commissions to examine their roles in World War II and their relationships with looted Nazi assets, the most comprehensive effort being the Swiss Bergier Commission and the French Matteoli Commission.

But by far the most unexpected revelations came from Israel. In January 2000 Israel's largest bank, Bank Leumi, disclosed that it held some 13,000 dormant accounts, many belonging to Holocaust victims who had opened accounts in Leumi's predecessor, the Anglo-Palestine Bank. Most had been deposited by European Jews to have the money for an entry permit into British Mandate Palestine. A claims process was established, similar to the one for the Swiss banks.

The revelation about the Leumi accounts led the Israeli Knesset to create its own historical commission, which concluded in November 2001 that Israeli banks and various government and public institutions held approximately 25 billion shekels ($6.25 billion) in unclaimed Holocaust-era assets, most in the form of land purchased in prewar Palestine by European Jews who were killed in the Holocaust before they made it to the Holy Land.

In Sweden, Prime Minister Göran Persson was shocked in the summer of 1997 to hear over Swedish radio about a public opinion poll that revealed how few young people knew either about the Holocaust in general or Sweden's role in particular in aiding the Nazis, which the United States had revealed in my May 1997 Nazi gold report. This farsighted leader commissioned two historians to compose a moving booklet, *Tell Ye Thy Children,* and had 1 million copies distributed to virtually every household in the country. When the first copies were delivered to us in the winter of 1998, Bennett Freeman of my staff handed me a copy and said simply, "This is what it's all about." With the Swiss bank controversy still swirling around us and so much broken crockery to repair on issues from art and insurance to forced labor, the Swedish initiative was a dignified reminder of how to face the past and, at the same time, avoid the damage to national reputation that might otherwise have resulted.

Prime Minister Persson went further. At the urging of my team and me to shift the focus from money and assets to education and remembrance, Persson also agreed to sponsor an international conference in Stockholm, modeled on the 1997 London gold conference and our own, then forth-coming 1998 Washington conference. The Stockholm International Forum on Holocaust Education was held in late January 2000 and was attended by more than forty countries, the Vatican, and a dozen heads of European gov-ernments. After more than half a century, it was extraordinary to convene so many political leaders to commit their countries to promote Holocaust education, remembrance—like national days of commemoration—and research.

In addition, Persson suggested to us and the British the creation of an international Holocaust education task force to promote the lessons of the Holocaust in schools around the world. As a result of Persson's leadership and our active engagement, the fourteen-nation International Task Force for Holocaust Education is today actively working on this project and has ongoing outreach efforts from Argentina to the Czech Republic. In this effort, Germany has long been a model. Holocaust education is an integral part of its school curriculum and a mandatory component of its military training, as part of its ongoing effort to ensure that Nazism is permanently expunged.

It was not only governments that launched retrospectives. Daimler-Chrysler, Degussa, and Deutsche Bank hired historians to catalogue their involvement with the Third Reich. In 1999 General Motors hired a Yale historian to catalogue and publish documents on the wartime role of its German subsidiary Adam Open AG. And in December 2001 the Ford Motor Company released a study of the role of Ford Werke in employing slave and forced labor.

My work in dealing with the consequences of the unchecked anti-Semi-tism of the Holocaust made it especially troubling to see a resurgence of anti-Semitic actions across Europe in 2001 and 2002, from synagogue burnings in France and attacks on rabbis in Belgium to desecration of Jewish cemeteries in Italy and threatened boycott of Israeli universities. I do not believe that any of this is related to the negotiations in which my team and I were involved. With the exception of Switzerland, our efforts generated little anti-Semitism in Europe. In Austria, all parties, even Jörg Haider's Freedom Party, supported the outcome of our negotiations. Editorial comment and public opinion polls in Germany, Austria, and France supported the justice provided to victims of Nazism.

Rather, the spate of anti-Semitic actions in Europe has coincided with the response by Israel, under Prime Minister Ariel Sharon, to Palestinian terrorism and has come largely from immigrant Arab populations, especially in France. To lash out at European Jewish institutions and individual Jews thousands of miles away from the Middle East, who may or may not agree with Israeli policies, is itself a new form of anti-Semitism. But the problem is more profound and troubling than that.

It is as much a mistake to condemn the whole continent for being anti-Semitic, as some American commentators have suggested, as it is to ignore that the Middle East conflict has tapped into a lingering vein of anti-Semitism among significant parts of the European public. Israel, like any country, is not exempt from criticism, nor should the Holocaust be used to blunt opposition. But neither should Israel's policies be a basis to relieve European nations of their accountability for the Holocaust. Large swaths of Europeans are treating Israel as a pariah state, like South Africa during the apartheid era.

It is not coincidental that Yassir Arafat's regular mantra in criticizing Israel's response to Palestinian suicide bombers has been to invoke "Nazi methods." He has tried to wash away Europe's remaining Holocaust guilt and to indicate a moral equivalency between Hitler's actions and Israel's. What is more disturbing is the resonance this has in Europe. A member of Germany's mainstream Free Democratic Party accused the Israeli army of "Nazi methods." Jürgen Möllemann, the deputy leader of the Free Democrats, accused Israel of engaging in "state terrorism" and defended the terrorist actions by saying, "I, too, would resist, indeed violently," and went on to blame Prime Minister Sharon for inspiring anti-Semites. In the last week of the September 2002 national election campaign, he mailed leaflets attacking a prominent German Jewish leader, Michael Friedman—an overt act of demagoguery that cost his party dearly at the polls, to the credit of the German electorate. In April 2002 the European Parliament, the only popularly elected body of the fifteen-member European Union, voted to impose trade sanctions on Israel. Trade union leaders in Scotland and Norway are refusing to offload Israeli products, and Norwegian supermarket chains are placing identification stickers on Israeli products. University professors in Britain and throughout the Continent are calling for a boycott on links with their colleagues at Israeli universities, while European companies are canceling contracts with Israeli firms.

Long before the current round of anti-Semitic incidents, at the height of the Middle East peace process, my wife, Fran, and I were always struck during our tenure in Europe by the omnipresent concrete barriers and police protection around Jewish schools and synagogues. As the last witnesses to the Holocaust depart, Europe continues to struggle with the forces of darkness, to exorcise the demons of the past so they do not haunt their future. Jews are hardly the only target. Muslims and immigrants are subject to worse discrimination. But the antipathy toward the Jews—a sentiment long embedded in European culture—remains a more lasting and powerful force.

I do not deceive myself into thinking that our work on reviving interest in the injustices done to Hitler's victims can make the difference in how Europe deals with its struggle. But I hope it will give the nations of Europe at least a nudge in the right direction. The French government, though slow to condemn the spate of synagogue burnings, has now acted forcefully to track down their perpetrators. Austrian president Thomas Klestil issued a moving apology in the spring of 2002 at a public ceremony interring the remains of handicapped and mentally ill children—considered *lebensunwertes Leben*, "life unworthy of life"—who were killed in a Nazi clinic in Vienna, when Austria was part of the Third Reich.

There are additional long-term effects. Other victims of human rights violations have already followed our model. Class-action suits by Korean comfort women and American POWs against the Japanese clearly took their inspiration from the Holocaust cases. In fact, it is striking that Japanese companies have escaped the harsh scrutiny of those in Switzerland and other European countries. In early 2000, inspired by the Holocaust class actions, Armenians sued New York Life Insurance Company for failing to pay policies held by victims of the Armenian genocide of World War I, prompting a settlement offer by the company of $15 million, which the Armenians rejected as inadequate. As of this writing, claims for reparations are being prepared on behalf of over 250,000 Spanish Republican prisoners employed as forced laborers by General Francisco Franco during and after the Spanish Civil War.

On July 21, 2000, Secretary of State Albright called me from the Camp David Summit to ask if my experience with Holocaust property restitution afforded any answers to Yassir Arafat's demands for restitution for the homes that many Palestinians lost during Israel's 1948 War of Independence. I warned her about any comparisons and stressed that Jews in Arab countries had been expelled in large numbers in the years following the creation of the state of Israel. Yet there still are lessons that may be applicable. Palestinians have been taught to believe that they were unjustly driven from their homes and will return with any peace agreement. This is both historically inaccurate and politically impossible. But I learned from our negotiations that offering material benefits can provide a balm for lingering pain. I hope that, when the Israelis and Palestinians come to the point of an overall settlement, it will include an international fund, in lieu of actual property restitution, both for those in Arab refugee camps and for Jews who fled to Israel from Arab lands, not unlike those we encouraged Eastern European countries to create when the actual restitution of property was impractical. Perhaps payments as part of a general settlement would help encourage Palestinians to rebuild their lives and, over time, work with the Israelis, as the Israelis and Germans do now.

Most recently, the filing of class-action cases in March 2002 in federal court in New York against a number of American employers, financiers, and insurers of slaves during the American Civil War, like Aetna, CSX Railroad, and Fleet Boston Financial Corporation, has taken a page from the arguments and tactics employed by the lawyers in our Holocaust cases. In July 2002 antiapartheid class-action suits were also filed in New York, against IBM, Citigroup, UBS, and Credit Suisse, directly patterned on the Holocaust cases. They seek compensation, reparations, and the creation of a historical and audit commission, just as in the cases I negotiated. One of the lead lawyers in both sets of cases is the ubiquitous Ed Fagan, who said of the apartheid cases, "Apartheid victims deserve the same justice as was shown to Holocaust victims."

These cases stand on the same shaky legal grounds as the ones I mediated. But the applicable lesson from our work is that they will ultimately be decided in the court of public opinion more than in the court of law. If they can galvanize public opinion and generate political support, as the Holocaust cases did, they may succeed despite their legal infirmities. It is interesting to note that one group that has not organized to exert political pressure are American POWs who were employed as slave laborers by Japanese companies during World War II, perhaps because as soldiers they were trained to treat hardship as a part of their duty.

For the Holocaust suits, the combination of sympathetic victims in one of history's worst tragedies, heavy political pressure, and serious foreign policy implications was unique. Although it is unclear whether the U.S. government will again devote the kind of time, energy, and resources it did here, my teams and I created a precedent others can point to in the right set of circumstances.

An out-of-court political resolution to the American slavery cases, for example, might draw on some pieces of the puzzle we put together to resolve our disputes. The emphasis on memory through Holocaust education and creation of national historical commissions could be used as models in the United States. A U.S. government commission to examine slavery and its modern implications, together with a commitment to incorporate more emphasis on the history of slavery in the nation's textbooks, could help, as well.

The kind of public apology for slave and forced labor I encouraged the presidents of Germany and Austria to make to cap our negotiations would help salve the wounds of generations of African Americans who suffered the direct and indirect consequences of slavery. The U.S. Congress officially apologized to Japanese Americans for their internment in camps during World War II. Why not to African Americans?

Individual compensation to the descendants of slaves today is another matter. Our payments for coerced labor were strictly limited to actual survivors who performed the labor. All parties agreed there was simply not enough money to cover heirs. The only heirs eligible were those claiming identifiable bank accounts, insurance policies, and property. If this is the case for a twentieth-century event, it would certainly apply for slavery, whose unfortunate roots predate the American republic itself.

But again, our experience may offer a way out. The Future Fund established within the German Foundation, the Humanitarian Fund created by the Swiss banks, the Shoah foundation established in France, and the fund for heirless insurance policies in ICHEIC all provide latitude for programs of tolerance, education, and social benefits. The companies sued might draw a lesson in providing, for example, minority scholarships or training and hiring programs. Already the class-action lawyers are talking about putting any damages into a fund to improve health, education, and housing opportunities for African Americans.

Although I would like to think my teams and I helped write a new page in creating civil liability for the violation of human rights, we provided scant legal precedent. Only Judge Sterling Johnson in the French bank cases was ready to let one of them go forward, and then only because he did not see the French as providing a comprehensive remedy, as the Germans and Austrians had done. All the other judges either dismissed the cases that came before them or would most likely have done so.

But this does not diminish the legal and diplomatic implications of what we accomplished. It was one massive alternative dispute-resolution process, one giant set of mediations by the U.S. government, pointing to a new direction for American diplomacy that will only increase in the twenty-first century. The new types of issues that are coming onto the foreign policy agenda, like the global environment, AIDS, and human rights, can no longer be conducted successfully by traditional state-to-state relations. New actors—nongovernmental organizations (like the WJC and WJRO in our negotiations) and, yes, even lawyers at times—must be part of the solution. Indeed they are often driving the new agenda and forcing governments to react, as occurred in the Holocaust cases. Governments, especially the United States', will need to be more flexible and open to engage in the new diplomacy with nontraditional actors.

We developed novel concepts that may have applicability in future mass violations of human rights, like "rough justice" to pay mass numbers of victims, rather than the individualized justice that courts provide; acceptance of loose standards of proof, given the decades that have passed; and the creation of administrative remedies, like the German Fund for Remembrance, Reconciliation, and the Future, the Austrian Fund for Reconciliation, Peace and Cooperation, and the French rough justice fund.

At a time when corporate accountability and governance has become a major preoccupation, the Holocaust-related cases also may have a positive, prophylactic impact on the conduct of multinational corporations. They may be less likely to engage in conduct supportive of evil regimes, for fear of consequences similar to those that befell the Swiss, German, Austrian, and French firms that directly or indirectly supported the Third Reich. Nongovernmental organizations and the media will be certain to focus on those corporations that are complicit in human rights abuses around the world. I hope that one enduring message we sent was that, regardless of treaties and legal precedents, there is no effective statute of limitations on corporate accountability before the court of global public opinion. The challenge the Holocaust-related cases pose to multinational corporations is hardly theoretical. A raft of suits have been brought recently against major oil companies, from Unocal to Exxon Mobil, accusing them of cooperating with governments in the abuse of human rights in their investments in Southeast Asia. In September 2002 a federal appellate court allowed a suit against the energy company Unocal to proceed on the ground that it may have aided and abetted the repressive government of Myanmar (Burma) in employing forced labor to construct a gas pipeline.

.　　　.　　　.

ONE OF THE most revealing aspects of this piece of history is what it suggests about the political influence of the Jewish community in the United States. Since the end of World War II, there has been a dramatic change as Jews—for two millennia a dispersed powerless minority living in the shadows of history, supplicants in their countries of residence—have moved onto the world stage. In Israel, they do so within their own nation-state; in the United States, they do so as an influential political group. The searing lesson for the post-Holocaust generation of American Jews—the Bronfmans, Singers, and Foxmans—has been to compensate both for the passivity of the World War II generation and the weakness of European Jewry in the face of Hitler's evil, by coming out of the political closet and openly pressing its influence, like other groups do in the United States' polyglot politics. Like it or not, the intensity, at times belligerency, of their words and actions—whether directed against Kurt Waldheim in the 1980s or the corporate targets in Switzerland, Germany, Austria, and France in the late 1990s—in their minds had a twofold motivation. It was both a just retribution for what was done by their corporate predecessors to European Jewry, and an expiation of the American Jewish community's own collective guilt for doing so little to stop it six decades before.

This made for sometimes uncomfortable and even unsavory tactics, ones I opposed as a U.S. government official because they compromised the foreign policy powers of the president of the United States. But the Jewish activists of the 1990s were copying on a worldwide stage the types of moral shaming employed in fighting South African apartheid and in achieving racial justice in the United States, from the days of the Montgomery bus boycott right down to recent pressures on southern states to remove Confederate symbols from their flags.

·     ·     ·

THERE IS STILL much work to be done, and I am pleased that Secretary of State Colin Powell has chosen to keep the Office of Holocaust Issues alive, staffed by many of the same people with whom I worked. At a time when almost all of the Eastern European nations want to join Western institutions like NATO and the European Union or to achieve more favorable trade terms, property restitution in those very countries remains incomplete, a work in progress. In the Czech Republic, for example, Catholic Church property claims remain unsatisfied. These countries should be told straightaway that their progress in establishing fair, efficient, and transparent processes to return confiscated properties belonging to religious communities will be one factor in considering their applications.

The major agreements the United States helped broker still must be effectively implemented. Art archives, particularly in Russia, should be fully opened, and looted art returned to its owners. It is time for all European countries to undertake the kind of massive declassification of wartime documents that the United States has done through its National Archives and Records Administration. Most glaring, the Vatican must finally open its archives to permit an examination of the role of the Church and of Pope Pius XII during the war. This would be a legacy to a great pope, John Paul II.

As I look back, I realize I was driven by an abiding principle in Judaism imparted to me by my parents, Leo and Sylvia, called *tikkun olam*, literally, "to repair the world." In this case it was to partially repair lives torn asunder during World War II. Yet none of this would have been possible without bipartisan support from the greatest nation in the world. Only the United States, of all the nations on the globe, cared enough to try to repair the damage done to so many people, even if so late in the day.

In realizing how much we accomplished, I am equally mindful of how many were never helped, how imperfect was the justice we helped obtain, how in the truest sense there can be no final accounting for the devastation wrought by the Nazis to human lives and property. I think of Greta Beer, haunted by her father's still-missing Swiss bank account, plaintively saying to me even now, "Mr. Secretary, don't forget me; please don't forget me, Mr. Secretary." History will not forget you, Greta, nor Alice Fisher, Estelle Sapir, Gizella Weisshaus, and all the others who had the courage to step forward before it was too late.

I close this book and this chapter in my life with an ancient proverb from Pirkei Avoth, Ethics of the Fathers: "It is not your obligation to finish the task, but neither are you free to exempt yourself from it."

## ACKNOWLEDGMENTS

MY WIFE, Fran, and my sons, Jay and Brian, first encouraged me to write this story. Fran has been with me every step of the way, from urging me to accept this special Holocaust-related assignment when others argued against it, to supporting me when this enterprise, on top of my regular duties, stretched us to the limit. She never let me flag in bringing it to a successful conclusion. I owe her a debt of gratitude for all of this and, along with our sons, for pointing me in the right direction.

My agent, Ronald Goldfarb of Goldfarb & Associates in Washington, D.C., had a deep faith in the importance of memorializing my experiences and worked hard to help me develop a book proposal that gained the support of Peter Osnos, the publisher of PublicAffairs. I cannot say enough kind words about the professional competence of Peter, his superb executive editor Paul Golob, and editor Kate Darnton. They believed in this book, gave me invaluable advice in structuring it, and helped me separate the wheat from the chaff.

I would not have been able to provide them with a solid manuscript without the special assistance of my own editor, Lawrence Malkin, of New York City. An experienced journalist for many years with major publications in Europe and the United States, as both a foreign and economic correspondent, he had previously edited several other books. Larry gave me the "tough love" I needed to create a story out of a mass of facts, to make this a personalized history for a broad range of readers. He turned around my preliminary drafts at an astonishing speed, with keen insights, and kept me and the story moving.

But with all the work of Larry Malkin, Paul Golob, and Kate Darnton, the person who put the most hours, time, and effort into it, besides myself, was Carolyn W. Keene, my personal assistant since my Carter White House days almost a quarter century ago. Carolyn's devoted effort was self-sacrificial, working for months on end long into the night after her regular duties with me at the Covington & Burling law firm. She organized over six years of my voluminous notes, arranged the extensive interviews I conducted, and typed every revision of the manuscript. Her own enthusiasm for this project kept up mine. Joan Williams, my secretary at the law firm, also helped by typing parts of the manuscript.

I am especially touched by the moving Foreword written by Elie Wiesel, whose life, work, and values have long been an inspiration.

A special word of thanks goes to former Congressman Lee Hamilton, President of the Woodrow Wilson International Center for Scholars in Washington, and Peter Kovler, President of the Kovler Family Foundation in the nation's capital. Lee and his colleagues, Dean Anderson and Rosemary Lyon, permitted me to serve for five months as a Public Policy Scholar at the Wilson Center, which helped me get a running head start on this book. Peter Kovler's foundation made two generous grants that enabled me to hire research assistants, who helped me place my work into a proper historical context.

These assistants were universally excellent: Lisa Fierer and Salo Zelermyer for the Introduction and Chapter 1 on property restitution; Dr. William Slany for the Swiss chapters; Dan Rabinowitz on Switzerland and Germany; Aron Kuehnemann for Austria; Lisa Lubick Daniel and David Glasner for France; Russell Shaw for the art chapter; and Alexander Gerschel on insurance and general cite checks. Special work was done by my longtime friend Milton Gwirtzman on the German chapters; by Eric Rosand of the Legal Adviser's Office at the State Department, who after hours read much of the manuscript for accuracy and provided invaluable suggestions; by Ronald Bettauer, also of the Legal Adviser's Office, who helped do the same with several of the sections; and by Michelle Wildstein, who did extensive general and legal cite checks for historical accuracy in the final manuscript. Greg Bradsher of the National Archives and Records Administration was helpful in tracking down documents.

My work that formed the basis for this book could not have been done without the support of President William Jefferson Clinton and his top assistants: Sandy Berger, his National Security Adviser; John Podesta, the White House Chief of Staff; Mary Ann Peters and Antony Blinken on the National Security Council staff; James Steinberg, Deputy National Security Adviser; Secretary of State Warren Chirstopher, Secretary of State Madeleine Albright, Secretary of the Treasury Lawrence Summers, and Ambassador Richard Holbrooke, initially in his capacity as Assistant Secretary of State for European Affairs.

The success of my negotiations was a genuine team effort that started at the top. But the heavy lifting, the creativity needed to overcome innumerable hurdles in the negotiations, and the drafting of documents was done by an extraordinarily talented, selfless, and dedicated team of U.S. government lawyers, career diplomats, and senior government officials who took on this added burden to their other important responsibilities. They worked together, though they were drawn from diverse agencies and, at various times, some dozen different departments. I have listed them in the endnotes for each of the major negotiations. But I want to give special recognition to those with whom I worked most intensively: at the State Department, E. Anthony Wayne, my Deputy Chief of Mission in Brussels; Ambassador J. D. Bindenagel, then the head of the department's Office of Holocaust Issues, and his assistants John Becker and Jody Manning; Anne Derse at the U. S. Embassy in Belgium; Ambassador Randolph Bell, now Ambassador Bindenagel's successor; Victor Comras, Margaret Pearson, and Ambassador Henry Clarke, who worked with me on Eastern European property restitution; Ronald Bettauer and Eric Rosand of the Legal Adviser's Office; Basil Scarlis, a special consultant; William Slany, the Historian of the department; Ruth van Heuven, head of the Office of German, Austrian, and Swiss Affairs; Bennett Freeman, my Senior Adviser in my Undersecretary's office at the State Department, and Peter Bass, my Chief of Staff; and Rosalinda Seldowitz and Thelma Resper of the State Department's Office of Holocaust Issues; for the Justice Department, David Anderson, David Buchholz, and Will Kirschner; from my personal office Holly Toye Moore, my Special Assistant and de facto chief of staff at the Treasury Department; and Milton Gwirtzman at Treasury; and during my time at the Commerce Department, Judith Barnett, Judy Liberson, and Lisa Lubick Daniel. Others who helped my work include my dedicated secretaries at the Treasury Department, Marsha Valentic and Reavie Harvey; and my press aide at Treasury, Helaine Klasky.

Our negotiations were successful not only because of my talented U.S. team but also because of our key foreign counterparts: for Germany, the courageous Chancellor Gerhard Schröder; Bodo Hombach, the head of the German Chancellery; Count Otto Lambsdorff, the Chancellor's Special Envoy and one of Germany's wise men; Manfred Gentz, Chief Financial Officer of DaimlerChrysler and German industry's senior negotiator; for

Austria, Chancellor Wolfgang Schuessel, and his special envoys Maria Schaumayer and Ambassador Ernst Sucharipa, and their aides Ambassador Hans Winkler and Martin Eichtinger; for France, then Prime Minister Lionel Jospin, Ambassador Jacques Andreani, Dr. Adolphe Steg, Lucien Kalfon, and Claire Andrieu.

I decided at the outset to try to give the readers not only my view of events but those of all the key players. So I conducted interviews with more than 110 heads of state, senior government officials, key corporate representatives, class-action lawyers, and leaders of nongovernmental organizations. Several people deserve special thanks for sharing their own notes of meetings and communications or other pertinent information that enabled me to tell a more complete and accurate story: Edward Fagan, Michael Hausfeld, Robert Swift, Melvyn Weiss and his colleague Deborah Sturman; Israel Singer, Elan Steinberg, and Maram Stern of the World Jewish Congress; Ronald Bettauer of the State Department; and David Buchholz of the Justice Department. Margaret Grafeld and her staff at the State Department declassified the cables on my meetings with Eastern European officials, which was helpful in putting together Chapter 1, on property restitution. Alice Rickey at State coordinated the comprehensive interagency review of the manuscript for security purposes.

But to everyone who took the time to be interviewed I am appreciative:

## Art

Ambassador J. D. Bindenagel; Philippe de Montebello, head of the Metropolitan Museum of Art; Tom Klein and Will Korte; Lynn Nicholas; Jonathan Petropoulos; Elaine Rosenberg; Bill Singer; Dr. Lawrence Wheeler; and John Coffey of the North Carolina Museum of Art.

## Austria

Ed Fagan; Heinz Fischer, president of the Austrian Parliament; Kurt Ladner; Hannah Lessing, director of the Austrian National Fund; Dr. Ariel Muzicant, president of the Austrian Jewish community; Harold Radday, translator; Eli Rosenbaum; E. Randol Schoenberg; Chancellor Wolfgang Schuessel; Ambassador Ernst Sucharipa, the Austrian Special Envoy for property negotiations; Robert Swift; Melvyn Weiss; and Ambassador Hans Winkler and Maria Schaumayer, the Austrian Special Envoy for labor negotiations.

## Eastern European Property Restitution

Victor Comras, Margaret Pearson, Anne Derse, and Ambassador Henry Clarke of the U.S. Department of State; President Valdas Adamkus of the Republic of Lithuania; Rabbi Andrew Baker of the American Jewish Committee; Galina Levina and Vladimir Tchernitski of the Belarus Jewish community; David Susskind of Belgium; Dr. Solomon Passy; Victor Melamed; and Dr. Emil Kalo of the Bulgarian Jewish community; Dr. Aleksandr Dusman, Armir Kulman, and Gessi Kozlovski of Estonia; Dr. Ferenc Olti, Janos Gado, Agnes Peresztegi, Gabor Sebes, and György Sessler of Hungary; Herbert Block and Michael Schneider of the American Joint Distribution Committee; Tomas Kraus, executive director of the Federation of Jewish Communities in the Czech Republic; Emanuelis Zingeris, Dina Kopilievic, and Ilya Lempertas of Lithuania; Andrzej Zozula, Stanislaw Krajewski, and Jerzy Kichler of Poland; Fero Alexander of Slovakia; and Josef Zissels, Rabbi Yaakov Bleich, Dr. Anatoly Podolsky, Yana Yanover, Boris Yanover, Anna Yudkovskaya, Michael Frenkel, Leonid Finberg, Yevgeny Ziskind, and Henry Filvarov of Ukraine.

## France

Ambassador Jacques Andreani; Rabbi Abraham Cooper of the Simon Wiesenthal Center; Henri Hajdenberg, then president of the CRIF (the central French Jewish organization); Serge Klarsfeld; Theo Klein; Ken McCallion; Rose Helène Spreiregen; Dr. Adolphe Steg of the Matteoli Commission; Harriet Tamen; and Professor Richard Weisberg.

## General Background

Nessie Godin; Ben Helfgott in London; Ken Klothen and Gene Sofer of the President's Commission on Holocaust Assets; Michael Lewin, then

chairman of the U.S. Commission on the Heritage of the U.S. Abroad; and
Norman Salsitz.

## Germany

Ronald Bettauer, Edgar Bronfman, Edward Fagan, Benjamin Ferencz, Dr.
Manfred Gentz, Michael Hausfeld, Bodo Hombach, Dr. Michael Janssen,
Roman Kent, Ambassador John Kornblum, Count Otto Lambsdorff, Ben-
jamin Meed, Professor Burt Neuborne, Eric Rosand, Chancellor Gerhard
Schröder, Israel Singer, Deborah Sturman, Robert Swift, Gideon Taylor,
Seth Waxman, Melvyn Weiss, and Roger Witten.

## Holocaust Education Issues

Yehuda Bauer of Yad Vashem in Jerusalem; Bennett Freeman, my Senior
Adviser at the State Department; and Prime Minister Goran Persson of
Sweden.

## Insurance

Ambassador J. D. Bindenagel, Jack Brauns, former Secretary of State
Lawrence Eagleburger, Herbert Hansmeyer, Neil Levin, Neil Sher, and
Robert Swift.

## Introduction

Dr. Michael Berenbaum and my former colleagues in the Carter White
House, Ellen Goldstein and Mark Siegel.

## Switzerland

Hans Bär, Greta Beer, Ambassador Randolph Bell, Ronald Bettauer, Dr.
Rolf Bloch, Swiss Ambassador Thomas Borer, Michael Bradfield, Edgar

Bronfman, Marc Cohen, former Swiss President Flavio Cotti, Lloyd Cutler, former Senator Alfonse D'Amato, Swiss Ambassador to the United States Alfred Defago, Edward Fagan, Abraham Foxman, Alice Fisher, Bennett Freeman, Judah Gribetz, Peter Gumbel, Michael Hausfeld, former New York City Comptroller Alan Hevesi, Curtis Hoxter, Lord Greville Janner of Britain's Holocaust Education Trust, Helen Junz, Saul Kagan, U.S. District Judge Edward Korman, Russ LaMotte, Christoph Meili, Professor Burt Neuborne, Robert O'Brien, Gregg Rickman, Eli Rosenbaum, Israel Singer, Elan Steinberg, Maram Stern, Deborah Sturman, Robert Swift, Gideon Taylor, Paul Volcker, Melvyn Weiss, Dr. Barrie White, and Roger Witten.

.　　.　　.

EACH PERSON in this drama played an indispensable role—U.S. and foreign government officials, class action lawyers, representatives of the private foreign corporations and NGOs, politicians, and judges. With all of our combustible conflicts and bitter differences, in the end the sparks they produced fused together to make possible the stunning results I have tried my best to faithfully record.

STUART E. EIZENSTAT

*Washington, D.C.*
*November 2002*

# NOTES

❧

## Introduction: A Fifty-Year Wait for Justice

9   On Jewish emigration to the United States and Switzerland: Raul Hilberg, *The Destruction of the European Jews* (New York and London: Holmes & Meier, 1985), pp. 310–311; William D. Rubinstein, *The Myth of Rescue: Why the Democracies Could Not Have Saved More Jews from the Nazis* (London and New York: Routledge, 1997), citing Immigration and Naturalization Service figures, pp. 34–35. The *American Jewish Committee Year Book* (Jewish Publication Society of America, Vol. 48, 1946–47), by the staff of the American Jewish Committee, has higher figures. From July 1942 to December 1945, it estimates some 36,000 Jews came to the United States. But that figure could include a significant number who arrived after the war ended in Europe in May 1945. For the crucial July 1942–June 1943 period, the committee estimates only 4,700 Jewish refugees came to the United States, and 31,400 from July 1943 to December 1945. Even these numbers are tragically small.

10   On Canadian figures: Irving Abella and Harold Troper, *None Is Too Many: Canada and the Jews of Europe, 1933–1948* (Toronto: Laster Publishing, Ltd., 1991). With regard to Swiss emigration between September 1, 1939, when the war broke out in Europe, and May 1945, 51,129 civilian refugees were granted asylum in Switzerland, of whom 21,304 were Jews. See "Switzerland and Refugees in the Nazi Era," Independent Commission of Experts—Switzerland—Second World War (Bern, 1999), pp. 23–24.

10   Morgenthau report: "Report to the Secretary on Acquiescence of This Government to the Murder of the Jews" (January 13, 1944), Henry Morgenthau Diaries, Book 693, Index for Refugees, pp. 212–229 (located in the Franklin Delano Roosevelt Library, Hyde Park, New York). Secretary Morgenthau later retitled this report "Personal Report to the President" and shared it with the president on January 16, 1944 (Henry Morgenthau Diaries, Book 694, Index for Refugees, pp. 190–202). Secretary Morgenthau was not the first in his family to take an interest in the plight of refugees. His father, Henry Morgenthau, Sr., the American banker, diplomat, and philanthropist, led the effort from 1919 to 1921 to raise funds for relief in the Middle East and was chairman of the Greek Refugee Settlement Commission, created by the League of Nations in 1923.

11   Polish nationalists murdered Jews: Martin Gilbert, *The Holocaust* (Austin, TX: Holt, Rinehart & Winston, 1985), pp. 816–817.

11  "This will be the fate of all surviving Jews": Yehuda Bauer, *Flight and Res-cue: Bricha* (New York: Random House, 1970), p. 15.

11  Polish Home Army shootings: Gilbert, *Holocaust,* pp. 816–817.

11  Displaced persons: Mark Wyman, *DPs: Europe's Displaced Persons, 1941–1951* (Philadelphia: Balch Institute Press, 1989).

11  Patton and the DPs: Leonard Dinnerstein, *America and the Survivors of the Holocaust* (Ithaca, NY: Columbia University Press, 1982), pp. 17, 47.

11–12  Harrison's findings: Earl G. Harrison, *Treatment of Displaced Jews,* report RG–19.024*01 (Washington, D.C.: U.S. Holocaust Memorial Museum Archives, 1945); letter of President Truman to General Dwight D. Eisen-hower, August 31, 1945, White House News Release, September 29, 1945. Eisenhower letter responding to President Truman: Headquarters, U.S. Forces, European Theater, Office of the Commanding General (Oct. 8, 1945). URL: www.US-Israel.org

12  Conditions gradually improved after the Harrison report: See Judah Nadich, *Eisenhower and the Jews* (New York: Twane Publishers, 1953).

12  Merkers mine contents: Greg Bradsher, "Nazi Gold: The Merkers Mine Treasure," *Prologue: Quarterly of the National Archives and Records Adminis-tration* 31, no. 1 (Spring 1999), p. 11.

13  "Who can doubt that we Jews . . . ": Nahum Goldmann, *Autobiography* (London: Weidenfeld & Nicolson, 1970), p. 250.

14  Begin and Ben-Gurion: See Lily Gardner Feldman, *The Special Relation-ship Between West Germany and Israel* (London: George Allen & Unwin, 1984), p. 42.

14  At the end of war: West Germany refused to sign a formal peace treaty because the Eastern Zone had not been incorporated into the homeland. Feldman, *Special Relationship Between West Germany and Israel,* p. 39.

14  "Unspeakable crimes . . . ": Ibid., p. 40.

15  Arthur D. Morse, *While Six Million Died: A Chronicle of American Apathy* (New York: Ace, 1967).

15–16  President Kennedy's direction: Executive Order 11086, February 26, 1963.

16  An explosion of Holocaust-related books: Walter Laqueur (editor), *Second World War: New Essays in Political and Military History* (Thousand Oaks, CA: Sage, 1982); David S. Wyman, *The Abandonment of the Jews: America and the Holocaust, 1941–1945* (New York: Random House, 1986); Lucy S. Dawidowicz, *From That Place and Time: A Memoir, 1938–1947* (New York: W. W. Norton, 1989); Dawidowicz, *The War Against the Jews, 1933–1945* (Austin, TX: Holt, Rinehart & Winston, 1975).

16  William Styron's *Sophie's Choice* (Random House, New York, 1979) was also made into a movie.

16–19  Holocaust Museum's history: See, generally, Edward T. Linenthal, *Preserv-ing Memory: The Struggle to Create America's Holocaust Museum* (New York: Viking, 1995); Judith Miller, *One by One by One* (New York: Simon & Schus-ter, 1990).

19  Executive order establishing Holocaust Memorial Commission: President,

Executive Order 12169 (signed October 26, 1979), *Federal Register,* p. 44, FR §2277.

19 "Deplorable manipulations": Elie Wiesel, *And the Sea Is Never Full: Memoirs 1969–* (New York: Alfred A. Knopf publishers, 1999), p. 211.

## Chapter 1: Through the Valley of the Dry Bones

26 Ten Jewish organizations: The World Jewish Restitution Organization (WJRO) consists of the following member organizations: Agudath Israel World Organization; American Gathering/Federation of Jewish Holocaust Survivors; American Jewish Joint Distribution Committee; B'nai B'rith International; Centre of Organizations of Holocaust Survivors in Israel; Conference on Jewish Material Claims Against Germany; European Jewish Congress/European Council of Jewish Communities; Jewish Agency for Israel; World Jewish Congress; World Zionist Organization.

26 Israeli government and the Jewish people: Letter of Yitzhak Rabin to Edgar Bronfman, September 10, 1995. Yitzhak Rabin was assassinated on November 4, 1995.

30 The Jewish community in the Czech Republic was not the only religious community to have problems with property restitution. As late as July 2002, the Czech Catholic Church had no satisfaction on claims to seven hundred buildings and 125,000 hectares of land, mostly held by local authorities. See testimony of Randolph M. Bell, Special Envoy for Holocaust Issues, before the Helsinki Commission on Property Restitution in Central and Eastern Europe, July 16, 2002.

31 Pinkas Synagogue: Arno Pařík, *Prague Synagogues,* trans. Stephen Hattersley (The Jewish Museum in Prague, 2002).

32–33 Meeting with Czech prime minister Klaus: U.S. Department of State cable, "Ambassador Eizenstat's Restitution Conclusions and Proposed Action Agenda for the Czech Republic," December 1, 1995 (Brussels 12135).

35–36 Meeting in Slovakia: U.S. Department of State cable, "Property Restitution: Ambassador Eizenstat's Conclusions and Proposed Action Plan for the Slovak Republic," November 29, 1995 (Brussels 12029). In September 2002, the Slovak government of Prime Minister Mikulas Dzurinda reached an agreement with Fero Alexander of the Slovak Jewish community, assisted by Rabbi Andrew Baker of the American Jewish Committee and U.S. ambassador to Slovakia Martin Butara, settling all property claims through creation of an $18 million fund. This fund will be used for charitable and social programs, preservation of cultural property and cemeteries, and compensation for individuals whose personal property was confiscated. Alexander told me, "We are in euphoria."

37–39 Visit to Bulgaria: U.S. Department of State cable, "Visit to Sofia of Ambassador Eizenstat—Scenesetter," December 12, 1995 (Sofia 08384).

38 Meeting with Mayor Stephan Sofianski, mayor of Sofia, Bulgaria: U.S.

Department of State cable, "Ambassador Eizenstat's Discussions on Jewish Property Restitution in Bulgaria," January 5, 1996 (Sofia 00070).

42 No publicity in Poland: U.S. Department of State cable, "Polish Officials Express Concern About Eizenstat; Worry About Press," May 9, 1995 (Warsaw 6442).

43 Clarke mediation: Ambassador Henry L. Clarke, Senior Adviser for Property Restitution, Bureau of European Affairs, U.S. Department of State, 1998–2000, "Reaching Agreement on Restituting Jewish Communal Property in Poland," 2000 (unpublished paper given to the author by Ambassador Clarke).

44 Revival of Jewish life in Hungary: Interview for this book with Dr. Ferenc Olti, vice president of the Association of Hungarian Jewish Communities, and Janos Gado, Editor of *Szombat*, periodical of the Federation to Maintain Jewish Culture in Hungary (Budapest, Hungary), May 3, 2001.

44 Visit to Hungary: U.S. Department of State cable, "Eizenstat Mission to Budapest on Jewish Restitution: Meetings With Jewish Leaders," June 7, 1995 (Budapest 05114); idem, "Eizenstat Mission to Budapest on Jewish Restitution: Meetings With Hungarian Government Officials," June 9, 1995 (Budapest 05192).

45 "prophesy over these . . . dry bones": Ezekiel 34:1–14.

## Chapter 2: Greta Beer and the Swiss Bank Affair

48 A law in 1962: In 1962 the Swiss Federal Council asked Professor Edgar Bonjour of the University of Basel to examine the wartime role of the Swiss and gave him full access to the federal archives. He concluded that Switzerland had a mixed record and had made mistakes in denying many Jewish refugees entry after World War II. Bonjour did not look into the conduct of the banks.

48 Picard's landmark book: Jacques Picard, *Die Schweiz und die Juden, 1931–1945* (Switzerland and the Jews, 1931–1945) (Zurich: Chronos Verlag, 1997).

50–51 *Vorwärts* poem: "R. L.," "Political Poem on the Washington Accord," from *Vorwärts*, attachment no. 2 to dispatch 14103, July 24, 1946, from the U.S. Embassy in Bern, RG 59, Box 4212, SB 07060.

## Chapter 3: Enter the Players

61–69 Senator Alfonse D'Amato generally: Gregg J. Rickman, *Swiss Banks and Jewish Souls* (Piscataway, NJ: Transaction, 1999).

63 He asked Gregg Rickman: Gregg J. Rickman, *Swiss Banks and Jewish Souls* (Piscataway, NJ: Transaction, 1999).

66 Bronfman presented the first lady with article about Greta Beer: Jeffrey

Goldberg, "The Money Trail: Stolen Assets," *New York Magazine*, April 29, 1996.

68  Poor Hans Bär: Records indicate that Nazi black marketers deposited their assets with Bank Julius Bär. But Hans Bär was a teenager in the United States during the war and knew nothing of the conduct of his family's bank at that time (National Archives, Document S-MIS 0157633, American Embassy, London. Safehaven Report, "Techniques Employed in Transferring German Funds from Istanbul to Swiss Banks," April 30, 1945, Reports and Messages, State Department, Great Britain, Document Library Branch, Intelligence Administration Division, Assistant Chief of Staff (G-2), Records of the Army Staff, Record Group 319, Box 801).

72  International accounting firms: Independent Committee of Eminent Persons, *Report on Dormant Accounts*, p. A212, Appendix U.

73  Volcker findings: Independent Committee of Eminent Persons, *Report on Dormant Accounts of Victims of Nazi Persecution in Swiss Banks* (Berne, Switzerland: Staempfli Publishers, 1999), p. 10, Table C.

73  Regarding prewar wealth of the Jewish population, see Helen B. Junz, "Report on the Pre-War Wealth of the Jewish Population in Nazi-Occupied Countries, Germany, and Austria," in Independent Committee of Eminent Persons (ICEP), *Report on Dormant Accounts*, p. A727, Appendix S.

## Chapter 4: Enter the Lawyers

78–80  Estelle Sapir was born in 1925. Information and quotations from deposition by Estelle Sapir to Edward Fagan, New York City, July 23, 1997, supplied to the author by Mr. Fagan.

## Chapter 5: All That Glitters

90  On September 26, 1996, Edgar Bronfman wrote: Letter from Edgar M. Bronfman, President, World Jewish Congress, to President William Jefferson Clinton, September 26, 1996 (copy supplied to author by World Jewish Congress).

90–91  A month later, on October 25, Bronfman got more specific: Letter from Edgar M. Bronfman, President, World Jewish Restitution Organization, and Hon. Greville E. Janner QC MP, Chairman, Holocaust Educational Trust, to H.E. Secretary of State Warren Christopher, October 25, 1996 (copy supplied to author by World Jewish Congress).

91  The president replied to Bronfman: Letter from Bill Clinton to Edgar M. Bronfman, President, World Jewish Congress, October 30, 1996 (copy supplied to author by World Jewish Congress).

92–93  Delamaruz and blackmail: Amos Elon, "Switzerland's Lasting Demon," *New York Times Magazine*, April 12, 1998; Congressional Research Service,

*The Holocaust Recovery of Assets from World War II: A Chronology (May 1995 to Present)*, report prepared for the U.S. Congress by Barbara A. Salazar, July 31, 2000.

93  Only a few weeks after the Swiss National Bank decided to contribute to the Humanitarian Fund, it released its own study indicating that the bank helped Portugal, Spain, Sweden, Turkey, and other European neutrals to buy 1.7 billion Swiss francs' worth ($425 million) of looted Nazi gold during the war. Balz Bruppacier, "Swiss Bank Says Portugal Led List of Other Neutrals Buying Nazi Gold," The Associated Press, March 20, 1997.

94  Would not destroy any potential evidence: The Swiss Federal Council issued a federal decree on December 13, 1996, prohibiting the destruction or transfer of existing records that could be useful to the ICEP investigation (decree published in Independent Committee of Eminent Persons (ICEP), "Report on Dormant Accounts of Victims of Nazi Persecution in Swiss Banks" [Berne, Switzerland: Staempfli Publishers Ltd., 1999], Appendix F, p. A-27).

96  On Studer's accusations, see Alexander G. Higgins, "Whistleblower's Lawyer Demands Explanation from Bank Chief," Associated Press, January 19, 1997.

98  Series of mysterious fires: See Niles Lathem, "Fires Are Cozy for Swiss Banks," *New York Post*, June 29, 1997, pp. 6–7.

99–111  *U.S. and Allied Efforts to Recover and Restore Gold and Other Assets Stolen or Hidden by Germany During World War II—Preliminary Study*, May 1997, report coordinated by Stuart E. Eizenstat, prepared by William Z. Slany, with the participation of the Central Intelligence Agency, Department of Commerce, Department of Defense, Department of Justice, Department of State, Department of the Treasury, Federal Bureau of Investigation, Federal Reserve Board, National Archives and Records Administration, National Security Agency, and U.S. Holocaust Museum.

107–109  My foreword: One of Switzerland's own American lawyers told me later that I had been "99 percent fair to Switzerland." But it was a few words that caused the uproar. The land of milk chocolate had been shown to have knowingly accepted looted gold, and likely also gold ingots with victims' teeth in them. Frankly, the Swiss would have done well to direct their uproar less at my report and more at a belated reevaluation of their own conduct during and after the war. But this was not to be. Press reaction in the United States was uniformly positive. Jim Hoagland of the *Washington Post* called the report a "Matterhorn of integrity" and nailed Swiss defensiveness on the head when he wrote that the Swiss had forgotten that "the problem of morality and greed does not begin or end at Switzerland's borders" ("Old Crimes," *Washington Post*, May 25, 1997, p. C7).

112  The London Conference on Nazi Gold: See, generally, British Stationery

Office, "Nazi Gold: The London Conference" London, United Kingdom, December 2–4, 1997.

## Chapter 6: Kabuki Dance

121 Volcker sent the letter anyway, angering Singer: Letter of Paul Volcker, Chairman, Independent Committee of Eminent Persons, to Judge Edward R. Korman, July 24, 1997.

124 "to see their values diminished": Letters of Alan G. Hevesi, Comptroller of the City of New York, to Robert Studer, Chairman of the Board, Union Bank of Switzerland and to Rainer Gut, Chairman of the Board, CS Holdings, May 6, 1996 (provided to the author by Eric Wollman of the New York City Comptroller's Office).

125 "their record of collaboration with the Nazis": Letter of Senator Alfonse M. D'Amato to Alan Greenspan, Chairman, Board of Governors of the Federal Reserve System, February 5, 1998 (provided to the author by Gregg Rickman).

126 My U.S. team for the Swiss issues included Bennett Freeman, senior adviser in my undersecretary's office at the State Department; Ronald Bettauer, a senior legal adviser from the State Department; Ruth van Heuven, the State Department's official in charge of German, Austrian and Swiss affairs; Jonathan Schwarz, associate deputy attorney general in the Justice Department; and Ambassador Madeleine Kunin and two senior aides from her Embassy Bern staff, Carey Cavanaugh and Dan Smith. In later negotiations, Russ LaMotte from the State Department's legal adviser's office worked intensively with me.

128 Robert Studer's alleging Christoph Meili's ulterior motives: "What I currently know allows me to assume that the motives Meili has stated for his actions aren't the only ones." (Alexander G. Higgins, "Whistleblower's Lawyer Demands Explanation from Bank Chief," Associated Press, January 19, 1997).

130–131 "a positive development for Switzerland": *Neue Zürcher Zeitung*, December 15, 1997.

132 Cotti's New Year's statement in the *Tribune de Geneve* cited in "Jewish Group Criticizes New Swiss President," Reuters, December 31, 1997; and Alexander G. Higgins, "Swiss Reject Labor Camp Accusations," Associated Press, January 14, 1998.

134 Letters of Marcel Ospel, President and Group Chief Executive Officer, Swiss Bank Corporation, and Lukos Mühlemann, Chief Executive Officer, Credit Suisse Group, to Israel Singer, secretary general of the World Jewish Congress, March 26, 1998 (provided to the author by Eric Wollmann of the New York City Comptroller's Office).

134–135 "Structure for Settlement of Swiss Bank Class Actions and Related Issues," April 6, 1998 (copy in author's possession).

## Chapter 7: Scorpions in a Bottle

140 "Each of the undersigned agrees that . . . ": Stipulation and Order filed *In re Holocaust Victim Assets Litigation* with Judge Korman in the United States District Court of the Eastern District of New York, April 27, 1998.

144 The twenty-one-page letter: From Michael Hausfeld, Melvyn Weiss, Robert Swift, and Israel Singer to Stuart E. Eizenstat, undersecretary of state for economic, business, and agricultural affairs, May 19, 1998 (copy in author's possession).

144 New Jersey State Assembly bill: "Dormant Accounts—Sanctions Against Swiss Banks: New Jersey Parliament Votes for Boycott; Big Banks Disappointed," SDA (Swiss newswire agency), May 19, 1998.

145 Letter of Senator Alfonse D'Amato to Alan Greenspan, chairman, Federal Reserve Board of Governors, February 5, 1998 (provided to the author by Gregg Rickman).

149–150 A leak: David E. Sanger, "Swiss Banks Said to Offer Holocaust Payment," *New York Times,* June 5, 1998, p. A9.

## Chapter 8: The Settlement

180 It is a measure of the depths to which their reputation had fallen: Independent Committee of Eminent Persons (ICEP), *Report on Dormant Accounts of Victims of Nazi Persecution in Swiss Banks* (Berne, Switzerland: Staempfli Publishers, 1999), p. 13. George Krayer, president of the Swiss Bankers Association, said the report was "fair" and refuted claims that Swiss bankers had conspired to hoard Holocaust victims' accounts. As the SBA put it, "The ICEP report disputes any notion that there was a concerted effort by Swiss banks to single out victims of Nazi persecution. . . . Specifically the independent auditors found no evidence of organized discrimination against Jews or other victims of Nazi persecution" ("Swiss Bankers Association: Swiss Banks Seek Closure on World War II Dormant Assets Issue Following Publication of Volcker Committee Report," Press Information, Swiss Bankers Association, Basil, Switzerland, December 6, 1999). Krayer also apologized for "disappointment and hurt feelings" caused by the insensitivities of bankers. Sigi Fergel, a prominent member of the Swiss Jewish community, said the banks' behavior "was based on anti-Semitism and sheer hunger for money" (Elizabeth Olson, "Swiss Banks Criticized on Holocaust Accounts," *International Herald Tribune,* December 7, 1999, p. 1).

180–181 Independent Commission of Experts Switzerland—Second World War, *Switzerland, National Socialism and the Second World War* (final report), March 22, 2002, e.g., pp. 275–276, 446.

182 The culmination of three and a half years of work: Three conversations were of special meaning for me personally. One was from Lloyd Cutler,

my former Carter White House colleague and a Swiss bank lawyer: "We never would have made it without you." Another came from Bobby Brown, who said that Prime Minister Netanyahu "puts you at the top of the list" for thank-yous. Then, out of the blue, Mel Weiss called to say, "I never meant to disparage you. I told the NGOs you played a very important role. It became critical to achieving any progress to get Singer and the lawyers together."

182    Fagan after the settlement: Barry Meier, "Lawyer in Holocaust Case Faces Litany of Complaints," *New York Times*, September 8, 2000, A1.

182–183    Borer: Elizabeth Olson, "Swiss Publisher Apologizes for Reports on Official," *New York Times*, July 15, 2002, p. A7; see James Morrison, "Sacked Envoy on TV," *Washington Times*, July 22, 2002, p. A15; see "Model Who Claimed She Had Affair with Ex-Swiss Ambassador Drops Appeal Against Gagging Order," Associated Press Worldstream, July 16, 2002; "Fired Envoy to Become Swiss Airline Consultant," Agence France Presse, August 18, 2002; "Swiss Role Boulevard," *Financial Times*, August 21, 2002, p. 11; Aisha Labi, "Boring He's Not," *Time International*, September 2, 2002, p. 107.

182    Meili: Tom Tugend, "Remember the Swiss Whistle-Blower?," *Jerusalem Post*, January 25, 2002. Meili has just gotten a new job with the U.S. Navy loading weapons onto warships at Long Beach Station, California, while continuing his studies at Chapman University. "Former Night Watchman Gets Job with U.S. Navy," Associated Press Worldstream, November 5, 2002.

183    On David Vogelsanger's remarks: *The Washington Times*, April 11, 1997, p. 16.

183    Amounts paid to date to dormant account holders: Letter from Michael Bradfield, Special Master, Holocaust Victim Assets Litigation, to Judge Edward Korman, August 19, 2002 (supplied to the author by Mr. Bradfield, with Judge Korman's approval).

186    Statement of Kasper Villeger, in Fredy Rom, "Swiss President Retreats on Vow Made to Help Holocaust Survivors," *Jewish Telegraphic Agency*, July 9, 2002.

## Chapter 9: The Barbarians of Culture

188    "In France alone, more than 1 million cubic meters of personal belongings": Matteoli Commission, Fact-Finding Mission into the Looting of Jews in France, April 17, 2000, p. 10.

189    13,000 "heirless" pieces sold at auction: "Looted Art in French Presidential Palace," Reuters, February 12, 1999. For the number of pieces of art collected by the French after the war, see Michael Fitzgerald, "The Spoils of War: World War II and Its Aftermath: The Loss, Reappearance, and Recovery of Cultural Property," *Art in America*, February 1998, pp. 63–66.

189 Jonathan Petropoulos, *Art as Politics in the Third Reich* (Chapel Hill: University of North Carolina Press, 1999).

189 Lynn H. Nicholas, *The Rape of Europa: The Fate of Europe's Treasures in the Third Reich and the Second World War* (New York: Alfred A. Knopf, 1994).

189–190 Konstantine Akinsha, *Beautiful Loot: The Soviet Plunder of Europe's Art Treasures* (New York: Random House, 1995).

190 Hector Feliciano, *The Lost Museum: The Nazi Conspiracy to Steal the World's Greatest Works of Art* (New York: Basic Books, 1998).

## Chapter 10: Remembering Dora-Mittelbau

205 "Never mind the human victims": see document entitled "Quotations Showing Nazi-Germany Mentality," prepared by the U.S. Army prosecution of the Dachau war crimes trial, *United States of America* vs. *Kurt Andrae et al.*, at Dachau, Germany, beginning August 7, 1947, in Friedmann Collection, U.S. Holocaust Memorial Museum.

206 "During World War II, Nazi Germany forcibly employed about 10 million people": Policy paper of Professor Lutz Niethammer of the University of Florence and Professor Ulrich Von Alemann of the University of Düsseldorf, January 14, 1999 (provided to the author by Linda Bixby of Cohen, Milstein, Hausfeld and Toll). A figure of 12 million was mentioned in the statement of Burt Neuborne to the Financial Services Committee, U.S. House of Representatives, September 14, 1999.

206–207 On the use by the Third Reich of slave and forced labor, see, generally, Benjamin B. Ferencz, *Less Than Slaves: Jewish Forced Labor and the Quest for Compensation* (Bloomington: Indiana University Press, 2002).

207 Herman Göring Werke: A. Barkai, *Nazi Economics: Ideology, Theory, and Policy*, trans. Ruth Hodass-Vashitz (New Haven: Yale University Press, 1990), chapter 5.

207 Profits the SS made on slave laborers: "SS Profitability Calculation Regarding Use of Prisoners in the Concentration Camps," quoted in Bernd Klewitz, *The Slave Workers of Dynamit Nobel* [*Die Arbeitssklaven der Dynamit Nobel*] (Schalksmühle, Germany: Verlag Engelbrecht, 1986). This document is also in the National Archives and Records Administration, College Park, MD. In computing their profits, the SS even deducted the "cost of incineration" as 2 Reichsmarks per person.

207 On figures regarding the loss of Polish citizens, see the Web site of the United States Holocaust Memorial Museum, at http://www.ushmm. org/research/library/bibliography/Poland/right.htm, and that of Tel Aviv University, at http://www.tau.ac.il/Anti-Semitism/aws99–2000/poland. htm.

208 12 million to 14 million German civilians expelled: Markus Krah, "The Germans as Victims?" *Jerusalem Report*, June 17, 2002, pp. 30–33.

212 On initial German goal of achieving "legal peace": The Germans pressed

me and my legal team for a global government-to-government claims settlement that would provide a defense in litigation. Our legal team, led by Ron Bettauer of the State Department and David Anderson of the Justice Department, pointed out that this would not be effective because the United States could represent and settle only the claims of U.S. nationals and there was no precedent for settling claims against private companies, rather than against a government, by executive agreement.

219 Edward Fagan's press conference comment labeling Degussa "badness personified": *Frankfurter Allgemeine Zeitung*, December 24, 1998.

219 "conspirators, collaborators, and money launderers": *Die Welt*, June 5, 1998.

220 A reminder that World War II was not far away: Roger Cohen, "Schröder, like Germany, Looks Harder at the Past," *New York Times*, July 2, 2001, p. A1.

215, 228 My team for the German negotiations was led by Ron Bettauer, deputy legal adviser, and Eric Rosand, attorney-adviser, from the U.S. Department of State's Legal Adviser's Office; and David Anderson, Federal Programs Branch director, and David Buchholz, senior counsel, Civil Division, from the Department of Justice. Other members of the team were John Becker, Office of Holocaust Issues, U.S. Department of State; Ambassador J. D. Bindenagel, special envoy for Holocaust issues, U.S. Department of State; Milton Gwirtzman, special adviser to me as the deputy secretary, U.S. Department of the Treasury; Carolyn Keene, executive assistant, U.S. Department of the Treasury; Ambassador John Kornblum, Embassy Berlin, U.S. Department of State; Jody Manning, Office of Holocaust Issues, U.S. Department of State; Holly Toye Moore, senior adviser to me as the Deputy Secretary, U.S. Department of the Treasury; David Ogden, assistant attorney general, Civil Division, U.S. Department of Justice; Basil Scarlis, Office of German, Austrian and Swiss Affairs, U.S. Department of State; U.S. Ambassador to Germany John Kornblum and Mark Scheland, Embassy Berlin, U.S. Department of State; Heather Schildge, Legal Adviser's Office, U.S. Department of State; Richard "Ras" Smith, Office of Holocaust Issues, U.S. Department of State; Jim Warlick, Office of German, Austrian and Swiss Affairs, U.S. Department of State; Seth Waxman, solicitor general, U.S. Department of Justice; Jim Wojtasiewicz, Poland desk, U.S. Department of State.

## Chapter 11: As Old as the Pyramids

239–240 Number of conscripted workers: Policy Paper, Professor Lutz Niethammer, University of Florence, and Professor Ulrich von Alemann, University of Düsseldorf, January 14, 1999 (provided to the author by Linda Bixby of Cohen, Milstein, Hausfeld and Toll).

## Chapter 13: A Strange Ending

263 On Reichsbank building: See "The History of the New Premises of the Federal Foreign Office," p. 2, published by the Federal Foreign Office, 1999.

266 "The most bitter and intense negotiations of the entire saga": See, generally, Michael Maiello and Robert Lenzer, "The Last Victims," *Forbes*, May 14, 2001.

268–269 Prisoner of war claims: The parties ultimately agreed in article 3(3) of the executive agreement that the U.S. government would never raise any reparations claims, including POW claims against the Federal Republic of Germany, that were left unresolved by article 5(2) of the 1953 London Debt Agreement. The German government considered this commitment extremely important.

268 German insurance companies not joining ICHEIC: It was not until October 2002 that ICHEIC, the German insurers, and the Claims Conference reached an agreement on the publication of lists of policyholders, the allocation of costs between ICHEIC and the German Foundation, and other issues, thereby permitting the implementation of the agreement I had reached two years earlier. I was present at the formal signing ceremony in Washington.

## Chapter 14: Unser Wien

279 The sins of the father: "Fathers shall not be put to death for their children, nor children put to death for their fathers; each is to die for his own sins" (Deuteronomy 24:16).

280 Kurt Ladner's background: Manuscript of Mr. Ladner's unpublished memoirs, supplied to author.

280–281 On the general history of Austria during the *Anschluss* and World War II, see Gordon Brook-Shepherd, *The Austrians: A Thousand-Year Odyssey* (London: Harper Collins, 1996); Evan Burr Burkey, *Hitler's Austria: Popular Sentiment in the Nazi Era, 1938–1945* (Chapel Hill: University of North Carolina Press, 1998); Robert H. Keyserling, *Austria in World War II: An Anglo-American Dilemma* (Montreal: McGill-Queens University Press, 1998); Hella Pick, *Guilty Victim: Austria from the Holocaust to Haider* (New York: I. B. Tauris, 2000).

281 Nazi party membership among Austrians: Michael H. Kater, *The Nazi Party: A Social Profile of Members and Leaders, 1919–1945* (Cambridge, MA: Harvard University Press, 1983).

281 Austrians wearing Tyrolean and Styrian peasant hats: Robert S. Wistrich, "Austria and the Legacy of the Holocaust," a report prepared for the American Jewish Committee news conference, press release, February 12, 1999.

282 Austria as neutral barrier against the Soviet bloc: Gunter Bischof, *Austria in the First Cold War, 1945–1955: The Leverage of the Weak* (New York: St. Martin's Press, 1999), p. 91.

282 Cardinal Franz König, speech in St. Polten, Austria, September 26, 1987.

282 Chancellor Franz Vranitzky's speech: see Hannah Lessing, "The National Fund of the Republic of Austria for Victims of National Socialism," March 15, 2001, p. 2, provided to the author by Lessing.

282–283 The National Fund for the Victims of National Socialism was created to make payments of about 70,000 schillings (about $4,500): The average exchange rate in 2000 was just under 15 schillings to the dollar.

283 Stephan Templ and Tina Walzer, *Unser Wien* (Berlin: Structure Publishing House, 2001).

283 The confiscated properties included: Steven Erlanger, "Vienna Skewered as a Nazi-Era Pillager of Its Jews," *New York Times*, March 7, 2002, p. A3.

283 "dishonest pimps for the Nazis!": Fagan quoted in *Der Standard* (Vienna), September 16, 1998.

283 Class-action lawsuits brought by Edward Fagan on October 16, 1998: *Bressler et al.* vs. *Phillip Holzmann AG et al.*, CV 98–6335, U.S. District Court for the Eastern District of New York; *Gutwillig et al.*, vs. *Steyr-Daimler-Puch AG et al.*, CV 98–6336, U.S. District Court for the Eastern District of New York. Steyr-Daimler-Puch AG, a Vienna company, was a wartime manufacturer that exploited a large number of forced laborers during the World War II. It is believed to have used over 1,000 forced laborers from Mauthausen concentration camp at its plants in Steyr and Muenicholz, Austria, and at a plant in Radom, Poland.

287 I never had to negotiate with the private sector: My team did have difficult negotiations with the Austrian private-sector lawyers over language in the executive agreement to incorporate the broad agreements Maria Schaumayer and I reached.

291 Schuessel's view that he could isolate the radical wing of Haider's Freedom Party: In September 2002 Chancellor Schuessel's government coalition fragmented when moderate Freedom Party ministers resigned over a conflict with Haider.

292 My Austrian team consisted of David Anderson, federal programs branch director, Civil Division, U.S. Department of Justice; John Becker, Office of Holocaust Issues, U.S. Department of State; Randolph Bell, director, Office of German, Austrian and Swiss Affairs, U.S. Department of State; Ambassador J. D. Bindenagel, special envoy for Holocaust issues, U.S. Department of State; Ursula Dorfinger, Embassy Vienna, U.S. Department of State; Ambassador Kathryn Hall, Embassy Vienna, U.S. Department of State; Will Kirschner, trial attorney, Civil Division, U.S. Department of Justice; Holly Moore, senior adviser to me as Deputy Secretary of the Treasury, U.S. Department of the Treasury; Nancy Pettit, Embassy Vienna, U.S. Department of State; Eric Rosand, attorney-adviser, Legal Adviser's Office, U.S. Department of State; and Basil

Scarlis, Office of German, Austrian and Swiss Affairs, U.S. Department of State.

## Chapter 15: Bridge over Troubled Water

293, 302 On Jewish-owned property in Austria generally, see Brigitte Bailer-Galanda, Eva Blimlinger, Susanne Kowarc, *"Arisierung" und Rückstellung von Meiterrinnen aus ihren Wohnungen und das verhinderte Wohnungrück-stellungsgesetz* (Vienna: Austrian Historical Commission, 2000), pp. 14–16, 34; AVA, VVSt, karton 1370, Mappe Mörixbauer, "Anlage zu Schreiben des Stellvertretenden Gauleiters Scharizer an den Regierungs präsidenten Dr. Dellbrügge vom 25 April 1941," cited in Hans Witek, "'Arisierungen' in Wien," in Emmerich Talos, Ernst Hanisch, Wolfgang Neugebauer (eds.), *NS-Herrschaft in Österreich*, 2nd ed. (Vienna: Verlags-gesellschaft, 2000), p. 814; George Weis, "Report on Jewish Heirless Assets in Austria," December 4, 1952, Annex M, 1–3, cited in "Survey of Past Austrian Measures of Restitution, Compensation and Social Welfare for Victims of National Socialism," prepared by the Office of the Special Envoy for Restitution Issues, Ernst Sucharipa, October 2000; Gertraud Fuchs, "Die Vermögensverkehrstelle als Arisierungsbehörde jüdischer Betriebe," thesis submitted to the University of Economics, Vienna, 1989, pp. 26–28.

295 Hans Winkler and Martin Eichtinger, Austrian officials who had been working with Maria Schaumayer: Martin Eichtinger, "The Reconcilia-tion Fund: Austria's Payments to Former Slave and Forced Laborers of the National Socialist Regime" (2001) for the Austrian view of the nego-tiations. Martin Eichtinger, head of the international relations section of the Federation of Austrian Industry, was from February 16 to November 6, 2000, chief of staff to Special Representative Maria Schaumayer. This article was reviewed by Maria Schaumayer and by Ambassador Hans Winkler, legal adviser of the Ministry of Foreign Affairs. Andreas Khol, Günther Ofner, Günther Buerkert-Dottolo, Stephan Karver, eds., *Aus-trian Yearbook of Politics 2000* (Vienna: München, 2001), pp. 193–242. It was translated from the German into English for the author by Harold F. Raddy, a retired Foreign Service officer.

298 The Austrian bank cases before Judge Kram (*In re: Austrian and German Bank Holocaust Litigation*, 98 CV 3938, 2/19/95; further consolidated with 99 CV 1065 and 99 CV 1067, 3/11/99; consolidated class action complaint filed 3/17/99): The Austrian bank settlement was one of the most bizarre matters with which I had to deal. The settlement was limited to the activ-ities of the headquarters of Creditanstalt and Bank Austria, and the class-action lawyers hoped the broader settlement I was negotiating with Austrian business would lead to further contributions from other Aus-trian banks. In order to justify the modest $40 million settlement by the

two Austrian banks, Bob Swift and his colleagues Ed Fagan, Carey D'Avino, and Lawrence Kill, representing the plaintiffs, and Charles Moerdler, representing the Austrian banks, concocted an assignment to the plaintiffs of supposed claims that the Austrian banks had against German banks for stripping their assets during the war. This was the basis upon which they convinced Judge Kram to support the settlement. In fact, the assignment was largely worthless, since in the 1955 State Treaty Austria had expressly waived all of its Nazi-era claims against Germany and German companies.

Israel Singer and the Claims Conference vehemently objected to the $40 million settlement as inadequate to satisfy the claims of Holocaust victims. But they had another, unstated objection. They feared being replaced by the class-action lawyers as the authorized representatives of the victims, and by Judge Kram in controlling the funds. Judge Kram's deep animus towards the Claims Conference for their opposition to the settlement of the Austrian bank cases brought about a comic scene. Former Senator Al D'Amato had gotten himself appointed by Judge Kram as special master. D'Amato called me and announced Judge Kram wanted to talk with me. She pronounced herself "speechless" in admiration at all my accomplishments. I soon found myself speechless, as well, for Judge Kram then launched into a diatribe against the Claims Conference, warning me that allowing them to control humanitarian funds in the German Foundation would be like putting the "fox in charge of the chicken coop" and that there could be a "scandal that would rock you." She warned that she would refuse to dismiss the class-action suits against the German banks unless she could have close supervision over any funds allocated to the Claims Conference (which had been periodically criticized by Holocaust survivors for its handling of German reparations funds). She also insisted that the plaintiffs in her Austrian bank case could collect more money from the German banks. Judge Kram closed pleasantly, "You've done a monumental job; let's work it out." We never did.

At the conclusion of our slave and forced labor negotiations with the Germans, Judge Kram refused to dismiss the cases brought against German banks, even though the plaintiffs' attorneys, including Bob Swift, petitioned her to do so. She held out for an additional payment by the German banks above and beyond our 10 billion DM German settlement or a separate allocation from the German Foundation, pursuant to this spurious assignment by Austrian banks in the separate Austrian bank case. This in turn held up payment of our German funds for half a year. It required an unusual mandamus order from the Second Circuit Court of Appeals to get the cases dismissed against the German banks in the spring of 2001. I worked on this during the early months of the Bush Administration as a Special Advisor to the State Department.

300 Case filed by Jay Fialkoff: *Whiteman et al.* vs. *Fed Rep of Austria et al.*, filed

October 20, 2000, 1:00 CV 8006, U.S. District Court for the Southern District of New York.

303–304 Isaac's blessing: Genesis 27:22.

305 Secretary of State Madeleine Albright met with Chancellor Wolfgang Schuessel and Benita Ferrero-Waldner on November 8, 2000. On November 13 a formal cable was sent lifting restrictions.

313 Muzicant's actions after initialing the agreement: In the end, Muzicant reneged on his support for the agreement. He later told me that Moerdler and his Austrian lawyer, Gabriel Lansky, had urged him to go home without initialing the agreement. He felt he should have left but did not want to create a "scandal for the survivors." The suits filed on orders from Muzicant and Moerdler were not withdrawn, postponing the day when money could start to flow for the Austrian forced laborers. Judge Shirley Wohl Kram appointed as special master Walter Zifkin to review the agreement.

In July 2001 Zifkin, working closely with the Austrian government, me (the Bush administration asked me to continue to stay on as special adviser to complete the implementation of our agreements), and my team, persuaded Muzicant to have the labor claims dismissed. Money finally began to flow to the former laborers nine months after our October 2000 agreement, during which period hundreds of them may have died in the interim. But the General Settlement Fund for property claims has yet to come into being, because Judge Kram refuses to dismiss lawsuits that remain pending at Muzicant's orders.

To allow at least for the enhanced pension payments to the aging Holocaust survivors, provided by the otherwise stalled property agreement I reached, the Austrian parliament amended the law establishing the General Settlement Fund. But to obtain the agreement of all the political parties, additional payments were also granted to some 13,000 surviving Austrians who served as soldiers in Hitler's Wehrmacht.

As to the $40 million Bank Austria settlement, the first payments were made in September 2002. About $30 million has been set aside for 58,000 potential Holocaust survivors and their heirs, with some of the balance for a historians' commission to examine the conduct of Austrian banks during World War II. See Elizabeth Olson, "World Briefing/Europe: Austria: Holocaust Victim Payments," *New York Times*, August 8, 2002, p. A8.

## Chapter 16: The French Exception

315 Two-fifths of French territory under Vichy control: Robert O. Paxton, *Vichy France: Old Guard and New Order, 1940–1944* (New York: Columbia University Press, 1972), p. 8.

316 Vichy government's anti-Semitic laws: Michael Marrus and Robert Paxton, *Vichy France and the Jews* (New York: Basic Books, 1981), p. 3.

316 One-billion franc fine: Marrus and Paxton, *Vichy France and the Jews*, p. 111.

316 By the end of 1942, 42,000 Jews had been sent from France to Auschwitz (Marrus and Paxton, *Vichy France and the Jews*, p. 261).

316 Between 6.5 and 7 billion francs: Matteoli Commission report, pp. 56, 74. On January 25, 1997, French prime minister Alain Juppé established a commission to examine the circumstances under which Jewish property in France was confiscated or acquired between 1940 and 1944. The chairman of the commission was Jean Matteoli. Its final report, entitled *Summary of the Work by the Study Mission on the Spoilation of Jews in France*, was published on April 17, 2000. See also Harriet Tamen memorandum to Michael Hausfeld, Ken McCallion, and Morris Ratner, December 2, 2000 (in the author's possession).

317 Chirac speech, July 16, 1995: *Discours et messages de Jacques Chirac: En hommage aux Juifs de France victimes de la collaboration de l'Etat français de Vichy avec l'occupant allemand* (Paris: Les Fils et Filles des Deportees Juifs de France, 1998), p. 22.

318 Juppé speech announcing creation of the Study Mission on the Spoliation of Jews in France: "Discours du Premier Ministre devant le Conseil Representatif des Institutions Juives de France" (Paris, Hotel Meridien), January 25, 1997.

319 Class-action suits against France's major banks: *Bodner* vs. *Banque Paribas*, filed December 17, 1997, CV 97–7443, in U.S. District Court for the Eastern District of New York; *Benisti* vs. *Banque Paribas*, filed December 23, 1998, CV 98–785, U.S. District Court for the Eastern District of New York; *Mayer* vs. *Banque Paribas*, filed March 24, 1999, Civil Action no. 302226, California Superior Court.

319 Richard Weisberg, a professor at Cardozo Law School: Richard H. Weisberg, *Vichy Law and the Holocaust in France* (New York: New York University Press, 1996).

320 Judge Johnson's order not to dismiss: *Bodner et al.* vs. *Banque Paribas et al.* and *Benisti et al., v. Banque Paribas et al.* Memorandum and Order issued by the United States District Court, Eastern District of New York, Judge Sterling Johnson presiding, August 30, 2000.

337 My team for the French negotiations included John Becker, Office of Holocaust Issues, U.S. Department of State; Ambassador J. D. Bindenagel, special envoy for Holocaust issues, U.S. Department of State; David Buchholz, senior counsel, Civil Division, U.S. Department of Justice; Robert Gianfranceschi, Embassy Paris, U.S. Department of State; Jody Manning, Office of Holocaust Issues, U.S. Department of State; Holly Toye Moore, senior adviser, U.S. Department of the Treasury; and Eric Rosand, attorney-adviser, Legal Adviser's Office, U.S. Department of State.

In a meeting of July 22, 2002, with Ambassador Francis Lott (Ambassador Andreani's successor as ambassador-at-large), Prefet Lucien Kalfon (director of the Drai Commission), and Ambassador Marcel Surbiguet (director of Fund B), I was informed that the claims period for soft claims had been extended by six months to January 18, 2003, to permit better worldwide notice. As of July 12, 2002, 12,200 claims have been filed to the Drai Commission, of which 3,200 are bank account claims. Of the bank claims, 43 percent are hard claims and 57 percent are soft claims for what the French call Fund B, the rough justice fund, which will pay up to $3,000 per person. Thus far 680 awards have been made to claimants for Fund B.

## Conclusion: A Final Accounting for World War II

339, 345   On criticism of Holocaust litigation, see Gabriel Schoenfeld, "A Grow-ing Scandal," *Commentary*, September 2000.

340   "act of public appeasement" (Hansmeyer): Michael Maiello and Robert Lenzer, "The Last Victims," *Forbes*, May 14, 2001.

340   On Christoph Blocher, speech quoted in "Blocher: The Jews Are Only Interested in Money," *Sonntags Blick* (Zurich), cited in Elizabeth Olson, "A Billionaire Leads the Campaign to Keep Switzerland Apart," *New York Times*, February 24, 2002.

340   Cartoon: *Nebelspalter: Das Humor—und Satire—Magazine*, June 1998.

345   Attorneys' fees in German and Austrian Holocaust settlements: German Foundation Arbitration Plaintiff Counsel Awards; Attorneys' Fees and Austrian Fund "Reconciliation, Peace and Cooperation," Slave/Forced Labor Cases. An allocation of attorneys' fees was determined by arbitra-tors Kenneth Feinberg and Nicholas Katzenbach and provided to me and my U.S. government team and to the judges handling these cases.

345   On the tobacco litigation and class-action settlements in general, see Richard B. Sobol, *Bending the Law: The Story of the Dalkon Shield Bank-ruptcy* (Chicago: University of Chicago Press, 1991); Dennis E. Curtis and Judith Resnik, "Contingency Fees in Mass Torts," 47 *DePaul Law Review* 425 (1998); Barry Meier, "The Spoils of Tobacco Wars," *New York Times*, December 22, 1998; Barry Meier and Jill Abramson, "Tobacco War's New Front: Lawyers Fight for Big Fees," *New York Times*, June 9, 1998; "Greed Breeds Bad Case of Eye-Popping Legal Fees," *USA Today*, December 9, 1997.

346   On Foxman's struggle to collect damages for Holocaust-era crimes and looted assets, see Abraham H. Foxman, "The Dangers of Holocaust Restitution," *Wall Street Journal*, December 4, 1998 ("a desecration of the victims, a perversion of why the Nazis had a Final Solution, and too high a price to pay for justice we can never achieve"). See also, in a similar vein, Charles Krauthammer, "Riding the Holocaust to Mere Dollars and Cents," *Los Angeles Times*, December 11, 1998 ("It should be beneath the dignity of the Jewish people to accept [money] let alone to seek it . . . a shakedown of Swiss banks, Austrian industry, [and] German automakers

[by lawyers] could revive anti-Semitism [in Europe]"). All are quoted in Michael J. Bazyler, "The Holocaust Restitution Movement in Cooperative Perspective," *Berkeley Journal of International Law* 20, no. 1 (2002).

347 On the number of Holocaust-era historical commissions, information is based upon the Web site of the International Task Force for Holocaust Education and the U.S. Holocaust Memorial Museum, provided by the Office of the Special Envoy for Holocaust Issues, Bureau of European Affairs, U.S. Department of State, July 17, 2002.

348 On Holocaust-era assets in Israel and on Ford and General Motors studies, see various articles and reports collected in Michael J. Bazyler, "The Legality and Morality of the Holocaust-Era Settlement with the Swiss Banks," *Fordham International Law Journal* 25 (2001), pp. S-87–S-90, symposium; and Bazyler, "The Holocaust Restitution Movement in Comparative Perspective," pp. 43–44.

349 On European sanctions, see Netty C. Gross, "How Bad Could It Get?", *The Jerusalem Report,* June 3, 2002; David Horovitz, "Europe Buys the Big Lie," *The Jerusalem Report,* May 20, 2002.

349 Möllemann's comments: Steve Erlanger, "Germany's Leader Retains His Power After Tight Vote," *New York Times,* September 23, 2002, p. A1, A8; Peter Finn, "Ruling Coalition Wins Narrowly in German Vote," *Washington Post,* September 23, 2002, p. A1, A11.

349 On the increase in Swiss anti-Semitism, see a 1998 study by the Swiss government that noted the increase in anti-Semitism there in the aftermath of the Swiss bank affairs (Swiss Federal Commission Against Racism, *Anti-Semitism in Switzerland: A Report on Historical Current Manifestations with Recommendations for Counter-Measures* (1998), cited in Michael J. Bazyler, "The Legality and Morality of the Holocaust-Era Settlement with the Swiss Banks," *Fordham International Law Journal* 25 (2001), symposium.

350 Japanese slave laborers: Some 25,000 American prisoners, both civilians and POWs, along with thousands of other Asians, worked as slave laborers for at least forty private Japanese companies in Japan and Japanese-occupied Asia, including Mitsubishi and Nippon Steel. These suits have been dismissed at the district court level, in significant part, because of the U.S. government's intervention that I was unable to stop. They are now on appeal. For a thorough discussion of these cases, see Bazyler, "The Holocaust Restitution Movement in Comparative Perspective," pp. 25–32. I consider the failure of these Japanese companies to make a moral gesture deeply regrettable.

350–351 On Armenian suits, see *Maroutian* vs. *New York Life Insurance Company,* filed January 17, 2000, No. 99–12073, U.S. District Court for the Central District of California, cited and discussed in Bazyler, "The Legality and Morality of the Holocaust-Era Settlement with the Swiss Banks," p. S-98, and see note 74 for other citations; and Bazyler, "The Holocaust Restitution Movement in Comparative Perspective," pp. 33–34.

351 On the apartheid cases, see *Lungisile Ntsebeza vs. Citigroup Inc., UBS AG, and Credit Suisse Group,* filed July 2002, Docket no. 02 Civ 4712 (CRC), U.S. District Court for the Southern District of New York; *Nyameka Goniwe vs. IBM Corporation, Deutsche Bank AG, Dresdner Bank AG and Commerzbank AG,* filed July 2002, Docket no. TBA (CRC), U.S. District Court for the Southern District of New York.

351–353 On the American slavery cases, see *Deadria Farmer-Paellmann vs. Fleet Boston Financial Corporation, Aetna, CSX,* filed March 26, 2002, CV 02 1862, U.S. District Court for the Eastern District of New York; see also, generally, by James Cox, "Corporations Challenged by Reparations Activists," *USA Today,* February 2, 2002; James Cox, "Aetna, CSX, Fleet Boston Face Slave Reparations Suit," *USA Today,* March 24, 2002; "Lawsuits Seek Reparations For Slavery," Associated Press, March 27, 2002).

351–353 African-American reparations: There is already some political momentum behind these suits, as shown by resolutions of support from the city councils of Chicago, Cleveland, Detroit, and Dallas. In 2001 California passed a law forcing U.S. insurers who sold policies insuring slaves to develop information about them. In 2002 the Georgia insurance commissioner asked insurance companies doing business in the state for any information on insurance provided to slave owners. Also, Michigan Congressman John Conyers has introduced legislation since 1989 to study the issue. See Bazyler, "The Holocaust Restitution Movement in Comparative Perspective," pp. 34–37.

353 On courts' receptivity to considering civil liability for human rights violations, see Anne Marie Slaughter and David Bosco, "Plaintiffs' Diplomacy," *Foreign Affairs* 79, no. 5 (September–October 2000): pp. 103–105.

353 On new forms of diplomacy, see the essay by the Bennett Freeman, "The Diplomacy of Holocaust-Era Assets: A Personal Memo," *Balliol College Annual Record* (2001).

354–355 On Jews moving from powerlessness to power, see Rabbi Irving Greenberg, "The Ethics of Jewish Power," *CLAL* [National Center for Learning and Leadership] *Perspectives* (1983), reprinted in R. R. Ruether and M. W. Ellis, *Beyond Occupation* (Boston: Beacon Press, 1990), pp. 22–64, and abridged, in Elliot M. Dorf and Louis E. Newman, *Contemporary Jewish Ethics and Morality: A Reader* (London: Oxford University Press, 1995), pp. 403–422; and Rabbi Irving Greenberg, "Yitzhak Rabin and the Ethic of Jewish Power," *CLAL Perspectives* (1995).

354 Unocal forced-labor case: See *DOE I vs. Unocal Corp.,* Nos. 00–56628, 00–57195, 9th Circuit Court of Appeals, by Judge Harry Pregerson, September 18, 2002.

354 On suits against oil companies, see those cases collected and discussed in Bazyler, "The Legality and Morality of the Holocaust-Era Settlement with the Swiss Banks," pp. S-96–S-97.

356 Greta Beer's lament: On September 18, 2002, Judge Korman awarded Greta Beer $100,000 for the special role she played in the Swiss bank

affair. Although it was not paid out of the amount of the $1.25 billion settlement set aside for claims, she told me she felt vindicated at last. She was not forgotten.

356  Pirkei Avoth, Ethics of the Fathers, 2:21.

# PHOTO CREDITS AND PERMISSIONS

෴

*Synagogue in Chelm, Poland*: Bildarchiv Preussischer Kulturbesitz, Berlin

*Sacks of looted Nazi gold*: National Archives and Records Administration

*"J" stamp*: Miriam Kleiman

*Family of Greta Deligdish Beer*: Greta Beer

*Hans Bär*: Hans Bär

*Mathis Cabiallaveta and Marcel Ospel*: Agence France-Presse

*Lukas Muehlemann*: Agence France-Presse

*Thomas Borer*: AP/Wide World Photos

*Christoph Meili*: AP/Wide World Photos

*Stuart Eizenstat, Robin Cook, and Edgar Bronfman*: AP/Wide World Photos

*Michael Hausfeld*: Agence France-Presse

*Edward Fagan, Robert Swift, and Michael Witti*: AP/Wide World Photos

*Alfonse D'Amato*: Agence France-Presse

*Alan Hevesi*: Alan Hevesi

*Edward Korman*: Judge Edward Korman

*Dwight D. Eisenhower, Omar N. Bradley, and George S. Patton, Jr.*: National Archives and Records Administration

*Adolf Hitler in his Berlin bunker*: Verlag Silvia Fabritius

*Forced laborers at Dora-Mittlebau*: Ullstein Bild

*Full-page newspaper advertisement*: B'nai B'rith International

*Eizenstat and Bill Clinton*: Agence France-Presse

*Eizenstat, Gerhard Schröder, Otto Lambsdorff et al*: German Federal Press and Information Office

*Eizenstat et al*: Deborah Sturman

*Eizenstat, Maria Schaumayer, and Wolfgang Scheussel*: Agence France-Presse

*Roundup of foreign-born French Jews*: Photo Centre for Historical Research and Documentation on War and Contemporary Society—Brussels

*Kurt Ladner, Eizenstat, and Israel Singer*: Agence France-Presse

# INDEX

❧